# AUSTRALIA 1989

# THE CONTRIBUTORS

**Kirsty McKenzie** covers an enormous amount of territory for this book, as writer of the Queensland, Northern Territory, South Australia, and Western Australia chapters. Kirsty contributes to a number of publications, among them, *Australian Gourmet and Traveller* and *Panorama*.

The chapters on Melbourne and Victoria and Tasmania are by **Mark Kestigian.** Mark has written for American newspapers and magazines, including *Travel & Leisure* and the *Miami Herald,* as well as such Australian publications as the *Melbourne Sun.* He's currently at work on a novel.

**Mary Ellen Dyster** wrote most of the Sydney chapter, the chapter on New South Wales, a number of the historical essays, and the Cultural Timeline. Her writing credits include *Good Housekeeping* and *Australian Gourmet and Traveller.*

The Sydney restaurant section is the work of **David Dale.** A writer for Sydney's *Good Food Guide* and the Australian contributor for Britain's *Good Food Guide,* David is currently editor of the weekly newsmagazine *The Bulletin.* His book on his experiences in the United States, *An Australian in America,* has recently been published.

The introduction, Travel in Australia 1989, is by **Steve Bunk,** as are a number of the wildlife essays in the book; Steve also put together the wildlife tour in the Travel Arrangements section. He contributes articles to *The Bulletin,* Australian editions of *Time* and *Playboy,* and American publications, including *Travel & Leisure* and *Mother Jones.*

Much of the information in the Travel Arrangements section was contributed by **Mark Sheehan** who has worked with a number of tour operators Down Under. The Business Brief is by **Sondra Snowdon,** author of *The Global Edge: How Your Company Can Win in the Marketplace.*

The New York editor for the book is Debra Bernardi. A number of people helped in putting this all together—too many to thank here. But we would especially like to acknowledge Paul Gardiner, Gill Chalmers, Tony Baker, Judith Curr, and the Australian Tourist Commission. Maps are by Swanston Graphics and R. V. Reise und Verkehrsverlag.

A BANTAM TRAVEL GUIDE

# AUSTRALIA

1989

917.3
BAN
cop.1

# BANTAM
NEW YORK ● TORONTO ● LONDON ● SYDNEY ● AUCKLAND

32948

AUSTRALIA 1989
*A Bantam Book / April 1989*

*Grateful acknowledgment is made to the following for reprint permission:*
*From,* Cooper's Creek, *by Alan Moorehead, copyright © 1963. Reprinted*
*by permission of the Atlantic Monthly Press. From,* The Fatal Shore, *by*
*Robert Hughes, copyright © 1986 by Robert Hughes. Reprinted by*
*permission of Alfred A. Knopf, Inc., and Collins Harvill Publishers (U.K.).*
*From,* Kangaroo, *by D.H. Lawrence, copyright 1923 by Thomas Seltzer,*
*Inc. Copyright renewed 1951 by Frieda Lawrence. Reprinted by permission*
*of Viking Penguin, Inc., and Lawrence Pollinger and the estate of Frieda*
*Lawrence Ravagli (U.K.). From,* The Outback *by Thomas Keneally,*
*reproduced by permission of Hodder and Stoughton Limited and Rainbird*
*Publishing Group.*

ISBN 0-533-34635-0

*Published simultaneously in the United States and Canada*

*Bantam Books are published by Bantam Books, a division of Bantam Double-*
*day Dell Publishing Group, Inc. Its trademark, consisting of the words "Ban-*
*tam Books" and the portrayal of a rooster, is Registered in U.S. Patent and*
*Trademark Office and in other countries. Marca Registrada. Bantam Books,*
*666 Fifth Avenue, New York, New York 10103.*

PRINTED IN THE UNITED STATES OF AMERICA

0 9 8 7 6 5 4 3 2 1

# CONTENTS

# FOREWORD

Anyone who's ever used a travel guidebook knows how addictive they become when they're good, but how annoying they are when they're bad. We at Bantam launched this new guidebook series because we honestly believed we could improve on, no, that's too weak, we believed we could *significantly* improve on the best of what's already out there.

It was apparent to us that, unless we improved on the best of what's currently available, there was no sense in producing a new series. More to the point, there'd be no reason for you, the traveler, to buy our guidebooks. We analyzed the guidebooks already on the market, making note of their best features as well as their deficiencies. The single greatest deficiency of most guidebooks is that you have to buy something else to supplement these deficiencies. Usually you need to buy a good map or a guide to hotels or restaurants because your primary guide lacks good detailed maps, has outdated information on hotels or restaurants, or simply doesn't include such information at all.

The Bantam team had one major goal—that of producing the only travel guides that both the experienced and the inexperienced traveler would ever need for a given destination. You're holding an example of how well we succeeded. Can we document this success? Let's take a look.

- One of the first things you'll notice is that **Bantam Travel Guides** include a full-color travel atlas.
- Upon closer scrutiny you'll find that the guide is organized geographically rather than alphabetically. Think of what this means to you. Descriptions of what's available in a contiguous geographical area make it easier to get the most out of a city neighborhood or a country region. For those who still need to locate something alphabetically we provide a detailed index.
- A real convenience is the way that restaurants and hotels in major cities are keyed into the maps so that you can locate these places easily.
- At the end of key chapters you'll find a feature called City Listings where museums, churches, major sites and shops are listed with their addresses, phone numbers and map-location code.

- Bantam guides will be revised every year. Travel conditions change and so do our guides.
- Finally, we think you'll enjoy reading our guides. We've tried hard to find not only well-informed writers, but good writers. The writing is literate and lively. It pulls no punches. It's honest. Most of all it's a good read.

Still, no guidebook can cover everything that's worth seeing or doing—though we believe we come closer than anyone else. We ask you to bear in mind, too, that prices can change at any time, and that today's well-managed restaurant or hotel can change owners or managers tomorrow. Today's great service or food can be tomorrow's disappointment. We've recommended places as they are now and as we expect them to be in the future, but there are no guarantees. We welcome your comments and suggestions. Our address is Bantam Travel Guides, 666 Fifth Avenue, New York, N.Y. 10103.

Richard T. Scott
Publisher
Bantam Travel Books

## Tips on Getting the Most Out of This Guide

Bantam Travel Guides are designed to be extremely user friendly, but there are a few things you should know in order to get the maximum benefit from them.

1. You'll find a special **Travel Arrangements** section, easily identified by the black tinted pages, toward the back of the book. This section can be invaluable in planning your trip.
2. The **Priorities** chapter will insure that you see and do the most important things when you visit your destination. Whether you're spending two days or two weeks there, you'll want to make the most of your time.
3. Note that in addition to our main selection of important restaurants you'll also find described in the text informal places to stop for lunch, a snack, or a drink.
4. To help you instantly identify restaurant and hotel write-ups, whether they're in a list or mentioned in the text, we've designed the following two little versions of our friendly Bantam rooster. Miniatures of these roosters will appear at the beginning of restaurant and hotel lists and in the margin of the text whenever a restaurant or hotel is described there.

**Restaurants**

**Hotels**

# 1

# TRAVEL IN AUSTRALIA 1989

The middle-aged American's high blood pressure was showing. Florid with indignity, he recalled: "All I wanted was a credit card. I had a big account with the bank but it took me over an hour to get a job done that an American bank would have done in ten minutes."

"Calm down, dear," his wife counseled. "After all, we're not in America."

How sweetly that simple truth rang. Nor was it lost on the disgruntled husband, who indeed calmed down immediately. In his defense, it *is* easy for English speakers in Australia, especially Americans, to forget Rule One of overseas travel: don't judge them by our standards. In fact, it's easier to forget that dictum here than perhaps anywhere else in the world.

The explanation for this sounds like a class schedule from school days: history, government, communications. Skipping the lecture, let's suffice to say that, whether for good or bad, the Australian character (if indeed a nation can be said to produce a certain type of character) is literally akin to the American one. Yet, just as the similarities between cousins can mask great differences, so it is easy and misleading for Americans to assume our Australian relatives are exactly like us.

Those who do make that mistake let themselves in for frustration when appearances don't match reality. A classic example of that mismatch is the gateway to Australia for most Americans, Sydney International Airport.

Outwardly, it's modern, spacious, serviced by sleek jumbo jets from all over the globe. Within, it often is utter chaos, an organizational mess of awe-inspiring proportions. Australians in general and Sydneysiders in particular are well aware that at the worst of times, transit through the airport can take many hours. This very awareness is the answer to the wonderment of an Ohio chief executive officer whose luggage was put on the wrong flight at Sydney International.

"My wife and I waited at the airport for hours to get an onward flight to Darwin," he recounted. "We couldn't believe it—but none of the other passengers seemed worried at all. The only person who got upset was another American."

The Ohio couple's original flight to Darwin was canceled and he claimed the only way he got another one was by watching the departure board, then going to the ticket window and rebooking. "If I had relied on the airline people to do it, we'd probably still be in Sydney."

Even worse in his eyes, a soft handbag he had carried from America just in case the couple's luggage was lost en route had been taken from him. It was judged too large for hand-luggage, which meant the couple arrived in Darwin with just the shirts on their backs, only to learn that all their belongings mistakenly had been sent to Brisbane. Australians who heard him tell this tale of woe the next day at a fishing resort outside Darwin nodded their heads in sympathy and understanding.

If this nation had an unofficial motto, it would be, "No worries." One of the most often-heard phrases in the Aussie lexicon, it can mean either, "That's easily done," or "That will take a long time to do, so don't get excited." Sometimes, it's simply a substitute for "You're welcome," but almost always, it is an expression of cheerful nonchalance.

Although many Australians deplore this laid-back style, which makes California's laid-back types look like hypertensives, it does suit the place. The warm climate has something to do with it and Australia's proximity to the tropical paradises of the South Pacific plays a part as well. An urban populace beached on the ring of seas around a vast, blank interior perhaps has developed its "She'll be right, mate," attitude as one defense against isolation and, in the early days, deprivation.

All this has been analyzed thoroughly by Australian authors and sociologists. To an American visitor today, it mainly means service is lax. Only in the big metropolitan hotels or other establishments that cater to upscale tourists are service standards high.

An American tour group staying at a Sydney Hyatt Hotel—known for its high percentage of Japanese clientele, who often expect top-drawer service—expressed uniform pleasure in their treatment as guests. The tour group leader remarked, "Our tour people met us promptly and helped us in every way they could. The hotel people had us all pre-registered, handed us our keys as we walked in the door, and said, your room is here and here and here. I would find that even above U.S. standards."

Several folks noted the likenesses between the two nationalities. One suggested Australians are "as friendly as Texans." Another joked, "I don't think you'd know the difference between us and them, except you can't understand their language."

Of course, it's about as hard to generalize on whether or not people are friendly as it is to say whether or not a particular accent is difficult to understand. In Australia, it might be argued that the people become more friendly as their speech becomes harder for other English speakers to comprehend. That's because there are basically two Australian accents, not due to geographic regions as much as to urban versus rural divisions. The accents of native Melbournites or Sydneysiders settle easily on most Americans' ears. The friendliness of city-dwellers, however, is often more fleeting than that of the less-harried country folk.

On the other hand, a thick Australian country accent can thoroughly baffle unwitting visitors—which certainly shouldn't prevent the traveler from venturing afield. Although it's true that the laconic country-dwellers seem to speak out of the sides of their mouths, through almost-closed lips (as the joke goes, this technique was developed to keep them from swallowing the ever-present Outback flies), they also are every bit as open-hearted and genuine as are most rural families.

Something else at once similar to, and yet different from, America is travel in Australia. The modes of transport are the same: car, bus, plane, train, and, rarely, boat. Even the distances are alike. If a scaled map of Australia were pulled and squashed into the shape of the continental United States, it would fit just inside the borders of an American map. (Clearly for New Zealanders and the British the concepts of distance are far different.) Where these similarities to the United States end is in the actual experience of traveling Down Under. The same distance from point to point in the two countries can seem much longer in Australia. One reason is the terrain, for Australia is the flattest continent. Although much of it is above sea level, much of it also is plateau. Distance assumes new majesty, and sometimes terror, where the horizons are forever wide and far.

The Great Dividing Range, which separates the heavily populated east coast from the continent's barren center, is one of Australia's few important topographical features that go up rather than down. Most of the really interesting land formations are gorges, valleys, waterfalls, and the like. Even a visit to the Great Barrier Reef is a downward plunge.

None of this makes traveling through the country by land an overwhelming experience. Rather than a kaleidoscope of sights and sensations, the Australian countryside presents the wizened visage of an immeasurably rugged survivor. Its beauty is less obvious than cumulative. Yes, there are endless white beaches, forests, dramatic escarpments, and bizarre rock formations to admire. Each of these features, and more, can be delicious in their beauty. But unless you stick to the beaches or plane-hop from one national park to another, don't expect these delights to be served on a silver plate. The meat and potatoes before dessert are those long, flat stretches of open scrubland. And, no surprise, many people do prefer the main course to the sweets.

The other shock for visitors here is the sparsity of settlements. The traveler in Australia can go for hours or even days without seeing signs of human habitation. To people from a highly populated land, this can be an eerie experience.

Witness the story of an important Asian delegation visiting the Australian national capital of Canberra. As they were being escorted around the well-ordered city on the Sunday of their arrival, the little group became increasingly agitated. Finally, one of the visitors could contain himself no longer and burst out to his interpreter: "But what has gone wrong here? Where are all the *people*?"

With only 16 million souls in a country almost as big as the United States, and 90 percent of them living in a handful of cities, there is an uncanny amount of empty space. Roughly four of every ten Australians live in either Melbourne or Sydney. Imagine a United States with only a couple of largish cities and three or four medium-sized ones on the entire east coast, plus one each on the south and west coasts and nothing but the very rare small town in between. That's Australia. Don't expect to see it all unless you have plenty of time and/or money.

For those who don't visit on an organized tour, flying is obviously the best way to cover the most territory with the least effort. It also is expensive. Australia has only two major domestic airlines, one of which is government-owned. Deregulation is an oft-mooted topic but just as often, opponents point to what they see as the ill effects of deregulating America's airlines. For now, ticket prices remain comparatively high, although there are substantial discounts for overseas visitors.

These air pass discounts, which can be purchased after arrival in Australia, contain limitations on the total distances traveled (a maximum of 6,000 or 10,000 kilometers, about 3,750 to 6,250 miles, are the two options) and require that a minimum number of days be spent outside capital cities. No backtracking is allowed and a total time limit of six weeks is imposed. Because conditions differ slightly between Ansett and Australian airlines, as does the selection of small towns served by the two carriers, it's advisable to get brochures describing the air passes from any of the airlines' customer service bureaus.

Many Australian villages are served infrequently by the major airlines, due to the small population and the large distances covered. Sometimes it will be more convenient for a traveler to reach a certain destination by flying to the nearest town serviced regularly by air, then driving for a few hours rather than waiting several days for the next regular flight to their destination. Charter flights is the other option for those to whom cost is not a consideration.

For most, terrestrial travel of some sort will dominate. Long-distance bus service is good and not expensive. The coaches are modern, air-conditioned, and safe. Of course, buses aren't the most comfortable way to cover vast distances—trains are preferable by far.

Criticism of urban train systems is a regular refrain in the media and it's true that those vehicles can be late, untidy, and even unsafe on occasion in the wee hours, with vandals on the prowl. Still, they're generally convenient, spacious, and the views they afford sometimes are fine.

In Brisbane and Perth, the trains are powered by electricity, which makes them quiet and non-polluting. In Melbourne, they are supplemented by trams (or streetcars), and by a modern light-rail system (commuter railroad). In Adelaide, a light-rail line and a "busway" run from the suburbs into town, after which the trains take over. The busway is a pair of concrete rails along which buses, guided by mechanical arms, travel at speeds up to 100 kilometers (60 miles) per hour. In Sydney, a new monorail zips around and through the central business district, creating more or less equal parts of ease and controversy among the citizenry.

A long-distance rail journey is highly recommended. With a sleeping berth, a sortie up or down the east coast, west to Alice Springs, or even across the country on the Indian-Pacific makes for a memorable way to go. Drawbacks? Well, a booking might be hard to get, due to demand. Also, it isn't cheap, often approximating the price of airfare. Ah, but the clacking rails, the cars and fittings, the flavor of it all!

Even so, for those who have the wherewithal and the time to really explore this nation-continent, the best mode of travel is by private vehicle. A caravan (or mobile home) may easily be rented or purchased. Caravan parks are numerous, inexpensive, and often can be found in idyllic settings.

Those who can't afford to rent or buy a mobile home should think seriously about investing even a couple of thousand dollars for any make of car familiar to Australians and therefore repairable without much trouble in country towns. Holden, an Australian car, is probably best because of the availability of used parts. However, Ford and some Japanese makes such as Toyota are plentiful also. For anyone staying at least a month, a car is well worth the investment, especially because it cuts down on other, more expensive forms of travel and its cost can be partially offset by reselling the machine.

**Americans need to remember that Australia is a right-hand drive country, and drivers in the metropoli are fast and pushy, far less polite than American drivers. A fender-**

**bender or worse is a high probability for anyone unfamiliar with right-hand drive who doesn't ease into the experience.**

One other word of caution: if you decide to drive in the Outback, be a good scout, be prepared. Australia's annual "shock horror" stories about people being eaten by sharks or crocodiles are no more plentiful than those of people who wander into the Outback unprepared and are found later, quite thoroughly dead. The aforementioned vastness of this country and its unyielding nature are nowhere more painfully evident than in the middle of the Tanami or Simpson Desert.

Often enough, the Outback's victims are foreigners who haven't brought enough water or extra gasoline or have bad maps. Road signs on the various edges of the Outback warn drivers against continuing without proper preparation but alas, some people think they know better. With no radio transmitter, it could be days before help arrives. But death can come in a matter of hours to a traveler who's out of the shade and not practicing personal energy conservation.

Enough gloom and doom; for the vast majority of American visitors, Australia is pleasant in the extreme, as long as it remains a different country in their minds. That can be easier said than done in a place full of McDonalds, Coca-Cola, cinema by Spielberg, advertising by Dancer Fitzgerald Sample, "Dallas" on TV, even cowboys and football, albeit the latter two are of distinctly Australian types.

The adage is often heard and generally true that, in many ways, Australia is one or perhaps two decades behind the United States in development. Nowhere is that lag more evident than in social attitudes. Visitors don't have to go too far outside the big cities—into the suburbs is far enough—to find textbook cases of me Tarzan, you Jane. Women are for tending the hearth except at barbecues, when the blokes take over the tongs and the "sheilas" gather in a clutch to burble cheerful inanities. This doesn't always happen among well-educated urbanites anymore but it frequently remains true of blue-collar families.

It certainly helps mutual understanding that Australians are largely fans and supporters of the United States. Naturally, there are some who regard the American military presence (exemplified by satellite surveillance installations and the occasional visit of warships) as unwelcome, but most citizens seem to believe the U.S. umbrella is essential. Even the detractors are likely to differentiate between national policies and individuals.

Australians tend to identify with American ingenuity and admire American drive. Most U.S. visitors will come away with a strong sense of the two countries' parallel courses as former British colonies, one-time dumping grounds of the persecuted and the unwanted who have flourished far from their parent land, with the help of eager immigrants from just about everywhere.

Yet, the careful observer will begin to notice those subtle differences underneath the similar exteriors. For example, Australia retains strong emotional ties to Mother England, even while she moves ever closer to American ways. The nation is caught between an old allegiance and a new one, all the while still striving to forge a complete identity of her own. It's neither accidental nor insignificant that Australia is not yet a fully independent republic. In this way, it is a far younger place than America.

Perhaps it would be less useful to give other examples of the differences between the two countries than to let each visitor find them individually, according to his or her desire and ability. After all, that's part of the fun of a new country, and the challenge. For the visitor to Australia, it is also the essence.

# History of Australian Cuisine

The English and the Irish almost ruined Australia's food, but at the last minute it was saved by the Chinese, the Italians, the French, the Vietnamese, and the Thais.

Twenty-five years ago, if you asked the question "What is Australian food?" the answer would have been "grilled steak, fried fish, roast lamb, mashed potatoes, frozen peas, tinned pineapple, and ice cream." The accompaniment to a typical Australian meal would have been beer and/or tea.

Ask the question today and the answer would include fettuccine with lobster sauce; a salad of mussels, potatoes, mushrooms, and caviar; chilled mince pork with asparagus; veal with a sauce of mushrooms and smoked salmon; char-grilled octopus; and passionfruit soufflé. The accompaniment might be a Hunter Valley Chardonnay or a Barossa Valley cabernet sauvignon.

When the English colonized Australia two hundred years ago, they encountered Aboriginal tribes who had developed over the preceding 30,000 years a varied diet of berries, seeds, leaves, bulbs, roots, fruits, mollusk fish, and game. The English settlers ignored these local sources of nourishment and lived on rations imported from Britain, gradually supplemented by British crops and animals that could be cultivated in Australia.

For the first century of the country's history, the standard diet was known as "ten, ten, two, and a quarter." This referred to the weekly rations of the rural workforce, handed out on Saturday nights (with rum if they were lucky): ten pounds of flour, ten pounds of mutton, two pounds of sugar, a quarter pound of tea, and salt. To this the Irish immigrants added their great culinary contributions: whiskey and potatoes.

And so was formed the assumption about eating that dominated Australian thinking until well into the 20th century—food was not to be eaten for pleasure, it was to provide energy for work. When you weren't working, you got drunk.

The Chinese arrived with the gold rushes of the mid-19th century. When the gold ran out, some of them turned to market gardening and cooking. A few of the more open-minded Anglo Saxon settlers began to try Chinese food as a novelty, just for special occasions, and by the 1930s many a country town and city suburb had a Chinese café, featuring the standard "exotic" dishes: sweet and sour pork, chicken and almonds, and beef with black bean sauce.

But it was not until the mass migration from Europe in the 1950s that the real changes began in Australia's attitude to eating. Italian immigrants, brought in as factory fodder, realized they had landed in a culinary wasteland, and set about opening restaurants. Standard fare became spaghetti bolognese, veal scaloppine with mushrooms, and lemon gelato.

In the 1960s, the Italian invasion was followed by the French revolution. French restaurants started to appear on every suburban corner, often run by French arrivals who had never worked in a commercial kitchen before, or by Australian amateurs working from air-mailed copies of the latest French cookery books.

The formula restaurant meal became quiche Lorraine, duck à l'orange, and crème caramel.

When "nouvelle cuisine" appeared in the mid 1970s, Australia's urban "foodies" embraced it even more enthusiastically than did the foodies of New York. Australian chefs found that nothing succeeded like excess. Kiwi fruit and tamarillo decorated every plate. Game birds were stuffed with shrimp mousse, seated on beds of cream and cucumber, and covered with passionfruit sauces.

The period of unrestrained experimentation produced many failures, but from it emerged a small group of French-influenced scholar-chefs who still dominate Australian cuisine. The most imaginative are Gay Bilson, of Berowra Waters Inn, north of Sydney; Philip Searle, of Oasis Seros in Sydney; and Stephanie Alexander, of Stephanie's in Melbourne.

The late 1970s also saw an influx of Vietnamese refugees who, unable to find other work, opened restaurants and introduced Australians to a new range of delicate taste sensations. The Vietnamese fad has now been replaced by a Thai obsession, and in the late eighties, small Thai restaurants are materializing in the Australian suburbs as rapidly as French restaurants did in the 1970s. The spag-scal-gelato formula that described Australian restaurant food in the 1960s, and became quiche-duck-caramel in the 1970s, is now cilantro fishcakes, chili pork, and satay. And there are early indications that all of these are blending into a new Australian cuisine, and that the next fad to hit the suburbs will be the char-grill bistro.

—David Dale

**Note:** Throughout this book we've indicated restaurants by using little roosters carrying trays.

## Australian Wines Come of Age

When it comes to liquid assets, Australia has long been hailed as a beer drinker's delight. From Carlton & United Brewery's Foster's Lager to Alan Bond's Black Swan Premium Lager, Aussies have never been shy about their love of liquid amber.

There's more than beer being brewed Down Under, though. Indeed, the world has awakened to the fact that quality wines are being bottled from coast to coast, as well as across the sea in Tasmania.

This grape rush did not occur overnight. In fact, grapes were being grown not long after the First Fleet dropped anchor in 1788. It wasn't long before some of the fledgling colony's offerings were receiving praise, either. One early vintner won a gold medal in London in 1828 for his red table wine, while another had his sparkling wine christened by French ruler Napoleon III as being "equal to the finest champagne."

Australian wines now routinely win ribbons at international taste tests and are considered by many connoisseurs as providing better value for money than most Californian and French drops. Indeed, while in the United States you might expect to pay between $20 and $30 for a decent California pinot noir, the same bottle of Australian would cost about half that much.

Then, too, Australia also offers less-demanding drinkers a very affordable and tasty alternative—wine casks. These are smartly packaged, sturdy cardboard containers that feature a wide selection of red and white table wines for about $10.

For those who prefer a bottle or two with dinner, the country's prime wine growers, found in New South Wales, Victoria, South Australia, Western Australia, and Tasmania, offer everything from traditional favorites like rhine rieslings, chardonnays, and chablis to dark, fruity pinot noirs, cabernet sauvignons, and burgundys. (Other offerings such as ports, sauternes, and sparkling wines are also readily available.)

For white-wine lovers, there are many great labels to choose from, including rhine rieslings from New South Wales's Hunter Valley and South Australia's Clare Valley. Then, too, many winemakers in the Hunter Valley, as well as in Western Australia's Swan Valley, are renowned for their range of drier varieties like white burgundy or chablis and chardonnay.

Red-wine lovers have an equally wide range of varieties and labels to choose from. Hot spots to look for include South Australia's tiny Coonawarra region and Victoria's Great Western district, if you prefer firm red drops such as cabernet sauvignon and claret; while lovers of burgundy and softer wines can look for labels from the Hunter Valley, South Australia's McLaren Vale, the Swan Valley, and northeastern Victoria's Rutherglen region.

If you find yourself getting light-headed from simply poring over the myriad varieties and labels to choose from, there's one last Aussie import that tastes great no matter whether you're climbing Ayers Rock by day or spending a night at the Opera House—beer. It's just a case of deciding whether you want a Foster's or Black Swan, Emu Lager or Toohey's, Melbourne Bitter or . . .

—Mark C. Kestigian

# 2

# ORIENTING YOURSELF

We cannot overstate the fact that Australia is a huge country: roughly the size of the United States (and with almost half of its people concentrated on the east coast in the major cities of Sydney and Melbourne). If you're not traveling with an organized tour, you're going to need a clear idea of what's where and how far away things are from each other. Unless you've quit your job back home or have taken a lengthy leave of absence, don't expect to see all of the country. The major points of interest are usually quite far from each other indeed—and after that very long plane flight you've just taken to get to Australia, you may not relish another six-hour flight once you're here (also remember, as we've said earlier, domestic air travel is quite expensive). Consider choosing one state to explore; two contiguous ones maximum. For further information on planning your trip, see Travel Arrangements at the back of the book.

**Sydney** is usually the gateway for visitors to Australia—especially for those who are exploring the east coast. The country began here and there's much of historical interest. Although citizens of Melbourne (to the south) may refute this, Sydney is usually considered the center of Australian life: its financial center, its arts and cultural center. Here is the world-famous Opera House, where, more than admire the architecture you can see some of the country's premier artists. Close by you can go to the beach (Manly is a twenty-minute ferry ride away; the surfing beach at Bondi is a short drive or bus ride); pet a koala or a kangaroo at nearby wildlife parks; go bushwalking in the Blue Mountains (about two hours out of town). Outdoor oriented, Sydney manages to combine cosmopolitan urban life with a typical Australian love of the outdoors.

**New South Wales** is the state Sydney is located in. It is more than 300,000 square miles in size—that's bigger than any U.S. state except Alaska. Should you decide to explore the state, moving beyond Sydney, you can travel north and south along the coast to beach towns punctuated with strange geological formations (like the Blow Hole in Kiama); or move inland, perhaps to the Southern Highlands, where you can stay in country house hotels and drive through an area reminiscent of the English countryside. Canberra, Australia's capital, is actually in a federal enclave, called the Australian Capital Territory (A.C.T.), land within, but independent of New South Wales. (We cover it as a section of the New South Wales chapter.) It's a city to visit if you're interested in seeing the site of Australia's governmental workings. Canberra is a logical place to stop off on your way to the Snowy Mountains: there's skiing here in winter, and in the summer the meadows are covered with wildflowers, the rivers filled with trout and perfect for white-water rafting. Also in New South Wales is the area known as the Hunter Valley, New South Wales's wine-growing region—where you can sample the local goods and take in the country air. As you move farther west, you pass through the area known as the New England region, rolling pastureland with some spectacular waterfalls and unusual rock formations; it's also possible to go fossicking (hunting) for sapphires around Glen Innes. Farther west, but still in New South Wales, you'll be in the state's Outback: the areas are large, barren, and harsh. The people are warm, almost as if to make up for the land, and you can get a taste of what much of the center of the country is like; there are old mining towns to explore, fossicking to try your hand at—it's perfect if you're not going to have the time to travel farther into the Outback. Broken Hill, at almost the extreme west of New South Wales, is about 1,161 road kilometers (700 miles) from Sydney. The serene beauty of Lord Howe Island is off the coast.

**Melbourne** suffers from a reputation as Australia's second city; it's about 889 kilometers (550 miles) south of Sydney. A bit more British in feel than its northern neighbor, it has less of an outdoorsiness to it (remember that when you move south in Australia, the weather gets colder); it's a refined city of trams, sophisticated shops, good restaurants, and night-spots. When you explore outside of Melbourne, you're in the small state (that's small by Australian standards) of **Victoria.** Most of the state is within day-tripping distance of Melbourne. There are national parks here to explore; areas teeming with colorful birds, where days can be spent horseback riding and drinking in the scenery; wineries in the Rutherglen region; and plenty of places to sign up for a farm holiday to give you an inside look at rural Australian life.

Farther south, on its own island, is **Tasmania,** the smallest Australian state. (You can take a ferry here from Melbourne— around 12 hours or so; or take a short flight from Sydney or Melbourne.) Tasmania is a popular spot for Australians to vacation. Main cities are Launceston, in the northeast of the island, Hobart in the southeast. Both have popular casino hotels—or you could consider staying in mountain lodges in the country or at a fly fishing resort. The cities are historic, the countryside fascinating (the land formations as well as the animals are different from those of the mainland), and fishing enthusiasts, bushwalkers, even scuba divers and river rafters can find plenty to do here.

**Queensland** covers almost a quarter of Australia—it's a state about twice the size of Texas. Fly into a city near the areas you're most interested in exploring. The main city farthest to the south is Brisbane (748 air kilometers, about 465 miles, from Sydney; about 1,030 road kilometers, 640 miles). The city offers some historic sights, the Lone Pine Koala sanctuary (another place to cuddle a koala), quality restaurants. Nearby are the highly developed Gold Coast beaches and the quieter Sunshine Coast beaches. North of this area, Central Queensland, is a huge area, beginning at Maryborough, about 264 kilometers (165 miles) north of Brisbane, and stretching another 1,100 kilometers (680 miles) north. There are beach resorts along the coast; the rainforested sand island of Fraser, off the coast; access points for the Great Barrier Reef; some inland sheep and cattle farms for experiencing bush life. Planes fly into Townsville, at the northern end of this stretch; Townsville is 1,460 kilometers (over 900 miles) north of Brisbane. Far North Queensland is the area of the Great Barrier Reef. Cairns, 800 kilometers (500 miles or so) north of Townsville, is also an international airport, so it can be your gateway to Australia. The offshore resorts of the Reef, including the Whitsunday Islands, are very close to the coastline here. In addition, there are great coastal beaches; a rainforest that meets the sea at Cape Tribulation; plenty of unusual geologic formations in the hinterland; and places to explore and fish in the Outback.

**South Australia** is the southern part of the country, west of Victoria, New South Wales, and Queensland. Sparsely populated, this is an area of wineries; charming country-house hotels; and the pleasant city of Adelaide—site of a three-week cultural festival held during March of even-numbered years. (Adelaide is about 1,475 road kilometers, 914 miles, from Sydney; it would take about two hours by plane.) The northern area of the state—actually most of the state—is harsh desert, so the population and visitors stay in the southeast. Kangaroo Island is off the coast, about half an hour's flight from Adelaide. It's a place filled with rare flora and fauna; you can stay in beachfront hotels or in farm houses scattered around the island.

**The Northern Territory** is the huge expanse of land north of South Australia; the home of the Aborigines. The Top End consists of the city of Darwin, crocodile-infested swamps, and rainforests. It's home of Mick "Crocodile" Dundee, and residents are known for their beer drinking and all-around "toughness." Explore this area to see the wildlife, and perhaps to hook up with a tour that will take you into the Aboriginal lands here. Darwin is 2,068 air miles (3,328 road miles) from Sydney; that's about a five-hour plane ride. The Center, south of the Top End, is where Ayers Rock is, the monolith, sacred to the Aborigines, that may be the greatest landmark in Australia. Alice Springs is the main city in the area; it is about 1,179 road kilometers (730 miles) from Darwin, 674 air kilometers (417 miles); it takes two and half hours from Sydney by plane to get to Alice Springs. Alice Springs is about 480 road kilometers (300 miles) from Uluru National Park, in which are Ayers Rock and the undulating rock formations of the Olgas.

**Western Australia.** One-third of the Australian continent is Western Australia. By far the great majority of the state's population live in the capital, Perth. A city of sunshine and water sports, Perth underwent a major facelift in preparation for Australia's defense of the America's Cup in 1987. Today, hotels, restaurants, and tourist facilities abound. The rest of the state's population has over 2.5 million square kilometers of land to spread out in: mostly this is mining country, or cattle ranches, or wheat farms. This is also the state that's said to have the best surfing (in the southwest), and the state of the Kimberleys, considered the country's last real frontier.

---

### Important Note

All prices given in this book are in Australian dollars unless otherwise noted.

# 3

## PRIORITIES

The great dilemma for travelers to Australia is in deciding how to spend your time. With distances so great, you have to be especially careful to choose your priority sights and activities and then see what's nearby. This is a personal listing of what we consider to be worthwhile.

**Ayers Rock and Uluru National Park.** Of spiritual significance to the Aborigines, Uluru National Park encompasses the great monolith known as Ayers Rock as well as the rolling peaks called the Olgas. Situated in The Center of the Northern Territory, the sights, unlike anything you'll see anywhere else in the world, are some 480 kilometers (300 miles) southwest of Alice Springs, which will probably be your gateway to the area. Facilities and accommodations are in the Yulara complex about 20 kilometers (12 miles) from the Rock.
**Nearby:** You can travel north to Darwin (it's about 1,179 kilometers, or 730 miles from Alice Springs) and the Aboriginal lands of The Top End, such as Kakadu National Park and the Tiwi Islands. South is South Australia; Adelaide is almost 1,597 kilometers (1,000 miles) from Alice Springs.

**Great Barrier Reef.** More than 2,500 coral reefs give visitors a chance to explore a living underwater museum. Located at the top end of Queensland, the reef offers more than twenty off-shore resorts and more charter and day-trip boats than we can count. Scuba divers and snorkelers, of course, won't want to miss this; but even if you don't swim, you can take a glass-bottom boat out. International airports are in Townsville and Cairns; domestic airlines can link you with minor coastal ports.
**Nearby:** If you're interested in traveling farther south— perhaps to Sydney, you'll most likely have to fly: it's 2,636 kilometers from Cairns to Sydney by road (that's 1,635 miles). The sophisticated beaches of Queensland's Sunshine Coast are closer; maybe the closest sight of major interest is the

wilderness rainforest, which meets the beach and the reef at Cape Tribulation.

**Kakadu National Park.** Home of "Crocodile" Dundee, Kakadu is a huge area of woodlands, forests, and waterways, containing wildlife, Aboriginal history, and rock art. Come here to spot a crocodile, or maybe a lizard; bird watchers can have a field day. Take a tour into the Aboriginal lands around here—either Arnhem Land or the Tiwi Islands where you can spend time with the people—spear fishing, eating real bush "tucker," seeing sights that few foreigners have been able to see. You'll probably fly into Darwin.
**Nearby:** You're north of Alice Springs (see above); much closer to Katherine Gorge.

**Kangaroo Island.** Off the coast of South Australia, this small island gives visitors the opportunity to see seals, sea lions, fairy penguins, rare birds, and, of course, kangaroos. There are great beaches here, too.
**Nearby:** You're 110 kilometers (68 miles) south of Adelaide; a trip to Kangaroo Island may combine well with an exploration of South Australia's wine country.

**Katherine Gorge.** This national park consists of 13 canyons carved out of the land by the Katherine River. The best way to see it is to sign up for a cruise and clamber tour, which will combine boating on the river and then clambering over the rocks to the next gorge.
**Nearby:** You're not too far from Kakadu and the Tiwi Islands; the small town of Katherine is about 300 kilometers (185 miles) south of Darwin, the nearest major city.

**Kimberleys.** In the northwest of Western Australia is the country's last real frontier: historic towns such as Broome and Derby and the bizarre, colorful gorges of the Kimberleys themselves, their wildlife and Aboriginal art. The eastern access point to the region is Kununurra, also the access for the Bungle Bungles, domes of multicolored rock.
**Nearby:** Kununurra is on the Northern Territory border; you could combine this trip with a visit to the Northern Territory Top End (Kakadu, Katherine Gorge).

**Lord Howe Island.** Almost 500 miles northeast of Sydney, the unspoilt beauty of Lord Howe makes it popular as a holiday spot among Australians and visitors alike. Bushwalking, scuba diving, and just relaxing are among the favored activities. Space on Lord Howe is limited, however; book well in advance.
**Nearby:** You can use Sydney as your gateway.

**Melbourne.** This charming city, sophisticated with a touch of old-world charm, is a contrast to its outdoorsy big sister to the north, Sydney. Come here just to explore the city by tram, drink in its culture—or take part in the excitement of the Melbourne Cup, a horse race that's a national event. The tennis matches of the Australian Open are played in Melbourne, too.

**Nearby:** You can explore the Victoria hinterland, take the one-hour-fifteen-minute plane trip to Sydney to the north, or fly or ferry south to the island state of Tasmania.

**Perth.** This is more of a water-oriented city than others in Australia—and that's saying something. Now known as the home of the America's Cup defense, Perth and neighboring Fremantle have historic districts, lots of fancy hotels, and nearby beaches. You can take a day trip to nearby Rottnest Island, a wildlife reserve, as well as into rural inland areas.

**Sunshine Coast.** Along the coast of Queensland, north of Brisbane, are the cosmopolitan beaches called the Sunshine Coast (less brash than the Gold Coast beaches, south of Brisbane). Aside from the surf, sand, and sun, you can explore some Australian wilderness in the hinterland.

**Nearby:** You can travel north to the Great Barrier Reef (but you'll probably have to fly; Cairns is over 2,000 kilometers—1,400 miles—from Brisbane), or move south to Sydney (over 1,000 kilometers—640 miles—from Brisbane).

**Sydney.** Probably Australia's most important city, Sydney offers one of the world's most magnificent harbors (complemented by the world-famous Opera House), great restaurants and nightlife, and good beaches in the area.

**Nearby:** Travel south to Melbourne; fly to the Great Barrier Reef or the beaches of the Queensland coast; take an excursion into the countryside—if you travel all the way to Broken Hill (about 1,161 kilometers, 720 miles, west), you'll get a taste of the Australian Outback; or consider a trip to Lord Howe Island.

**Tasmania.** For sports enthusiasts, a trip into the Tasmania bush should be up on the list of things to do while in Australia. There's some great fishing here; unique wildlife; scenic walks; kayaking; canoeing; and river rafting. You can base yourself at one of the country houses we recommend, or stay in the cities of Launceston or Hobart and make excursions from there.

**Nearby:** You're a 12-hour ferry ride from Melbourne; a short plane ride either from Melbourne or Sydney.

**Western Australia's Southwest.** An immensely varied area of beaches, wildflowers, and wine districts; the coastline between Cape Naturaliste and Cape Leeuwin is supposed to comprise the country's best surfing beaches. There are also spectacular caves here, and inland, on the Blackwood River, white-water rafting. You can even travel through the area in your own horse-drawn wagon.

**Nearby:** Combine a visit here with a trip to Perth.

**Wine Country of South Australia.** You can explore one of Australia's premier wine-growing regions (and sample the goods) in the Barossa or Clare valleys. Both can be visited from Adelaide, but there are wonderful country houses in the area, as well.

**Nearby:** From Adelaide, consider visiting Kangaroo Island. Or if you're up to it, see the inhospitable Outback of South Australia, some 350 kilometers (220 miles) from Adelaide.

## Australian Language

American visitors to Australia may make the mistake of thinking that, as both countries are English speaking, communication will be a breeze. And, to some extent, they are right. Certainly Australians, acclimated after years of watching American TV shows, understand the American idiom. But whether the American tourist will always understand what his Australian hosts are on about (that is to say, what they mean) is a moot point.

For instance, in a restaurant when ordering a three-course meal, you will no doubt refer to the main course as the "entrée." The waiter will be confused—in Australia, the entrée refers to the beginning course; the main course is called just that. Occasionally you'll hear dessert referred to as "pud," as in, "What's for pud?" This is short for pudding—and is applied to any form of dessert, whether or not it is of a custardy consistency.

Please avoid using penny, nickel, and dime to refer to one-, five-, and ten-cent pieces. The terms are not used here.

You walk on the footpath, not the sidewalk; throw your golf clubs into the boot of the car, not the trunk; and keep a torch (flashlight) in the glove box (not compartment).

You may occasionally decide to forgo the pleasures of restaurant dining, opting instead for a burger in your motel room. You'll get these at the local takeaway (not take-out). You can also get burgers at most milk bars—funny little places that make milk-based drinks like milk shakes, serve ice cream cones (though seldom hand dipped), and a range of candy.

The counter hand, not sure you've been served yet, may well ask "Are you right, mate?" (or "luv," if you're a woman), meaning "have you been served?" You answer, "Yes, I'm right, thanks."

For some reason, Australians have a penchant for forming a diminutive of everything. This is most often done by attaching the suffix "ie" to words. Hence Christmas becomes "Chrissie," presents "pressies," university, "uni." Abbreviations generally are popular: the milkman and the garbage man are the "milko" and the "garbo"; people plan their summer "hols," short for holidays.

On the other hand, just when you think you have them all figured out, they throw you a fast curve and insist on plain speech: Not for them such euphemisms as "restroom" or "lavatory." If you can't find them by yourself, ask where the toilets are, not the restroom. This goes for the most up-market establishments. Occasionally in conversation you may hear it referred to as "the lav" (short for lavatory) or, as in Britain, "the loo" (supposedly a contraction of the old French medieval warning shouted when a chamber pot was being emptied: "Gardez loo," though this may be totally apocryphal). But, really, toilet will do just fine.

And as you're leaving the country, tell anyone who asks how you enjoyed your stay that you were wrapped. That means you really liked it.

—Mary Ellen Dyster

# 4

# SYDNEY

Sydney is the hub of contemporary Australian life—its financial heart, home to some of the nation's most creative artists, actors, fashion designers, and musicians. The original colony of New South Wales began here and many of the nation's treasured historic landmarks are found in these streets and in the nearby countryside.

Some of the most beautiful spots on earth lie in and around Sydney, from magnificent beaches, many practically deserted most of the year, to mountains for hiking in or skiing on.

Most visitors to Australia arrive via Sydney. Passenger liners glory in pulling into one of the most beautiful harbors in the world. Yearly, more and more international airlines are finding that Sydney is a "must" stop on their Pacific route. In fact, around 63 percent of American tourists use Sydney as the port of entry to Australia every year.

Combined with a climate that boasts a Mediterranean-style summer, when the rest of the world is shoveling snow, competitive prices on tourist accommodations, and a very favorable rate of exchange on the U.S. dollar, it's hard to think of a reason *not* to visit Sydney.

## ORIENTING YOURSELF

When residents of Sydney talk about "the city" they mean two very different things. They refer to the entire urban sprawl of 3,500,000 people that spreads beneath the plane as you circle before landing. This extends from the twenty or so surf beaches on the Pacific Ocean side, to the heights of the Blue Mountains, eighty kilometers (fifty miles) away to the west. They are also including the eighty kilometers or so from north to south where residential areas end in large national parks.

"The city," secondly, is the Central Business District (CBD), about three kilometers (two miles) square on the south side of Sydney Harbour, in which many of the major hotels and the best-known tourist attractions are to be found. This is where the Opera House, the colonial Rocks region, and the city's Chinatown district can be found, as well as major shopping venues and several theaters.

> The train ran for a long time through Sydney, or the endless outsides of Sydney. The town took almost as much leaving as London does. But it was different. Instead of solid rows of houses, solid streets like London, it was mostly innumerable detached bungalows and cottages, spreading for great distances, scattering over hills, low hills and shallow inclines. And then waste marshy places, and old iron, and abortive corrugated iron "works"—all like the Last Day of creation, instead of a new country. Away to the left they saw the shallow waters of the big opening where Botany Bay is: the sandy shores, the factory chimneys, the lonely places where it is still bush. And the weary half-established straggling of more suburb. . . . Far in the west, the sky having suddenly cleared, they saw the magical range of the Blue Mountains. And all this hoary space of bush between. The strange, as it were, *invisible* beauty of Australia, which is undeniably there, but which seems to lurk just beyond the range of our white vision. You feel you can't *see*—as if your eyes hadn't the vision in them to correspond with the outside landscape. For the landscape is so unimpressive, like a face with little or no features, a dark face. It is so aboriginal, out of our ken, and it hangs back so aloof.
>
> —D. H. Lawrence
> *Kangaroo,* 1923

Outside of this central area, Sydney is divided into approximately four hundred suburbs, each a separate political district, with its own shops and services and local identity. This concept of suburb differs from the American in that not all these districts are distant from the CBD—in fact some are no more than a five- or ten-minute bus ride away.

Because Sydney is built on a series of bays and inlets, its coastal suburbs particularly are irregular in shape. This and the hilliness of the city can make finding your way around fairly puzzling. Even the natives get confused!

Don't panic; simply invest in what every Sydneysider owns—a street directory. The two most consulted versions come in hardback form: *Gregory's Sydney* (known colloquially as "a Gregory's") or the *UBD* guide. Each contains detailed maps with coordinates for every street and lane in the metropolitan area, as well as the location of train stations, post offices, and major park areas.

If you've rented a car, check the glove compartment for a copy of one of these directories. Most rental agencies furnish them. As well, they will often lend copies of directories for other cities if you intend driving between major locations.

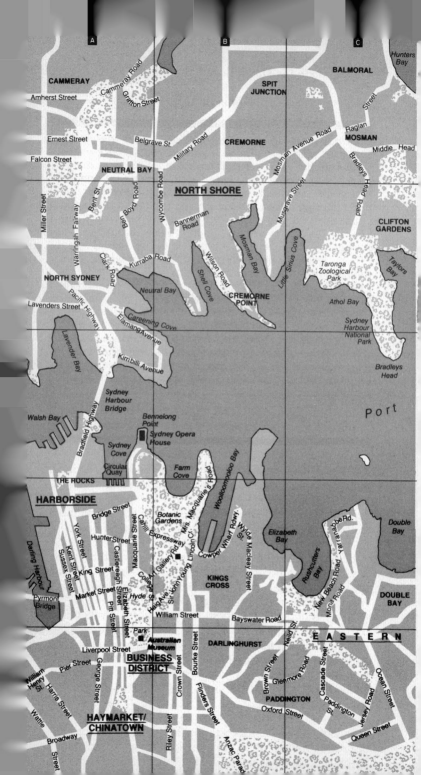

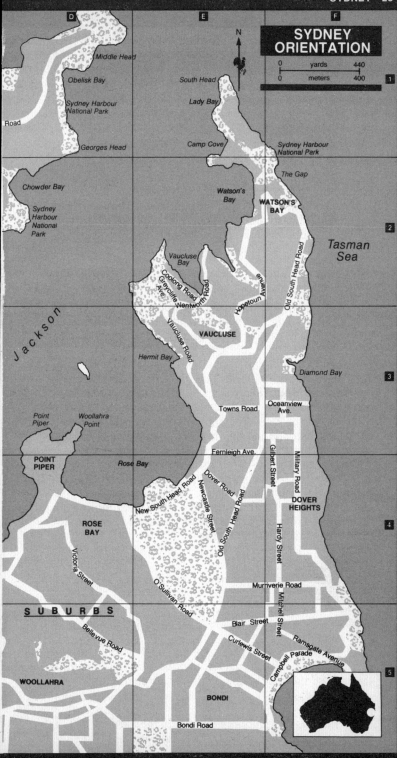

SYDNEY
ORIENTATION

N

0     yards     440
0     meters     400

Middle Head

Obelisk Bay

Sydney Harbour
National Park

Road

Georges Head

South Head

Lady Bay

Camp Cove

Sydney Harbour
National Park

The Gap

Chowder Bay

Watson's
Bay

WATSON'S
BAY

Tasman
Sea

Sydney
Harbour
National
Park

Vaucluse
Bay

Old South Head Road

J a c k s o n

Coolong Road
Greycliffe
Ave.
Wentworth Road

Hopetoun Avenue

Vaucluse Road

VAUCLUSE

Hermit Bay

Diamond Bay

Towns Road

Oceanview
Ave.

Point
Piper

Woollahra
Point

Fernleigh Ave.

Gilbert Street

Military Road

POINT
PIPER

Rose Bay

Dover Road

DOVER
HEIGHTS

New South Head Road

Newcastle Street

Old South Head Road

Hardy Street

ROSE
BAY

Victoria Street

O'Sullivan Road

Murriverie Road

Mitchell Street

**S U B U R B S**

Bellevue Road

Blair   Street

Curlewis Street

Ramsgate Avenue

Campbell Parade

WOOLLAHRA

BONDI

Bondi Road

You'll probably want two or three days to explore the central city. The **Harborside** area takes in the area along Darling Harbour, due west, continuing up to Walsh Bay at the extreme northern tip of the peninsula, then south again to Sydney Cove (bordered by The Rocks area on the west), up to Bennelong Point (where the famous Opera House stands), and around Farm Cove which edges the lovely Royal Botanic Gardens.

Due south of this waterfront area is the main **Business District,** incorporating the major entertainment and shopping venues of the city. Its informal southern boundary is the Central Railway terminus and Railway Square.

On the southwestern fringe of the mid-city area parallel with Railway Square lies the Haymarket area, more popularly known as **Chinatown.** The new Powerhouse Museum, Sydney Entertainment Centre and the shops and restaurants of Darling Harbour are each a short walk from here.

Back in the middle of the city, the corner of Park and George streets form a major intersection. George Street is a main artery leading from the waterfront through the city toward the west. Together with Pitt, Castlereagh, and Elizabeth streets, which lie parallel to George on the east, it forms some of the key shopping real estate in the city.

Park Street heads east, changing its name to William Street as it passes through leafy, mid-city Hyde Park and moves into the **Eastern Suburbs.** William Street bypasses the notorious **Kings Cross** area (strictly speaking, part of the Eastern Suburbs, but separated from them in our neighborhood breakdown for emphasis) and speeds along toward Double Bay and the rest of the wealthy harborside Eastern Suburbs.

Oxford Street begins at the southeastern boundary of Hyde Park and stretches up through the non-harborside Eastern Suburbs. It is in itself a fascinating shopper's route (see Shopping) and runs through the iron-lace suburb of **Paddington** (like Kings Cross, separated for our purpose from the rest of the Eastern Suburbs) before continuing on toward the ocean. Here are Sydney's beach suburbs, including famous Bondi and quieter Tamarama.

Since the suburbs west of the Central Business District will be of only passing interest to the short-term visitor to Sydney, we won't go into detail about them here, merely outlining some of their major attractions as potential day-tours later in this chapter.

The **North Shore** is another matter. Reachable via the Sydney Harbour Bridge and any number of ferries that cross the harbor from Circular Quay, it is another gold mine of beautiful beaches, sophisticated shopping, and touring opportunities.

The harborside suburbs on this side of the bridge, like their Eastern counterparts, are, for the most part, fairly tony.

Farther up the line one runs into a mixture of native bush suburbs, houses nestled in pockets of gum tree and sandstone, and English-style mansions landscaped with all the deciduous flora you'd expect in a colder northern climate.

If you continue due north, the native bush thickens until you run into Ku-ring-gai Chase National Park, the city's natural northern boundary.

Suburbs along the eastern coast of the North Shore are called the Northern Beaches. Like those beaches on the same coast of the south side, most are surfing beaches (see Beaches and Sporting).

All we have attempted to do here is give a general idea of the layout of that part of Sydney which a short-term visitor might find interesting. This isn't to say that some of the so-called Western suburbs haven't also points of extreme interest, particularly the Paramatta area, about 25 kilometers (15 miles) west of the city. But this area will be discussed, along with other outlying regions, in the section on Short Trips out of Sydney.

**When looking for particular addresses, especially if giving directions to a cab driver, be sure you ask for the street name and *give the name of the suburb*. Many street names are repeated in several suburbs, thus you'll have an Elizabeth Street in the city, also one in Paddington and again in Surry Hills —all of which a tourist may wish to visit. If you ask for 41 Elizabeth Street when you get into a cab, be sure to specify which suburb you want, to avoid confusion.**

**Similarly, many streets run through several suburbs. Oxford Street, for example, runs from the city, through Darlinghurst, Paddington, Woollahra, and Bondi Junction. Each time you change suburbs, street numbering begins again. If you're taking the bus or walking, be sure of which suburb you're in and which one you want to be in before looking up the building address. As in the States, odd numbers are on one side of the street, evens on the other—although opposite sides of the street frequently fall into different suburbs. Check your "Gregory's"!**

# PRIORITIES

Every tourist has his or her own idea of what to see in a city. For some it's the cultural aspect, for others the natural scenery. The following is a list of places that gives a cross section of Sydney's attractions—a little something for everyone. Later on, in Short Trips out of Sydney, areas more than an hour's traveling time from central Sydney will be discussed—and we do believe that everyone should make the effort to see the countryside outside Sydney. The areas listed here can usually be reached from central Sydney in about half an hour by foot, taxi, or public transportation. Each attraction is keyed into the area of the city in which it is located (as delineated above under Orienting Yourself). Also, sights are keyed into the color maps of the city at the back of the book, referring to the page number of the maps as well as the appropriate coordinates.

## Argyle Centre                    HARBORSIDE, P. 24, B2

Argyle and Playfair streets, The Rocks; open between 9:30 A.M. and 5:30 P.M., seven days a week. Argyle Centre is a series of stone and brick warehouses, built between 1820 and 1840, which were restored in the late 1960s. The Centre houses a series of arts, crafts, and antique shops, and several cafés and restaurants including the Argyle Tavern and the Garrison Restaurant. The Brasserie Bar is a recent glassed-in addition which runs off the Playfair Street end of the Centre.

The Jolly Swagman Show in the Argyle Tavern runs nightly, featuring aspects of colonial Australian culture—sheep-shearing display, bush ballads, and songs played on the gum leaf. To book, phone 27-7782.

**Nearby:** Argyle Cut; Argyle Place; Orient Hotel (pub); the Opera House is within walking distance.

## The Art Gallery of N.S.W.      BUSINESS DISTRICT, P. 25, D4

Open Monday through Saturday from 10 A.M. to 5 P.M.; Sunday from noon to 5 P.M. Admission to general exhibits is free; special exhibitions are individually priced. 225-1700. To get to the gallery, follow Art Gallery Road, which lies east of College behind St. Mary's Cathedral in the section of parkland known as The Domain. Featured in the museum's permanent exhibits are works by Australians, Europeans, and Asians.

**Nearby:** Botanic Gardens; Conservatorium of Music; State Library; The Domain; St. Mary's Cathedral.

## Australian Museum      BUSINESS DISTRICT, P. 24, C5

6–8 College Street, Corner of William; open Tuesday through Saturday and public holidays from 10 A.M. to 5 P.M.; Sunday and Monday from noon to 5 P.M. Admission is free. 339-8111. The museum houses the largest natural history collection in Australia. Also here are fine specimens of Aboriginal and Pacific Island art and artifacts.

**Nearby:** Hyde Park; St. Mary's Cathedral; Boulevard Hotel.

## Botanic Gardens      HARBORSIDE, P. 25, D3

Across Cahill Expressway from the Art Gallery. Open from 8 A.M. to sunset. Free admission. More than seventy acres of gardens are here, featuring native and exotic plants. A restaurant in the center of the gardens is open from 10 A.M. to 4 P.M. on weekdays, noon to 4:30 P.M. on Sundays and holidays.

**Nearby:** Conservatorium; Opera House; State Library; Hotel Inter-Continental; Circular Quay; Art Gallery; The Domain.

## Chinese Garden CHINATOWN, P. 26, B6

At the southeastern boundary of the Darling Harbour project, this garden was a bicentennial gift from the Chinese government. It is an exact reproduction of a classic garden in the Chinese style, complete with waterfalls and Oriental vegetation. Open from 11 A.M. to sunset daily. From George Street, take bus 431, 433, or 438 to Hay Street, and walk west to Chinatown.

**Nearby:** Sydney Entertainment Centre; Powerhouse Museum.

## Conservatorium of Music HARBORSIDE, P. 24, C3

The center for advanced musical study, the conservatorium is located by the Botanic Gardens at the end of Bridge Street, just off Macquarie. During term time, free lunchtime concerts are given each Wednesday, with Friday evening concerts sometimes given at a moderate charge in the school's concert hall. Phone 230-1263 for details.

**Nearby:** Sydney Opera House; Circular Quay; Hotel Inter-Continental; State Library; The Domain; Art Gallery.

## Darling Harbour Redevelopment NEAR CHINATOWN, P. 24, A5

Adjacent to Chinatown, this area was once a collection of empty lots and unused tram lines; today it is the site of the greatest urban redevelopment scheme in Australia's history. There are more than two hundred specialty shops and restaurants; the Sydney Maritime Museum; the Sydney Convention Centre; and an exhibition center. An aquarium is on the opposite side of Darling Harbour. A monorail connects the central city area (you can pick it up on Pitt or Market St.) with Darling Harbour.

**Nearby:** Powerhouse Museum (two blocks west); Sydney Entertainment Center; Chinese Garden.

## Elizabeth Bay House EASTERN SUBURBS, P. 25, F4

7 Onslow Avenue, Elizabeth Bay. One of Sydney's grand historic houses, the Elizabeth Bay House is open to the public Tuesday through Sunday from 10 A.M. to 4:30 P.M. Admission $2.50. Phone 358-2344. The superbly restored Regency house has been furnished in keeping with its period and often mounts exhibitions of relevant historical interest. Take the bus from Park Street.

**Nearby:** Kings Cross; Boomerang house; Sebel Town House hotel.

## Ferry to Manly HARBORSIDE, P. 24, C2

Sydney looks magnificent from the water—and you especially should make a point of seeing the Opera House from this vantage point. The ferry to Manly (catch it at Circular Quay) gives you a leisurely, scenic ride; and when you disembark you'll be within walking distance of a pleasant beach. For information on Manly ferries telephone 29-2622.

## Hyde Park Barracks
BUSINESS DISTRICT, P. 24, C4

At the top of Macquarie Street at Queen's Square, opposite the northern end of Hyde Park. Open Wednesday through Monday from 10 A.M. to 5 P.M.; Tuesday from noon to 5 P.M. Free admission to general exhibits. Phone 217-0111. The Barracks is a series of restored early-19th-century buildings that once housed convicts. Today it is a museum where, in the specially reconstructed dormitory, you can climb into a hammock like the ones used by convicts or look at any of the special changing exhibits on display.

The Barracks Café has had special commendation from Sydney food writers for its innovative light meals. It is open Monday through Sunday from 10 A.M. to 5 P.M. Phone 223-1155.

**Nearby:** Hyde Park; Parliament House; Mint Museum; David Jones department store; St. Mary's Cathedral; State Library.

## Mint Museum
BUSINESS DISTRICT, P. 24, C4

Also at Queen's Square and Macquarie Street, next to Hyde Park Barracks. Open from 10 A.M. to 5 P.M. daily, except Wednesday from noon to 5 P.M. Free admission. Phone 217-0111. During the Australian gold rush, this former wing of the Old Rum Hospital became a mint for coining gold sovereigns. Today it is a museum of decorative arts, coins, and stamps.

## Parliament House (State)
BUSINESS DISTRICT, P. 24, C4

Macquarie Street, between Hunter and Martin Place. Phone 230-2111. The original building was once the northern arm of the Old Rum Hospital, but since 1827 it has been the seat of state government debate. It is open to the public Monday through Friday from 9 A.M. to 4:30 P.M. Gallery seats may be booked for debates when Parliament is sitting by phoning 230-2111; a seat will be reserved for evening sittings after 7:30. It is difficult to access for handicapped persons.

**Nearby:** Mint Museum; Hyde Park Barracks; State Library; Botanic Gardens; Conservatorium; Hyde Park.

## Pier 1
HARBORSIDE, P. 24, B1

Number 1 Wharf, Hickson Road, Walsh Bay. The major benefit of this tourist attraction is that it saved one of Sydney's historic wharves, unused since the closure of the area to passenger ships in the early sixties. Modeled loosely on Fisherman's Wharf in San Francisco, the Pier 1 shops sell a variety of knickknacks, inexpensive souvenirs, and seafood. Its restaurants and bars provide unparalleled harbor views.

**Nearby:** Wharf Theatre; Wharf Restaurant; Lower George Street; The Rocks.

## Powerhouse Museum
CHINATOWN, P. 26, A6

Harris Street, Ultimo. Phone 217-0111. Open daily from 10 A.M. to 5 P.M. This fascinating museum of applied arts and sciences was fashioned from a 19th-century power station. Among its ten thousand displayed objects are a Catalina flying boat, the Boulton and Watt rotative steam engine (1785)— restored and working; a reproduction of an old Australian pub, Art Deco works by Rene Lalique, and a working model of the Strasbourg Clock. It has a café-restaurant. Plan at least half a day for this one—it's worth it.

**Nearby:** Chinatown and the Chinese Garden; Sydney Entertainment Centre; Darling Harbour.

## The Rocks Visitors Centre
HARBORSIDE, P. 24, B2

104 George Street, The Rocks; Phone 27-4972. Open Monday through Friday from 8.30 A.M. to 5:30 P.M.; Saturday through Sunday from 9 A.M. to 5 P.M. This should be the first point of call in any visit to the Rocks district—the site of the first European settlement in Australia. Here you can pick up maps, leaflets, and information about the area—what to see, where to shop. The Centre shows a film about old Sydney and can organize walking tours of the district.

**Nearby:** Crafts Centre Gallery; Old Sydney Parkroyal Hotel; Cadman's Cottage; Orient Hotel (pub); Argyle Centre; Argyle Cut; Argyle Place; the Opera House is also within walking distance.

## Sydney Harbour Bridge
HARBORSIDE, P. 24, B1

Completed in the 1930s, the Bridge links the north and south sides of the harbor. It carries a train line, passenger cars, and trucks and also has a walkway and a bicycle route. A toll of $1 is collected from drivers coming from the north side day and night. There are massive stone pylons at either end of the bridge; it's possible to go up into the southeast pylon for a panoramic view of the harbor. (Open 9 A.M. to 5 P.M. daily) Find the entrance to the walkway on Cumberland Street. The bridge is, at present, the major alternative to ferry travel for crossing from the south to the north side of the harbor. Plans are under way for a Harbour Tunnel, which will reduce the congestion on the bridge considerably when completed sometime in the 1990s.

## Sydney Opera House
HARBORSIDE, P. 24, C2

Bennelong Point. Phone 250-7111. There are guided tours lasting about one hour, between the hours of 9 A.M. and 4 P.M. daily; backstage tours on Sunday between 9 A.M. and 4 P.M. Cost is $4.50.

This is probably the Sydney landmark with the highest world profile—the roof that looks like a series of ships in full sail, the glass walls overlooking the harbor. But try to see the Opera House doing what it was created for: hosting fine musical and dramatic performances. Bookings for performances can be made by phoning 2-0525. Check local newspaper entertainment listings for current programs.

The Bennelong Restaurant occupies one of the shell-roofed sections of the building. It is not inexpensive, and few raves have ever been directed its way; but if you like making a night of it at the harbor, you can book a table by phoning 250-7111. Open Monday through Saturday for lunch, dinner, and pre/post theater supper.

The medium-priced Forecourt Restaurant, below podium level on the western side of the forecourt, is a brasserie open from 9 A.M. to midnight every day except Sunday, 11:30 A.M. to 8 P.M.

The Harbourside Restaurant at the northern end of the Opera House boardwalk is less expensive. Open daily from 11 A.M. to 8 P.M. for light meals and drinks to enjoy at outdoor tables.

Free musical entertainments are given each Sunday from noon to 4 P.M. on the boardwalk (good weather only). Programs are advertised in the Saturday edition of the *Sydney Morning Herald* entertainments section.

**Nearby:** Botanic Gardens; Circular Quay; The Rocks; Conservatorium; State Library.

### Sydney Tower BUSINESS DISTRICT, P. 24, C4

Centrepoint; Market, Pitt, and Castlereagh streets. Open Monday through Saturday from 9:30 A.M. to 9:30 P.M.; Sunday and public holidays, from 10:30 A.M. to 6.30 P.M. Admission is $4 for adults, $2 for children. Phone 229-7444. Sydney's tallest structure, the tower is approximately 304 meters (1,000 feet) high. From it you can achieve 360-degree views over the whole of Sydney from the ocean to the Blue Mountains in the west. Slides and a film help visitors understand the panorama that unfolds beneath them. A great place to get your bearings.

Two restaurants, one budget and one à la carte, are on the levels immediately beneath the observation deck. To book a table in the à la carte restaurant, phone 233-3722.

### Taronga Park Zoo NORTH SHORE, P. 28, B2

Bradleys Head Road, Mosman. Phone 969-2777. Open daily 9 A.M. to 5 P.M. For most Australians the zoo is as close as they get to native fauna. The koala exhibit offers the chance to see "eye to eye" with the furry favorites. The platypus house (open 10 A.M. to 4 P.M.—best viewing time 1:15 P.M.) allows you to see this nocturnal creature going about its routine. There is a free seal show twice daily, afternoons at 1:15 and 3:15, with an extra show at 11:15 A.M. on Sundays and public holidays. Special ramps and rest-room facilities for wheelchair users. Much of the park affords visitors spectacular views over the surrounding harbor. Admission is $10; $4.50 for children.

The easiest—and most fun way to get there—is to take the Taronga Park ferry from Circular Quay.

**Nearby:** Military Road shopping; Balmoral Beach.

## Vaucluse House EASTERN SUBURBS, P. 29, D2

Wentworth Road, Vaucluse. Phone 337-1957. Admission $2.50. Open from 10 A.M. to 4:30 P.M. daily, closed Monday. Home of William Charles Wentworth, the Father of the Australian Constitution, this Gothic style 1830s mansion is set in 27 acres of parkland. The house is furnished in period detail. The grounds themselves are open from 7 A.M. to 5 P.M. Parking is available within the grounds and a tea room provides light lunches and morning and afternoon teas. Take a bus from Park Street that travels east along New South Head Road; ask the driver for Vaucluse Park; the house is in the Park and signs for it are prominent.

**Nearby:** Nielsen Park and Beach.

## Victoria Barracks PADDINGTON, P. 27, F7

Oxford Street between Greens Road and Oatley Road, Paddington. Phone 339-3543. The Barracks are an outstanding example of mid-Victorian military architecture. A military museum is on the premises. Book in advance for a visit to the Barracks; on Tuesdays from February to December you can watch the changing of the guard ceremony, then tour the museum and the sandstone Barracks buildings. Take a bus running east on Oxford Street and ask the bus driver to call out the stop.

**Nearby:** Oxford Street shopping; "Paddington lace" terraces; Centennial Park; Sydney Cricket Ground and Show Ground.

---

# TRAVEL

Without question, the best way to see any city is on foot. Sightseeing buses, et al., are fine for general orientation, but actually to learn about a city, its personality, and the surprises it conceals from the casual observer, you have to walk around it.

Sydney is hilly—not quite in the same category as San Francisco; there aren't as many extremely steep streets. But there are precious few streets that are absolutely flat; even streets that look dead level slope subtly so that after a few hours of wandering, you will find you're feeling the strain. Wear comfortable walking shoes. And plan your itinerary so that you'll wind up near someplace you can sit down; don't decide to walk the length of Macquarie Street to look at the architecture and follow this with a couple of hours at the Art Gallery of N.S.W. without stopping for a good rest—perhaps sitting under a tree in Hyde Park.

Remember that cars travel on the left-hand side of the street in Australia. Americans need to forget all that childhood training to look left, then right before crossing the street. In Sydney, look right, then left—otherwise, you may find yourself picked up by a passing truck while you're carefully looking the wrong way!

Many intersections that don't have crossing lights have zebra stripes painted on the road for pedestrians. The rule is that traffic must stop for anyone who has stepped on to a zebra crossing. Of course, you have to exercise a little judgment; make sure cars see you and can stop safely before you step blithely out.

**While there's no rule about this, people tend to walk down the street and up and down stairs using the same traffic pattern—keeping to the left.**

## Getting from the Airport

A taxi from the airport to centrally located hotels in the city will run around $10–$11; the airport is about 6 miles from the city.

There is also, express bus service between the airport and the city—Circular Quay, George St. and/or Central Station—leaving approximately every twenty minutes 6 A.M.–9 P.M. (airport bound) and until 10:15 P.M. (city bound). It costs $3.

## Buses

Sydney is well served by its bus system in the Central Business District and suburbs within a wide radius. Free buses (no. 666) run about every thirty minutes between The Art Gallery and George St., and between The Australian Museum and Clarence St. every ten minutes (no. 777). Fares are determined by the number of sections you wish to travel through; an average ride will probably run $2–$3 each way. Packets of 10 tickets at reduced prices are available at any newsagent or train station.

Conductors collect fares at busy bus stops in the city, especially during peak travel times; otherwise you pay the driver directly. If you're not sure how many sections you will be traveling through, just tell the driver your destination and he/she will charge the correct fare. It isn't mandatory to give correct change, but busy bus drivers appreciate not having to make change for large bills. They do not accept one cent and two cent coins. You can halve your bus ticket costs by buying a MetroTen ticket—a ten-trip ticket with no time limit. Get it at The Travel Centre, 11–31 York St.

A $7 day-rover ticket (available at train and ferry stations, major bus depots, and selected newsagents) allows unlimited travel all day on buses, trains, and ferries (excluding hydrofoils) in the metropolitan area. A Purple Travelpass ($28.20) will get you a weekly ticket (valid Mon.–Sun.).

For information about timetables for buses, trains, or ferries, or about where you can purchase day or weekly tickets, you can phone Public Transport's Customer Service Bureau at 262-3434, every day 6 A.M.–10 P.M.

The Sydney Explorer runs during the day every 15 minutes or so. Beginning at Circular Quay, the bus visits twenty of the city's most interesting sights, including the Opera House, Art Gallery, Sydney Tower, Elizabeth Bay House, Pier 1, and Chinatown. You can get off, stay at any of the attractions as long as you like, and pick up the next Explorer when you're ready to go on. Explorer stops are marked on bus stop signs. (See Touring below.)

## Ferries

The ferries are the least expensive way to see the harbor, and the most enjoyable method of crossing it to get to the North Shore. All ferries leave from Circular Quay, bound for northern harborside and beachside suburbs. The cost is $1.10 one way (some longer rides, such as the trip up the Parramatta River to Ryde and Meadowbank, are slightly more).

Ferries run from very early in the morning until just around midnight. Be sure to check the time of the last ferry if going out for dinner or an evening visit, particularly if you don't fancy a long cab ride back. For ferry information, telephone 262-3434.

Some destinations, such as Manly, are also serviced by hydrofoils, which cut the half-hour ferry trip in half. If you've never traveled by hydrofoil, you may want to try one (it's a little more expensive), but, to our mind, nothing beats a leisurely ferry trip on a sunny day (or a balmy night, for that matter).

There are, as well, two harbor cruises provided by the public transport system: One leaving at 10 A.M. cruises around five islands in the harbor and some of the foreshore scenic spots. It returns to Circular Quay at 12:30 P.M. Another leaves from Circular Quay at 1:30 P.M. and spends 2 ½ hours on the harbor, going up to the mouth of the harbor (The Heads) and passing some of Sydney's loveliest waterfront homes. More information on these cruises can also be had by ringing 262-3434. Coffee or tea is available on board these ferries and a commentary is provided to help you identify what you will be seeing.

## Trains

Trains are probably the most rapid way of moving from one part of the city to another. They are not the easiest routes to figure out, particularly if you don't catch a train at one of the major city stops. Still, if you want to get from one end of the CBD to another in a hurry, this is the best way to go.

Fares are similar to those for buses, though each stop counts as a section. There are several lines that service the city. The North Shore line will take you across the bridge, with the first stop in North Sydney—mainly a satellite business district. After that, the train heads away from the harborside toward what is known as the Upper North Shore. On the south side of the harbor, this line splits into lines that go west into the Blue Mountains, southwest, and northwest.

A separate Eastern suburbs line has stops at Edgecliff (a few blocks' walk from Double Bay) and Bondi Junction, from which you can catch a bus to take you to Bondi Beach.

For information telephone 262-3434. For information on trains beyond the metropolitan area, call 217-8812 or 262-3434.

A new monorail runs through Darling Harbour into the central city.

# Cabs

At most times of the day and night cabs are plentiful in the city. Exceptions to this occur between the hours of 2:30 and 4 P.M. when "changeover" occurs. Cab drivers go back into the depots to change shifts, leaving the streets bereft for the time it takes to get the cabs back on to the streets. It's a ridiculous waste of time and public complaint is getting so loud it will probably be remedied soon, but just in case, you should know that mid-afternoon doesn't always bode well for the cab-seeker in Sydney.

The best places to find cabs are, of course, outside major hotels, near department stores (There is a particularly good cab stand opposite David Jones' Market St. exit), and outside the major city movie houses. Fares are on a par with those of large American cities; they're posted on the meter. Gone are the days when you felt free to pay your fare and not leave something as a tip—there's no set percentage, but it's considered pretty tight-fisted of you not to tip *something*.

Australians pride themselves (erroneously, perhaps) on being a classless society. In that spirit, it was popular here to choose to sit beside the taxi driver, instead of sitting in the rear seat, putting the driver in the position of chauffeur. This was practiced more often by men than by women and has, for the most part, begun to die out. As long as you pay your fare, cab drivers don't care *where* you sit. Join the driver in the front seat by all means if your social philosophy dictates this course of action. But don't feel you have to—he or she won't be offended either way.

It is required by law that all passengers in a car wear a seat belt. This holds for passengers in private cars and in taxis. You can be fined $50 for failing to observe this rule, so keep it in mind.

# Car Rental

There are so many car-rental agencies in Sydney it would be impossible to list them all here. Suffice to say that all the well-known names are here, from Avis, Hertz, and Budget to Rent-a-Wreck. You're not likely to get amazing deals; a budget-size car, rented for a set number of days, with unlimited mileage will never cost much less than $35 a day plus any additional insurance you might require.

Your driver's license and a credit card are all you need to rent a car.

Remember, you drive on the left-hand side of the road in Australia. This means that the steering wheel and gears are on the right-hand side of the car. This is important; unless you specify you want an automatic transmission, you will most probably be given a car with manual shift. Assuming you know how to drive a car with manual shift, you will need a little time to get the hang of shifting with your left hand. Be forewarned.

If you've never driven on the left side of the road before, everything will seem strange. Cars will appear to be turning into your path; you will have to keep your wits about you even more so than usual. It's not impossible, just tricky.

Speed is measured in km.p.h.—in built-up areas (areas where houses exist) the general speed limit is 60 km per hr. On highways it ranges 80–110 km per hr. A km is reckoned at about five-eighths of a mile (62 percent).

Remember, the passing lane on highways is the far right lane. And on some major city roads one of the lanes is designated a transit lane (marked TL). During peak traffic times—7–9:30 A.M. and 3–6:30 P.M.—cars with fewer than three passengers are not allowed to use these lanes.

Visitors to Sydney for only a couple of days will probably choose not to rent a car, but any stay of a week or more will probably necessitate one. Some of the loveliest coast line, the mountains, and the more inaccessible parts of the north shore are better visited in your own time with a car.

# TOURING

The best way to see the city that has one of the best harbors in the world is **from the water.** The cheapest way to do this is to take one or several of the ferries from Circular Quay to the end of its run and then back. Most of these rides will cost no more than $1.20 each way; they're relaxing and provide a stress-free method of orienting yourself. There are also special ferry tours provided by the ferry system (see Transportation, under Ferries). One specialty is the Five Island Ferry Cruise that gives you a look at five of the small islands lying in the harbor—something most Sydney locals haven't managed to do!

Captain Cook Cruises offers the best range of commercial sightseeing cruises on the harbor. Among several is the 2½-hr. coffee cruise that takes in the inner harbor, sails up to Middle Harbour, and passes some of Sydney's most beautiful and expensive real estate on the way. The tour, complete with coffee and commentary, costs $18. A luncheon cruise includes full buffet lunch at $24 per person, while the Sundowner Cruise offers full bar service while you watch the harbor change color as the sun sets. Then there's the Candlelight dinner tour that leaves Circular Quay at 7 P.M. for dinner and dancing on the harbor. You can return at 9:30 P.M. if you wish, or rage on until 11 for the same tariff of $42.

All these cruises, plus several more, are available from Captain Cook Cruise office at no. 6 jetty, Circular Quay; 251-5007. You may also book through your travel agent, who can use their fax number, (02) 251-4725. Most hotels will offer booking service and you can also arrange tours through the Travel Centre of N.S.W. at the corner of Pitt and Spring sts. in the city.

The *Sydney Showboat* is an authentic paddle wheeler that has been refurbished and fitted as a restaurant seating four hundred. It offers a selection of morning coffee, luncheon, and afternoon cruises with bar service, each of which lasts about 1½ hrs.

The Evening Cabaret Cruise (advance bookings are a must for this one) is a 3½-hr. extravaganza, combining sights of the harbor at night with performances by some of Australia's best cabaret artists.

To book in Sydney, phone 264-3510 or 27-5189. You can fax them on (02) 267-8442.

Landlubbers will get a terrific orientation at comparatively little cost through the **Sydney Explorer bus.** This service, provided by the Urban Transit System, runs every day, 9:30 A.M.–5:00 P.M. For $10 adult, $5 child, or $25 for a family (comprising two adults and any number of children from the same family) you can ride around the city, visiting 20 of its top attractions. You can get off whenever you like to visit museums or shop, and then get on another Explorer bus (they come every 15 minutes or so) and continue on the tour.

The tour begins at Sydney Harbour, Circular Quay, and visits locations as diverse as Kings Cross, Chinatown, and Central Railway, with the major city stops included. You can pick up the bus at any of the stops marked by a distinctive bus sign in red with a sketch of the Opera House and Harbour circled in green. The bus itself is bright red.

After 5 P.M. you can use your Explorer ticket to travel on standard buses between Central Railway and Circular Quay or the Rocks until midnight. For more information on ferry or bus services, call Metro Trips at 262-3434 until 10 P.M., seven days.

AAT King's Australian Tours run a selection of half-day and full-day tours, but unlike the Sydney Explorer, you have to stay on the bus you board. Half-day tours, leaving at 9.15 A.M., cost about $22. Full-day tours, 9:15 A.M. to 5:30 P.M., include a harbor cruise and cost $44; $54 with lunch included. To book and get information on the pick-up spot in George Street, phone 27–2066; after hours 667–4918.

**A range of bus services offer an orientation tour, but the best value has to be the Urban Transit's Sydney Explorer, which gives you a whole day to see Sydney at your own pace.**

Skycruise is a relatively new method of seeing the city—**from the air.** It's not cheap—at $200 per person for the 75-minute flight. But you will see Sydney from an angle few people have experienced. Because the flight cruises at around 500 meters above ground level, you have a much more detailed look at land masses, waterways, and daily movement down below.

The airship is composed of a gondola holding eight to ten people, attached to a helium-filled balloon boosted with turbo-charged engines on take-off and landing. Persons under seven years of age are not allowed on board; neither is food (nor presumably smoking) permitted. Still, since the balloon is constantly visible every fine day, lots of folks think the experience is worth fighting the munchies for an hour and a half. Thomas Cook Travel handles the bookings in Sydney at 234-4000. You can arrange an advance booking through a Thomas Cook agency in your city while you're planning your trip. From time to time, however, the airship visits other cities and these cruises are unavailable.

Back on land, **Rocks Walking Tours** at 33 Playfair St., The Rocks, 27-6678, will take you through the historic Rocks area, showing you what life was like 150 years ago in one of the oldest parts of Australia.

Tours leave from the Tours' office on the ground floor of the Argyle Centre hourly, 10:30 A.M.–2:30 P.M. daily. Each walking tour lasts about one hour. It's essential to book ahead if you want to take a large group along with you, but individuals and families can just show up. To book, phone 27-6678, 10 A.M.–4 P.M.

Maureen Fry will take you through The Rocks, and she'll also take you on a walking tour of just about any place in Sydney or environs you want to go. She and her associates specialize in **historical tours:** you can visit Macquarie St. yourself, but you'll learn a lot more about the way Sydney developed if you do the walk with one of Maureen's guides. Similarly, try a tour with Maureen of some of the lovely old National Trust neighborhoods like Paddington, Glebe (where she can also organize a tour of Sydney University's gothic campus—the oldest in Australia), and Balmain, a historic area of picturesque lanes and Victorian homes. There are tours of Chinatown, tours to the Pyrmont fish markets (where, if you want to get up early enough, you can watch the fish being auctioned), as well as tours of some of the outlying areas of Sydney, such as Parramatta.

Maureen will arrange walks for as few as two persons for around $10 per person. Special rates apply for groups of ten or more people and tours will be tailored to suit individual group preferences.

Maureen Fry's Walking Tours of Historic Sydney can be reached at 660-7157 or through the Travel Centre of New South Wales at 231-4444. Write to Maureen Fry at 15 Arcadia Rd., Glebe 2037 to make long-range plans for guided tours.

**Whether you intend to tour Sydney on foot, air, or water, don't even *think* of leaving your hotel room without a hat to shade your face and a liberal application of a sun block. The thing that makes Sydney so attractive to visitors—sun and blue, blue water—is also responsible for one of the highest rates of skin cancer in the world. Wear a sun screen all day (men, don't forget to put some on that bald patch on the top of your head).**

# ✤ HOTELS

While Sydney is not overly supplied with hotels in comparison with other large cities, it does have its share of accommodation facilities in varying price ranges. It's impossible to list them all here, so we've given you our choices for hotels that will offer the best for the money. In case our top choices are full when you try to book, we also mention a few other selections in passing, together with their location.

When planning a trip to Sydney, book your accommodation well ahead. At present, with the tourist boom in full swing, hotels can't be built fast enough to meet demand. Secure a room early, particularly if you intend to spend more than two days in Sydney.

The hotels are listed by price categories—with Expensive first, followed by Moderate, then Inexpensive. Amenities vary with price, although some of the moderate and inexpensive hotels and apartment hotels have surprising amounts of local flavor and period charm to make up for the lack of room service, television, and wet bar.

All of these hotels accept American Express, Visa, Master-Card, and Diners Club. The same neighborhood and map keying system used in Priorities, above, is also used here.

## Expensive

The giants in this category (over $200 per night) are The Regent and The Hotel Inter-Continental. Others such as the Hiltons, The Sheraton Wentworth, and Boulevard meet the requirements for international-standard hotels with ease—but none with the panache of these two which have captured the imagination of Sydney's elite.

### Hotel Inter-Continental      HARBORSIDE, P. 24, C3
The Old Treasury Building, 117 Macquarie St., Sydney 2000; (02) 230-0200.

The Inter-Continental's public rooms are all set in what was once Sydney's treasury building, parts of which are 150 years old. A mammoth refurbishment program completed in 1986 has linked these historic rooms with the new 31-story tower that houses guest suites. The new wing complements the old in using traditional colors, Australian motifs in choice of fabrics for furnishings, and bathrooms outfitted in Edwardian splendor.

Two restaurants, including the elegant Treasury Restaurant (which overlooks the Botanic Gardens), three bars, and the Cortile—the hotel's light and airy central lobby area where refreshments can be taken—are all contained in the historic section of the hotel. Also here are boutiques, each contained in one of the old strongrooms, once used to store the colony's bullion.

There are those who say the youth and inexperience of many of the staff sit uneasily with the expectations raised by the hotel's ambience of tradition, but the hotel is worth a night or two if you'd like to experience some of Sydney's historic architecture. Most of the rooms have views over Sydney Harbour and/or the Botanic Gardens; the rest overlook the city itself.

**Prices for a single or double room start at around $275 per night. Add $100 for harbor view.**

### The Regent      HARBORSIDE, P. 24, B3
199 George St., Sydney 2000 or Box N185, Sydney 2001; (02) 238-0000, telex REGSYD AA 73023, fax (02) 251-2851.

Built in 1982, the Regent is a soaring column of biscuit-colored sandstone and granite. Located at the Rocks end of George St., 70 percent of the hotel's rooms overlook Sydney Harbour, gardens, and the North Shore.

The Regent is the essence of luxury (with the highest staff/guest ratio of any hotel in the city)—from its atrium-like reception area to its premier restaurant, Kables. This restaurant, by the way, isn't considered to be just another hotel dining room; Kables is in the forefront of a movement to create a distinctive Australian cuisine. It's not cheap—three courses will set you back $100 with a bottle of wine at dinner, but setting, service, and the meal itself are worth it.

Rooms are large and comfortable with all the amenities you would expect from a hotel where **rooms begin in excess of $250 and range up to $2,000 per night for a suite.** A caution:

the sixth and seventh floors also house room-service pantries, thus the noise is often distracting. Avoid booking here.

There are a number of other restaurants, bars, and cafés in the hotel. For an evening of laid-back glamour you can try the Don Burrows Supper Club where many visiting jazz performers can be seen while in Sydney. Australian jazz great Don Burrows himself is often on hand.

### Sebel Town House   EASTERN SUBURBS, P. 25, F4
23 Elizabeth Bay Rd., Sydney 2011; (02) 358-3244, telex AA 20067, fax (02) 357-1926.

This hotel will remind you of one of those classy private hotels you find in London. It's small—but size isn't the only measure of a luxury hotel, and with the Sebel the watchword is service. For a hotel with only 165 double rooms and 23 suites, this hotel boasts more well-known guests than any other hotel in Australia. They all stay here—on one visit the guest list included Cleo Laine and her husband, John Dankworth, Mr. and Mrs. Robert Morley, and Bea Arthur. The Sebel is known among actors, musicians (Dire Straits live here when in Sydney), even minor royalty and politicians.

Nothing is too much trouble for staff—and celebrities know it. While you aren't encouraged to linger in the lobby waiting for the stars to appear, you can have a meal in the restaurant off the lobby or a drink in the bar and chances are you'll see a familiar face. Or if you just want to *feel* like a celebrity yourself, this smallish hotel just up the road from Kings Cross, with lovely bay views from many of its rooms, is the place to be.

As you'd expect for a hotel where you're treated like a king, prices are steep. **A double with dressing room will run you upwards of $260, while suites are around $500, and luxury suites (with magnificent views) average $750–$1,200.**

### The Sydney Hilton   BUSINESS DISTRICT, P. 24, C5
259 Pitt St., Sydney 2000; (02) 266-0610, telex 25208, fax (02) 265-6065. Also: Hilton International, Sydney Airport, 20 Levey St. Arncliffe, N.S.W. 2205; (02) 597-0122, telex 70795, fax (02) 597-6381.

One of the city's most well-respected international hotels, the Sydney Hilton is also the only hotel that sits smack dab in the middle of the city's main shopping district, straddling a large piece of real estate that stretches between George and Pitt sts., just across from the Queen Victoria Building. Its architecture is dated, its lobby cramped, but the rooms are spacious and comfortable and the service friendly and of a quality that keeps this hotel in the same league as the newer, flashier international hotels.

There aren't many hotels in Australia that can boast a dining room with food as consistently good as that served in the Hilton's San Francisco Grill where a woman staying on her own in the hotel can mention that fact to the maître d' and find herself seated at his table.

Juliana's, the hotel's disco, is also the scene of many performances by international stars—Tina Turner has headlined there several times.

**Tariffs range around $250 for twin/doubles to $700 for a suite on the executive floor.**

There is a second **Hilton at Sydney Airport,** which is only about twenty minutes away from the city by car or coach. For those with early flights, or who like the idea of being able to play a bit of tennis between sightseeing trips (the Airport Hilton has several outdoor courts), this Hilton may be an alternative worth considering. Prices here average a bit less than its Sydney sister hotel: **from about $210 for double occupancy, around $400 for a suite.** Both hotels charge a uniform $20 for a third person sharing a double/twin room.

## OTHER EXPENSIVE HOTELS

**The Boulevard,** 90 William St., Sydney 2000; (02) 357-2277, telex 24350, fax (02) 356-3786. Stunning views over the Eastern Suburbs and harbor and classy meals in the beautiful 25th-floor restaurant.

**Sheraton Wentworth,** 61 Phillip St., Sydney 2000; (02) 230-0700, telex 121227, fax (02) 227-9133. In the financial district of the city, this is the place to be if you plan to combine business with pleasure—the best duty-free shops are all at this end of the city as well. The Garden Court restaurant is a lovely, restful place for lunch.

# Moderate

These hotels run $100 and over for a double room—and though they do not offer the luxury of the more expensive properties, you can expect an array of first-class amenities.

### Best Western Central
### Plaza Hotel                          CHINATOWN, P. 26, B7
Corner George and Quay sts., Sydney 2036; (02) 212-2544.

At the south end of George St., near Chinatown and Railway Sq., Best Western's Central Plaza Hotel comes in well below the $200 mark, with standard rooms beginning at **around $155 for a double.**

The 116 rooms all come with direct-dial telephones (two or three in each room) color TVs, toasters, and coffee-making facilities, among other standard facilities. There is 24-hour room service (although don't expect anything too elaborate on the menu). But who cares, with some of the most delicious and exotic cuisine only minutes away by foot in Chinatown or at Darling Harbour.

### The Manly Pacific
### International Hotel                        NORTH SHORE
55 North Steyne, Manly 2095; (02) 977-7666, telex 73097, fax (02) 9777822.

The Manly Pacific International is worth thinking about if you want a beachside holiday and don't mind the twenty-minute ferry ride into the city. It's a deluxe hotel, right at Manly beach, with 170 rooms, most of which overlook the water. All first-class facilities are here—including a spa and gym. Aside from the advantages of being right at one of Sydney's most famous beaches, you also have the benefit of being very near some of its nicest cafés.

Prices begin at about **$180 per night,** qualifying it as moderate.

## Oakford Apartments PADDINGTON, P. 28, B4

400 Glenmore Rd., Paddington 2021; (02) 361-9000, fax (02) 332-3484.

In this price range you can also try the growing range of apartment hotels available in Sydney. The Oakford Apartments are located in Paddington, right next to White City, one of the city's premier locations for outdoor tennis matches. For a week's stay, the Oakford offers two-bedroom apartments for around **$190 per night** (which would sleep two couples, or a couple and two children) or three-bedroom apartments for around $230 per night. Many of the apartments overlook White City, and though you wouldn't have much chance of catching any Davis Cup action from up there, the outlook is nice and leafy. Buses from New South Head Rd. and trains from the Edgecliff Station on New South Head Rd. connect the Oakford with central Sydney.

All 46 apartments are serviced daily and have full kitchens and laundries. There is security parking and, as a bonus, tennis buffs can rent a court at White City for around $10 per hr. and rent racket and balls, as well. Decor is modern, with leather sofas in tones of grays and fawns. What you *don't* get in apartments such as these is secretarial and room service or access to a fax machine. But, hey, you're on holiday, right? And the price *is* good.

## Old Sydney Parkroyal HARBORSIDE, P. 24, B2

55 George St., The Rocks, Sydney 2000; (02) 20524, telex 72279, fax (02) 251 2093.

Back in the city, the Old Sydney Parkroyal gives you access to the Rocks, Circular Quay, and the harbor. Its lobby is uncannily like that of the infinitely more expensive Inter-Continental— terra cotta–toned atrium, lots of comfy seating. All modern facilities, including a pool (with harbor views), fax service, secretarial service, valet parking, and 24-hour room service. There is also a floor devoted to rooms with facilities for the handicapped.

**Single/doubles are $210** ($10 for an extra person). Suites begin at around $240. Harbor-view rooms are available. The hotel's restaurant, the Cove Café in the foyer, serves all meals daily.

## The Park Hotel Apartments EASTERN SUBURBS, P. 27, D6

16–32 Oxford St., Darlinghurst 2010; (02) 331-7728, fax (02) 360 2583.

Only a ten-minute stroll into the heart of the city are the Park Hotel Apartments. More hotelish than the Oakford, the Park has 135 rooms, all with full kitchen and laundry facilities, TVs, spa/sauna, and swimming pool. There are also a licensed restaurant and a bar on the ground floor. And you're within a few minutes' walk of some of the city's most adventurous eating, on Oxford St. **A one-bedroom apartment will run around $175 a night; $190 for a two-bedroom.**

# Inexpensive

An apartment hotel (see above), depending on the number of people sharing it, is probably your best bet if you're trying to spend only around $100 per couple per night. There are, as well, in the city a number of small hotels (boutique hotels, some call them). Each of these tends to have relatively few rooms and offers a bed-and-breakfast–style accommodation, similar to what canny tourists enjoy in Europe.

## The Russell
HARBORSIDE, P. 24, B2

143a George St., Circular Quay, Sydney 2000; (02) 241-3543, telex AA121822 (SY3297).

The Russell Hotel is probably the oldest of these boutique hotels. At Circular Quay, it's a stone's throw from the shopping and nightlife of this area, as well as the city and harbor. Each of its rooms is meticulously outfitted in Victoriana—lots of brass beds, Laura Ashley prints, and fresh flowers. Rates range **from around $80 for a single to $190 for its "suite"**—which will sleep four easily, has its own kitchen, and opens onto a private terrace. The tariff includes continental breakfast, which you can have in your room or downstairs in the hotel's café, which also serves light lunches. There are some rooms that share bathroom facilities, but this is no problem as the baths are plentiful, the rooms commodious and decorated in the same tasteful style as the rest of the hotel.

## OTHER INEXPENSIVE HOTELS

**The Jackson Hotel,** 94 Victoria St., Potts Point 2011; (02) 358-5801. Eighteen rooms from **$75 per night, double, with shared facilities, to $90 with bath and $120 for a room with a balcony.** The Jackson is near the Elizabeth Bay House and Kings Cross; the Elizabeth Bay bus from Park St. and the Eastern Suburbs railway line to the Kings Cross stop connect the Jackson with the central business area.

**Newington Manor,** 10–14 Sebastapol St., Stanmore 2048; (02) 560-4922. This hundred-year-old home was built in the style of an English country house in the days when Stanmore (now inner Sydney) was considered part of the countryside. The house has been completely refurbished with exquisite antiques and comfortable beds. There are only seven rooms ranging **from $75 for a single with shared bath, to $110 per night for a grand double with en suite bath.** Tariff includes pick up and delivery to and from airport or elsewhere in Sydney, plus breakfast in your room, or in the sunny dining room or the courtyard. Visitors are encouraged to use the house as they would their home—refreshments are available until 10 P.M.; dinner by prior request. A large swimming pool is also on the premises.

**Pensione Sydney,** 27 Georgina St., Newtown 2042; (02) 550-1700. With 14 rooms and an unlicensed restaurant, this converted terrace house in the city's inner west suburbs is right at a train station for the ten-minute trip into town, plus it's near another great strip of inexpensive dining places—King St., Newtown. **Prices from $130 for a double;** all rooms with private baths. The tariff here also includes a pick-up and drop-off service.

## The Rocks

Any tour of central Sydney must include the area around Sydney Cove known as The Rocks. It's the birthplace of the nation. When Captain Arthur Phillip of the First Fleet selected a site in which to land the nine-hundred-odd settlers (most of them convicts) who first came to Australia, he selected the cove for its relatively plentiful supply of fresh water. Thus the nation was born.

It's not surprising then that some of the earliest remnants of Australia's past exist in the streets that have grown up around that first landing site.

Argyle Street is the main street in this area. The **Argyle Cut,** a passage hewn through the solid sandstone that once blocked passage between Walsh Bay and Sydney Cove, still shows evidence of the hand-held picks used by the convicts who began this immense labor.

In this vicinity also is **Argyle Place,** a group of early colonial cottages and terraces, still looking onto a village green. Passing along Argyle Street, heading east you will come to the **Argyle Centre.** The buildings that house the Centre and a group of bars and restaurants called the **Argyle Tavern Centre** were once warehouses. They were built around 1823 of sandstone and were restored in the late 1960s to house a series of galleries, gift shops, restaurants, and bars. The lovely old sandstone walls are still evident and give an 18th-century feel to a shopping expedition in the region.

Particularly on weekends there is a lot of street life in the area—buskers operate here, one perhaps playing traditional colonial airs on his fiddle, another skirling away on the bagpipes. Traditional bush-style dinners are served and bush-style entertainment performed at the Jolly Swagman Show seen at the Argyle Tavern. (A swagman was an itinerant worker who usually hired himself out to shear sheep. He was named after the pack, or "swag" in which he carried his belongings, and was immortalized in the song "Waltzing Matilda.")

Other places of interest in the region are one of Sydney's oldest churches, the **Garrison Church,** built in the 1840s and still functioning; the old **Police Station,** well over one hundred years old, though today serving as a gallery for Australian handicrafts; the collection of 1830s cottages of **Lower Fort Street,** which includes the oldest pub in Australia, The Hero of Waterloo; and **Observatory Hill,** where the Observatory, built in 1857, now also serves as a museum of time-keeping and astronomical artifacts.

**Cadman's Cottage,** nearby on George Street, rates a special mention. It is Sydney's oldest dwelling, built in 1816 for John Cadman who was in charge of the governor's boat crew.

# Convicts

Between 1788, when the First Fleet landed at Sydney Cove with its first shipment of convicts, and 1867, when Western Australia, the last colony to abolish convict transportation, ceased its activities as a penal settlement, more than 160,000 men and women arrived in Australia as prisoners.

About one in six were women, many as young as 14 years of age. Their "crimes" often amounted to no more than having been caught stealing a loaf of bread or a few shillings worth of clothing. Very often, these were first offenses—repeat offenders were often hanged, as were murderers and perpetrators of other serious crimes.

Political dissidents also formed a segment of these convicts. Irish activists and prisoners taken during the black slave uprising at Montego Bay in Jamaica in 1832 were transported to Australia. In fact, one in every thirty transportees was not of Anglo/Celtic origin, arriving via the British jail system from Europe, Asia, Africa, and the Caribbean. French Canadians rebelling against British rule found their way to the penal settlements of New South Wales, as did American sympathizers who fought alongside these French Canadians.

The population of the early Australian colonies, while branded "criminal" by the lawmakers of Britain, was far from what we understand by that term today. In most cases, their crimes were to be poor in a time when there was no social welfare, to have fought on the losing side in a war of independence. (It's interesting to speculate what would have happened to George Washington, Thomas Paine, and other fathers of the American Revolution had that war resulted in a British victory.)

While conditions were hard and treatment often brutal at some of the more infamous prisons such as Tasmania's Port Arthur, life could be good for a convict who had a trade or profession to offer to the fledgling nation. Builders, stonemasons, farm-workers—all found their services in great demand.

A professional man such as Francis Greenway, an architect who was transported for forging a contract, was so well received that he was actually appointed Government Architect soon after his arrival to begin his sentence. Today, Sydney's Macquarie Street is a monument to Greenway's efforts in that post.

While women had few professional qualifications to secure the same preferences, their relative scarcity placed them in somewhat of an anomalous position—they were fair game sexually, yet they were valued as the potential mothers of the second generation of Australians, without whom the nation would surely founder.

Though the circumstances that brought these men and women to Australia differed, their personalities, beliefs, characters, and ambitions differed little from those of the men and women who settled the North American continent.

 Connoisseurs of liquid refreshment might want to try a pub crawl, a tour of some of the character-filled bars in the area.

You're advised to avoid this on Fri. and Sat. nights, when locals can get a bit overwrought, but if you're game, a pint or two of lager at the **Hero of Waterloo** (81 Lower Fort St.), **the Lord Nelson** (19 Kent St.), the **Orient** (corner of George and Argyle Sts.), or the **Observer** (69 George St. North) hotels can lead to a few interesting exchanges with the odd (and we use the word advisedly) frequenter of these precincts.

You will often hear pubs referred to as hotels. This goes back to the days when licensing laws required that establishments that served alcoholic beverages also provide sleeping accommodation. Most pubs from this era still have bedrooms upstairs, thus qualifying them for the appellation "hotel," though few of these hotels still let rooms out.

In recent years, The Rocks area has been purposely cultivated as a tourist center, though, with a healthy mix of general commerce, it has been saved from the plasticity that this kind of conscious grooming gives places like San Francisco's Fisherman's Wharf. Greengrocer's shops and newsagencies are next door to specialty shops, and at lunch the offices empty into the quaint pubs and restaurants for their mid-day breaks. The 20th century is all around you—but the 18th doesn't seem very far away.

## Circular Quay

If you begin your trek along Macquarie Street at the Circular Quay end, you can include The Sydney Opera House before setting off toward the city center. The Quay itself is worth a couple of hours' attention; it's the departure point for ferries, hydrofoils, and harbor cruise boats that ply the water, so it's good to become familiar with it.

A lot of upgrading has gone on in this part of the city lately, resulting in a number of attractive eating places with appetizing food and reasonable prices—perfect for a quick meal or coffee and watching the harbor traffic (an attractive prospect on sunny days). After a fortifying breakfast at someplace like Billy Blue's on the western boardwalk, you can wander around the harbor's edge up to the **Opera House** for a look at the Danish-designed performing arts center that looks like a ship in full sail. Tours are conducted daily (see Priorities).

The spectacular structure has been the subject of controversy since Danish architect Joern Utzon won the international competition for its design in 1957. From union difficulties to building problems to a skeptical public, the 14 years that the Opera House took to complete were enough to make Utzon decide to forego the privilege of directing its construction and return home.

## European Settlement of Australia

Although Australians celebrated two hundred years of European settlement in 1988, explorers knew about and visited the continent long before the arrival of the First Fleet in 1788. As early as the 15th century, maps referred to the only half-mythical *Terra Australis,* the great South Land which Portugese explorers suspected existed beyond the Indies.

The Spanish searched for this mysterious land throughout the 16th century, but it was the Dutch in the first years of the 17th century who actually landed here—on the western coast of Cape York. In 1642 Abel Tasman was sent to chart and explore sections of what is today the state of Tasmania and part of the New Zealand coast. These explorations and resultant maps gave later explorers an imprecise, but working knowledge of this mysterious continent.

The British didn't begin any meaningful exploration of the Pacific Ocean until the mid 1700s, the most noteworthy of these explorations having taken place in 1769 when a ship under the command of Lieutenant James Cook was sent to Tahiti to observe the transit of Venus across the sun. After observing the astronomical event, the ship charted both of New Zealand's islands and on April 29 landed at what is now Botany Bay, where the crew rested for a week. This voyage produced the most complete chart of the coastline of Australia extant at the time. In addition, Joseph Banks, a noted botanist, also on board, recorded many of the plants indigenous to Australia and surrounding islands, later included in his famous *Florilegium.*

The scheme to use Australia as a convict settlement was the result in part of necessity. The Revolutionary War in America denied Britain access to the colonies she had set up there for this purpose. Prisons all over England were full to overflowing—so much so that excess prisoners languished in prison hulks, moored in the Thames. However, the decision to send these convicts to Botany Bay was only partly to rid Britain of unwanted criminals. In fact the plan was a "two birds with one stone" idea. It was essential in these decades of warring for naval supremacy to maintain a bridgehead in the East, to protect British trading interests there. Establishing a colony in Australia with convict labor would both solve the problem of manpower in an area where Britain had a shortage as well as clear the Thames of its disease-ridden prison hulks.

In January 1788 Captain Phillip led the First Fleet into Botany Bay. Almost all of the nine hundred passengers on board the ships were convicts.

On January 25, the ships moved around to Sydney Cove where the spring water was purer and the ships could anchor near to the shore. Thus, from that first arrival of 757 convicts, an escort of two hundred military and a few women and children, was the nation born.

But in the end, there was little doubt that this building, like the Eiffel Tower and the Statue of Liberty, was to be in the eyes of the world a symbol for a nation, as well as a city. There is nothing else anywhere even remotely like it. Each "sail" in the building's roof is covered with shining tiles that gleam day and night. Intermission at a performance leads visitors out onto terraces overlooking one of the world's most beautiful harbors. Everything about the Opera House—whether it's being viewed or used—works together to make it (in the words of the *London Times*) "the building of the century."

## Macquarie Street

Coming back down from the Opera House forecourt, you will be pointed in the direction of Macquarie Street. This is, perhaps, the most architecturally significant street in Sydney—a couple of kilometers of magnificent sandstone buildings dating well back into the last century.

On your left as you proceed along are the **Royal Botanic Gardens,** the exotic trees and plants themselves worth a morning or afternoon's stroll. (Open 8 A.M. to sunset daily.) The **Conservatorium of Music** stands beside these gardens. Once a stables, it was converted into the state music conservatorium in 1916. Throughout most of the year, except in high summer, free lunchtime concerts are given by students on Wednesday in the castellated structure.

The **Inter-Continental Hotel** at 117 Macquarie Street was once the state treasury building. A masterful restoration of the building enables it to house the hotel's public rooms and is definitely worth a look. (See Hotels, above.)

The **Cortile,** the hotel's atrium-like lobby, serves morning and afternoon teas.

In Macquarie Place is the **The Obelisk,** designed by renowned architect and former convict Francis Greenway. Greenway designed the structure under the order of Governer Macquarie (for whom the street is named) in 1818 as the point from which all distance from Sydney was to be measured.

# Business District

## Macquarie Street Continues

A block or so along Macquarie Street, just across from the start of the Cahill Expressway, stands the **State Library of N.S.W.,** containing the largest collection of records and illustrations relating to the settlement of Australia. There are regular exhibitions held there 6½ days per week.

Beyond this is **Parliament House.** The original building which now accommodates Parliamentary debates was originally part of a hospital. Known as the Old Rum Hospital, it got its name because the contractors who began it in 1810 were paid by being granted a monopoly on the rum trade in the colony—a very lucrative deal, that. Visits can be arranged to hear evening sittings of state parliament when in session, though access is difficult for the disabled. The modern, colonial-style wing houses administrative offices and is not open to the public.

**Sydney Hospital,** which stands opposite Martin Place, replaced the old Rum Hospital some seventy years later. It still functions as a hospital. The huge boar, *Il Porcellino,* in front of the building is a gift from the Italian government to the people of N.S.W., though why it was chosen to stand in front of a hospital is a vexing question. The boar is a replica of a 15th-century Florentine sculpture—and the legend is that it's lucky to rub his nose (Note how the nose has worn away).

Two more sandstone buildings finish this tour of the more prominent buildings in Macquarie Street: Hyde Park Barracks and The Mint are both enclosed by a sandstone wall at the very top of Macquarie Street, across from Hyde Park at the intersection known as Queen's Square. Both are now museums worth visiting. **Hyde Park Barracks** was also built by convict architect Francis Greenway. (Open Wednesday through Monday from 10 A.M. to 5 P.M.; Tuesdays from noon; 217-0111.) Its superbly elegant lines belie its original purpose—to house convicts. Today, in addition to mounting exhibitions relating to social history from colonial times to the 1950s, the graceful Georgian buildings also include an exceptionally good café.

The **Barracks Café** serves inventive light meals throughout the afternoon.

The **Mint Museum** (open Thursday through Tuesday from 10 A.M. to 5 P.M.; Wednesdays from noon; 217-0111), originally yet another wing of the old Rum Hospital, houses displays devoted to Australian decorative arts, as well as stamps, coins, and flags.

## Hyde Park Area

Across the street from the Mint and Barracks museums is **St. James Church,** yet another Francis Greenway design. Behind that and extending onto Elizabeth Street, one block west of Macquarie, are some law courts, including the Supreme Court, the oldest sections of which repeat Greenway's Georgian design.

Hyde Park, which extends from Elizabeth Street to College Street to the east and from Queen's Square to Liverpool Street at its south boundary, is a cool and colorful oasis in the very midst of the shopping and business district. At its southern end stands the **Anzac Memorial,** a monument to

Australian soldiers from the First World War, but now dedicated to soldiers of all wars.

The **Great Synagogue** stands across from the park on Elizabeth Street, between Park and Market. Its massive and ornate wrought-iron gates are usually locked unless the synagogue is open for services or for specific touring times.

On the opposite side of the park, on College Street, just parallel with Market, **St. Mary's Cathedral** is the Catholic cathedral, executed in Gothic style.

About one block south of St. Mary's, the **Australian Museum** stands at the intersection of College and William streets. It is the country's largest natural history museum, housing exhibitions of Australian and Pacific art, artifacts, and fauna. Open Tuesday through Saturday from 10 A.M. to 5 P.M., from noon on Sundays and Mondays; 339-8111.

## Art Gallery Road

Art Gallery Road lies directly behind St. Mary's. If you follow it along you will come to the **Art Gallery of N.S.W.** It houses permanent and temporary collections of Australian and European art, as well as a special gallery of tribal art. Open Monday through Saturday from 10 A.M. to 5 P.M.; from noon on Sundays; 225-1700.

Art Gallery Road cuts through the large city park known as **The Domain,** a favorite spot for soapbox orators to air their thoughts on Sunday afternoons. Art Gallery Road becomes Mrs. Macquarie's Road, leading to Mrs. Macquarie's Point, on the edge of the water. It's said that the wife of this early governor of Sydney used to sit on the chair-like rock here (**Mrs. Macquarie's Chair)** and gaze out at the view.

## Shopping Areas

Sydney's main shopping streets, Castlereagh, Pitt, and George streets, lie immediately west of Hyde Park, as does the Sydney Hilton, the only international-class hotel to be located in the middle of the central shopping district. Several other hotels are located a few blocks north and east of the area (see Hotels section), and at time of writing a couple of large hotels are being built in the Darling Harbour region.

What to buy where will be discussed fully in the Shopping section, but there are two arcades in this part of the city that no one—shopper or not—should miss.

The first is **The Queen Victoria Building,** or QVB. It is located at the corner of George and Park streets, directly across the street from the gingerbread sandstone confection that houses the Sydney Town Hall. The QVB started life at the turn of the century as a market, fell into serious disrepair for decades, and was just about to be turned into a carpark when a Malaysian consortium saw the potential in the grand building and restored it to its former glory. It now houses several scores of boutiques and specialty shops on its four levels of tessellated tile, marble, and polished cedar. Worth visiting—if only to take a coffee at one of its indoor/"outdoor" cafés and view one of the most perfect Victorian restorations in the world.

The second arcade is a decade or two older. The **Strand Arcade** was originally built in 1891. Running between Pitt and George streets, half a block north of Market Street, it houses eighty specialty shops. It was actually refurbished twice. In 1976 a fire destroyed a large part of the newly renovated arcade, so they did it all again. A little bit of what Sydney was one hundred years ago.

# Haymarket and Chinatown

Australia's proximity to Asia, particularly Southeast Asia, has made it a historically favored destination for Asian emigrants since the mid-1800s. In those days, as in the United States, the call of the gold fields summoned Chinese workers; eventually the larger cities of Sydney and Melbourne drew enough of a Chinese population to develop thriving Chinatowns.

Sydney's Chinatown grew up around what is known as "The Haymarket" section of the city, on its southwestern edge. The Haymarket is so called because, until less than ten years ago, it was the center of produce wholesaling, an area of enterprise into which the Chinese immigrants made substantial inroads during the late 19th century.

Chinatown's main drag is **Dixon Street.** Over the last few years the quaint little dusty shopfronts that used to house everything from cheap, but very good, woks to exotic spices, have given way to vast expanses of granite as the Chinese community has poured some of its communal wealth into re-creating this section of the city into a mini Hong Kong or Singapore. Pagoda-like towers at each end block automobiles from the street, turning it into a mall where the business of buying and selling goes on indoors and out, apparently far into the night.

Some of Sydney's best Chinese restaurants lie along Dixon Street and in its neighboring Goulburn, Hay, and Campbell streets. During daytime shopping hours, almost anything from a paper lantern to antique porcelain is sold in the new and luxurious arcades that have sprung up.

But one of the special attractions of Chinatown is the street life that seems to go on from early morning until late. Shoppers, diners, and strollers mix with locals in the crowded narrow streets; the smell of barbecued pork and frying garlic scents the air as it does in Kuala Lumpur, Singapore, or anyplace where a substantial Chinese crowd gathers on a tropical night.

A mere two blocks away, crowds of a different kind gather. The **Sydney Entertainment Centre,** built in 1982 on the site of some of those wholesale produce markets, is at present the premier venue for performances that draw big crowds. The center holds over 12 thousand and accommodates anything from a circus to a rock concert. Even major indoor tennis matches are played there. Its proximity to Chinatown means a huge spillover after the show into the surrounding restaurants—guaranteeing lively night scenes most evenings until very late.

Only a few blocks beyond the Entertainment Centre, on Harris Street in Ultimo, is the jewel in the Haymarket crown: the **Powerhouse Museum,** which opened in 1988. The site was once one of the city's power stations, long abandoned and mouldering away until somebody got the bright idea to convert the massive building into a museum. After an outlay of $54 million, the museum soared into being, offering 16,000 square meters of exhibition space devoted to five major thematic areas: Australian creativity and achievement; science, technology, and people; decorative arts; everyday Australian life; and bringing people together. More than nine thousand objects are on display at any one time, spanning almost every field of human creativity. The museum is very much a "hands on" sort of place, offering exciting experiences in the areas of science, decorative arts, performing arts, and Australian history in one incredible location. Open daily from 10 A.M. to 5 P.M.; 217-0111.

## Darling Harbour Redevelopment

Once a collection of old tram lines and empty lots, the area around Darling Harbour, south of the city and adjacent to Chinatown, has become the site of the greatest urban redevelopment scheme in Australia's history.

Already open are the **Harbourside Festival Marketplace,** a vast glass-roofed collection of more than two hundred specialty shops and restaurants facing the harbor along its western foreshore, next to Pyrmont Bridge.

Visitors can shop for souvenirs, clothing, or even groceries here. **Virgin Records** has opened the largest record store in the Southern Hemisphere, and video screens play the top performers perpetually until late at night. (Other shops close at 9 P.M. 6 P.M. Sunday).

You can dine on Chicago-style deep dish pizza at **Uno's,** or go more up-market at one of the waterside seafood restaurants.

On weekends, the city's best buskers provide day (and evening) entertainment along the boardwalk.

The **Sydney Seaport Museum** has sponsored the exhibition of the *James Craig*, one of the graceful old sailing ships that once plied the waters between Australia and Britain. The *James Craig* is moored in the water facing the Festival Marketplace; it's in a state of being restored, but visitors are welcome to look her over. Admission is $2. Open 10 A.M. to 6 P.M.

Beyond the Festival Marketplace is the **Sydney Convention Centre,** a seven story, 3,500-seat building, which curves along the western foreshore of Darling Harbour. Information on events can be had by calling 211-2311.

Directly next to the Convention Centre is the **Exhibition Centre.** Its main hall, 25,000 square meters of space, overlooks the harbor. The glass eastern façade can be divided into several smaller exhibition halls for planned car shows, furnishing exhibitions and the like. For information on what's on, call 211-2311.

The **Chinese Garden,** a gift from the Peoples' Republic for Australia's bicentenery, lies just beyond the Exhibition Centre; see Priorities, above.

On the opposite side of Darling Harbour, directly across from the Harbourside Marketplace, is the **Aquarium.** The complex houses a full range of marine environments, featuring everything from sharks to sardines in their natural habitats. Visitors pass through the marine world via a specially designed walkway, which gives the impression of being under water. Open 9:30 A.M. to 9 P.M., seven days; admission $9 adults; $4.50 children; 262-2300.

# Kings Cross

Immediately to the east of the Domain is the dockside suburb of Woolloomooloo (of interest to tourists predominately because of its euphonious name). Beyond this, one encounters the dubious pleasures of Kings Cross. The Cross, as it's called locally, gained its reputation as the sin center of Sydney during the Viet Nam War, when American soldiers on R&R discovered the bohemian charms of its European-style restaurants, coffeehouses, and bars. By the 1970s its main drags of Victoria and Macleay streets had become saturated with girlie clubs, sex shops, and decidedly unsavory types.

Still, there is a lot of charm in the back streets of neighboring suburbs, Potts Point and Elizabeth Bay. The whole area is vaguely European in feel, with overtones of New York's Greenwich Village.

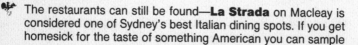 The restaurants can still be found—**La Strada** on Macleay is considered one of Sydney's best Italian dining spots. If you get homesick for the taste of something American you can sample

classic new American cuisine at **Jo Jo Ivory's** in the Sheraton Motor Hotel.

It's possible to avoid the strip joints and the squalor by simply visiting the area during the day when its appearance is more like that of a small Parisian neighborhood on the Left Bank. Visit **Elizabeth Bay House** on Onslow Avenue in Elizabeth Bay. It's a magnificent Regency period mansion designed by another of Sydney's 19th-century architects, John Verge, for Alexander Macleay who was Colonial Secretary in the 1830s. The house overlooks Sydney Harbour and, in addition to the period furnishings permanently on display there, often contains exhibitions of colonial interest. Open Tuesday through Sunday from 10 A.M. to 4:30 P.M.; 358-2344.

Around the corner on Billyard Avenue, the privately owned **Boomerang** is a splendid example of the Hollywood-style Spanish hacienda. It's not open to the public, but it's worth walking around the corner if you're visiting Elizabeth Bay House, to see what someone in the music industry during the flapper era called luxury.

# The Eastern Suburbs

William Street, which takes you out of central Sydney, past the turn-off for Kings Cross, and on to the harborside Eastern Suburbs, changes its name to New South Head Road as soon as it passes Rushcutters Bay Park. Soon afterward the bus will pull into Edgecliff Station to discharge passengers bound for the Eastern Suburbs railway and to pick up passengers who will continue up New South Head Road.

Along this stretch, the suburbs of most interest to the short-term visitor are Double Bay, Vaucluse, and Watsons Bay.

## Double Bay

The shopping drag along New South Head Road as it passes through Double Bay and the intersecting streets here of Bay and Knox streets have been likened to Los Angeles's Rodeo Drive. They're not. However, the boutiques and cafés in the area do cater to the Sydney nouveau riche taste in clothing and jewelry of the imported (and important) variety. Outrageous prices carry the day ("Double Bay—double pay," they say here).

A sidewalk cappuccino at the **Cosmopolitan** on Knox St. on a Sat. morning gives you a ring-side seat for watching Sydney glamour-pusses on the prowl. That's when the Ferraris, Porsches, and inevitable Mercedes pull up—ostensibly to shop, but mainly to see and be seen.

## Vaucluse

Farther along, the houses grow larger and the gardens more park-like. The monied set are at home in the plush suburbs of Point Piper, Rose Bay, and Vaucluse. A stroll around the streets of Vaucluse will give you a taste of opulence Sydney-style, though the best views of these mansions are from the water. The lovely 1830s turreted mansion, **Vaucluse House,** on Wentworth Avenue, is open to visitors daily. It was the home of William Charles Wentworth, known as the father of the Australian Constitution. The house is set on almost thirty acres of park accessible for picnics, though there is also a charming tea room where light meals and afternoon tea or coffee are available. The house is open from 10 A.M. to 4:30 P.M.; closed Mondays.

Nearby **Nielsen Park** sports a pleasant little beach, outfitted with a shark net to protect swimmers. Tea rooms in the park also supply light meals and snacks.

## Watsons Bay

New South Head Road (which changes its name a couple of times as it winds its way up) ends at Watsons Bay. Not far from here (about a twenty-minute walk) is the infamous **Lady Jane Beach,** where it is legal to bathe nude. A lot of hullabaloo went on for a while over the fact that a dozen or so people took their clothes off to sunbathe here, but now the relative difficulty of getting down to the beach (you need to descend ladders hanging from a cliff face) and general common sense has discouraged all but the most committed. You are welcome to join them, but popping along merely for a peek will only mark you as yet another repressed American.

**It is commonplace to sunbathe topless on just about every beach in Sydney and environs—even the most populated.**

If you prefer your scenery sans nudes, Watson's Bay is still worth visiting. Its position on the headland puts it midway between harbor and ocean.

Grab a bag of fish-and-chips from **Doyle's** on the harborside pier and sit on the beach for a picnic. You can watch the sailboats glide by against the backdrop of the Harbour Bridge. Or take your fish across to the other side of the street and gaze at the waves breaking against the rocks of The Gap. Some of Sydney's most beautiful outlooks can be appreciated from this headland and the walk that winds along the coast here at the edge of The Gap park.

## Bondi

You may want to return to the city via Old South Head Road which runs on the oceanside of the headland, skirting the oceanside suburb of Bondi, home of the most famous beach in Sydney. Bondi Beach is about a kilometer long on your left as you head back toward the city; no one could consider a visit to Sydney complete without stopping for at least a look.

The beachfront at Bondi has the seedy-attractiveness of lots of Mediterranean port cities. Old shopfronts and inexpensive cafés face onto a busy thoroughfare called Campbell Parade; across this the beach spreads in all its golden glory for about a kilometer. At the south end of the beach you can pick up a walkway that takes you south along the coast, passing the small, gentle beaches at **Tamarama Bay** and **Bronte,** ending at the **Bronte baths.** These baths are stone pools which fill naturally with seawater.

Before you start off on your walk—or perhaps once you return to Bondi—you can have a cup of excellent coffee and a slice of one of the European cakes or pastries served at the **Gelato Bar.** The health conscious might prefer a fruit drink at **The Lamrock Café.** For an all-out wonderful meal, with a view you won't forget for a long time, try the **Bluewater Grill** on the headland at the north end of the beach.

**Bondi is pronounced "bond-eye," not "bond-ee." Most Americans mispronounce it; getting it right will impress the natives.**

## Oxford Street

Oxford Street is the seam that holds the central Eastern Suburbs together. The harborside suburbs may have posh, the oceanside suburbs a raffish salt-laden charm, but for the kind of streetwise sophistication and funkiness that you encounter in cities like Manhattan, the closest you will come in Australia is along this five kilometers of road. It begins in the city and stretches east through four suburbs before melding with New South Head Road.

### DARLINGHURST

Darlinghurst is the suburb closest to the city on the Oxford Street route. Slow to become gentrified, much of the Darlinghurst stretch consists of workaday shops, office buildings, and a few cafés. This changes suddenly around the intersection at Crown Street, where a small collection of boutiques, ethnic delicatessens, and small restaurants builds up steam heading toward Taylor Square, a couple of blocks east.

**Taylor Square** is a fascinating amalgam of lifestyles. On one side of Oxford Street sits the sandstone majesty of the Darlinghurst Courthouse. Across from it, at any time of the day or night, bag ladies, punks, and bikers mix quite naturally with the young professionals who come here to buy their fantasy evening dresses from designer Christopher Essex (just a block or so down, on Flinders Street) or the students from

East Sydney Tech, who appreciate the Slavic home cooking at the wonderful Balkan, just across Flinders on Oxford Street.

Oxford Street is mecca to Sydney's gay community. The Taylor Square area particularly includes a number of clubs and it is on this street and intersecting Flinders that the yearly **Gay Mardi Gras** parade makes its way in late February. The parade has become an institution in Sydney, drawing thousands of spectators, gay and straight alike, to see the outrageous, clever, and beautiful floats.

The stretch of Oxford Street from Taylor Square to Paddington is particularly well served with fine restaurants and cafés in all price ranges—from haute French to Lebanese, high Thai to Balinese.

If you're around at lunchtime, go to **La Passion de Fruit** at 100 Oxford St., Paddington. Fresh, light meals and blissful fruit drinks will set you up for the next leg of the trip.

Across the street from La Passion stands the stone wall surrounding **Victoria Barracks,** still a military post 140 years after its founding. It's open for tours on Tuesdays from February to December; or book in advance (339-3543). The buildings alone are worth an inspection.

## PADDINGTON

Just past the Glenmore Road intersection (which has a number of worthwhile boutiques), you'll hit a semi-dead patch for about three blocks with little more than the sandstone wall of the Barracks to hold your attention. Then you move into Paddington. The streets and lanes to the north of Oxford Street abound with colorful shops and a variety of 19th-century housing that range from drab little cottages to large, elegant lace terraces.

In fact, the term "Paddington lace" refers to the New Orleans–style iron lacework which decorates many of the balconies of these houses. The lace is said to have come out originally as ballast on sailing ships. Builders in Sydney began to use it as a distinctive decorative feature and, though it exists throughout Sydney on houses of this era, Paddington has become associated with the style. **Cascade Street** is particularly famous for its iron lace.

The shopping is something else, too. From curios to cut-rate china to books or batik, you'll find a shop for it on Oxford Street. The fashion is, on the whole, *not* mainstream. A number of experimental shops, boutiques specializing in punk gear or futuristic fashion dot the area. You can also see Sydney's oldest and largest street market in operation all day on Saturday (see Shopping).

## WOOLLAHRA

At the top of Oxford Street, at the intersection with Queen, you are in the more genteel suburb of Woollahra. While Paddington housed aspiring actors, artists, and assorted bohemians in the sixties and early seventies (though now its prices tend to attract stockbrokers and middle management), Woollahra has always catered to those who've made it. The Queen Street shops that branch off to the left of Oxford show a preponderance for interior design, quality antiques, and good dresses. A wander in the back lanes of Woollahra will divulge stunning little sandstone pied-à-terres trailing bougainvillea, and the only traffic jams occur around 3 P.M. when the mums pick up their offspring from private school.

Jutting off at an angle from the Oxford/Queen Street intersection is **Centennial Park,** established in 1888 to celebrate the nation's one-hundredth birthday. The 220-hectare park houses duck ponds, lagoons, horse riding facilities, and the recent addition of a classy little kiosk-cum-dining room for those who prefer something a little more upmarket than sandwiches in the park.

Beyond the park is the **Sydney Cricket Ground** and the new **Football stadium.**

# The North Shore

Of course, even if you're only in Sydney a few days, you'll succumb to the temptation of the harbor. Whether this means a cruise, renting a sailboat, or merely taking one of the many ferries and hydrofoils that cross from one side to the other is entirely up to your pocket and time limitations.

If you opt for a ferry ride, you may like to know what to do when you get off on the other side. For the casual tourist there are four major "ports of call," each of which makes an excellent reason for a ferry excursion.

One is, of course, **Taronga Park Zoo.** There is a separate ferry that takes you to the zoo. Once you dock, you can take the "flying fox"—an airborne gondola-like conveyance that whizzes you up from the water to the zoo's top entrance. The zoo is open daily from 9 A.M. to 5 P.M.; 969-2777. Entrance costs $10 and $4.50 for children.

For those among us who never get enough of shopping, the stretch along **Military Road** from Neutral Bay through Cremorne and Mosman provides ample alternatives to either the city or Eastern Suburbs. Many of the same Australian designers have outlets here, but the merchandise is often different. As well, there are a number of boutiques that sell imported clothing, household accessories, and giftware.

If you take a ferry to one of the Neutral Bay wharves, you can walk up to Military Road through streets laden with charm. More expensive on the whole than Paddington, the Neutral Bay area has much of its winding village charm, but the building style is more Federation than Victorian— Federation was a building style popular when Australia became a nation, post-1900, with wide, elaborately gabled houses set on deep lots.

There are also buses that will carry you to Military Road; the walk is a longish one, though if you carry a *Gregory's* it will be hard to lose your way.

**Mosman** can also be approached via the harbor. The walk up to Military Road from Mosman wharf is an impossibly long and steep one, though, so take the bus. Save some time to wander around the suburb, rich in lovely old houses— particularly the streets around the zoo. There are one or two worthwhile beaches in the area as well, such as Balmoral (see Beaches and Sporting).

A third destination for northern-bound harbor cruisers is the oceanside suburb of **Manly.** There was a saying about the area in the early part of this century: "Seven miles from Sydney and a thousand miles from care." It was the favored beachside holiday spot for country people—particularly country children—whose inland lives saw little of any kind of water, let alone an ocean. The beach was planted with enormous pine trees, sadly dying off due to late–twentieth-century pollution, but there is still a fading holiday charm about the place.

The area around Manly wharf is the center of latter-day development. Manly's Marineland and Underwater World are located here. On the other side of the headland, on the open ocean, are several lovely beaches, many almost deserted on weekdays, among them Manly and Shelly Beach.

You can lunch royally at any of several good eateries along these beaches, among them **Just Prawns** at 14 South Steyne. Contrary to what its name might suggest, you can get more than prawns (large shrimp) here, but all of it comes from the sea. A little farther east at Fairy Bower is **Fairy Bower Tea House,** open for delightful lunches seven days a week and serving an amazing breakfast Sun. from 8 A.M.

If you're going to Manly for the day, take the hydrofoil; it cuts the trip time in half. But if you just want a lazy trip on the harbor for very little money, take the ferry for just over a dollar each way, spend an hour getting the feel of the place, and go back the way you came; it's a morning well spent.

**Hunters Hill** is the fourth suggestion for a harbor trip. Again, the normal ferry system will get you there. Hunters Hill lies on a peninsula on the Parramatta River which flows into the harbor. Its collection of magnificent sandstone mansions, many built in the French style by European craftsmen who immigrated here in the last century, is not matched anywhere in Australia. Hunters Hill is essentially a residential area; there is little to buy or even to see beyond these houses. But their beauty combined with half an hour or so each way on the water makes for a rewarding and unusual excursion.

Getting there is a bit tricky. Ferry services are irregular outside of peak hours on weekday mornings and evenings. There are a few tour guides who can arrange special visits to the area (see Touring), and for those who have limited time, this may be the way to go.

## BEACHES AND SPORTING

Sydney's beaches are among the most famous in the world. Sadly, in the past few years, problems with pollution have made some of them slightly dicey for swimming. A daily pollution watch in summer is published in the *Sydney Morning Herald* and it's advisable to consult it before venturing to swim off some of the Eastern Suburbs beaches, particularly.

Below is a short list of the most popular beaches in the greater Sydney area, with recommendations for whether they are purely good for getting a tan, for swimming as well, or for surfing.

**Bondi Beach** is great for sunbathing, though footwear is recommended to protect from cuts caused by glass and other debris that tends to get buried in the sand. The northern corner of the beach is best for swimming and in northerly winds, some surfing is also possible. (See Eastern Suburbs, above.)

Nearby, **Tamarama** and **Clovelly** beaches are also good for both sunbathing and swimming (provided pollution reports allow). These are all ocean beaches; on the harborside of the Eastern Suburbs there are several quiet beaches, good for swimming: **Redleaf Pool,** despite its name, is actually a beach. Its entrance is via New South Head Road, opposite Victoria Road. There's a nominal charge for admission to this beach ($1) but the water is clear and the beach pleasant.

The beach at **Nielsen Park** in Vaucluse is also very pleasant for both sunning and swimming. On weekends it is packed with locals and their children and parking is hard to find, but weekdays, particularly after summer holidays end in early February, are no problem. The park provides shade for those who like the option of getting out of the sun; the beach is wide and very clean. Both Redleaf and Nielsen Park also have kiosks for food and beverages.

**Camp Cove** up at Watson's Bay is another lovely beach for a quiet swim. It's about a ten-minute walk from the end of the bus line. You can follow the headland around from here to **Lady Jane,** the nude beach, if you like, but Camp Cove, particularly on weekdays, is more pleasant.

On the North Shore, **Balmoral Beach** at Mosman is another harbor beach good for a quiet swim and sunbathe. At various times of year, **Manly, Shelly,** and **Queenscliff** beaches at Manly are good for surfing. A little farther north, **Collaroy** beach has gentle waves, good for beginning surfers, while you can get some really big waves at both **Dee Why** and **Narrabeen** beaches.

**Surfboards** and related materials (wetsuits for winter, and so on) can be rented from:

Surf Rentals, 31 South Steyne, Manly; 977-7808

Surfboards Manly Style, 49 North Steyne (shop 6), Manly. 977-3363

## Tennis

Time was when every Sydney neighborhood had a tennis court or two, but the value of inner-city land has just about done away with them. Few hotels in the city have courts, but many will be able to arrange a court for you locally if you request it. Here is a list of a few inner-city courts that you may want to try yourself. You'll have more luck during the day on a weekday than evenings or weekends when most courts are booked up.

Cooper Park Tennis Courts, off Suttie Road, Double Bay; 389-9259

Grasshopper Tennis Centre, Pidcock Street, Camperdown (just west of the city, near Sydney University); 51-2131

Moore Park Tennis Courts, at the corner of Lang Road and Anzac Parade, Paddington; 662-7005

Rushcutters Bay Tennis Centre, Waratah Street, Rushcutters Bay; 357-1675

## Golf

Again, the best bet for arranging a game, if you don't have access to one of the city's private clubs, is to ask your hotel to recommend a golf course. Here are a few public courses in the immediate area:

Eastlake Public Golf Links, Gardners Road, Kingsford (near the airport); 663-1374

Moore Park Golf Links, Cleveland Street and Anzac Parade (near Paddington); 663-3791

Tourist Sports Promotion, 18 Chalmers Crescent, Mascot (also near airport); 669-5068

All of these will rent equipment, including golf carts. Tourist Sports Promotion will arrange transfer to a course from your hotel.

# Hang Gliding

There are a number of hang-gliding schools and associations in N.S.W. Below are listed those most accessible to central Sydney. All will be able to supply you with necessary equipment, give you instruction from beginner to brush-up, and most will be able to arrange weekends out of the city if you want.

Airspace School of Hang Gliding, 1 Ducross Street, Petersham (about a 15-minute drive west of the business district); 560-8773

Free Flight School of Hang Gliding, 8 Laitoki Road, Terrey Hills (a northern suburb, bordering the Ku-ring-gai National Park, due west of Narrabeen); 450-2186

Aerial Technics Hang Gliding School, 38 Stanwell Avenue, Stanwell Park; (042) 94-2545. This last is actually not in Sydney proper, but will arrange group sessions at the Kurnell Sandhills, in the Sydney southern suburbs.

# Boating

Not everyone may be satisfied to see the harbor via a ferry. For those who wish to explore it on their own, here is a list of marinas that will hire boats you can captain yourself:

## SYDNEY HARBOUR

Rose Bay Outboard Hire, Vickery Ave, Rose Bay; 326-1507. This concern deals in open runabouts—good for fishing or a slow amble around the harbor islands. Boats available during daylight hours only.

Sail Australia, 23a King George Street, North Sydney (just across the Harbour Bridge); 957-2577. Offers a comprehensive fleet of yachts for charter from 24 to 67 feet. Can rent for half day or by the week. Sailing lessons are also offered.

## PITTWATER

Pittwater Yacht Charters, Lovett Bay, via Church Point; 99-3047. If sailing on the bay called Pittwater, between Ku-ring-gai and the tony northern suburbs of Palm and Whale Beach, intrigues you, you might not mind the drive (about an hour from central Sydney) up to Church Point. There's great scenery here and Pittwater Yacht Charters can provide eight-berth cruising yachts on a daily or weekly basis.

Skipper a Clipper at Clippers Anchorage, Akuna Bay, in the Ku-ring-gai National Park, Terrey Hills; 450-1888. Gives you the same opportunity with four-, six-, and eight-berth luxury cruisers.

Church Point Charter & Brokerage, at the corner of Pittwater and McCarrs Creek roads, Church Point; 99-4188. Offers sailboats or cruisers for hire for use on Pittwater or the Hawkesbury River.

## SPECTATOR SPORTS

### Cricket

September to March is the summer cricket season. The game is slow, by baseball's standards, but has a certain grace missing in the American sport. On weekend afternoons in summer you'll see cricket matches being played in almost every park. The big matches are played out at the Sydney Cricket Ground in Paddington (357-6601). While matches traditionally take several days to reach a conclusion, the relatively new institution of One Day Cricket means you can now see a whole match played out in a single day (and evening). Tickets are available at the gate prior to the match; big games can be booked through ticketing agencies (see Theatre in the Entertainment section).

### Football

While gridiron is gathering a large crowd of followers in Australia, little is played here professionally. The best games you'll see are relayed from the United States. Australian football still means soccer or one of the forms of the game which go under the title of Australian Rules (probably the most spectacular, very fast with high kicks and leaps—18 men on a side) Rugby Union (amateur—14 men on a side) and Rugby League (professional off-shoot of Rugby Union).

Most suburbs have playing fields (called ovals) where from March to September you can see games being played most Saturdays. The big matches are usually played at the Sydney Football Stadium (332-3791), next to the Sydney Cricket Ground on Moore Park Road. Tickets can be bought at the gates prior to game times.

### Racing

The sport of kings is well represented in Sydney. Horses run at Randwick Racecourse (663-8400) directly south of Paddington; across Centennial Park, most weekends; and at Rosehill Racecourse, out at Parramatta (682-1000). There are pacers at Harold Park in Glebe (660-3688), just west of Sydney, twice weekly, on Friday and some Tuesday nights.

Betting is done through bookmakers on the course, as well as through what is called the TAB (Totalizator Agency Betting), which operates both on the course and through centers in just about every suburb's main shopping street.

Greyhound racing is also very popular in Australia. In Sydney most meets take place at Wentworth Park, also in Glebe (Monday nights). (The dogs chase a mechanical "rabbit" around the course, so there is no cruelty involved.) Telephone 660-4308.

## Sailing

On Boxing Day, the day after Christmas Day, yachts compete in the annual Sydney to Hobart (Tasmania) race. Boats leave from the eastern end of the harbor. Best vantage points to see them off are from the foreshores of the suburbs of Double Bay, Rose Bay, Point Piper, Vaucluse, and Watson's Bay.

In the summer there is some sort of race held almost every weekend. Check the sports pages of the *Sydney Morning Herald* if you're interested. The best vantage points will be the same as those for the Sydney–Hobart race.

## Surfing

The main surfing championships of international status to be challenged on Sydney beaches are: The Coca Cola Classic at Manly Beach—held in April; The Quicksilver Surf League at Bondi—held in October; and The Mambo Showdown at Bondi—held in December.

Local papers and sports pages of the *Sydney Morning Herald* give details of dates and times. Just show up at the beach, pick a spot with a good vantage point, and spend the day.

## Tennis

The season for tennis begins in late November when a number of major indoor and outdoor matches are played. Major centers for matches are White City in Paddington (331-4144) for outdoor tennis and the Sydney Entertainment Centre (266-4800) for indoor matches.

Tickets for all matches can be bought at the gates or through ticketing agents such as Bass agencies (see Entertainment).

## SHOPPING

In the Central Business District, the main shopping outlets are clustered along George, Pitt, and Castlereagh streets, the heaviest concentration between Park and Hunter streets.

At the corner of George and Market streets stands **Grace Brothers Department Store;** two blocks east, **David Jones**'s two buildings cater to the same clientele they served when they opened 160 years ago—the upper-middle and upper classes. Times have changed to the extent that the store realizes that all client money looks alike and to that end, they promise to meet any price quoted at any other shop for comparable merchandise.

# Australian Women's Fashion

As part of the 1988 bicentennial celebration, Australia staged a fashion parade featuring one of the country's star performers—wool. What amazed so many visiting designers was that Australia had such a strong and talented body of local designers—something any tourist should be aware of.

Australian fashion has the happy facility for combining classic design with a sense of casual lifestyle. Designers such as Carla Zampatti, with her soft wool crêpes in winter and crisp cottons for warmer seasons, understand the needs of a climate where heavy clothing isn't needed at any time of the year. But her fabrics work well in northern climates also, where central heating obviates the need for thick woolens.

Wendy Heather echoes this philosophy, but Wendy's knit designs aren't for everyone; you need a perfect figure, tall and lean, for them to work. Her silk dresses, in flattering small prints, are the essence of springtime in New York or Chicago.

Classic design is what Robert Burton is all about. He uses only the finest fabrics—Irish linens, pure Australian wool, silk from Italy—to fashion the sort of garments that never date. Before you make a mental note that that means boring, it's not—just the opposite in fact because few designers on any continent still trouble to make each garment as though it were being designed with a specific client in mind. Burton's designs are expensive in comparison to many, but you will have a garment of impeccable lineage.

Adele Palmer fashions are perfect illustrations of the marriage of the classic with the casual. They're comfortable, never tricksy, and her color sense is second to none. In this she shares honors with Peter and Adele Weiss for day wear. The Weiss range of evening wear stands alone—flatteringly feminine.

Jenny Kee's sweaters combine color in exciting ways, usually with themes of Australian flora and fauna. Her shop, Flamingo Park in Sydney's Strand Arcade, has become a mecca for fashionable ladies who love Jenny's bright winter woolens.

There are few women in advertising, public relations, or other socially related professions who don't own at least one linen suit designed by Lizzie Collins. Liz's fashion philosophy is comfort combined with style; her skirts are cut to accommodate that little bit of extra tummy or backside that most real women (as opposed to fashion models) have. Waistbands are as often as not elasticized for greater comfort. At the same time fabrics, styling, and detail are such that these clothes look good at any function.

Other labels to look for in better dresses departments are the Covers label—Marilyn Said, head designer, goes for the slinky in evening wear, lots of small waists, peplums on jackets—very vampy. Harry Who is a label devoted to classic styling, the kind of thing one wears to the office. Country Road specializes in sportswear—tweedy jackets, pleated skirts, lambswool.

All these labels can be found in larger department stores in major cities. Many have their own outlets in better shopping arcades throughout Australia.

While Grace Brothers has been perceived as downmarket in comparison to DJs, the city store particularly fights its middle-of-the-road image with a second-floor designer boutique. You could say Grace Brothers (GBs) is the Macy's or Carson Pirie Scott of Sydney; David Jones's (DJ's), a less glitzy Bloomingdale's—more Marshall Field's, really.

In the city, these two are the heavyweights in their field, but Sydney is much more about boutique shopping and so the arcades are the places in which to search out clothing from budget to brilliant. The **Queen Victoria Building** (QVB) on George Street, between Park and Market, fills an entire city block with its restored Victorian magnificence. Its two hundred specialty shops include some of Sydney's best designers: marvelous Jenny Kee knitwear, easy-to-wear Lizzie Collins designs for busy female executives, and for the men, ultra-modern Najee designs. Everything from classic jewelry to deep-dish Chicago-style pizza is sold here on four superbly appointed levels.

Another lovely old arcade, **The Strand,** which extends between George and Pitt streets, near the intersection with King, also features imaginative dressing—try Shepherds' silk Diane Fries dresses at a fraction of designer prices. Smaller than the Queen Victoria Building, with only eighty shops, The Strand is nonetheless equally meticulous in the quality of the restoration work that went into this hundred-plus-year-old building.

**Centrepoint Shopping Centre** between Pitt and Castlereagh at Market Street and the **Mid-City Centre** at 197 Pitt Street are two of the modern arcades that have sprung up in the city in the past ten or so years. Centrepoint is directly beneath Sydney Tower, so you can finish your bird's-eye viewing with a little down-to-earth shopping.

Both the lower level of Centrepoint and that of the QVB (called Eat Street) are the places to go for a mid-day snack attack, although the QVB is probably preferable, since it has more seating. Still, with Hyde Park no more than a few minutes' walk away from Centrepoint or the Mid-City Centre, on a nice day a salad, pizza, or plate of nachos is great to have on the grass.

As you walk along the streets between these arcades and department stores, you will no doubt notice a number of small speciality shops. Castlereagh between Park and Market is particularly rich in small, elegant **antique shops** where it is possible to find some fine Georgian silver or a small Oriental artifact—for a price, of course.

In general, city shops open at 9 A.M. six days a week. They close at 5:30 P.M. Monday through Wednesday and Friday;

on Thursday nights some stay open until 9, some close at 7. On Saturday, the city shops open from 9 A.M. until 4 P.M.

Outside the city shopping area, there is a little more latitude in opening hours. Along Oxford Street, Paddington, shops tend to open later in the mornings during weekdays; usually not admitting customers until 10 A.M. or even 11 A.M. On Saturday, they're all open by 9 A.M., however, and few close before 6 P.M. any night. Late-night shopping hours apply here on Thursdays as well, and many Oxford Street book and specialty stores even open for a few hours on Sunday.

Double Bay shops, particularly the large chain stores like Sportsgirl, which has a nice range of town and country wear, open in accordance with their city counterparts. Boutiques and specialty shops follow their own inclination about late shopping (the attitude seems to be that if you work and have to shop in the evenings and on Saturdays you're not the kind of client they want anyway). A pleasant exception to this attitude is The Squire Shop at 409 New South Head Road, Double Bay (327-5726), which opens seven days a week with a fantastic—though pricey—range of local and imported women's and men's casual and dress clothing.

American Express, Visa, Diners Club, MasterCard are accepted in all tourist areas. Large department stores such as Grace Brothers and David Jones will also accept these cards in addition to their own card.

Small shops and restaurants will usually accept Visa or MasterCard, though it's a good idea to ask if you don't see signs displayed to this effect.

## Specialty Shopping

### OPALS

Australia is one of the few countries in the world where first-class opals are found in large amounts. Even here a good quality opal is not inexpensive, but there couldn't be a more appropriate souvenir of your trip Down Under.

Most quality jewelry shops have a selection of opals set in rings, earrings, or pendants. **Percy Marks** specializes in high-quality stones, set in magnificent designs. There are three Percy Marks shops, one at 65 Castlereagh Street, in the city, one in the Regent Hotel, and one in the Hotel Inter-Continental.

**Flame Opals** at 119 George Street in The Rocks area sells both set and unset stones from inexpensive little chips to large investment pieces. They also have chunks of opal still embedded in rock, which make great paperweights or decorative pieces. A similar selection is available from the opal shop just inside the front door of the Argyle Centre.

Most specialist jewelry and gemstone shops are empowered to sell their wares tax-free to bona fide overseas customers. When you make your selection, present your ticket (and in some cases your passport) to the salesperson to have the tax deducted from your purchase.

Steer clear of souvenir shops when buying opals. Most offer substandard merchandise and a few (though not many) even sell fakes as the real thing. The only way to be sure of quality is to buy from a reputable jeweler or specialist; ask at your hotel for the names of nearby outlets.

---

### About Opals

Opal comes in different forms and some are more rare, therefore more valuable. Only shop for quality opals from reputable dealers.

Black opals are very rare. They have a dark appearance shot through with blazes of color. Boulder opals are similar in appearance to black opals and are second in value to the black opal, the most expensive of these stones.

Probably the most well known and popular form of opal is the white or light opal, which has a "milky" appearance shot through with red, blue, and green lights. These are sometimes called "fire opals." Although these are less rare than the black opal, many white opals are of exquisite character. Care must be exercised in selecting one, and price is usually a good indication of quality.

When shopping for black opals, be careful you aren't offered a triplet instead (though this won't happen with reputable jewelers or gemstone dealers). A triplet is a thin slice of light opal which is placed on top of a piece of dark backing and then covered with a crystal, giving the appearance of solid opal. This is an inexpensive way of buying souvenir opal and as such is perfectly acceptable. A doublet is similar to a triplet without the quartz overlay which protects the opal layer.

---

## PRIMITIVE ART

Sydney is also a good place for collectors of primitive art to search out pieces. Aboriginal art, most of which comes from inland Australia, is sold at a few galleries around the city. **Aboriginal Art Centres** have two outlets, one at 7 Walker Lane, Paddington (357-6839), the other on level 2 of the Argyle Centre, Argyle Street, The Rocks (27-1380). The Centres specialize in Aboriginal arts and crafts. **Aboriginal Art Australia** at 477 Kent Street in the city (261-2929) also sells fine examples of the art of the first inhabitants of this continent.

**Galleries Primitif** at 174 Jersey Road, Woollahra (32-3115), sells art and craftwork from New Guinea and Oceania. **New Guinea Primitive Arts** has two outlets, one in the Dymock's Building at 428 George Street (232-4737), and nearby in shop 42 of the Queen Victoria Building (267-5134). Both these shops are in the very center of the city shopping district, making access easy.

## CRAFTS

Instead of the ubiquitous koala, why not consider some of the works executed by Australian craftsmen as souvenirs to take home to friends? Beautifully made boxes of Australian woods, neatly crafted jigsaw puzzles, and hand-screened silk make much lovelier gifts—and say a lot more about the country.

**The Craft Centre** at 100 George Street, The Rocks (27-9126), is sponsored by the Craft Council of New South Wales. The gallery displays the best among works in wood, glass, metal, and fabric fashioned by artisans from this state.

Another site for exploring creative Australian possibilities is at Australian Craftworks in the **Old Police Station,** 127 George Street, also at the Rocks (27-7156). Exhibitions are mounted in the cells of this 106-year-old station that only ceased in its function as a lock-up in 1976. There are many beautiful works for sale, as well.

## KEN DONE

The name Ken Done (pronounced "doan") has developed a high profile within Australia in the past five years. His cheerful prints featuring Australian flowers, water scenes, and beach vignettes have made him a star in the local art firmament. He branched out in the last few years, adding everything from beachbags to bed sheets to his collection of tropical prints. An original Done print will set you back a few hundred dollars, but a copy, a poster, or a T-shirt makes just as nice a souvenir—and little is as "dinky-di" a momento of Australia as one of these joyful designs. Department stores carry a limited supply of Ken Done merchandise; for a more complete range try Ken Done's own shop at 123 George Street (27–2737) and at Shop 141, Harbourside Festival Marketplace, Darling Harbour (281–3818), or **The Art Directors Gallery,** 21 Nurses Walk, both at The Rocks (27-2740).

**Dinky-di (pronounced die) means for real, honest. As in "I'm not havin' you on; I'm dinky-di."**

## ANTIQUES

If you're in the market for antiques, Sydney has myriad outlets for merchandise from past generations. As mentioned earlier, the stretch along Castlereagh between Park and Market streets in the city offers half a dozen small but very fine dealers in antiques where you can find excellent silver, statuary, and estate jewelry. There are one or two shops just parallel with these, on Elizabeth Street, as well.

The arcade that runs through the Sydney Hilton hotel, known as **The Royal Arcade** (259 Pitt Street, through to George Street), **The Queen Victoria Building,** and **The Strand Arcade** are also good places in the city to look for antique shops.

In the Eastern Suburbs, Queen Street, Woollahra, has become something of a specialist area for antique dealers. Among the best are **Anne Schofield Antiques** at 36 Queen Street (32-1326), who specializes in stunning antique jewelry, and **Copeland & De Soos** at 66 Queen (32-5288), who specialize in furnishings, jewelry, and objects d'art in the Art Deco and Art Nouveau styles.

**Woollahra Galleries,** at 160 Oxford Street, Woollahra (327-8840), and the **Sydney Antique Centre,** 531 South Dowling Street, Surry Hills (33-3244), both deal in antique trading on a large scale. They are warehouse-style buildings, set up to house individual stalls with wares ranging from antique books to magnificent colonial cedar chests, oak refectory tables, and even leaded windows rescued from an old mansion under demolition. These are definitely worth a browse, even if you don't intend to buy anything—they're like museums of Australia's past. Both of these centers are open from around 10:30 A.M. to 6 P.M., seven days a week.

## Prices

On the whole, prices for merchandise are higher than in the United States. The small size of the country's population, the fact that most consumer goods are still imported from overseas, and the relatively high tariffs on imported goods contribute to keeping prices high. Best buys are locally produced goods: Australian-designed fashions, local craft work, and jewelry. Film developing is also cheaper in Australia than most other places, so leave enough time to have your snaps developed in Sydney before going home.

Balanced against these higher prices is the fact that the Australian dollar has been averaging around 20 percent less in value than the American dollar, giving the U.S. tourist more purchasing power. British visitors will find that their strong pound will also give them strong purchasing power. The Canadian dollar and the Australian dollar at press time are almost on a par.

## Markets

One of the most unusual ways to shop for gifts, as well as a great way to see the locals, is to spend part of a Saturday at one of the two great markets in Sydney. The first is **Paddington Markets,** located in the Paddington Village Centre, whose official address is 2 Newcombe Street. In reality, the market spreads across the churchyard into the vacant area next door, encompassing everything from clothing, plants, ceramics, and handicrafts to jewelry and artifacts brought back from destinations as far flung as Southeast Asia, Afghanistan, the Andes, and Addis Ababa.

Don't be fooled into thinking this is just another "hippie" market; several of Sydney's most successful antique dealers and clothing designers (the labels Lizzie Collins and Van Troska are examples of the latter) got their start here. There's a lot of junk, but also some wonderful bargains on occasion, and the street life that gravitates to the area is worth mixing in for entertainment value alone. Buskers perform for crowds all day in good weather, and if you don't fancy the admittedly alternative leanings of most of the food on sale in the center, you can always cross the street for lunch at one of the six or eight cafés that stretch from Oatley Road to Jersey Road along Oxford Street.

The best of these are **Anastasia's, The New Edition Tea Rooms** (packed out from noon to around 6 P.M. on Saturdays), or **Sloane Rangers.**

**Balmain Markets,** on the grounds of St. Mary's Anglican Church on Darling Street, Balmain, is the second weekly market worth visiting. The pickings aren't necessarily as vast as Paddington's, but quantity is replaced by quality here. Lots of hand-made goods are on sale at stunning prices. Hand-marbled paper and embroidered pillow cases and quilt covers in cream and peach linen are two of the more tempting recent offerings.

There's also a woman who has a stunning selection of Art Deco jewelry (she won't, naturally, reveal her sources, but prices are well below those in antique shops).

Inside the church hall a veritable United Nations of food stuffs is on sale. Indian pakoras, African samosas, and kebabs from the Middle East mingle with South American dishes, Chinese stir fries, and Australian meat pies.

Both markets open around 9 A.M. on Saturday and begin to close around 4 P.M., though there's still a little life left in each an hour or so after this.

Both Oxford Street, Paddo, and Darling Street, Balmain, are excellent shopping districts, with Saturday shopping hours more or less reflecting those of the markets.

# RESTAURANTS

Fascinating things are happening to food in Sydney. Over the past five years, a style which we might as well call the new Australian cuisine has been evolving, thanks to the efforts of some younger chefs who tired of Sydney's preoccupation with French and Italian restaurants.

They started experimenting with fresh local ingredients, especially seafood, replaced the frying pan with the barbecue, and abolished heavy sauces. They encouraged nearby farmers to produce unusual vegetables and salad ingredients that had been largely ignored by the traditional chefs. The result is a colorful and lively taste sensation that shows the inspiration of France and Italy but also has much in common with what American gourmets call the "nouvelle Californian" style.

You're unlikely to find this new Australian cooking in Sydney's grand restaurants. The style is flourishing in smaller, more informal places normally called bistros and brasseries. Our selection of best eating places includes several of them, as well as a sprinkling of the more traditional establishments.

What you won't find in our list is the old Australian cuisine, because, as practiced in Sydney, it's just a tourist rip-off. There are a few places that offer roast mutton and damper (a kind of bread eaten in the bush country) served by "wenches" in low-cut blouses and cloth caps. Sydney residents rarely go to them, except for a laugh.

Sydney's other specialty is Asian cuisine, particularly Thai and Vietnamese, because of waves of immigration from those countries in recent years (this chapter includes a separate listing for the best of the new Asians). These styles have added to the already wonderful diversity of Sydney food—transformed in the 1950s by Italian restaurateurs, expanded in the 1960s by the French fad, mingled in the 1970s with Lebanese, Greek, Indonesian, Japanese, Spanish, and even American influences. You're in for a treat.

Credit cards—widely accepted—are abbreviated here as AE—American Express, V—Visa, MC—MasterCard, DC—Diner's Club. We'll say "All cards" when all of the above are accepted. Restaurants are keyed to maps in the same way Priorities are.

## Baseline Brasserie    EASTERN SUBURBS, P. 27, F6

In the clubhouse of White City Tennis Courts, 30 Alma St., Rushcutters Bay; (02) 331-1632.

This is a historic spot. The Baseline Brasserie overlooks the grass courts on which generations of Australian tennis champions have trained. Martina Navratilova has eaten in this very room—although not as well as you will eat, since the food style (categorized now as adventurous Australian) has changed a lot since her visit.

The restaurant used to be the members' dining room of the New South Wales Lawn Tennis Association. In 1986 it was taken over by a brilliant new chef who installed an open kitchen in the middle of the room and opened the place to the public. The tennis crowd still eats here, but now they pay about $25 a head for the likes of char-grilled tuna steak with caper vinaigrette, barbecued scallops, oyster and avocado salad, and rich passionfruit pudding. Wine is reasonably priced at around $12 a bottle. And if you come at lunchtime (a short cab ride from midtown), you can sit on the balcony and observe the Davis Cup champions of tomorrow practicing below. Open Sun.–Fri. for lunch, Tues.–Sat. for dinner. MC, V only.

## Bayswater Brasserie    KINGS CROSS, P. 27, E5

32 Bayswater Rd., Kings Cross; (02) 357-2749.

The Bayswater Brasserie buzzes from morning to midnight. Sydney's young in-crowd go there to spot their friends. It's always crowded, always noisy, and yet always able to offer brisk friendly service and light tasty food—in the adventurous Australian category—a pasta with duck sausage, perhaps, or chargrilled octopus with a chili sauce, and superb walnut cream cake if you're just looking for an afternoon tea snack. A full meal will cost about $30 a head, plus wine by the glass or bottle; but snacking can be managed for around $10.

There's a pretty courtyard out back, but those in the know sit in the front room and observe the street life through the big glass windows, or just admire their fellow diners.

Getting there is half the fun—a short ride on Sydney's subway (the Eastern Suburbs Railway) to Kings Cross Station, and a short walk through what passes for sin city. The strip clubs and the local versions of Irma La Douce are harmless. Open every day for lunch and dinner till 11 P.M., Sat. and Sun. for breakfast from 8 A.M. MC, V only.

---

## Sydney Eating with a View

The American humorist Calvin Trillin has laid down three rules for people visiting a new city. If you're looking for good food, you must never eat (a) in your hotel; (b) in anything higher than twenty feet above the ground; and (c) in anything that revolves. The second and third of these rules are very useful for Sydney.

Unless you're absolutely desperate to overlook the city while rotating, you should ignore any guidebook that directs you to The Summit restaurant or the Sydney Tower restaurant. Sydneysiders rarely go to them because they know that great views can be obtained elsewhere, along with great food.

We mentioned three scenic establishments in our list of Sydney's best eateries: **The Wharf,** the **Imperial Peking Harbourside,** and the **Bluewater Grill.** In addition, consider the following (not quite so fine for food, but good enough):

**Butler's,** 123 Victoria St., Potts Point; 357-1988. Posh French food, close to town, with a skyscrapered skyline visible from its balcony.

**Doyle's on the Beach,** 11 Marine Pde., Watsons Bay; 337-2007. Specializes in fish. About 15 minutes from midtown (take the bus for fine views along the way).

**Sails,** 2 Henry Lawson Ave., McMahon's Point; 920-5793. Fish with rich sauces. On the north side of the harbor, reachable by a lovely ferry ride from Circular Quay.

---

## Beppi's

EASTERN SUBURBS (BUT NEAR BUSINESS DISTRICT), P. 25, D5

Corner of Stanley and Yurong sts., East Sydney; (02) 360-4558.

Beppi Polese will not be offended if you call him the godfather of Italian food in Sydney. He opened his restaurant in 1956, and was the first to stun the barbarian palates of Australians with calamari, mussels, and scampi. Beppi has introduced so many great dishes to Sydney, and has been copied by so many other restaurateurs, that you might expect him to rest on his laurels.

But no—he's still wandering round the tables, offering samples of his latest creation to delighted customers, tying bibs round the necks of those who eat his spaghetti with squid ink sauce, pouring tiny glasses of lethal grappa made at his own orchard west of Sydney.

No wonder Beppi's is the favorite lunchtime meeting place of Sydney's lawyers and business executives, who have no trouble paying $40 a head, plus around $20 for a bottle of wine. Open Mon.–Fri. for lunch, Mon.–Sat. for dinner from 6 P.M. All cards.

### Berowra Waters Inn     NORTH OF SYDNEY
Berowra Waters, north of Sydney; (02) 456-1027.

It's a long journey to the experimental French food at Berowra Waters from the center of Sydney—about eighty minutes by car, much longer by train (and taxi from the station), shorter but far more expensive by seaplane (which some Sydney millionaires do almost every weekend). But the pilgrimage is worth the time and money for what has often been described as the greatest restaurant in Australia.

Your car journey ends at a little wharf, where you are met by the restaurant's motor launch. This whisks you across the river to a typically Australian bush bungalow. As you're seated and start to gaze at the river and forest scenery, your complimentary glass of champagne and your hors d'oeuvres arrive. Prepare to spend at least two hours luxuriating with the best Australian wines and the most imaginative French food—from an appetizer of bone marrow on brioche, perhaps, to a dessert of lemon crème brulée. And prepare to pay $70 a head, plus around $25 a bottle, for the privilege. Open for lunch and dinner Fri., Sat., Sun. All cards.

### Bluewater Grill     EASTERN SUBURBS, P. 29, E4
168 Ramsgate Ave., Bondi; (02) 30-7810.

This is sheer hedonism. You're sitting back in a comfortable chair on a wide veranda, under a beach umbrella, with a glass of crisp white wine in one hand and a forkful of the freshest local tuna in the other, gazing over the entire length of Bondi Beach. A few yards away, surfers are catching long breakers into a shore packed with sun worshippers.

The Bluewater Grill (seafood is the specialty) opened only a couple of years ago, and it took Sydneysiders—who tend to be suspicious of restaurants with views—a few months to realize that it was offering some of the most innovative food in the city. Now they cram in, and since the Bluewater doesn't take bookings, it's a good idea to arrive early for lunch (around mid-day) or very late (around 3 P.M.).

You must try the raw salmon on a bed of mascarpone (somewhat like a soft cream cheese), which sounds an odd combination till you sample it. Then you're addicted. There's also chargrilled swordfish with garlic and potato purée, or char-grilled sting ray with basil and pepper, plus fine fruit tarts and sorbets for dessert. It will cost you around $30 a head, plus wine at around $20 a bottle. And you can even get shrimps on the barbie (although Aussies call them "king prawns"). Open every day except Tues. for lunch and dinner. MC, V only.

## Buon Ricordo
PADDINGTON, P. 27, E6

108 Boundary St., Paddington; (02) 357-6729.

Buon Ricordo (which means "good memories") looks rather like an Alpine chalet. But be assured that these are the Italian Alps, not the Swiss. Armando Percuoco, the owner and chef, actually comes from Naples, but he has broadened his culinary horizons to include the more sophisticated dishes of northern Italy.

Armando's specials change often, but if you're there on a night when he does the zucchini blossoms fried in light batter, or the deviled spatchcock (baby chicken), or baby goat casserole with ricotta and peas, you've a culinary memory to last a lifetime. His luscious cakes and soufflés dispell the myth that Italians are weak on desserts. It's easily worth the $40 a head that you'll pay. Open Tues.–Sat. for dinner (until midnight for late supper). AE, MC only.

## The Burdekin Diningroom
EASTERN SUBURBS
(BUT NEAR BUSINESS DISTRICT), P. 27, D6

Top floor of the Burdekin Hotel, 2 Oxford St., Darlinghurst; (02) 331-1046.

Getting into the Burdekin restaurant is a little like entering a Chicago speakeasy of the Roaring Twenties. You must book. Then, at the appointed hour, you go round the back of the old Burdekin pub and walk through a green and orange tiled room called The Dugout Bar. Identify yourself to the barman, and he will, by some mysterious process, summon a bow-tied waiter, who will lead you to an ancient elevator. The elevator clanks up three floors, the doors open, and you're welcomed into a different world—an elegantly restored Art Deco dining room.

The food is a fine example of the new Australian cooking—a salad of braised lamb shanks and leeks, perhaps, or roast duck with crunchy spinach, or pigeon tortelli, or rare grilled tuna. They'll mix a mean steak tartare at your table, spicing it to your specifications, and they are Sydney's finest fryers of chips (what Americans call french fries, only bigger and crisper). Save room for sensational desserts like the almond and pear tart. There's a small but interesting list of Australian wines at around $20 a bottle, with waiters happy to advise; you'll pay around $30 a head for a complete meal.

The Burdekin is just across the road from Sydney's lovely Hyde Park, and if you're staying in mid-city, a stroll through the park, past the Pool of Remembrance, is a delightful way to work up an appetite. Afterwards, you might like to observe Oxford St., Sydney's gay bar area. Open Mon.–Fri. for lunch, Mon.–Sat. for dinner from 7:30 P.M. AE, MC, V.

## Chez Oz
EASTERN SUBURBS, P. 28, A4

23 Craigend St., Darlinghurst; (02) 332-4866.

This is Sydney's most fashionable restaurant, a favorite of actors, gossip columnists, businessmen in stretch limos, and Ladies Who Lunch (and who hop from table to table showing off their new outfits). Because many of its customers go there simply to be seen, Chez Oz could probably get away with serving merely average food, so it is much to the chef's credit that he maintains rigorously high standards and creates an exciting new menu every couple of months.

The style is vaguely French (liver with pear sauce), vaguely Italian (ravioli stuffed with asparagus), and vaguely Californian (char-grilled quail). There's a pleasant garden, but the true glitterati prefer to be crowded together in the front room. They happily pay high prices ($50 a head, plus wines around $25 a bottle). Some of them may even go there for the food. Open Tues.–Fri. for lunch, Tues.–Sat. for dinner. All cards.

## Clareville Kiosk                    NORTH OF SYDNEY
27 Delecta Ave., Clareville; (02) 918-2727.

Only twenty years ago, Clareville was a sleepy seaside village to the north of Sydney. It had a little wooden post office and a community of fisherfolk, artists, and escapists from city pressures. But the city kept growing, and now Clareville is a suburb—about an hour by bus or car from midtown—and the old post office is now a superb little restaurant called The Clareville Kiosk, specializing in the new Australian cuisine.

Some of the seaside simplicity remains. Locally caught crabs and fish feature often on the menu, along with juicy racks of lamb, spatchcock with chili, and decadent desserts. Lunch at Kiosk can be combined with a swim at Palm Beach, Sydney's northernmost surfing spot, or a gentle stroll past the waterside mansions and yachts of the leisured classes. The meal will cost around $30 a head. You bring your own liquor—you can buy fine wines at the nearby Avalon shopping center. Open Thurs.–Sun. for lunch, Fri.–Sun. for dinner. No credit cards.

## Cleopatra                          WEST OF SYDNEY
Cleopatra St., Blackheath; (047) 87-8456.

Early in this century it became fashionable for Australians to make a pilgrimage to the Blue Mountains, about 50 miles west of Sydney, to breathe fresh air, walk in the forest, and eat huge meals at resort hotels. The resorts are somewhat faded now, but the air is still fresh, the forests are largely unspoiled, and a new element has been added: a brilliant French chef named Dany Chouet.

Chouet took over an ancient boarding house called Cleopatra and is serving the kind of food you dream about finding in the countryside of southern France: onion and olive tarts, flavorful casseroles of lamb and lemon, pastries stuffed with locally picked raspberries. She always offers second helpings.

On fine Sundays Chouet serves lunch in her lush garden (set price: $40; bring your own wine). In cooler weather, you're cozy by the fire in her ornate dining room.

Reaching Cleopatra makes an entertaining day trip. Set off about 10 A.M. from Sydney's Central Station, enjoy two hours of spectacular scenery as the train climbs the mountains, buy a bottle of wine at the Blackheath village pub, and stroll down to Cleopatra for a leisurely two-hour lunch. There'll be time for a little bushwalking before you catch the 5 P.M. train back to town.

Better yet, book to stay at Cleopatra overnight and enjoy both dinner and a breakfast of home-made croissants and fresh orange juice. Open Fri.–Sun. for dinner, Sun. for lunch. No cards.

## Desaru

NORTH SHORE

28 Falcon St., Crows Nest; (02) 438-4331.

Mixing cuisines can be a risky business, but Desaru succeeds brilliantly. It offers light spicy Thai dishes like fish cakes or chili pork with string beans, alongside hearty Malaysian curries. A must is the chicken and coconut curry served with crunchy pancakes (the chicken is deboned at your table).

Desaru's decor tends to the plastic, but its service and its imaginative food distract your attention from the walls, and its prices (around $25 a head) barely graze your wallet.

If you're staying in midtown, getting there involves a twenty-minute taxi ride across the Sydney Harbour Bridge into the city's near northern surburbs; a visually satisfying experience. Open Mon.–Fri. for lunch, Mon.–Sat. for dinner. All cards.

## The New Asian Restaurants

It's a fair estimate that Sydney has more Thai restaurants than any city in the world apart from Bangkok. Sydneysiders, with a largely uninspiring collection of Chinese restaurants, have taken to Thai with manic enthusiasm. It's understandable, since Thai food involves clear, strong flavors, light and healthy undercooked vegetables, moderate shots of chili, and no monosodium glutamate.

Vietnamese food can claim similar attractions, and Sydney has almost as many Vietnamese restaurants as Thai. They tend, however, to be located in the outer suburbs—difficult for visitors to reach. Here are some suggestions of a few convenient Asian eateries to start your addiction:

**Bangkok,** 234 Crown St., Darlinghurst; 33-4804.

**Kim Van Vietnamese,** 147 Glebe Point Rd., Glebe; 660-5252.

**Silver Spoon Thai,** 203 Oxford St., Darlinghurst; 360-4669.

**Thai Orchid,** 628 Crown St., Surry Hills; 698-2097.

## Imperial Peking

HARBORSIDE, P. 24, B2

15 Circular Quay West, The Rocks; (02) 27-7073.

The first rule at the Imperial Peking is: ask for a table outside. Then you'll be by the water with an uninterrupted view of the Sydney Opera House. But if by any mischance there is no room in the courtyard, don't walk away. The interior of the Imperial Peking is relaxing (a renovated sandstone warehouse) and the food magnificent.

This is aristocratic Chinese cuisine, with an emphasis on seafood (like lobsters and crabs plucked live from huge glass tanks). Those with fish allergies might prefer the spicy squab or the sizzling Mongolian lamb. Desserts should be avoided—''Korean balls with bean paste'' are even duller than they sound. Expect to pay around $30 a head for a fine meal, or around $50 if you venture into the lobster. Open every day for lunch and dinner. All cards.

## Le Trianon

29 Challis Ave., Potts Point; (02) 358-1353.

For thirty years Le Trianon has been Sydney's grandest French restaurant—the kind of place where couples over-dressed and overdrank to celebrate their wedding anniversaries. But by the mid 1980s, the velvet banquettes were starting to grow a little threadbare, the chandeliers a little dusty, and the food a little too rich for modern tastes.

In the nick of time, Le Trianon was taken over by an ambitious couple of young chefs who renovated both the decor and the cuisine. Nowadays it's a little less formal—gentlemen are admitted without ties—and a lot more lively. The French influence is apparent, but Australian imagination has been added—escalope of ocean trout with ratatouille of zucchini and red peppers; fillet of hare with quince purée; breast of guinea fowl with wild mushroom sauce; caramel parfait with poached pear and praline; chocolate truffle cake with chocolate sorbet.

Such grandeur doesn't come cheap—at least $50 a head, plus around $25 for a bottle from an excellent list of Australian and French wines. But it's only a few minutes by cab, subway, or even foot from midtown. Open Tues.–Fri. for lunch, Mon.–Sat. for dinner. All cards.

## Mixing Pot

178 St. John's Rd., Glebe; (02) 660-7449.

Giuseppe Zuzza, who comes from a village about thirty miles from Venice, can be credited with introducing four great contributions to Sydney dining: vitello tonnato (sliced roast veal with a tuna mayonnaise and capers); potato gnocchi with a sauce of cream and gorgonzola cheese; radicchio and fennel salad; and tirami su (sponge cake soaked with coffee-liqueur covered with mascarpone). For this alone Australia should give him a knighthood, but in addition he has opened one of Sydney's most delightful little restaurants—the Mixing Pot.

At lunchtime its leafy courtyard is crammed with advertising types and journalists from the nearby newspaper offices. At night, you're more likely to find Italian families. All of them rely on Giuseppe's recommendations from his seemingly endless list of specials, and they stroll away satisfied after spending about $30 a head.

Glebe is an inner western suburb of Sydney filled with elegant cottages and Victorian terrace houses, and the back streets around the Mixing Pot deserve an hour's exploration after lunch. Open Mon.–Fri. for lunch, Mon.–Sat. for dinner. All cards.

## Oasis Seros

495 Oxford St., Paddington; (02) 33-3377.

Oasis Seros is the place for Serious Gourmets. It's in a magnificent old mansion which looks good enough to be a tourist site all by itself. But you're not here for the scenery. You're here to worship the cooking. The decor inside is minimalist—some might say stark—in order not to distract from your prime purpose. The waiters creep about like priests, offering advice on food and wine in whispers.

The menu sounds decidedly odd—how about pickled swordfish and trout salad, or stir-fried oysters with bacon and mustard greens, or witloof (like Belgian endive) stuffed with bone marrow and parmesan, or roast duckling and ginger buns? But the combinations seem to work wonderfully. Chef Philip Searle just may have invented a whole new cuisine. Such ingenuity costs: about $50 a head, plus at least $25 a bottle for great Australian and French wines. Open Fri. for lunch, Tues.–Sat. for dinner. All cards.

## Power Lunching

It is said that the power lunch is dead in New York—that businesspeople are too serious about making money to leave their offices in the middle of the day. Well, it's alive and hopping in Sydney.

People here will tell you that a long lunch with a couple of glasses of wine relaxes them so they work better during the afternoon. So around 3 P.M. in certain city restaurants you'll see suited men and women still sitting about laughing and sipping.

We mentioned two prime power eateries, **Beppi's** and **Chez Oz,** in our list of Sydney's best. Here are some others:

**Balthazar,** 71 York St., City; 29-7292. Modern French, favorite of stockbrokers.

**Iliad,** 126 Liverpool St., City; 267-7644. Upmarket Greek, favorite of media people.

**Le Lavandou,** 143 King St., City; 232-6670. Traditional French, favorite of lawyers.

**Tre Scalini,** 174 Liverpool St., Darlinghurst; 331-4358. Northern Italian, favorite of politicians.

## Suntory

BUSINESS DISTRICT, P. 24, B5
529 Kent St., mid-city; (02) 267-2900.

Our mothers always told us not to play with our food, but at the Japanese Suntory, they encourage us to. If you order the *Ishiyaki* (and you should), the kimono-clad waitress brings a stone just a little larger than a baseball, and warns you that it is very very hot. She brings with it a plate of raw marinated meat and fish, and explains that you should cook them yourself by placing them on the stone. The result is sizzlingly delicious and the process great fun.

Suntory has two large rooms, each with a glass wall looking onto a beautiful Japanese garden and waterfall. In one of them you eat communally, sitting on benches around a grill where a chef does miracles with a sharp knife and assorted shellfish. That's called the *teppanyaki* room. If you'd prefer a more intimate meal, you should choose the *shabu shabu* room, with a huge menu of delicacies and waitresses ready to offer guidance. In either room, you'll pay about $50 a head for a full meal, and more if you go for the house speciality of raw lobster sashimi. Open Mon.–Sat. for lunch and dinner. All cards.

## The Wharf
HARBORSIDE, P. 24, B2

Pier 4, Hickson Rd., The Rocks; (02) 250-1761.

Restaurants in theaters don't normally attract rave reviews from the food critics. They normally see their role as providing adequate nourishment fast enough to get the audience into their seats before the curtain rises. But The Wharf restaurant, attached to the Sydney Theatre Company, shatters all normal assumptions.

For a start, it has the most spectacular view of any Sydney restaurant. Perched at the end of a covered wooden pier thrusting into Sydney Harbour (the rest of the pier is the theater), The Wharf offers through its glass walls closeups of the Harbour Bridge (eerily lit at night in green and gold) and the Manhattanesque skyline of North Sydney. Ferries and cruise boats glide by every few minutes.

When you can tear your eyes from the view, you'll find a menu of subtle splendor (adventurous Australian the specialty). Start with a soup of sweet potato with parmesan and chili toast, or stuffed baby squid with basil and roast garlic. Proceed to loin of lamb with parsnip purée, or flathead fillets with dill mayonnaise and sweet and sour cucumbers. And leave space for ricotta and raisin cake or plum compote with almond pastry. Cost is $35 a head plus interesting local wines at around $20 a bottle. Close to midtown, The Wharf makes a breathtaking introduction to the beauties of Sydney on the first night of your visit, and the ideal place to spend your last night and make your vows to return. Open Mon.–Sat. for lunch and dinner. AE, MC, V.

## ENTERTAINMENT

Sydney is a hedonist's delight—particularly for hedonists who love sun, blue sky, and lots of water. Consequently, the pleasures of the indoor life get short shrift when a Sydneysider looks for entertainment. Most of this kind of entertainment revolves around eating and drinking—or at least involves it. There aren't a large number of nightclub venues as such, and, though there is some theater, you are unlikely to have a wide range of theater experiences from which to choose—however, musical productions here have often been judged superior to their London or Broadway counterparts.

The place to check out what's happening in the music and entertainment scene is the Friday edition of the *Sydney Morning Herald.* An arts-and-entertainment section called "Metro" lists all the films, live performances, and exhibitions scheduled around Sydney for the week.

### Theater

Major live theaters include (listed alphabetically):

**Ensemble Theatre,** 78 McDougall St., Milsons Point; 929-0644. This is a group of actors who tackle mainly the works of up-and-coming young British and Australian playwrights.

**Footbridge Theatre,** Parramatta Road, Glebe; 692-9955. Part of Sydney University, the Footbridge started as a venue for revues, but is now tackling more sophisticated theater, such as the works of South African writers like Athol Fugard.

**Her Majesty's Theatre,** 107 Quay Street; 212-3411. Mainstream theater is featured here—musicals and Broadway-type productions.

**Seymour Centre,** at the corner of Cleveland Street and City Road, Chippendale; 692-3511. Serious theater, classic and modern, by visiting companies.

**Sydney Opera House Drama Theatre,** Sydney Opera House; 2-0525. Classical theater is usually offered here.

**Sydney Opera House Playhouse,** in the Opera House, 233-4155. Mainstream theater in a small, intimate setting.

**Theatre Royal,** King Street, City; 692-9955. This theater stages productions of large, mainstream productions—*Les Miserables, Cats,* and so on.

**Wharf Theatre,** Pier number 4, Walsh Bay, Hickson Rd. Millers Point; 250-1777. Home of the **Sydney Theatre Company,** classic theater is featured here. Make an evening of it here, by combining theater-going with dinner at The Wharf Restaurant. See Restaurants, above.

## Film

For films the **Greater Union Centre** at 525 George Street, **Village Cinema City** at 545 George Street, **Hoyts Centre,** 505 George Street, and **The Pitt Centre** at 232 Pitt Street— all in the center of the city—offer a range of first-run American and Australian mainstream films.

For quality European or experimental Australian or American films you can try **The Dendy,** Martin Place, City; **The Chauvel,** at the corner of Oxford Street and Oatley Road, Paddington (in the Paddington Town Hall); **The Academy Twin Cinema,** 3a Oxford Street, Paddington; or **The Valhalla Cinema,** 166 Glebe Point Road, Glebe.

Check the *Sydney Morning Herald* for programs or get recorded information on 1–1681.

## Music

The music scene in Sydney is varied, if limited in the number of good spots for serious listeners.

### JAZZ

For jazz the prime spot is **The Don Burrows Supper Club** in the Regent Hotel, 199 George Street. Don Burrows is dressy with an upmarket menu and matching prices. Check "Metro" for appearances.

A new jazz spot that opened only in 1987 is **Round Midnight,** back in Kings Cross at 2 Roslyn Street (around the corner from Kellett Street and the Lido Motel—356-4045). A guy at the door checks you out. Drink prices are steep but the music's always good and the atmosphere very sophisticated.

## CLASSICAL

Classical music lovers have a somewhat wider selection of good venues; among the best:

**The Sydney Opera House, Concert Hall;** call 250-7111 for program information.

**Sydney Town Hall,** at the corner of George and Park streets. There is one of the largest pipe organs in the southern hemisphere here, often used for recitals.

**The Conservatorium of Music,** Macquarie Street. See Priorities—lunchtime concerts are often offered on Wednesdays (they're free) and sometimes Friday night concerts as well. Call 230-1222 for information.

**St. Mary's Cathedral,** College St, City; organ recitals and choral performances are often held; solemn mass every Sunday.

## ROCK

Venues for Australian rock music know no bounds. Local pubs provide the most easy access, as do the "clubs"—a scene peculiar to Australia. Workers' Clubs and RSL (Returned Servicemen's League) clubs require memberships, but you can usually get a member to sign you in at the door—several relax their policy for visitors from overseas. Often visiting U.S. and British acts appear here since many of the clubs can accommodate large audiences—and pay well.

The "Metro" section of the *Sydney Morning Herald* is your best bet to help you choose your poison.

# Bars and Dance Clubs

For dancing you can go to **Juliana's** at the Hilton Hotel. A disco, Juliana's also hosts overseas acts from time to time. The disco crowd is usually young and dressed up; special shows—depending on the performer—sometimes attract an older, more sophisticated clientele.

Downstairs on the lower level you can see what a posh hotel bar of the last century was like in the **Marble Bar.** This baroque room was created of marble, bronze, and glass as the bar for the Adams Hotel, demolished to make way for the Hilton. The Marble Bar was completely re-created in the Hilton's basement and functions as a favorite after-work spot. The live music (traditional jazz) doesn't suit the bar's opulent ambience—it's far too loud. But it's worth having a drink there to view the works of art that fill the place.

Not far away, in the Boulevard Hotel at 90 William Street, very near Kings Cross, **William's** operates as one of the city's most exclusive spots. Admission is steep, particularly at weekends when it's around $20 per head, but the Art Deco–inspired decor, classy service, and top music piped to the dance floor keep the monied set coming back. This is the kind of place to dress up for. There's a restaurant as well—no cover charge if you have dinner there. Telephone 357-2277.

Significantly downmarket from this, and strictly for the young—or the young at heart—is the **Freeze** at 11 Oxford Street, Paddington (332-2568). A heady mix of live new wave and disco keeps the kids dancing way into the midnight hours. Great for insomniacs.

## Getting Tickets

Tickets for performances (theater, concerts, sporting events) can be bought directly from the box office or usually through Bass, a ticketing agency that has offices around the city and in most large department stores (Grace Brothers, David Jones etc.).

Information about events around the city can be obtained by ringing Bass on 1-1688; phone to book tickets (charge accounts only) at 266-4800. AE, V, MC, DC accepted. In Martin Place (between George and Castlereagh), Halftix sells tickets to performances at half price. Working on the principle of the half-price booth in New York, tickets for that evening's performances that haven't been sold or booked go on sale on the afternoon of the day of performance. The really popular shows almost never make it to Halftix, but there are the odd exceptions. Good for seeing what local Aussie drama is all about. There's a number for Halftix: 235-1437. It doesn't open before noon and is often busy, so if you're in town in the afternoon, it is probably worth dropping by to see what they have on sale on the day.

## SHORT TRIPS OUT OF SYDNEY

Within a day's travel from the central business district, Sydney's environs offer a range of places to visit that will satisfy the interests of the historian and the naturalist—or both! See also the New South Wales chapter, which follows.

Visitors with only a few days to spend in Sydney can get a bit of an idea of what life is like in Australia's Outback at **Blue Gum Farm,** about an hour's drive west of the city. You can watch a (small) sheep muster (something like a cattle drive—but with sheep), see sheep being sheared after they've been rounded up by the incredibly smart dogs (who will actually climb on the animals' backs, a la *"Crocodile" Dundee*), and inspect hay sheds, a blacksmith's shop, and a reconstructed settler's hut.

Blue Gum Farm, Maxwell Avenue (off Henry Lawson Drive), Milperra, is open from 10 A.M. to 5 P.M. daily. Kiosk meals available; barbecues arranged for large groups. Admission: $5 adults, $2.50 child.

**Featherdale Wildlife Park** is the place to go if you want to hold a koala or pet a kangaroo. This park specializes in presenting Australian fauna in natural surrounds. And since a large proportion of Australian animal life is nocturnal, you have a better chance of seeing it here than in the natural wild. Featherdale Wildlife Park, 217 Kildare Road, Doonside (west of city), is open from 9 A.M. to 5 P.M. seven days. Admission: $5.50 adults, $2.75 child. For more information on seeing Australian wildlife, see Touring in the Travel Arrangements chapter.

**The Blue Mountains** are about a two-hour drive directly west of the city. So called because of the smokey blue haze that seems to emanate from them, the mountains are a perfect spot for bushwalking (there are scores of tracks well signposted) or sightseeing. Major towns in these mountains are on the city rail line, so the trip by train is both a practical and scenic alternative to driving.

Major towns include Katoomba, Blackheath, and Leura, which can easily be visited in a day and should be on every tourist list. Visit the Three Sisters, a rugged sandstone outcrop on the outskirts of Katoomba, then take the Scenic Railway down the side of the mountain—a three-minute hairraising ride along an old mining cart track. If you can keep your eyes open you *will* see some splendid scenery. Back in town have a waffle, a meal, or buy some hand-made chocolates at the Paragon Café on the main street—a beautifully maintained Art Deco diner.

In Leura springtime means azaleas and many of the grand old homes in the area open their gardens for public inspection. Ring the Blue Mountains 24-hour "What's On" line for events: (047) 39-1177.

The Blue Mountains have always been a prime holiday area; the difference these days is that instead of repairing to one's own holiday house, visitors from the city are more likely to check into one of the many splendid old guesthouses that have been refurbished in recent years. Among the top ones is the **Cleopatra Guest House** (amazing meals in the French style—see Restaurants), Cleopatra Street, Blackheath 2785. The Cleopatra has only half a dozen rooms and these are booked out early, so get a bid in months ahead; it's only open on weekends. Telephone (047) 87-8456. Larger than the Cleopatra is **Glenella** (also with a great dining room). Book early here, too: (047) 87-8352. The address is: 56 Govetts Leap Rd., Blackheath 2785.

The **Victoria and Albert Guesthouse** is at Mt. Victoria, a half hour or so beyond Blackheath. The hotel often sponsors "theme" weekends—murder weekends, literary weekends, and so on. If this isn't your thing, check first. A larger hotel, rooms can usually be booked only a week or so ahead: (047) 87-1241. Address: 19 Station Street, Mount Victoria 2786 Blackheath 2785.

There's little chance of the **Fairmont Resort** at Leura being booked solid. Only a little over a year old, the 210-room hotel has every facility expected in a luxury resort. Telephone (047) 82-5222.

Prices for these guesthouses can be steep (Cleopatra: $150 per person per day), but usually guesthouses include three meals a day from Friday night to after lunch on Sunday.

Closer to the city, yet still in the west is the city/suburb of **Parramatta.** Don't be put off by the modernity of its shopping center, the car yards, and suburban bungalows; Parramatta has a lot of history going for it. It was the center of N.S.W. sheep-grazing wealth at the beginnings of the colony—and until around the middle of the 19th century, it also provided one of the governor's official residences.

See **Elizabeth Farm,** Alice Street, once home of the McArthur family, one of the colony's most prosperous sheep graziers. The house is a perfect example of the colonial country style, with a deep veranda on all sides facing a shady garden. Elizabeth Farm has a small cafeteria where you can take morning or afternoon tea or a light lunch. Open daily except Monday, from 10 A.M. to 4:30 P.M.; phone (02) 635-9488.

**Old Government House,** in Parramatta Park, open Tuesday to Thursday, as well as on Sundays and all public holidays, 10 A.M. to 4 P.M., was one of the two official government residences. It has been restored and contains many objects of great value and artistic merit. Phone (02) 635-8149.

**Experiment Farm** 9 Ruse St., was the first private farm in Australia. The original land was given to an ex-convict upon attaining freedom. He sold it soon after to Dr. Harris who built the house that still stands here. It is nearly 200 years old and is another good example of the colonial-style farm house. Experiment Farm is open on the same days, same hours, as Old Government House. Phone 635-5655.

Admission to Elizabeth Farm is $2.50 adult; $1 child. Government House is $4/$1; and Experiment Farm $3 and $1, child. You can buy a three-way excursion ticket for all these houses at any one of them. This ticket costs $7 and allows you entry to all of them provided you visit on the same day.

**Old Sydney Town** lies north of the city at Somersby, near the Central Coast town of Gosford. It is a reconstruction of colonial Sydney, complete with ship in the "harbor," colonial buildings, and craftspersons working away at their trades. Occasionally there's even a flogging staged—some poor escaped convict given the cat-o'-nine-tails to a cheering crowd of bloodthirsty locals. Restaurants prepare traditionally based meals and there are souvenirs to take away with you. The drive up is an easy two hours and you can cover the sights of Sydney Town in a few hours, which makes this an ideal day trip, fun and educational at the same time.

Follow the Pacific Highway north toward Gosford. Admission is $9.80 adults, $4.90 children. Open Wednesday through Sunday and all public holidays; from 10 A.M. to 5 P.M. Telephone (043) 40-1104.

The **Royal National Park** to the south of the city and **Ku-ring-gai National Park** on its northern boundary offer hectares of bushland for picnickers, hikers, or those interested in the plant life and birds of the area. Camping facilities are available in the Royal National Park.

In the chapter dealing with the rest of New South Wales, several districts will be mentioned which could also serve as destinations for keen day-trippers. A concern called Balloon Flights offers trips in an old-fashioned basket carried aloft by a helium-filled balloon. Trips can be arranged from the Camden Valley, in the foothills of the Southern Highlands (about a two-hour trip south of Sydney), or from the town of Pokolbin, part of the Hunter Valley wine-growing district, to the north of Sydney. Each flight carries up to five people, plus pilot, and lasts approximately one hour, after which you are treated to a champagne breakfast and driven back to the point of origin. The cost is $125 adults and $80 for children 3 to 12 (children under 3 cannot be accommodated). For more information write Balloon Flights, Box 460, Rozelle 2039; (02) 818-4599.

Because the Hunter Valley is worth spending several days in, and because it cannot easily be visited in a day trip, details about it are in the New South Wales chapter. Similarly, the Camden Valley/Southern Highlands are more appropriately linked with a look at the N.S.W. South Coast or a trip to Canberra and the Snowy Mountains.

## CITY LISTINGS

Area code for all the establishments listed here is (02), unless otherwise noted. Sights/establishments are keyed into their neighborhoods and the color maps at the back of the book, with references to the map page number and the appropriate map coordinates. The page numbers within the listings refer to the text page on which the sight/establishment is discussed.

## Churches/Synagogues

**Garrison Church**  HARBORSIDE, P. 24, B2
Argyle Place, The Rocks; p. 45

**The Great Synagogue**  BUSINESS DISTRICT, P. 24, C4
Elizabeth St. (between Park and Market sts.); p. 51

**St. James Church**  BUSINESS DISTRICT, P. 24, C4
Queen's Square, at north end of Hyde Park; p. 50

**St. Mary's Cathedral**  BUSINESS DISTRICT, P. 24, C4
College St.; pp. 51, 83

## Landmarks

**Argyle Centre**  HARBORSIDE, P. 24, B2
Argyle and Playfair sts., The Rocks; Mon.–Sun. 9:30 A.M.–5:30 P.M., p. 28, 45

**Cadman's Cottage**  HARBORSIDE, P. 24, B2
George St., The Rocks; 27-8861; Mon.–Fri., 9 A.M.–5 P.M.; Sat.–Sun. 9:30 A.M.–5:30 P.M. p. 45

**Conservatorium of Music**  HARBORSIDE, P. 24, C3
Bridge St., Botanic Gardens; 230-1263; pp. 29, 49, 83

**Elizabeth Bay House**  EASTERN SUBURBS, P. 25, F4
7 Onslow Ave.; 358-2344; Tues.–Sun. 10 A.M.–4:30 P.M., pp. 29, 55

**Elizabeth Farm**  WEST OF CITY
Alice St., Parramatta; 635-9488; 10 A.M.–4:30 P.M. daily except Mon, p. 86

**Experiment Farm**  WEST OF CITY
9 Ruse St., Parramatta; 635-5655; Tues.–Thurs.; Sun.; and holidays 10 A.M.–4 P.M., p. 86

**Old Government House**  WEST OF CITY
Parramatta Park, Parramatta, 635–8149; Tues.–Thurs; Sun; and holidays 10 A.M.–4 P.M., p. 86.

**Old Sydney Town**  NORTH OF CITY
Near Gosford on Pacific Hwy., Somersby; (043) 40-1104; Wed.–Sun. 10 A.M.–5 P.M., p. 87.

**Parliament House**  BUSINESS DISTRICT, P. 24, C4
Macquarie St. between Hunter St. and Martin Pl.; 230-2111; Mon.–Fri. 9 A.M.–4:30 P.M., pp. 30, 49–50

**Pier 1**  HARBORSIDE, P. 24, B1
No. 1 Wharf, Hickson Rd., next to Harbour Bridge; 11 A.M.–6 P.M. (shops), to 10 P.M. (restaurants), p. 30

**The Rocks Visitors Centre**  HARBORSIDE, P. 24, B2
104 George St.; 27-4972; Mon.–Fri. 8:30 A.M.–5:30 P.M., Sat. and Sun. 9 A.M.–5 P.M., p. 31

**State Library of New South Wales**  BUSINESS DISTRICT, P. 24, C3
Macquarie St.; 230-1414; exhibition galleries open 9 A.M.–5 P.M. Tues.–Sat.; 11 A.M.–5 P.M. Sun. and Mon. p. 49

**Sydney Entertainment Centre**  CHINATOWN, P. 26, B6
Harbour St., Haymarket; 211-2222; pp. 53, 65

**Sydney Harbour Bridge**  HARBORSIDE, P. 24, B1
p. 31

**Sydney Opera House**  HARBORSIDE, P. 24, C2
Bennelong Point; 250-7111; tours daily 9 A.M.–4 P.M., Backstage, Sun. only 9 A.M.–4 P.M., pp. 31–32, 47, 82

**Sydney Tower**  BUSINESS DISTRICT, P. 24, C4
Centrepoint; Market, Pitt, and Castlereagh sts.; 229-7444; Mon.–Sat. 9:30 A.M.–9:30 P.M., Sun. and holidays 10:30 A.M.–6:30 P.M., p. 32

**Vaucluse House**  EASTERN SUBURBS, P. 29, D2
Wentworth Rd., Vaucluse; 337-1957; Tues.–Sun. 10 A.M.–4:30 P.M., grounds open 7 A.M.–5 P.M., p. 33, 56

**Victoria Barracks**  PADDINGTON, P. 27, F7
Oxford St. between Greens and Oatley rds.; 339-3543; p. 33

# Museums
**Aquarium**  CHINATOWN AREA, P. 24, A5
Across Darling Harbour from Harbourside Marketplace; 262-2300; 9:30 A.M.–9 P.M. daily, p. 54

**The Art Gallery of N.S.W.**  BUSINESS DISTRICT, P. 25, D4
Art Gallery Rd., Domain; 225-1700; Mon.–Sat. 10 A.M.–5 P.M., Sun. 12–5 P.M., pp. 28, 51

**Australian Museum**  BUSINESS DISTRICT, P. 24, C5
6–8 College St.; 339–8111; Tues.–Sat. and holidays 10 A.M.–5 P.M., Sun. and Mon. 12–5 P.M., pp. 28, 51

**Hyde Park Barracks**  BUSINESS DISTRICT, P. 24, C4
Macquarie St. at Queen's Sq.; 217-0111; Wed.–Mon. 10 A.M.–5 P.M., Tues. 12–5 P.M., pp. 30, 50

**Mint Museum**  BUSINESS DISTRICT, P. 24, C4
Queen's Sq. at Macquarie St.; 217-0111; daily 10 A.M.–5 P.M. except Wed. 12–5 P.M., pp. 30, 50

**Observatory**  HARBORSIDE, P. 24, B2
The Rocks; 241-2478; Mon–Fri 2–5 P.M.; Sat. and Sun. 10 A.M.—5 P.M.; every evening except Wednesday 8:30–10:30 P.M. by arrangement, p. 45

**Powerhouse Museum**  CHINATOWN, P. 26, A6
Harris St., Ultimo; 217-0111; 10 A.M.–5 P.M. daily, pp. 31, 53

**Sydney Seaport Museum**  CHINATOWN AREA, P. 24, A5
Darling Harbour; 552-2011; 10 A.M.–6 P.M., p. 54

# Parks and Gardens
**Blue Gum Farm**  WEST OF CITY
Maxwell Ave. off Henry Lawson Dr., Milperra; 774-3981; 10 A.M.–5 P.M. daily, pp. 84–85

**Botanic Gardens**  HARBORSIDE, P. 25, D3
Cahill Expressway, behind Opera House; 8 A.M.–sunset, pp. 28, 49

**Centennial Park**  EASTERN SUBURBS, P. 28, B5
Near Oxford/Queen sts. intersection; 6 A.M.–sunset, p. 59

**Chinese Garden**  CHINATOWN, P. 26, B6
Pier St. entrance to Darling Harbour, corner of Pier and Harbour sts.; 11 A.M.–sunset daily, pp. 29, 54

**The Domain**  BUSINESS DISTRICT, P. 25, D4
Behind Macquarie St., p. 51

**Featherdale Wildlife Park** WEST OF CITY
217 Kildare Rd., Doonside; 622-1644; 9 A.M.–5 P.M. daily, p. 85

**Ku-ring-gai National Park** NORTH OF CITY
Bobbin Head and West Head, about 30 km (19 miles) from city, p. 87

**Nielsen Park** EASTERN SUBURBS, P. 29, D2
Greycliffe St., Vaucluse; pp. 56, 61

**Royal National Park** SOUTH OF CITY
Off Princes Hwy., 30 km (19 miles) from city, p. 87

**Sydney Cricket Ground** EASTERN SUBURBS, P. 27, F8
Driver Ave., Moore Park; 357-6601 pp. 59, 64

**Taronga Park Zoo** NORTH SHORE, P. 28, B2
Bradleys Head Rd.; 969-2777; 9 A.M.–5 P.M. daily, pp. 32–33

## Shops

**Aboriginal Art Australia** BUSINESS DISTRICT, P. 24, B5
477 Kent St.; 261-2929; p. 69

**Aboriginal Art Centres** PADDINGTON, P. 28, A5;
HARBORSIDE, P. 24, B2
7 Walker Ln., Paddington; 357-6839; level 2, Argyle Centre, The Rocks;
27-1380, p. 69

**Anne Schofield Antiques** EASTERN SUBURBS, P. 28, B5
36 Queen St., Woollahra; 32-1326; p. 71

**The Art Directors Gallery** HARBORSIDE, P. 24, B2
21 Nurses Walk, The Rocks; 27-2740; p. 70

**Australian Craftworks** HARBORSIDE
The Old Police Station, 127 George St., The Rocks; 27-7156, p. 70

**Balmain Markets** WEST OF CITY
St. Mary's Anglican Church, Darling St., Balmain; p. 72

**Centrepoint Shopping Centre** BUSINESS DISTRICT, P. 24,
C4
Market St. between Pitt and Castlereagh sts.; p. 67

**Copeland & De Soos** EASTERN SUBURBS, P. 28, B5
66 Queen St., Woollahra; 32-5288; p. 71

**The Craft Centre** HARBORSIDE, P. 24, B2
100 George St., The Rocks; 27-9126; hours, p. 70

**David Jones** BUSINESS DISTRICT, P. 24, C4
Elizabeth and Market sts., Castlereagh and Market sts.; pp. 65–68

**Flame Opals** HARBORSIDE, P. 24, B2
119 George St., The Rocks; p. 68

**Galleries Primitif** EASTERN SUBURBS, P. 28, B5
174 Jersey Rd., Woollahra; 32-3115; p. 69

**Grace Bros. Department Store** BUSINESS DISTRICT,
P. 24, B4
Corner of George and Market sts.; pp. 65–68

**Ken Done** HARBORSIDE, P. 24, B2;
CHINATOWN AREA, P. 24, A4
123 George St., The Rocks; 27-2737; and shop no. 141 of Harbourside Festival Marketplace, Darling Harbour, 281-3818; p. 70

**Mid-City Centre** BUSINESS DISTRICT, P. 24, B4
197 Pitt St.; p. 67

**New Guinea Primitive Arts**
Dymock's Bldg., 428 George St.; 232-4737; and shop no. 42 of Queen Victoria Bldg.; 267-5134; p. 69

**Paddington Markets**
Paddington Village Centre, 2 Newcombe St.; pp. 71–72

**Percy Marks**
65 Castlereagh St.; Regent Hotel; Hotel Inter-Continental; p. 68

**The Queen Victoria Building**
George St. at Park St.; pp. 51–52, 67, 70

**The Royal Arcade**
259 Pitt St.; p. 70

**The Strand Arcade**
Between Pitt and George sts.; pp. 52, 67, 70

**Sydney Antique Centre**
531 South Dowling St., Surry Hills; 33-3244; 10:30 A.M.–6 P.M. daily, p. 71

**Woollahra Galleries**
160 Oxford St., Woollahra; 327-8840; 10:30 A.M.–6 P.M. daily, p. 71

# 5

# NEW SOUTH WALES

Although one of Australia's smaller states, New South Wales is over 300,000 square miles in size, larger than any American state except Alaska. It also has a greater diversity of topography and climate than any state in the United States—encompassing mountains (many snow-covered in winter), arid desert, and subtropical rain forest in its boundaries.

Such a variety of climates gives the tourist a number of options when planning a visit to Australia. Once you leave the hub of Sydney, the choice is yours whether to broaden your acquaintance with east coast surfing beaches, head for the Outback—to what in some minds is the "real Australia"—or to check out towns and regions of historical significance. Whatever you choose, you are sure to be overwhelmed by the scenery.

The time of year you visit will play some part in your selection. The months of June, July, and August form the Australian winter, although in this hemisphere winter doesn't wreak the same changes in weather as in northern climes. Still, these are the months to head north for hotter weather—for beach life, swimming, and surfing. This is also the time of the year to head south for the short ski season.

Winter is also a preferred season for braving the rigors of Outback Australia. The desert is inhospitable at most times of the year, but the blistering heat of summer is mitigated during these months. Clear blue skies make picture taking in this most photogenic part of the state a can't-lose proposition.

The terms "autumn" and "spring" have little meaning in most of Australia. There is no real change in season, beyond a gradual warming (noticed especially at night) as the season moves out of winter, with a parallel cooling and drop in humidity as, sometime in mid-May, the winter season arrives. Some mountainous areas do produce spectacular displays of spring flowers—azaleas, camellias, and rhododendron in particular.

In the north and even as far south as Sydney the magnificent violet-blue jacaranda blooms all through late October and is well worth viewing.

What this chapter will attempt to do is divide the state into a series of trips, displaying various areas in the light of what tourist expectations can be met there. Not unexpectedly, northern trips will involve a lot of sunshine, beaches, and tropical lifestyle. But the south coast can offer a lot of this as well, and isn't as well traveled—a plus for those travelers who like to feel they've "discovered" a place.

Away from the coast, there's the pleasure of hunting antiques or sampling wine in the state's Hunter Valley; country music fans may want to see what Australians have to offer in the state's northwest; you can even ski in winter on the slopes of the Snowy Mountains, the range that forms a border between New South Wales and its southern neighbor, the state of Victoria.

It's important to remember several things about traveling around New South Wales:

(1) It can be expensive. Plane fares are high, as is the cost of many longer train trips. As yet there are few package deals, although some bus lines do offer reductions for persons prepared to travel around the state for a week or more. As in most places, you'll see more here if you travel by car, though again, bargain car rentals are not plentiful. Still, petrol (gas) isn't much more expensive than in the United States and if you can master the art of left-side-of-the-road driving, it may be the way to go.

(2) Roads, particularly country roads, can be hazardous. There are few superhighways; many of the major arteries between key destinations deteriorate to two-lane roads (often potholed or unpaved) for kilometers, where the speed limit is usually between 60 and 80 kilometers per hour (35 to 45 miles per hour). Changes in driving conditions and speed regulations will mean you have to budget a longer amount of drive time to reach distant destinations.

To balance this, many areas have few cars on the road, and outside of peak holiday times (the main period being from mid-December to the end of January when schools break for summer holidays) and long weekends, you'll encounter few of the traffic jams that are an everyday occurrence in trying to get out of cities such as New York or Los Angeles. Coastal roads offer breathtaking scenery and most comfort stops will be clean and well supplied—even in fairly remote areas.

(3) Because of the relatively small populations of most townships, you'll have to adjust your expectations regarding the levels of accommodation and dining facilities you'll encounter. With exceptions that are few and far between, these will be fairly basic. Most of the good country cooking goes on

in private homes and the word "foodie" hasn't gotten into bush dictionaries yet. Unless you're in a restaurant that has been specially recommended, always go for the simpler things on the menu.

Hotel and motel rooms will be clean and furnished with all the basics (including usually a toaster, a jug for boiling water, and packets of tea and coffee—perhaps even bread for making your own breakfast). But you'll probably only find one or two channels on the television and the local nightlife may leave a lot to be desired.

You'll have to observe country mealtimes, too. Most restaurants serve lunch from 12 to 2 P.M. and dinner from 6 to 7:30 P.M.—it's not unusual to find that you've missed breakfast if you haven't ordered by 9 in the morning. If you can't manage to budget your travel times to be on the spot when restaurants serve, there are always the ubiquitous Chinese cafés and take-aways (take-outs) that exist in every town. The food in these is usually pretty grim, so go for simple things, eat sparingly, and plan to be someplace better for the next meal.

Some restaurants will be recommended in each area if possible. If you can't get to one of these, or if there are no highly recommended dining rooms in the area in which you wish to travel, you can always try the local RSL Club. RSL stands for Returned Servicemen's League. Every town in Australia has at least one RSL; though they are private membership clubs, the dining rooms are usually open to guests and in many rural areas, the best meal you're likely to get outside a private home will be in one of these. They're usually located on one of the main streets of town (check the local phone book for address) and be sure to get there during the serving hours listed above, as they don't have extended dining hours.

Credit cards, widely accepted, will be abbreviated as follows: AE—American Express, DC—Diner's Club, MC—MasterCard, V—Visa.

An area as vast and differentiated in climate and topography as New South Wales could never be covered adequately in one chapter. Make use of the advice of locals you meet on your travels. This is, after all, the essence of a successful journey: to meet people, learn from them, and pass your experience on.

The first port of call in any region of the state will be the closest State Tourism office. You can get a copy of their addresses from the **Travel Centre of New South Wales headquarters** at the corner of Pitt and Spring streets, Sydney, (02) 231-4444; see also Vital Information, at back of book. They will be happy to help you plan a journey to any destination in the state, and can arrange all bookings for tours, cars, and accommodation.

## Eucalypts

Not sure what kind of tree that is? In Australia, guess "gum" and the odds are with you. It's when you try to get more specific that the trouble starts.

There are about 550 species of eucalypts, most of which are trees, with some shrubs tossed in. They are the most dominant plants in Australia, found from desert to tropics. Only in Papua New Guinea, parts of Indonesia and the Philippines do they also grow naturally, although they've been introduced to more than forty other countries. For example, the popular Californian blue gum is the Tasmanian blue gum transplanted.

"Gum" is a misnomer, for these trees actually produce kino, a resin that contains tannins. Kino is used in treatments for cuts and abrasions, colds, sore throats, diarrhea, and dysentery.

"Eucalypts," as they are known in Australia, also are used for many types of construction, from railway sleepers to musical instruments. Other applications include paper, pulp, fiberboard, wood distillation, vegetable tanning, chemical compounds, and honey from the flowers. Aborigines even turn to some species for food and water during bad seasons.

Although the genus is distinctive, telling the species apart is another story. Bark is the best indicator. Gums have smooth bark, bloodwoods rough, ironbarks are hard, stringybarks furrowed, peppermints are a mixture of fibrous and smooth, while boxes have thin bark with fine furrows. Whether or not the bark can be peeled off easily is another clue, as are the tightly capped flower buds, called "gum nuts." Better not try to eat them, though.

—Steve Bunk

# The South Coast of N.S.W.

It will take about a full day to travel non-stop the length of the N.S.W. south coast. That's if you don't stop at all to eat, sightsee, or explore. The Princes Highway runs the entire distance and turn-offs for national parks, beaches, and principal townships lying inland from the highway are well signposted.

Of course, no one is going to travel the length of the southern half of the state without doing some stopping and looking; if you want to see the area at a leisurely pace, count on about a week—especially if you want to spend a day or two luxuriating at a guesthouse or going after game fish down at the southern tip.

If you do want to spend just a day journeying down this way, by starting early from Sydney you can comfortably get about as far south as Seven Mile National Park, about 150 kilometers (93 miles) south of the city's center. This will give you time to see a few sights, have a leisurely lunch, and spend a few hours on Seven Mile Beach before returning to the city in time for dinner.

## TRAVEL

There's a train line that goes from Sydney Central Station along the coast as far south as Nowra, just north of Jervis Bay. After that, local buses can take you farther.

Alternatively, you can take the train to Nowra and pick up a rental car there. Both Thrifty and Avis have depots at Nowra, with other depots along the south coast. To arrange ahead for a car from Thrifty, ring their Sydney number: (02) 357-5399; Avis at Nowra is on Egan La., (044) 21-3055 or ring toll free (008) 22-5533. Budget car rentals can be hired in Merimbula near the coast's southern end; ring the toll-free reservations number (008) 33-1331.

Air New South Wales flies to Merimbula, in the heart of game and fishing country, daily. Cars can be hired from the airport and arranged for when booking flights. In Sydney call for bookings and flight information at 268-1242.

## ❦ ACCOMMODATIONS

### KIAMA AREA

If you're not planning to travel the length of the south coast, or if you would like to do it very leisurely, consider staying at the northern end, near the beaches of the Kiama area.

**Gundarimba Guest House** is at 45 Allowrie St., Jamberoo 2533; (042) 36-0228, about twenty minutes west of Kiama. The Gundarimba is a 1928 former country house now owned by an erstwhile Sydney restaurateur and his wife. With those credentials it's not surprising that the table is far and away the best in the neighborhood. Accommodation is basic, but pretty—six double bedrooms with shared baths. There is a country-house atmosphere here, without the most modern facilities, but with a superb French-style restaurant. Cost will be around $95 per person including dinner. Lunch is served Sun.; dinner Wed.–Sun. Outside bookings are taken for dinner; reservations essential. MC, V.

**Jamberoo Valley Resort,** Woodstock Rd., Jamberoo 2533; (042) 36-0269, provides motel-style accommodation in the same area. While lacking the country-house flavor, rooms do have modern amenities such as TV, direct-dial telephones, private bath, and air-conditioning (although ocean breezes make this less than essential). Rates run around $75 per double. Lunches are also served in the restaurant for guests and outside patrons. MC, V.

### NOWRA AREA

A little farther south is the Nowra Area—the fishing towns and beaches of Jervis Bay.

**Pleasant Way Motor Inn,** 1 km north of Nowra in Pleasant Way 2541, (044) 21-5544 or toll-free (008) 33-5005, is part of the Flag Inns chain. It's a modern motel-style accommodation close to the river in Nowra, providing all facilities including heated pool and spa. Evening meals only are served (but it's next to the RSL Club where meals are available). AE, MC, V.

Just 12 km (about 7 miles) from Nowra is the **Coolangatta Historic Village Resort,** Shoalhaven Heads Rd., Shoalhaven Heads 2535, (044) 48-7131. This is a Georgian building which has been converted to house totally modern facilities. Rooms cost around $60-$90 double; with all meals for a weekend, about $110 per person. All cards.

## ULADULLA AREA
At about the midpoint of the south coast is Ulladulla Area. Base yourself here for swimming as well as to be a half day's drive or less from any south coast areas.

**Bawley Point Guest House** (off the main road at Bawley Point 2539, about 20 km (12 miles) south of Ulladulla), (044) 57-1011, sleeps 25 in either the original period building or in modern motel-style accommodation. There are fewer modern amenities here, but you'll find lots of charm and a good table provided by the owners who mix English and French-style dishes with more exotic Indian and Indonesian offerings. Book ahead in the summer season. Room plus dinner and breakfast is about $65 per person. AE, MC, V.

## EDEN AREA
Serious game fish enthusiasts will want to stay in the Eden Area.

**Merimbula International Hotel,** at the corner of Dunns Rd. and Princes Hwy., Merimbula 2548, (064) 95-3100, has 48 units, all with their own showers, direct-dial telephone, TV, and air-conditioning. You'll also find a spa, sauna, and tennis courts. The Blue Wren Restaurant, part of the hotel complex, is highly regarded as a better-than-average-for-the-area place to eat. Open for breakfast, lunch, and dinner. Rooms run around $80 for a double. AE, MC, V.

**The Seahorse Inn,** Boydtown Park, Eden 2551, (064) 96-1361, on Twofold Bay, 10 km south of Eden, is one of the oldest hotels in the area. What it may lack in modern conveniences, it more than makes up for in history, local color, and charm, dating as it does to a time when whalers still sailed from the port of Eden. Rates run around $60 for a double per night. The hotel has its own licensed restaurant. AE, MC, V.

# ❦ RESTAURANTS

By all means try a promising-looking café, guesthouse, restaurant, or diner—you never know, you might be the first to discover something great. Meantime, these are the most well-spoken-of restaurants along the coast road:

## KIAMA AREA

**The Baker and the Bunyip,** 23 Prince Alfred St., Berry; (044) 64-1454. The food here is worth coming all the way from Sydney for. Definite French influence on most dishes, such as steaks in various sauces—generous servings. Around $80 for two with wine. MC, V.

**Chambrettes Restaurant,** 148 Tongarra Rd., Albion Park; (042) 56-5220. Open for lunch and dinner Wed.–Sun. A relative newcomer to the area which is about 15 minutes' drive west of the Shellharbour intersection of the Princes Hwy. (just north of Kiama). The chef gives a pro's touch to good old-fashioned Australian country cooking—turning rabbit into a marvel with mustard cream sauce, creamy vegetable soups, and ethereal desserts. Bring your own bottle and expect to pay around $70 for two. AE, MC.

**Gundarimba Guest House,** 45 Allowrie St., Jamberoo; (042) 36-0228. Basically catering for its resident guests, the place also accepts reservations for dinner from outside patrons. The chef is European-trained in the French tradition and worked at several prestigious Sydney restaurants. Lunch Sun.; dinner Wed.–Sun. Reservations essential. MC, V.

## EDEN AREA

**The Blue Wren,** Merimbula International Motel, Dunns Rd., Merimbula; (064) 95-3100. Here is where you go to make a night out of it in the far south. The blue and white decor echoes the water outside, and inside the seafood is spectacular. Be sure to try the oysters—they're local, and as fresh as you'll ever get them. Expect to pay around $50 for two, with wine. AE, MC, V.

**The Waterfront Café,** Beach St., Merimbula; (064) 95-2211. As its name suggests, this eatery specializes in simple, café-style food. A super place to go for mouth-watering open sandwiches. Open for breakfast, lunch, and dinner daily; it is licensed.

---

Your first detour from the Princes Highway as you travel from Sydney will be the **Royal National Park,** which forms the city's southeastern boundary; 15,000 hectares of native flora, including rainforest and beach. It's Australia's oldest national park, and the second oldest in the world, dedicated in 1879. You can take in its sights while moving south, returning to the highway around the township of Waterfall.

Admission to the park is $4 per car, but if you just want to drive through as you continue to the south coast, tell them so at the park gates and they'll issue you a vehicle exemption ticket. It's worth the $4 to spend a few hours here, though. There are some fine beaches here, including Garie, Little Marley, and Burning Palms. All beaches are public.

Camping is possible in the park, but there have been some recent incidents of robberies and even a few assaults.

Alternatively, you can join **Lawrence Hargrave Drive** at Stanwell Park, a slower but more picturesque roadway that will take you through the coal-mining towns of Coalcliff, Austinmer, and Thirroul on the coast. D.H. Lawrence once lived at Thirroul during the short period he lived in Australia—he was probably at home in coal-mining country. Like any mining area, the living is not very swish, but the views over the ocean are spectacular and on clear days you'll probably see hang gliders out in full force. The cliffs in the region, including Bald Hill, are ideal for the sport.

In fact, Lawrence Hargrave, an early pioneer in aviation, flew in box kites from these hills in the 1890s, paralleling the Wright Brothers' experiments on the other side of the world.

Rejoin the Princes Highway at Bulli and continue on through the steel-mill city of Wollongong and its industrial twin, Port Kembla.

# Kiama Area

Once beyond here you'll come to **Kiama** with its wide beaches and shoreline edged with forbidding black rock that can make you think of the beginning of the world.

On the waterfront in Kiama is The Blow Hole, a strange geological formation of rocks that hover over the open sea and create a geiser-like effect. On days of heavy winds and rough seas this can be truly spectacular—but even on calm days it has its moments.

## SIDETRIP

Take Kangaroo Valley turnoff from Princes Hwy. at Kiama to a deep, crater-like valley of lush pastureland, cathedral-like, arching gum trees, and stone-age ferns in rainforest. The Kangaroo Valley makes a superb detour on the southern trip. You'll also pass Hampton Bridge, a gothic folly of architectural excess, where you can turn around and head out of the valley toward the town of Berry. The Kangaroo Valley Pioneer Settlement, adjacent to Hampton Bridge, is a re-creation of early living conditions among dairy farmers in the region. Open daily 10 A.M.–5 P.M.

# Dairy Country

Farther south is dairy country. Green pastureland surrounds the coastal towns of Gerringong and Berry, and Bomaderry, inland. Gerringong is the last town before **Seven Mile Beach,** which is a lovely site for picnicking and sunbathing on the sand. This is an ideal spot to spend the afternoon before returning to Sydney if you're only doing a day trip. Here you'll find spectacular golden sand beach (about seven miles in length, obviously) that is almost literally deserted most of the year. A sand bar goes out for some distance from the beach, so it's fairly safe from sharks and allows toddlers to paddle easily.

## Nowra and Jervis Bay

The **National Aviation Museum** is in Nowra, (044) 21-1920. Located on the HMAS *Albatross,* this museum is a chronicle of flight and the part Australians (like Lawrence Hargrave) played in its development. Open from 10 A.M. to 4 P.M., seven days, except Christmas and Good Friday.

Continuing south along the coast will take you eventually into fishing villages and past oyster beds—**Shoalhaven, Sussex Inlet,** and **Jervis Bay** (home of the Jervis Bay oyster, particularly large and meaty mollusks, much prized in Sydney restaurants). These towns are prime holiday centers, with many winding little inlets, creeks, and beaches where a holiday cabin can be rented fairly cheaply.

At **Ulladulla,** 230 kilometers (about 143 miles) south of Sydney, the fishing fleet is blessed every Easter in a traditional Italian ceremony. Even here the warm current that flows through the ocean makes swimming, even outside of the summer season, a possibility on still, sunny days. This lasts as far south as Narooma, though from May through October, evenings on land can get pretty crisp, and if you intend camping out, be sure to have well-insulated sleeping bags and ground sheets.

## Eden and the South End

South of here a cold current moves in, making swimming less inviting, but providing for some of the best **game fishing** on the Australian east coast. You're on what tourism promoters these days call the Sapphire Coast—from Bermagui, just south of Wallaga Lake, all the way down to the border with Victoria. The water is, indeed, a glorious iridescent blue, and fishermen have known its bounty for generations. Zane Grey fished here in the 1930s for blue marlin and yellowfin tuna. The towns of Bermagui (380 km—235 miles—south of Sydney), Merimbula and Pambula (470 km—290 miles—south), and Eden, another 20 kilometers (12 miles) farther on, are the centers for big-game fishing. In fact, Eden was once a whaling port, though today its main claim to fame is as a picturesque tourist center. On a rocky coast, the town is full of historic buildings; the light reflecting off the sea here makes the town particularly impressive. The Eden Killer Whale Museum, 94 Imlay Street, (064) 96-2094, is worth a visit to explore the area's whaling history. Opening times vary according to season, so phone before going.

If you'd like to cruise the waters in the area, sail on *The Merimbula Princess* (9 Beach Street, Merimbula, 064-95-2314). Skipper Alan Shand will take you off in a glass-bottomed boat for a leisurely day cruise through oyster beds to view local sea and other wild life. Cruises leave around 2 P.M. every afternoon; $10 adults, $5 for kids, family package $25.

Fishing enthusiasts should contact O'Brien's Boat Charters, 7 Embleh Terrace, Eden; (064) 96-1824. O'Brien's has two boats—a 38-footer that takes six passengers for fishing and a 42-footer that takes fourteen for bottom fishing. If you want the whole boat, be prepared to pay $500 per day for each boat, which can hold six to eight people—all tackle and bait provided. There is also an all-day charter that runs every Friday at $50 per head; all bait and lines supplied.

**Diving** is popular along the southern end of the coast. Bermagui Dive and Sports Centre, 8 Bunga Street, Bermagui, (064) 93-4184, provides scuba-diving instruction and all diving equipment, as well as boat rental. Or contact Begafex Aqua Centre, 1 Park Street, Bega (064) 92-1972. In Pambula, contact Gary Flanagan, at the corner of Toalla and Merimbola streets, (064) 95-6888. You'll find diving instruction and all equipment for rent.

# The Southern Highlands

The key towns in the Southern Highlands district are Mittagong, Bowral, and Berrima. Because of the altitude (around 2,000 feet), these townships have since the 19th century been popular country-retreat areas for the well-off. Bowral particularly has enjoyed a revival in the past ten years because of its superb Victorian and Art Deco guesthouses.

## TRAVEL

The links between the south coast and southern highlands are quite clearly marked on most road maps of the areas. Consequently, it's possible to begin your journey along the Princes Hwy. and continue up to the highlands through Kangaroo Valley or along the Illawarra Hwy. through the Macquarie Pass (well worth the climb for its visual delights). Or you can take the Hume Hwy., which begins in Liverpool, directly into the highlands. Trains also travel to Mittagong.

Trains leave Central Station, Sydney, several times a day for the resort towns of Bowral and Moss Vale (just 15 minutes south of Bowral).

To arrange pick up of a rental car, you can book through Budget's toll-free number from anywhere in Australia: (008) 33-1331, or for Hertz, (008) 33-3377.

# ❦ ACCOMMODATIONS AND RESTAURANTS

The range of guesthouses in the Bowral area is immense—from small to really large, full of extras. Probably the most luxurious is **Milton Park Country House Hotel,** Horderns Rd., Bowral 2576, (048) 61-1522. The hotel was originally the home of the Anthony Hordern family, a premier department-store family earlier this century. Today the Art Deco building has been completely restored and allows guests a taste of what country life was like for the upper crust before the Depression. Even if you don't have time to stay, be sure to see the beautiful gardens—hundred-year-old trees, flowers that will grow no place else in N.S.W., rose gardens, spring flowers in season.

The hotel restaurant, which is also open to the public, specializes in superb French cuisine based on fresh local produce and also serves morning and afternoon teas in addition to lunch and dinner seven days. Be sure to book in advance.

The hotel provides swimming, horseback riding, golf, sauna, spa, and tennis. All premier-class hotel facilities. Rates $120–$200 per night for a double with continental breakfast; all meals are extra. AE, DC, MC, V.

**Berida Manor Health Resort,** 6 David St., Bowral 2576, (048) 61-1177, is another lovely old home in the Georgian style. Despite its reference to health, it was the stellar resort for the self-indulgent until Milton Park opened. But it's still very popular and, although it doesn't boast the same level of haute cuisine as Milton Park, there are many who claim the food alone is worth the stay. Unlike Milton Park, Berida Manor's tariff includes all meals. Doubles cost $335–$355 per day. All cards.

**Ivy Tudor Motor Inn,** at the corner of Moss Vale and Links rds., Bowral 2576, (048) 61-2911, is a less expensive means of staying in the area. It has central heating, air-conditioning, TV, direct-dial telephone, as well as pool, spa, sauna, and in-house restaurant. Rates run around $65 for a double. All cards.

❦ In addition to the excellent food available in Berida Manor and Milton Park, you can get a good meal in Mittagong at **Hume House,** 84 Hume Hwy., Mittagong; (048) 71-1871. In summer its lovely garden setting adds to the superb international fare. The sauces on the menu show the French influence on the chef. In winter you will eat in front of a roaring log fire. Dinner will run around $70 for two people with wine. A coffeeshop is open seven days 10:30 A.M.–4:30 P.M. Lunch Fri.–Sun.; dinner Mon.–Sat. AE, V.

---

The scenery in the Southern Highlands is picturesque in the English manner—the high altitude permits the growth of many cold-climate plants, and deciduous trees abound, making the area something of a curiosity so close to Sydney. **Bowral**'s main street (Bong Bong Road—we kid you not) resembles the high street of an English country village—which is just as the early developers intended. The overall air is of gentility, and shop assistants in the myriad interior design and country-ware stores speak softly and hike their prices, so beware.

**Berrima,** about ten minutes west of Bowral, is another tourist town, though, since its main street is the highway, it lacks Bowral's more countrified airs. Still, it too has an interesting collection of handicraft shops, tea rooms, and antique shops (though you're unlikely to find any bargains).

**The Berrima Pub** has retained the air of an old-fashioned country pub. In warm weather you can take your beer outside to the veranda or the beer garden, where you'll be overlooked by the (frail-looking) walls of Berrima Prison. Don't worry—it's low security: no real bad guys, just the odd crooked magistrate or businessman learning to make picture frames for a while.

# Canberra

Continue along the Hume Highway through the city of Goulburn to the Federal Highway turnoff about ten minutes south. This will take you into Canberra. You'll notice the terrain becoming less lush as you head inland across the high plains.

The city of Canberra, the nation's capital, is situated within The Australian Capital Territory (A.C.T.), a federal enclave of land within, but independent of, the state of New South Wales. The city was designed by a Chicago architect, Walter Burley Griffin, a disciple of America's own Frank Lloyd Wright. The city was fittingly named; "canberra" is an Aboriginal word meaning "meeting place."

## TRAVEL

From Sydney it's less than an hour flight into Canberra, or about a four-hour train ride, with stops at Bowral, Mittagong, and Moss Vale.

**The easiest and fastest way to see major sights is to take a tour; we don't recommend you budget a great deal of time for a Canberra visit: plan to arrive one day, sightsee a little, spend the night, sightsee a little on day two, then move on.**

## TOURS

There are a number of tours being run through the N.S.W. Tourist Bureau in conjunction with the **Canberra Tourist Bureau,** in the Jolimont Centre on Northbourne Ave.; tel. (062) 45-6464.

**The Waltzing Mathilda tour** is a full-day inspection of the city of Canberra and surrounding bush, including a visit to a working sheep station featuring a sheep dog demonstration and barbecue lunch. Cost is $48 adults; $36 per child. It leaves daily at 10 A.M. from the Canberra Tourist Bureau office, Jolimont Centre, Northbourne Ave., or free pick-up from local hotels can be arranged.

**The Grand Slam Tour** focuses on Canberra only. It will give you more time at spots such as the National Gallery and new Parliament House than the Waltzing Mathilda tour, allowing you time to get your bearings for later, lengthier visits.

## ❧ ACCOMMODATIONS

As befitting a national capital, Canberra has a full complement of five-star hotels, ranging from the new **Hyatt** on Commonwealth Ave., Canberra 2600, (062) 70-1234, to the older, but equally well-patronized by the politicos, **Lakeside International** on London Circuit, Canberra 2600, (062) 47-6244. Both hotels offer the standard luxuries, plus businessperson's or politician's requisite access to fax, telex, and secretarial services. Rates for the Hyatt are $235–$320 per double; for the Lakeside International, $155–$280 per double.

**The Canberra City Travelodge,** at the corner of Northbourne Ave. and Cooyong St., Canberra 2600, (062) 49-6911, is less opulent but no less equipped with the expected comforts of air-conditioning, TV, direct-dial telephone, and restaurant. It's more accessible, with rooms priced $80–$124 per double.

**The Embassy Motel,** at the corner of Hopetown Circuit and Adelaide Ave., Canberra 2600, (062) 81-1322, is in the suburb of Deakin—at 5 km (less than a mile) southwest of Canberra, hardly worth listing as outside the city. It's part of the Homestead chain of motels—which consistently get top marks for clean, comfortable rooms and courteous service. As Deakin is in the heart of embassy country, you can stroll around the area taking in the consular architecture. Rates run around $70 double.

## ❧ RESTAURANTS

Both restaurants we've recommended are in the inner suburbs of Canberra; like Sydney, this city is composed of smaller "subsections," as much neighborhoods of the city as they are suburbs. A quick taxi ride can get you to either of the following.

**Café Provencal,** Red Hill Shopping Centre, Red Hill, 95-8317. Good quality provincial fare; dinner for two will run around $70–$80. Dinner Tues.–Sat. BYOB. MC.

**Nobbs,** The Lawns, Manuka; 95-9744. Modern French cuisine with a nouvelle touch using seasonal ingredients. Dinner for two people will run around $50. BYOB but there's a wine shop attached. Open for lunch and dinner seven days a week except for Sunday dinner. All cards.

Canberra's public buildings, particularly the new **Parliament House,** which opened in early 1988, are worth touring. The Parliament House (open daily from 9 A.M. to 5 P.M.) is set on Capital Hill, right in the center of the city. It cost more than $1 billion to build and is considered to embody the very best of Australian technical and artistic talent, designed to blend in with its surroundings. Government activities take place in two halls: the House of Representatives and Senate Chambers. Both have visitors galleries. Tours only take place when a particular chamber is not in session. Telephone 77-7111 for information.

**The National Gallery** is a repository of some of the finest Australian and international art in the nation. There's Aboriginal artwork here, works by famous Australian artists such as Sidney Nolan, as well as paintings by Jackson Pollock and Claude Monet. The National Gallery is on King Edward Terrace, right on the banks of Lake Burley Griffin. It's open daily from 10 A.M. to 5 P.M. Telephone 71-2411.

The **High Court** building, right near the National Gallery on King Edward Terrace, is also worth a visit to see the center of action of Australia's supreme court. It's open from 9:45 A.M. to 4:30 P.M. daily; telephone 70-6811.

Should you want to see where Australian money is made, visit the **Mint,** on Denison Street, in Deakin, southwest of Central Canberra. Visitors are welcome Monday to Friday from 9 A.M. to 4 P.M.; Saturday and Sunday 10 A.M. to 3 P.M.

The **Australian War Memorial,** on Anzac Parade, northeast of Lake Burley Griffin, is a large museum dedicated to displaying memorabilia and war machinery employed during World Wars I and II. You can see displays of uniforms, banners, and personal records of war, many written by participant soldiers. Open from 9 A.M. to 4:45 P.M., seven days. Telephone 43-4211.

Unlike capital cities in other countries, Canberra itself is of minimal interest. A planned city, it has little of the architectural or historic significance of older cities such as Sydney or Melbourne. In fact, it's a public servants' town and, with the exception of some of the consulate buildings (notably the Thai and Indonesian consulates), few nongovernment structures are worth studying.

Nightlife is practically nonexistent—in that way, the city resembles a large country suburb, rather than a cosmopolitan capital. Official entertaining takes place in official residences; junior public servants and ancillary workers prefer to entertain at home—or go to one of the larger cities for shopping and restaurants. Sound boring? Most Australians think so too.

There is some nice country surrounding the city, notably the Victorian-era town of **Bungendore,** 35 kilometers (21 miles) northeast of Canberra, and the **nature reserve** around Tidbinbilla Tracking station, about a half hour's drive southeast, where emus walk up to the car to see who's in it and you'll see some impressive kangaroos, of a size you won't find in zoos. To get to the nature reserve take Cotter Road and follow the sign for Tidbinbilla; it's about a 30- to 40-minute drive from Canberra. The reserve is open daily, 8 A.M. to dusk. You can telephone (062) 37-5120 for information.

# The Snowy Mountains

Canberra is a logical place to stop off on your way to the Snowy Mountains. You can take a day or so to sightsee and make the drive to the Snowy easily in half a morning.

The Snowy Mountains are part of the Great Dividing Range. For a few precious weeks in winter, these peaks are covered with the kind of snow suitable for skiing and everyone in Australia (it seems) heads for the ski resorts that have sprung up throughout these ranges.

**However, we don't recommend you come to Australia for skiing alone; snowfall can be iffy, the runs are far from the world's greatest, and prices are extremely high. And, with all of this, the area is packed during ski season; you would need to book months in advance.**

But come visit outside of designated skiing times. This is the real high country—*Man from Snowy River* country—and in spring and summer the meadows are filled with a collection of wildflowers unmatched by very many places in the world.

Rivers are filled with trout, the rapids make for some thrilling white-water rafting, and most of the homesteads that have opened their doors to paying guests also provide mounts for horseback explorations of the area.

## TRAVEL

If traveling by car, follow the Monaro Hwy. Ansett Pioneer buses connect Canberra with Cooma; trains also connect Canberra with Cooma.

## ✤ ACCOMMODATIONS

Perisher and Thredbo are convenient towns for skiers. The low end of the prices given below are summer rates; prices soar in winter, but you'll need to book well in advance if you're coming for ski season. Cooma is a small town in the region, below the ski fields, convenient for touring the area. See also the fishing village recommended below.

### THREDBO
**Alpine Gables,** at the corner of Kosciusko Rd. and Kalkite St., Thredbo 2627; (064) 56-2555. Central heating, direct-dial phone, TV, and private bath facilities in each of the 42 units here.

Winter rates: $70–$210; summer rates: $48–$80 for double occupancy. Rooms have cooking facilities; no restaurant. All cards.

Also in Thredbo, we recommend the **Thredbo Alpine,** in the village Center (Thredbo 2627); (064) 57-6333. All rooms have private baths and standard facilities. Plus laundry, barbecue facilities, heated pool, and spa. Dining facilities on premises. Double room: $52–$225 per person (includes breakfast). Toll-free booking within Australia: (008) 026-333. All cards.

## PERISHER
In **Perisher Valley, New Valley Inn,** Perisher Valley Rd. (Perisher 2630), 300 meters west of Perisher post office; (064) 57-5291. All 47 units have shower and toilet, direct-dial phones, TVs with video facilities. Dining room on premises. Open for week-long stays winters only. AE, V, MC.

## COOMA
**The Marlborough,** Monaro Hwy., Cooma 2630, 2 km (around 1 mile) north of the Cooma post office; (064) 52-1133. All rooms with showers and toilets. Central heating, room service, refrigerator in room, direct-dial phone, TV. Pool. $50–$70 double. All cards.

Consider a weekend of **horseback riding** at Reynella, a working sheep station that doubles as a resort, in the Snowy Mountains near Adaminaby. You can participate in full- or half-day trail rides, or, in summer, join Alpine horseback safaris into the high country. Weekend rates (Friday night to Sunday afternoon—all meals, accommodation, and horse rental inclusive): adults $124; children under 12, $72, under 15, $78. Horseback safaris: 5 days, 6 nights $525 per person. Long weekends $299.

If **trout fishing** is your idea of a great holiday, consider Anglers Reach Lakeside Village. Rainbow and brown trout are caught in Lake Eucumbene. Guided fishing tours are available in a specially equipped vessel which takes four comfortably. Prices include on-board barbecue, top-quality tackle, bait, guide, morning breakfast, or evening sausage sizzle. A half-day tour for two persons costs around $100 ($30 for each additional person). Self-catering cabins are also available at $50 per night.

**Snowy Mountains Wilderness Walk,** which departs from Cooma, consists of seven days of walking in the Kosciusko National Park. The moderate-grade walk (suitable for fit first-timers) passes through tall timber, on to the wildflower and snowgrass meadows. You'll enjoy waterfalls, swimming holes, and memorable mountain views. Cost is $495 per person, including all food, camping gear, transport, and guide. Meets on selected dates October through February.

**White-water rafting** on the Murrumbidgee River with its mixture of rapids and pools offers something for everyone. A weekend of easy-grade rafting which leaves from Canberra each weekend from October through April costs $195 per person, including all food and gear.

Book for these and other holidays in the Canberra/Snowy Mountain regions through the **Canberra Tourist Bureau,** Jolimont Centre, Northbourne Ave., Canberra City, A.C.T. 2601; (062) 45-6464, telex AA62305 or contact the N.S.W. Tourist Commission in Sydney: 16 Spring St., (02) 231-4444, telex AA22611.

# Newcastle and the Hunter Valley

The oceanside city of Newcastle, about a ninety-minute drive north of Sydney, is the gateway to the Hunter Valley, N.S.W.'s premier wine-growing district. But the city itself is worth having a look at—it has spectacular beaches, historic buildings, and places of scenic interest.

Consider spending a day or two in the Hunter, then continuing up the north coast.

## TRAVEL

Trains leave several times a day from Sydney to Newcastle, then continue north to Murwillumbah.

Planes also leave from Sydney to Newcastle (with connections farther north).

Budget can arrange car-rentals in Newcastle; toll-free in Australia (008) 33-1331.

## ACCOMMODATIONS

### NEWCASTLE

Although of little real tourist interest, Newcastle is the major city in the area, and does have some museums and a redeveloped harbor area.

**Newcastle Parkroyal,** Shortland Esplanade, Newcastle 2300; (049) 26-3777. Seven stories of air-conditioned, modern comfort, with direct-dial phones, TVs, mini bars, room service. Pool and restaurant on premises. Rates run around $90 for a double. All cards.

**Novocastrian Motor Inn,** 21 Parnell Pl., Newcastle 2300; (049) 26-3688. Fifty units, all with showers or baths, air-conditioning, direct-dial phones, TVs. Room service; restaurant on premises. Limited parking makes its "motel" designation questionable, but it is comfortable. Doubles run around $80. All cards.

## HUNTER VALLEY

In the Cessnock area, you'll be very convenient to all the wineries.

**Peppers,** Ekerts Rd., Pokolbin 2321, 7 km (about 4 miles) northwest of Cessnock, (049) 98-7596, is an exceptional guesthouse. Book early—it's full most weekends, though you may get lucky during the week. You'll find excellent food and a superlative standard of comfort from which to visit local wineries. There's a pool and TVs can be had on request. Rates run around $130 for a double. All cards.

**Casuarina Country Inn,** Hermitage Rd., 11 km (about 7 miles) northwest of Pokolbin (Box 218, Cessnock 2358), (049) 98-7562, has spacious rooms, all with private baths and air-conditioning. There's also a good restaurant here (closed Mon.), TV lounge, (TVs are also in the rooms), and a pool. Expect to pay about $120–$140 for a double. All cards.

All over the Hunter Valley, accommodation in the form of **self-catering cabins** is available for stays from a day to a week. Arrangements can be made with individual owners and, provided cabins aren't needed to house grape-pickers at harvest time, you can get a good bargain on accommodation (around $30 a night, depending on the season), if you don't mind roughing it a little. Some of the numbers to call for this kind of holiday are: **Belford Country Cabins**—(065) 74-7100; **Camway Cottages**—(049) 98-7655; **Krinklewood Cottage**—(049) 98-7619; **Pokolbin Cabins**—(049) 98-7611.

---

## ❦ RESTAURANTS

### HUNTER VALLEY

As mentioned under Accommodations, above, the dining room at **Peppers,** 7 km (4 miles) northwest of Cessnock on Eckerts Rd., in Pokolbin, is considered one of the best in the region. Australian-influenced continental cuisine comes in country-size servings in the classic Victorian dining room. About 11 km (7 miles) northwest of Pokolbin, the **Casuarina,** on Hermitage Rd. (off Broke Rd.), (049) 98-7562, is another spot that caters to big appetites—but everyone has one here; the food is that good. They specialize in flambé cookery for two or more people. A wide and classic selection of Hunter Valley wines is available. Expect to pay $80–100 for a dinner for two, depending on the wine you choose. See also Accommodations, above. Dinner Tues.–Sun.; lunch Sun. only. All cards.

**Pokolbin Cellar,** Hungerford Hill Wine Village, Broke Rd., Pokolbin; (049) 98-7584. Part of the winery, this offers a predominantly French provincial menu with exotic touches of Indonesia. Well thought-out—and well thought of! Dinner for two with wine will run around $80. Open daily for lunch and dinner except Sun. dinner. AE, MC, V.

**St. Helena's Restaurant,** on the New England Hwy. at Lochinvar, is about ten minutes from Pokolbin Vineyards (7 km, about 4 miles, north of Maitland); (049) 30-7207. It's a hard place to find—but worth the search. The historic house has much to recommend it and the traditional Hungarian fare even more. In season (around Dec.) when the apricot trees are bearing, you can call ahead and ask them to prepare their apricot dumplings. Don't even *think* of starting a meal with anything but the goulash soup. The price-fixed dinner at press time is $35. Dinner only, 7 nights from 7 P.M. All cards.

# Newcastle

The town of Newcastle was originally established as a coal-mining town, though today it acts as an unofficial capital of the Hunter region. Streams of traffic filter through it, either on the way to the Hunter, or farther up the north coast.

Perhaps your first stop should be the **Newcastle City Tourist Information Centre,** open from 9 A.M. to 5 P.M. on weekdays and between 9:30 and 3 P.M. on weekends. They are at Queen's Wharf Road (049-29-9299) and can provide you with information and maps for both Newcastle and the Hunter, book tours and harbor cruises, and advise you about accommodation in the region.

On the waterfront, **Newcastle Foreshore** and **Queen's Wharf** are bicentennial projects that have created for the city of Newcastle the same sort of new life that the Darling Harbour Project has provided for the once dead part of Sydney's waterfront. Marina, ferry wharf, taverns, cafés, and an observation tower from which to overlook the harbor make for a lovely afternoon's outing.

The **Newcastle Regional Museum,** 787 Hunter Street (62-2001), is the leading regional museum in Australia. It features industrial and technological exhibits—past and present—as well as displays on the social history and lifestyles in the Hunter region. Open Monday through Friday from 9 A.M. to 5 P.M.; Saturday, Sunday, and public holidays from 10 A.M. to 5 P.M. Adults $3.

**Supernova,** also at 787 Hunter Street (same phone), is a science and technology center with emphasis on hands-on exhibits. It's a great place for kids. Open Tuesday to Sunday from 9 A.M. to 5 P.M.; Saturday, Sunday, and public holidays from 10 A.M. to 5 P.M. Admission is $3 for adults, $1.50 for children.

**Newcastle Walking Tours** will give you three hours of Newcastle history. Sundays only. $5 adults, $2 children. Book by calling (049) 58-3435. Price includes a stop for a snack.

There are several good **beaches** in the Newcastle area. **Horseshoe Beach** is the city's harbor beach; there's good fishing from here. **Nobbys Beach** allows good surfing on the reef. Both of the above are within walking distance from the ocean end of the city's main street. **Susan Gilmore Beach** was named after an American ship wrecked here during the last century. You'll find nude bathing here due to relatively difficult access. Access is from the extreme northern end of Bar Beach, which is south of Newcastle Beach.

## The Hunter Valley

The first stop to make when entering the Hunter Valley is Cessnock, about 10 kilometers (6 miles) northwest of Newcastle (take the New England Highway out of Newcastle and turn off at the sign for Cessnock).

The Hunter's climate and soil are excellent for vineyards; Cessnock was the site of the first of these vineyards and today is home to **The Hunter Valley Wine Society,** 4 Wollombi Road (049-90-6699), which should be a priority stop for anyone hoping to seriously sample some of the wines produced by the dozens of fine vineyards here. They'll advise you which vineyards in the area produce your favorite wines, and can also direct you to some out-of-the-way hotels and guesthouses that serve these wines.

Among the vineyards in the area are names that have become legend in the Australian wine-production stakes: names like Lindeman's, Pokolbin (where the first vineyard was established in the middle of last century), Rothbury, and Wyndham. Whites in particular are developed to a high degree of perfection in the Hunter, although some reds of memorable character also call this region home.

Of course, what is wine without food. Naturally enough, some of the finest restaurants in N.S.W. are located in the Hunter region, while the guesthouse industry has enjoyed a boom with the growing interest in and knowledgeability about fine wine.

Most of the vineyards in the area operate cellar door sales, with tasting rooms set up for first-hand inspection of wares. Many also operate dining rooms open to the public, whether they wish to buy wines by the case, or not.

These days, now that wine from Australia has finally gained a deserved recognition outside of this country, prices are not so enticingly cheap for top-quality vintages. Still, cellar door sales offer competitive prices on wines sold in Sydney retail outlets.

Whether you want to sample wines, buy wines, or simply take a day or two of country air, this region has much to offer.

# New England and Western Areas

If you follow the New England Highway beyond the Hunter Valley, you'll reach **Tamworth,** 453 kilometers (about 280 miles) northwest of Sydney and gateway to the New England region. Tamworth is also the Country Music Capital of Australia. During the last weekend in January, the city plays host to country-music enthusiasts from all over Australia—and many American country singers—for a three-day celebration of their art.

New England is fine sheep country. Its undulating pasture land is a pleasure to drive through and while you do so you can stop off at a number of towns and cities that may surprise you.

## TRAVEL

Trains leave Sydney daily for Armidale, Tamworth, and Tenterfield, then continue to Brisbane. Air New South Wales reaches these towns, too.

## ACCOMMODATIONS

### NEW ENGLAND

If you want to take a brief excursion from Sydney into the New England sheep country, the easiest town to reach is Tamworth.

**The Power House Motor Inn,** New England Hwy., 1 km (less than a mile) northeast of Tamworth post office (Tamworth 2340), (067) 66-7000, has sixty units, all with private baths, air-conditioning, direct-dial phones, and TVs. There's also licensed room service, laundry facilities, and a pool. Rates run around $70 for a double. All cards.

**Alandale Flag Inn,** New England Hwy., 6 km (about 3 miles) south of Tamworth (Tamworth 2340), (067) 65-7922, has 25 units, all with showers, air-conditioning, direct-dial phones, and TVs. Room service is available (dinner only). Laundry, pool, half-court tennis. Doubles run around $50. All cards.

For something different try **Old Warrah,** Willow Tree 2339; (067) 47-1767. Old Warrah is a country homestead about an hour's drive from Tamworth. The 3,000-acre cattle farm provides a relaxing holiday with supervised horseback riding, a swimming pool, tennis courts, and bush-walking excursions. Accommodation is in a 100-year-old-verandaed farmhouse, which offers real country cooking using its own homegrown vegetables. Daily tariff is $50 per adult; $25 children, including all meals. Owners will pick up from Tamworth airport.

Those with more time may want to head farther north to Armidale, deeper in the New England region.

**Moore Park Motor Inn,** New England Hwy., Armidale 2350; (067) 72-2358. The main building of this motel is a National Trust classified homestead. All 22 units have private baths, central heat and air-conditioning, direct-dial phones, and TVs. Room service is available (dinner only); there's also a laundry and a pool. Rates are about $60 double. All cards.

If you're planning to make the trip out west, you may want to overnight in Glen Innes on your way.

**Rest Point,** Church St. (New England Hwy.), Glen Innes 2370; (067) 32-2255. A Flag Inn motel, built in the style of an old Australian country homestead with deep veranda all around it, the hotel has 19 units, with private baths, licensed restaurant, direct-dial phones, and TVs (some rooms even have waterbeds). There are laundry facilities and a pool. Rates run about $50 double. All cards.

## THE WEST
If you're hunting for black opals, stay in Lightning Ridge.

**Black Opal,** Opal St., 50 meters west of Lightning Ridge post office (Lightning Ridge 2834); (068) 29-0518. The 12 units all have shower facilities, air-conditioning, and TVs. There's a phone in the lobby. Cost is around $50 double. MC, V.

**Lightning Ridge Motor Village,** Onyx St., 1 km west of post office (Lightning Ridge 2834); (068) 29-0304. Sixteen of the 24 units have private baths. Air-conditioning, direct-dial phones, restaurant on premises, laundry. Rates around $60 double. All cards.

If a visit to Warrumbungle National Park is on your agenda, stay in Coonabarabran.

**Acacia Motor Lodge,** near junction of Oxley Hwy. and Newell Hwy., (Coonabarabran 2830); (068) 42-1922. All units have full bath facilities, air-conditioning, heat, direct-dial phones, and TVs. There's room service, and a licensed restaurant on the premises. Laundry, pool, gym. Doubles run $60–$85. All cards.

You can get a feel for the Outback in Dubbo, 412 km (255 miles) from Sydney.

**Ashwood Country Club Motel,** Whylandra St. (Newell Hwy.), 1 km (about half a mile) west of Dubbo post office (Dubbo 2537); (068) 81-8700. Forty units here, all with showers, some baths. Some rooms with waterbeds. Air-conditioning, heat, direct-dial phones, TVs. Room service. Restaurant on premises. Laundry, pool, tennis court. $64 double. All cards.

Or, if time allows, travel all the way west to Broken Hill.

**Mario's Palace Hotel,** 227 Argent St., Broken Hill 2880; (080) 88-1699. Built during the last century in the town center, this is a graceful and old original. It has been updated to provide private baths, air-conditioning, TVs, direct-dial phones. Parking. Breakfast only. Doubles around $40. No cards.

# New England

**Armidale** is the center of learning for the New England Region. The University of New England is here, off Queen Elizabeth Drive, as are several fine museums and some of the country's most prestigious private schools. Set at the very top of The Great Dividing Range, it's surrounded by prosperous cattle and sheep properties and orchards.

The **Folk Museum** is on the corner of Rusden and Faulkner streets, (067) 72-8666. A National Trust classified building, the museum houses displays on early transport, handicrafts, and general home life as lived in the area in the 19th century. Open Monday through Friday from 1 to 4 P.M.

The **New England Regional Art Museum,** Kentucky Street, (067) 72-5255, hosts collections of some of the best of Australian art—historical and contemporary. Open Monday through Saturday from 10 A.M. to 5 P.M., Sunday from 1 to 5 P.M.

There are a couple of **waterfalls** in the region that are well worth the effort to visit. Dangar's Falls, about 20 kilometers (12 miles) south of Armidale, is one of the most magnificent waterfalls in the state. (Follow New England Highway south and watch for the signs.) The scenic drive to the falls leads past a lovely old homestead at Palmerston. Wollomombi Falls is 40 kilometers (about 25 miles) east of Armidale. (Follow New England Highway north and watch for signs.) These are the highest falls in Australia with a drop of 460 metres (over 1,500 feet).

Continue up the New England Highway through Glen Innes and the amazing **rock formations** that surround the town.

Balancing Rock and Stonehenge Recreation Reserve are 12 kilometers (about 7 miles) south of town on the New England Highway. A 4-meter high, pear-shaped rock has been balancing for generations on a bed of flat rock.

---

**Note:** If you intend to do any fishing or fossicking in inland N.S.W., you will need to obtain a license for each activity. These can be obtained from any N.S.W. courthouse in any town for a cost of $5 for a thirty-day fishing license; $2.50 for an annual fossicking license ($5 for family license). Fishing licenses can also be obtained through most sporting stores and National Parks and Wildlife Services.

---

The **Glen Innes Tourist Centre** has information on where you may go fossicking (hunting) for sapphires. There are eleven designated **fossicking areas.** The center is located in The Railway Carriage, Church Street, (067) 32-2397. Open Monday through Friday from 9 A.M. to 5 P.M.; Saturday and Sunday, mornings only.

Tenterfield, 750 kilometers (about 465 miles) northwest of Sydney, is the home town of singer/songwriter Peter Allen and inspiration for his famous song "Tenterfield Saddler." You can choose to turn east here, along the Gwydir Highway toward the north coast (see below).

## The West

Or, head west along the Gwydir Highway to the dry, sometimes barren edges of the state's Outback. These areas are vast, and it's unlikely that the casual tourist will contemplate doing much exploration by car—the climate is harsh and water often scarce. But to many minds this is the "real Australia." It's unbearably hot in summer and unbearably cold in winter. Opals are dug out of its soil.

If you fly over it at night, you'll see vast stretches of blackness, with only the rare set of lights to indicate a sheep station with its main house, outbuildings, and—often—landing strip. If you do drive through here, you'll encounter a lot of scrub, dust, and phenomenal rock formations.

Head south at Moree along the Newell Highway to Coonabarabran, roughly level on the map with Port Macquarie, but several hundred kilometers due west. If you get here, you can visit the **Warrumbungle National Park,** a collection of gorges and awe-inspiring peaks tortured into fantastic shapes by thousands of years of winds. Animals and birds from both the moist eastern coast and barren western plains meet here in the Warrumbungle Range and the area is a gold mine for naturalists. There are campsites in the park, and they are almost never full.

Northwest of Coonabarabran is **Lightning Ridge,** 765 kilometers (about 470 miles) northwest of Sydney. This is a rich opal field, where the world's only black opal is mined. Fossicking is allowed and you can bathe in artesian bore baths, great basins of underground mineral water that has been tapped by man.

Almost due south of Coonabarabran is the town of **Dubbo,** home of the Western Plains Zoo where the larger varieties of wild animal wander vast spaces, separated by moats from visitors who walk, bicycle, or drive through the grounds to view them in an almost natural environment.

From Dubbo, you can travel the eight hundred-odd kilometers (almost 500 miles) to Broken Hill, almost on the border with South Australia. You will have traveled through real Outback to get here, past towns with whimsical-sounding names like Nevertire and Dickygundi. People travel by small plane a lot out here. The "local" doctor is the Flying Doctor and children attend The School of the Air via shortwave radio.

You can visit **Royal Flying Doctor Service,** beside Barrier Highway, 10 kilometers (about 6 miles) northeast of Broken Hill. Inspections are at 10:30 A.M. and 3:30 P.M., Monday through Friday; 10:30 A.M. Saturday and Sunday. Book through the Tourist Information Centre at the corner of Bromide and Blenide streets, Broken Hill, (080) 6077.

While you're in **Broken Hill,** you may want to visit **Delprat's Mine,** (080) 88-1604. Telephone to arrange for underground tours of a working mine, conducted Monday through Friday at 10:30 A.M.; 2 P.M. on Saturday. It gives an insight into the workings, past and present, of the mines so integral to this area's development. Or visit the **Gladstone Mining Museum,** at the corner of South and Morish streets, (080) 6277. This is a replica of a mine, built in an old hotel. It contains life-size replicas of mining procedure, present and past, as well as an extensive collection of minerals. But it's not all mining out here. The **Pro Hart Gallery,** (080) 2441, is one of the largest private art collections in Australia. Pro Hart himself is one of the country's most respected painters. Open Monday through Saturday from 9:30 A.M. to 5 P.M. and Sunday 2 to 5 P.M.

On the northern edge of Broken Hill Common, Sundown Nature Trail is a walking trail in the Sundown Hills. The walk is best just after sunrise and just before sunset. It'll take about 1½ hours.

Here in the west, it's nothing to travel 500 kilometers (that's over 300 miles) for a dance or a dinner party. And people are hospitable the way they are in a place where the life is hard and there aren't many visitors during the year.

This is a region whose grandeur compensates for its lack of modern comforts, where the ruggedness is closer in spirit to the old American West than any other part of this state. Broken Hill was once a bustling mining town (where street names reflect its past: Mica Street, Beryl Street, Argent and Chloride streets). Today most of the mines have closed down, but the red-earthed, Martian landscape, and brilliant blue of its days are creating another industry for residents brave enough to stay on—slowly, but surely, Broken Hill is becoming a popular location for film sets. And it affords the perfect location for visitors whose time won't permit a visit to the Red Centre—the Northern Territory and Ayers Rock. The Broken Hill area has much in common with the Territory: the desert landscape will give you a taste of what it's like in Australia's center and far north.

# The North Coast

Just as the Princes Highway is the gateway to the south coast, the Pacific Highway performs the same function for those who seek the sun-filled charms of the north coast. It runs through the north shore of the city, from north Sydney straight up through the shopping districts of some of the leafier northern suburbs, affording some gorgeous views of the ocean by the time you reach Berowa, on the edge of the Ku-ring-gai National Park (discussed as part of the Sydney chapter).

## TRAVEL

Trains leave for the north coast several times a day from Sydney's Central Station.

Express buses travel to Port Macquarie.

If your preference is to fly, Air New South Wales flights land at Coffs Harbour, Ballina, and Byron Bay airports. You can check with Air N.S.W. for smaller craft that fly to other local airports, such as the one at Port Macquarie.

Driving all the way to the Queensland border is not recommended. Roads are not the best in many areas and accidents are rife in busy travel times such as school holidays and long weekends.

You can load your car onto a train which will carry it to Murwillumbah, just south of Tweed Heads. The train line ends here and you can choose to drive around the upper N.S.W. north coast or go into Queensland by car.

Budget car-rentals can arrange a car for you in Newcastle, Port Macquarie, Nambucca Heads, Coffs Harbour, Murwillumbah, Lismore, or Tweed Heads (toll-free in Australia, tel. 008-33-1331) so you can arrange a combination fly/drive or train/drive holiday. Hertz provides a similar service; toll-free in Australia, tel. (008) 33-3377.

## ❦ ACCOMMODATIONS

### TERRIGAL AREA

If you don't have the time to travel too far north, and perhaps want to supplement a Sydney stay with some nearby beach, choose accommodations in the Terrigal Area.

**Cobb & Co Motor Inn,** 154 Terrigal Dr., Terrigal 2260; (043) 84-1166. Top-class comfort is available in these Georgian-style buildings overlooking the lagoon. All rooms have showers and bath, direct-dial phones, and TVs. There is also licensed room service, a pool, gym, tennis courts, and a sauna. Rates run about $85–160 double. All cards.

**Kim's Resort,** Charlton St., Toowoon Bay (just south of The Entrance); (write Box 1, Toowoon Bay 2261); (043) 32-1566. Located about ninety minutes from Sydney, Kim's features individual cabin-style accommodation, most taking advantage of beach and water views. Provided are TVs, radio/stereo cassettes, ceiling fans, refrigerators; all have private bath facilities. You'll also find all cabins with sweeping verandas or sundecks. Rates include all meals—the restaurant has developed a superb reputation. Seasonal rates: summer $110–$150 double; weekends add $15–$20. After March 1, rates drop about 20 percent. AE, MC, V.

## PORT MACQUARIE TO COFFS HARBOUR

If you have the time, travel farther north. From Port Macquarie to Coffs Harbour, the beach towns, though becoming more developed as time passes, retain a country feel. As you move farther north, the landscape becomes more and more tropical.

**Pelican Shores Resort,** Park St., Port Macquarie 2444, (065) 83-3999, fax (065) 84-0397, is on the lagoon at Port Macquarie, affording some water views. This is a modern, award-winning hotel with all modern facilities in rooms. Although not as well situated or as well appointed as its sister hotel in Coffs Harbour, Pelican Shores does have a superb restaurant, worth eating at whether you stay at the hotel or not. Doubles run around $110 and $130 in summer; meals not included. AE, MC, V.

**Destiny,** at the corner of Pacific Hwy. and Riverside Dr., Nambucca Heads 2448; (065) 68-8044. All rooms have shower, air-conditioning, direct-dial phones, and TVs. There is a restaurant and room service. Rates run $50–$60 for a double. All cards.

**Pelican Beach Resort,** Pacific Hwy., about 5 km north of Coffs Harbour, Coffs Harbour 2450; (066) 53-7000, telex PEL-RES 66651, fax (066) 53-7066. Bigger, better appointed, and better located than its Port Macquarie sister hotel, Pelican Beach is almost international standard. You'll find magnificent views of open sea from most rooms, an enormous salt-water pool landscaped to resemble a tropical lagoon, and family rooms complete with kitchens for self-catering. Both Pelican properties are designed in the style of the Aga Khan's Sardinian resort, Costa Smeralda, but are a fraction of those prices. Pelican Beach is slightly more expensive than Pelican Shores—around $150 for a family suite (queen-size bed with large single, separated by sliding wall). Take these even if you're only two—the extra space and cooking facilities are worth it, especially if you're staying a few days. All cards.

**The Nautilus,** on the beach, Pacific Hwy., Coffs Harbour 2450, (066)-536699, is next door to Pelican Beach. It provides the same standard of luxury, but in separate beach houses. The emphasis here is tropical style. Rates run around $100–$140 double. All cards.

**Sanctuary Resort,** Pacific Hwy. (2 km, about 1 mile, south of Coffs Harbour); (write Coffs Harbour 2450), (066) 52-2111, is smaller than the others mentioned here, but less pricey. It has 37 units with all luxury facilities, including room service from a top-rated restaurant located in the hotel complex, a solar-heated pool, gym, tennis, and squash courts. Doubles run around $75–90. All cards.

## THE FAR NORTH

If you're planning to head farther north from New South Wales into Queensland, and the surfing lifestyle appeals, stay at the north end of the N.S.W. coast in the Byron Bay Area.

**Byron Bay Beach Resort,** Bayshore Dr., Byron Bay 2481; (066) 85-8000, fax (066) 85-6916. Overlooking the beach and ocean with views to Cape Byron and Brunswick Heads, this resort is a collection of self-contained chalets with full kitchen facilities. All luxury facilities are available plus a number of recreational activities, such as escorted horseback riding on the beach, golf course, tennis courts, pools, and canoeing on freshwater lakes. Rates are $70–$130 for a double. AE, MC, V.

**Cape Byron Resort Motel,** 16 Lawson St., Byron Bay 2481; (066) 85-7663. A Georgian-style, though modern, building houses 30 units, all with shower facilities, some with baths. Direct-dial phones, TVs, refrigerators, cooking facilities, dining room, laundry, heated pool, and spa. Rates are $60–95 double. All cards.

In Murwillumbah, the place to stay is **Attunga Park Country House,** Nobbys Creek Rd., (11 km, about 7 miles, northwest of Murwillumbah post office; write Murwillumbah 2484); (066) 79-1455. Here you'll find old-world charm on the banks of the Tweed River. There are only four units, but each is elegantly appointed and has a shower, heat, fans, direct-dial phone, and TV. Restaurant, laundry, and heated pool are among the other amenities. Tariff includes all home-cooked meals and wine. Weekly rates: double, $380. AE, DC, V.

In Tweed Heads, stay at the **Blue Pelican,** 115 Wharf St. (Tweed Heads 2485); (075) 36-1777. This motel has 20 units, and is fully air-conditioned, with a pool, spa, direct-dial phones, TVs; all rooms have private baths. About three blocks to the beach. No room service or restaurant on premises. Doubles run around $45–$75 per night. All cards.

# ❧ RESTAURANTS

## TERRIGAL AREA

Terrigal is worth spending several days in just to eat at all the fine restaurants. Among the best are **The Galley,** The Haven; (043) 84-6333. Sublime French-influenced cuisine with Australian panache, inventiveness, and spirit. A palate refresher, for instance, is likely to be an apple and fresh basil sorbet. All served in an open, fresh atmosphere with glorious Pacific views. Ask for seating on the balcony overlooking The Haven beach. Lunch and dinner every day. All cards.

**Swells,** 100 The Esplanade; (043) 84-6466. Fresh, simple meals, and light snacks. Any fish, simply grilled will be worth ordering. Wonderful weekend breakfasts, too, if you can be there before 10 A.M. MC, V.

## PORT MACQUARIE TO COFFS HARBOUR

In Port Macquarie have dinner in the dining room of **Pelican Shores Resort Hotel,** Park St., Port Macquarie; (065) 83-3999. Impeccable service, carefully executed international cuisine, with emphasis on the local fresh seafood. Good piano bar on selected nights. A dinner for two with wine will cost around $75. AE, MC, V.

In Coffs Harbour, the best place to eat is the **Café Cezanne,** 18 Elizabeth St.; (066) 52-4144. The restaurant is a destination in itself. As its name suggests, the café is French influenced; the chefs inspired. Specialties include poached brains in phyllo pastry, served on a bed of seaweed with tamarillo sauce; and—for something a little more pedestrian—white chocolate and praline pâté in caramel sauce. Little compares—even in Sydney—with the care taken over dishes here. A dinner for two with wine will run around $70–80. V.

Also in Coffs Harbour is The **Treehouse Restaurant,** Sanctuary Resort; (066) 52-2111. International cuisine (schnitzels; chicken in cream sauce with champignons) is served in a real treehouse! The mood is fresh and tropical, the food slightly heavier, but a delightful place to spend an evening all the same. Dinner for two: $50–60 with wine. All cards.

If you make the trip to Woolgoolga, stop for a meal at **The Temple View Indian Restaurant,** River St.; (066) 54-1122. Named in honor of the Sikh temple which it overlooks, this dining room won't fail to please aficionados of Punjabi dishes—or Indian food in general. Dinner only except in N.S.W. school holidays. Fully licensed. Dinner for two, about $35. No cards.

## THE FAR NORTH

Once beyond Grafton on the Pacific Hwy., look for Chatsworth Rd. between the Iluka and Yamba run-offs. On the bank of the Clarence River is the **Chatsworth Island Restaurant,** highly recommended by some of Sydney's most respected food reviewers. European cuisine is offered by classically trained chefs, served up in the surrounds of a 19th-century general store. Described as an "unalloyed pleasure." Dinner for two around $70–80. Tel. (066) 46-4455. MC.

# Terrigal Area

You are approaching what is known as the central coast by the time you reach Gosford, about 85 kilometers (fifty miles) north of Sydney. The most popular areas for summer holidaying in this area are Terrigal, another 15–20 minutes east, right on the ocean, and the string of small towns that range up from here—Forresters Beach, Bateau Bay, Toowoon Bay, up to The Entrance.

If you're interested in **diving** in the area, contact Action Divers Tuncurry, Shop 4, 17 Manning Street, Forster (midway between Newcastle and Port Macquarie), (065) 55-4053.

Lessons are given at all levels; charter boats are available for dives.

## Port Macquarie to Coffs Harbor

Port Macquarie, about 420 kilometers (260 miles) north of Sydney, is the first real resort town on the north coast proper. Imposing vistas, good weather, and a collection of resort hotels adjacent to beaches have made this the choice of Sydneysiders as a holiday destination for generations. These days the resorts are going up-market, and a building boom has hit in the private home industry, but Port Macquarie still has a kind of untouched charm about it. Its first McDonalds only appeared in late 1987.

If **hang gliding** catches your fancy, try Mid North Coast Gliders, RMB Hannam Vale Rd., in Lorne (near Port Macquarie); (065) 56-9692. Lessons are given at all levels daily. Bunkhouse accommodation is also available here.

It's worth a drive to the **Way Way State Forest** and **Yarrahappini Mountain,** 7 kilometers (about 4 miles) south of Macksville. Yarrahappini Lookout, some 500 meters above sea level, provides a spectacular vista over the surrounding valley. Barbecue facilities are available if you want to make this into a picnic.

### SIDETRIP

**The Pub with No Beer** at Taylors Arm, 30 km (about 18 miles) west of Macksville, is a pub made famous by bush balladeer Gordon Parsons. Needless to say, after all the publicity the song engendered, this is one pub that wouldn't dare to run out of beer ever again! The real name is the Cosmopolitan; telephone (065) 64-2101.

At Nambucca Heads, farther north, begins the real subtropical north. Banana plantations begin to proliferate, but the beaches and the rock fishing make this another popular holiday spot, albeit one less heavily serviced with luxury hotels. All around you will see mountain ranges—a little like Hawaii. With this, combined with a softening in the air—even in winter—due to the fact that you are so much farther north, you'll feel a tropical lull begin to wash over you. This will grow with every additional fifty kilometers (thirty miles or so) you travel northward.

You're on what the travel bureaus call the Holiday Coast now. Officially it extends from Port Macquarie to the Queensland border, but most people reckon you need to see a few banana palms before you can really begin to unwind.

**Nambucca Heads** is named for the Nambucca River which empties into the sea near here. There's plenty of good fishing around here—but drinking seems to be an even more popular sport.

It's a bit unusual, but, especially if you're traveling with children, consider a stop at the **Swiss Toymakers,** 5 kilometers (3 miles) north of Nambucca Heads on Pacific Highway; (065) 69-5190. You'll see woodworkers here, using the traditional craft skills of their native Switzerland.

Just southwest of Nambucca Heads is the lovely **Bellingen Valley,** green and lush and fertile. It does your heart good just to drive through it. The town itself has many historic buildings, including the court house and restored butter factory.

Coffs Harbour, 572 kilometers (about 357 miles) north of Sydney, is yet another resort town. It's the home of the **Big Banana,** a giant concrete replica of the area's most successful product. (There's a tea room here and a souvenir shop; telephone (066-52-1657.) But, bananas aside, Coffs, as it's known, has some of the loveliest scenery and best beaches on this part of the north coast. Seaside resort hotels have been going up at warp speed in the past few years, making this once sleepy agricultural town a prime holiday spot. By American standards, however, it still retains the charm of a country town and, admittedly there isn't a lot of nightlife.

Mostly, what you should do here is enjoy the scenery. But there are a couple of specific tourist attractions. The **Pet Porpoise Pool,** Orlando Street, (066) 52-2164, is a sea circus with performing porpoises and seals. Shows are at 10:30 A.M. and 2:15 P.M. There's also a native fauna sanctuary, open daily from 9 A.M. to 5 P.M.

Or spend an afternoon at **Woolgoolga,** which has one of the largest **Sikh communities** outside of India. If you like Indian food, this should be the place to visit, and the **Guru Nanak Sikh Temple** on River Street (open on Saturday and Sunday) gives an exotic touch to this rural area of Australia.

If you're making this trip in late October or early November, call in at the town of **Grafton,** 650 kilometers (about 400 miles) north of Sydney, just off the Pacific Highway. The streets are lined with jacaranda trees. In spring, the pavement is carpeted with the violet-blue petals and the **Jacaranda Festival**, held the last week in October and first week of November, draws tourists from all over N.S.W.

While you're in town, visit the **Schaeffer House Museum,** 192 Fitzroy Street; (066) 42-5212. Set in a lovely early 1900 homestead, it's one of the largest and most comprehensive museums outside an Australian city. Open Tuesday, Thursday, and Sunday from 2 P.M. to 4 P.M.

## The Far North

**Byron Bay,** 813 kilometers (about 500 miles) north of Sydney, is the center of far north N.S.W. beach culture. Lots of surfing, swimming, and very laid-back living goes on year round, particularly in the warmer months. Surrounding areas have become increasingly popular as sites for building luxury housing, and property, unlike most of the north coast, is expensive.

Clearly, the water is the main attraction here, and **divers** might want to contact Byron Bay Sports and Dive, 9 Lawson Street, Byron Bay; (066) 85-7149. The center arranges daily dives at Julian Rocks, nearby. Telephone to reserve a place.

Other sights worth a look in the area include **Brunswick Heads Fisherman's Co-op,** which sells directly to the public from Brunswick Heads wharf (just north of Byron Bay), daily. The **Cape Byron Lighthouse** is on Australia's most easterly point. Open daily from 8 A.M. to 4 P.M. You can tour the lighthouse Thursday only from 10 to 11:30 A.M. and from 1 to 2:30 P.M.

Oddly enough, nearby towns of Mullumbimbah and Nimbin are the center for counter-culture activity not seen on such a scale since the late sixties in the United States. **Nimbin** particularly is hippie heaven, so if you're too young to remember what it was like the first time around, or if you want to recapture lost youth, head for Nimbin.

Near Murwillumby, visit **Shaw's Woodcraft Gallery,** 1 Ferry Road, North Tumbulgum, via Murwillumbah; (066) 76-6270. You can buy wooden furniture and see woodburning done by craftspeople. Open Monday through Friday from 8 A.M. to 5 P.M. Closed weekends. At the **Condong Sugar Mill,** Pacific Highway, 4 kilometers (2½ miles) north of Murwillumby, (066) 72-2244, see the sugar refining process in this cane-growing area. Open during crushing season: June to December, Monday through Friday from 9 A.M. to 3 P.M., weather permitting.

**Wollumbin Wildlife Refuge** is on Mount Warning Road, 10 kilometers (6 miles) from Murwillumbah; (066) 79-5120. This is a particularly lovely picnic area with swimming pool, tennis court. You'll be in a setting of subtropical birds— members of the parrot family.

**Tweed Heads,** practically on the border with Queensland, has grown (if that's the right word) from a picturesque, if sleepy, little fishing village to the club capital of the north coast. If you've tired of nature and jaded with scenic beauty, a night or two of this mini Las Vegas may be just what the doctor ordered. One-armed bandits proliferate at the Tweed Heads RSL, and the Seagulls Leagues Club (similar to an RSL club, but membership is based on allegiance to a local football team) is well known for spectacular floor shows and cabarets. Tourists are encouraged at these clubs.

For daytime activity, **diving** trips can be arranged through the Tweed Dive Shop, Treasure Island Shopping Centre, Tweed Heads; (075) 36-3822. Lessons are available for all levels. Equipment can be hired.

# Lord Howe Island

Lying parallel to Coffs Harbour in the Pacific Ocean, Lord Howe Island's subtropical beauty is a drawcard for thousands of Australians each year. The island's unspoilt charm is due especially to the decision on the part of locals to limit tourists to no more than 350 at any one time. While this makes spending time on the island more difficult, it ensures that the island's beauty is left intact for future generations of visitors and residents.

Lord Howe, like so much of eastern Australia, began as a prison colony. Ironically, the very buildings that housed convicts and saw some of the most brutal treatment of any penal colony, are some of the loveliest examples of Georgian architecture extant in Australia. The buildings are undergoing restoration and form one of the tourist attractions on the island.

Prime pastimes for tourists, besides visiting these sights, are **bushwalking** (maps are available from hotels and from Lord Howe Tourist Center; see below), lazing on some of the most spectacular **lagoon beaches** in Australia, and **fishing**—though, like so much on Lord Howe, certain areas are off-limits to fishermen for the protection of rare fish. **Ned's Beach,** for example, is home to some of the 15 varieties of fish found no place else in Australia. Here the fish are so tame they come up to you and take food from your fingers. **Windsurfers** can be rented for about $25 a day.

The **coral reef** that creates the lagoon is home to myriad varieties of marine life. Scuba divers get their money's worth swimming among the reef's formations, while those who don't wish to dive can see much of the reef's life from *The Coral Princess,* a glass-bottomed boat which takes visitors out to the reef for the purpose.

Because the island is so small, representative organizers of cruises, fishing trips, glass-bottom boat trips, and bushwalks will call at your hotel, allowing you to arrange a day's fishing or sightseeing. Your hotel's host can also arrange any of these activities for you, as well as help you rent equipment you might need.

It's best not to book any of these activities before you reach the island. Because of its position and its small size, Lord Howe can turn on some pretty blowy days—in which case, cruise boats will not go out. But don't worry; these periods never last long. And because there are so few tourists on the island at any one time, it's not a problem booking for a scuba lesson, cruise, or sail. Just be sure to do so while the weather is fine.

There are a number of special interest tours offered to Lord Howe. **Scuba divers** may wish to take a package which combines airfares, accommodation, and a number of dives (accompanied) for one price. Sea Life International Pty. can arrange these for you, beginning at just over $1,000 for a seven-night stay including six dives. Their address is: 1st Floor, 27 Alfreda Street, Coogee, N.S.W. 2034; telephone: (02) 665-6335; fax (02) 664-2623. Lord Howe Island Tourist Centre in Sydney (see below) can also help you arrange for scuba gear rentals.

## TRAVEL

Norfolk Island Airlines flies to Lord Howe. Contact East-West Airlines; in Sydney tel. (02) 27-2867; toll-free in Australia (008) 22-1713, fax (02) 251-2742.

Although there are a limited number of automobiles on the island available for hire, most people stick to bicycles. The island is small enough to make this mode of transport viable and the slow pace on the island discourages the hectic pace favored by cars. Bicycles can be rented from hotels at around $2.50 per day. Or through Clive Wilson: 63-2045.

**Luggage allowance for traveling to Lord Howe is only 13 kilos per person (that's about 28 pounds), so plan to bring a smaller bag with you to Australia to transfer your needs for travel to Lord Howe. Most hotels in Sydney will store your larger bags for you while you're away.**

**Comfortable shoes for walking (often on unpaved roads), tennis shoes for walking on coral, which can give you a nasty infected cut if your feet are unprotected, a heavy sweater for sudden weather changes, and a flashlight to see your way along the mostly unlighted streets at night are a few essentials.**

**Day wear is casual; for evenings casual wear is also acceptable, as long as it's not scruffy.**

## 🦜 ACCOMMODATIONS

Top-of-the-line accommodation is available at **Pine Trees.** The guesthouse can hold eighty people and provides access to fishing, diving, sailing, and swimming in the surf, and has a swimming pool, tennis courts, and bicycle rental.

Tariffs include all meals, transport to and from the airport, use of courts. Double rooms range from $100 to $143 per day. Packages are available through the Lord Howe Island Tourist Centre (see below).

Other hotels on the island include **Blue Lagoon Lodge,** who operate their own charter fishing boat; the **Ocean View** with excellent facilities for families, **Somerset,** one of the largest guesthouses, with motel-style units that have breakfast and snack-making facilities in rooms.

To some extent, where you stay will be dictated by what hotel has a vacancy at the time you desire. Bookings for the more popular guesthouses are often made up to a year in advance, so include a booking for Lord Howe when you plan your trip to Australia.

Demand for space on Lord Howe is high especially December through February. Visitors from outside Australia who wish to see this magnificent island should ask their travel agent to make a reservation for them as soon as they decide to visit Australia.

If you plan to visit Lord Howe during the winter months of June, July, and August your selection of guesthouses may be slightly restricted, as some of the smaller ones close for the duration. On the other hand, there is less competition for accommodation during these months.

Reservations can be made through the **Lord Howe Tourist Centre,** 20 Loftus St., Sydney 2000; (02) 27-2867; telex AA 21193; fax (02) 251-2742.

Camping on the island is not permitted.

## ❧ RESTAURANTS

Most hotel tariffs include full board. However, subject to space availability, nonguests can eat at other hotel dining rooms.

**Pine Trees'** dining room is highly regarded. Other restaurants include **Milky Way Restaurant and Bar,** Old Settlement Beach, 63-2012, which serves locally caught fish, battered and fried, with salads. Home-made pies are served with fresh cream.

**Lorhiti Lodge Restaurant,** Anderson Rd., 63-2081, specializes in the traditional Australian baked dinner (roast lamb, potatoes, and pumpkin), as well as island fish. Lorhiti Lodge is a country-style island homestead, full of old-time atmosphere.

MC is accepted throughout the island.

# 6

# MELBOURNE AND VICTORIA

Visitors can be forgiven if they think they've stepped into a touch of London Down Under, with Melbourne's many Victorian-era buildings and leafy-lined boulevards. Settled by English explorer John Batman in 1835, even the street names have a familiar ring to them; four of the city's main thoroughfares are King, William, Queen, and Elizabeth, in that order.

But Melbourne is far more than just England's most southerly suburb. It is a global village of some three million people and more than one hundred nationalities, with an international flavor not found anywhere else in Australia.

Long heralded as the country's center for food, fashion, and finance (though Sydneysiders may object to this), Melburnians also know how to let their hair down, with some of Australia's best late-night spots, comedy clubs, and colonial-era beer pubs contained within its borders. Then, too, in a country well known for its addiction to sports, Melbourne is the place to go for a fix, whether one's interest lies in cricket, golf, Australian Rules Football (footy), or tennis.

Despite the attractions and its wide array of Victorian-style architecture and beautiful gardens, Melburnians are forever reminded that their city pales in comparison with its big sister to the north, Sydney.

The main difference between the two is that while Sydney has its stunning harbor and world-renowned Opera House, Melbourne has nothing quite so dramatic to offer in return. Sydney attracts outdoorspeople, that is, those who delight in the pleasures of boating, swimming, and surfing, while Melbourne quietly goes about its business under cover, offering many of Australia's finest stores and arcades, restaurants, and late-night establishments.

Rather than move along at the faster-paced disco beat of Sydney, Melbourne hums along at a modest tempo, best exemplified by the ringing of a conductor's bell on one of its many tram cars that rattle along the streets.

## ORIENTING YOURSELF

Bordered by the murky waters of the Yarra River to the south, **Melbourne's City Center** comes alive each day with both commuters scurrying to their offices to make money and shoppers descending on the stores to spend it. The downtown area is laid out in an orderly grid network of streets commonly referred to as the Golden Mile. The main thoroughfare to look for is Swanston Street, which more or less bisects the city. Key streets to remember running perpendicular to Swanston include Collins and Bourke, which feature many of Melbourne's leading stores, glass-lit shopping arcades, and restaurants.

Melbourne is best explored on foot, both because of its compact size and also because of its plethora of sidewalk cafés for those who need to take a breather. The city is also blessed with more than sixty parks and gardens for those who prefer kicking off their shoes for a tip-toe through the eucalypts. There's always something in bloom at the Royal Botanic Gardens while far smaller floral displays are featured at places like Fitzroy, King's Domain, and Queen Victoria gardens.

One inner-city enclave of special interest is **Chinatown,** situated at the top end of Little Bourke Street between Spring and Swanston streets. The narrow road teems with Chinese restaurants which offer an extremely wide range of Oriental favorites. Then, too, Chinatown is home to several Oriental gift shops, small grocery stores, and the quaint Museum of Chinese Australian History, located at Cohen Place.

For those seeking to discover other parts of town, the city is ringed by a number of distinctive suburbs easily reached by the green and gold trams that remain Melbourne's most important means of transport.

**Fitzroy** is a small suburb located to the southeast of the downtown area. Best known as the home of one of Melbourne's lushest gardens, Fitzroy also is renowned for its working-class pubs, no-frills eateries and second-hand clothing and antique stores. The street best exhibiting these characteristics is Brunswick Street, which can be reached by the number 12, 30, or 31 tram.

To the north is **Carlton,** heart of the city's Little Italy district. The address best exemplifying the suburb's heavy Italian influence is Lygon Street, which is filled with pizza parlors, spaghetti bars, gelati shops, and up-market clothing boutiques.

Located just behind the Hilton Hotel and within an easy walk from the city, **East Melbourne** best typifies the grandeur of the 1880 gold-rush days in Victoria. Many magnificent mansions and terrace houses still grace the leafy, wide boulevards of this historic neighborhood.

Situated just two miles from downtown, **South Melbourne** offers a wide range of century-old buildings and trendy shops and restaurants. In recent years, the suburb's tenants have begun to shift from first-generation, working-class Australian families to young, upwardly mobile executives who still rub elbows every Saturday and Sunday at the South Melbourne Market, a mini version of the city's Queen Victoria Market.

Another prime suburb is **St. Kilda,** located directly south of the city. The best way to describe it is as Melbourne's answer to a combination of Manhattan's 42nd Street and Greenwich Village, with an endless array of colorful characters, entertainment arcades, sleaziness, and smoke-filled coffeehouses. Then, too, St. Kilda is also home to some of Melbourne's most popular beaches, and, for those not on some health-food kick, countless calorie-laden cake shops.

Melbourne's other key outer limit is the southeastern suburban triumverate of Armadale, South Yarra, and Toorak. **Toorak,** which has long been known as one of Australia's priciest addresses, houses many of the country's leading clothing designers and Paris-style cafés, while nearby **Armadale** features high-priced antiques, furniture, and jewelry shops. **South Yarra** is a blend between the other two with a dash of history thrown in as evidenced by the Colonial-era mansion called Como House.

## PRIORITIES

There are three major things that set Melbourne apart from other Australian cities: adherence to English traditions, trams, and parks and gardens. Here is a short list of must-sees that cover these unique aspects of Melbourne. Each attraction is keyed into the area of the city in which it is located (as delineated above under Orienting Yourself). Also, sights are keyed into the color map of Melbourne at the back of the book, referring to the page number of the map as well as the appropriate coordinates.

### Colonial Tram Car Restaurant

MELBOURNE CENTER

This converted 1927 tram allows visitors the opportunity to sit back in a Victorian-style compartment and enjoy a fine meal, at the same time viewing many of the city's best sights.

The restaurant is open six days a week (closed Mondays), and has two separate settings, depending on whether you prefer an early or late dinner. (Early dinners start at 5:45 P.M. and cost about $40, while late dinners, which begin at 8:35 P.M., cost between $65 and $75, including drinks.) The car

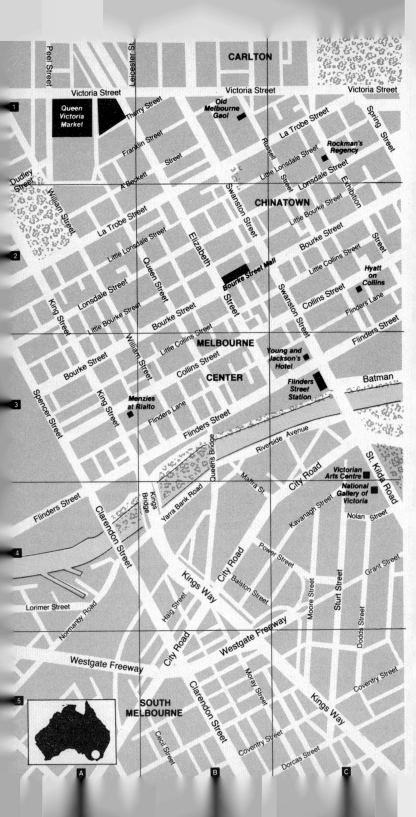

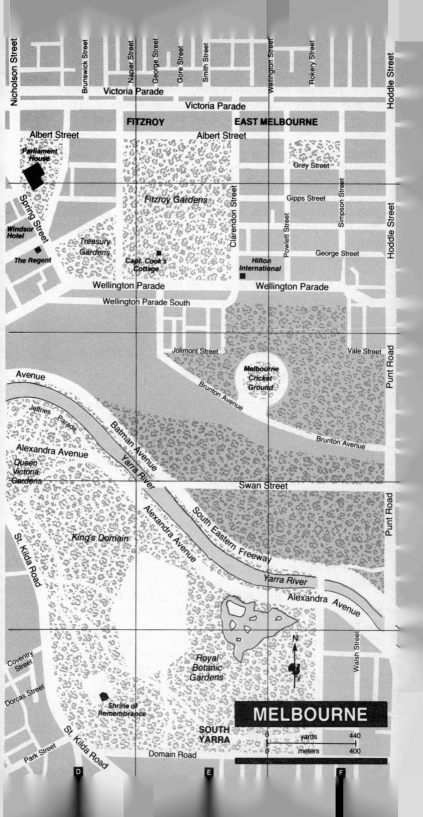

seats up to 36 and tourism officials suggest if you're interested, book well in advance. For reservations, phone 596-6500.

The Tram Car Restaurant picks up passengers at tram stop 12 on Nolan Street (adjacent to the National Gallery of Victoria on St. Kilda Road). Allow three hours for the moveable feast.

## Como House                                          SOUTH YARRA

Located just off busy Toorak Road in the suburb of South Yarra, this National Trust property extols the virtues of an earlier time when horses' hooves, not horse-powered engines, set the pace. The two-story, Victorian-era manse is filled with period furnishings and is surrounded by lovely gardens.

Como House is open daily except Christmas Day and Good Friday from 10 A.M. to 5 P.M. Admission charge is $4.50. Located on Como Avenue; visitors get there from the city by taking tram 8 and getting off at stop 30 on Toorak Road. For further information, call 241-2500. Allow one hour for the visit.

## Fitzroy and Treasury Gardens              FITZROY, P. 19, E2

These tree-lined gardens are located east of the downtown area just before the Hilton Hotel. Bordered by Spring, Wellington, Clarendon, Albert, and Lansdowne streets, they include everything from a J.F.K. memorial to the reconstructed cottage of Captain James Cook, the renowned British explorer who "discovered" much of Australia. There's a minimal charge for the cottage tour. Call 419-8742. No charge for gardens. For further information, call 658-9800.

## National Gallery of Victoria         MELBOURNE CENTER, P. 18, C4

This Kremlin-like building is far more enlightening than its forboding façade implies. Indeed, it was the first stage in the impressive Victorian Arts Centre complex and features everything from Renaissance masters to contemporary paintings, sculpture, and ceramics.

Located just south of the city at 180 St. Kilda Road (note: Swanston Street becomes St. Kilda Road just after it crosses the Yarra River), the gallery is an easy walk or an even quicker tram ride from the city. Allow about one hour to explore the exhibits. The gallery is open daily except Monday from 10 A.M. to 5 P.M. Admission is under $2. For further information, call 618-0222.

**Nearby:** King's Domain, Queen Victoria gardens, and the Victorian Arts Centre.

## Old Melbourne Gaol            MELBOURNE CENTER, P. 18, B1

This grim reminder of the country's convict roots is best known as the place where Australia's most notorious bushranger (outlaw), Ned Kelly, was hanged in 1880. The jail, which was in use until 1929, also includes other Kelly memorabilia as well as death masks of many early criminals, including a couple of American-born inmates.

The jail is located on Russell Street, across from the present-day police station, and is open from 10 A.M. to 4 P.M. daily except Christmas Day. Admission is $3.50. For further information, call 663-7228. Allow a half-hour or so for the tour.

## Parliament House    MELBOURNE CENTER, P. 19, D1

Built in 1856 during the height of the gold-rush fever in Victoria, this government building is probably the most lavish in the country, featuring, among other things, about $250,000 worth of gold leaf detail on the ceilings.

Tours are available of the Spring Street state government building weekdays at 11 A.M. and 2 P.M. while in session, and more frequently other times. No admission charged. For details, call 651-8911. Allow a half-hour for the tour.
**Nearby:** The Windsor Hotel and the Princess Theatre.

## Queen Victoria Market    MELBOURNE CENTER, P. 18, A1

This open-air bazaar rarely disappoints bargain hunters, whether they're looking for bananas, green beans, Australian wool hats, or sweaters.

The marketplace is open every day except Monday. Call ahead for opening and closing times: they vary somewhat from day to day. Phone 658-9800 for details. It is located at the corner of Elizabeth and Victoria streets in the northern tip of the city.

## Royal Botanic Gardens    SOUTH YARRA, P. 19, E5

Covering some eighty acres, this diverse landscape includes more than 12,000 species of native and exotic plants as well as flocks of colorful birds, including black swans. Located between Alexandra Avenue and Domain Road in South Yarra, the gardens are easily reached via tram from the city. Free tours are offered; for more information, phone 63-9424. Open daily from about 8 A.M. to dusk. Allow at least one hour for a short walk around the gardens or longer for a tour, and consider taking tea at the small kiosk located in the middle of the park. Take the number 8 tram from Swanston Street to Toorak Road; the conductor can advise you where to get off.
**Nearby:** Shrine of Remembrance, Government House, and Queen Victoria Gardens.

## Royal Melbourne
## Zoological Gardens    PARKVILLE

Opened in 1857, this is the third-oldest zoo in the world and features not only many of Australia's unique creatures but several other special exhibits as well. Perhaps the most unique of these is its cavernous walk-through butterfly enclosure, housing many of the country's brightly colored specimens.

Situated just north of the city on Elliott Avenue in the suburb of Parkville, the zoo is easily reached by taking either tram 55 or 56 from William Street or 18, 19, or 20 from Elizabeth Street in the city.

Allow plenty of time for exploring the zoo which is open daily from 9 A.M. to 5 P.M. Admission charge is about $5.50. For further information, call 347-1522.

## Shrine of Remembrance

MELBOURNE CENTER, P. 19, D5

Located between Domain and St. Kilda roads near the Royal Botanic Gardens; this pyramid-shaped shrine is a proud monument honoring the state's war dead. Inside the towering stone edifice, on the eleventh hour of November 11 (Armistice Hour), a ray of sunlight strikes the stone of remembrance.

There is no charge to visit the shrine, which is open every day except Christmas from 10 A.M. to 5 P.M. The shrine is reached by boarding nearly any tram heading south from the city along St. Kilda Road. Great views of the city are possible from its upper tiers. For further information, call 654-8415. Allow a half-hour for the visit.
**Nearby:** Royal Botanic Gardens.

## Tea at the Windsor

MELBOURNE CENTER, P. 19, D2

High tea at this Grand Old Lady of Melbourne hotels should be on every visitor's list. You'll be taken back to the days when Melbourne and Mother England were far closer. Tea is held from 2:30 to 6 P.M. The hotel is located at 103 Spring Street. Phone 653-0653 for further information.

## Tourist Tram

MELBOURNE CENTER

If you haven't time for the Colonial Tram Car Restaurant or feel too threatened by hopping aboard any of the regular electric cable cars, the state's Metropolitan Transit Authority operates another tram specifically for tourists.

It runs every day from the city, departing from the corner of Swanston and Victoria streets several times a day. Cost for the half-hour-or-so ride is only $2 and takes in many of Melbourne's most scenic areas. For further information, call 617-0900.

## Victorian Arts Centre

MELBOURNE CENTER, P. 18, C3

Located next to the National Gallery on St. Kilda Road, the arts center is best recognized by its roller-coaster-shaped roof. Guided tours lasting about one hour are offered of the Melbourne Concert Hall and State Theatre complex. Tours cost about $3. Open daily from 10:30 A.M. to 4:30 P.M. Closed Good Friday and Christmas Day. (It also has a marvelous restaurant for light lunch or dinner called The Vic.)

If you're interested in taking in a performance, telephone 11500 for tickets.

The arts center is easily reached by taking any tram heading south on St. Kilda Road or simply on foot by crossing the bridge over the Yarra River. For further information, call 617-8211.

**Nearby:** National Gallery of Victoria, King's Domain and Queen Victoria gardens.

### Young & Jackson's Hotel

MELBOURNE CENTER, P. 18, C3

A corner pub may seem like an unlikely place to gaze at paintings, but this historic hotel is home to Melbourne's most famous portrait: a full-length, milky-white nude known only as *Chloe.* Though more than one hundred years old, Chloe hasn't aged a bit since her birth in 1875 and has been the subject of countless toasts by servicemen and civilians alike.

The pub, now owned by Australian business tycoon Alan Bond (the bloke who briefly took the America's Cup Down Under), is located at the busy intersection of Swanston and Flinders streets, just across from the Flinders Street railway station. It's easy to spot—just look for the hotel with the huge Swan Premium beer sign on top. (Swan beer is another of Mr. Bond's products.) There is no admission charge, though it will cost a quid or two to sip a toast to Chloe.

---

# TRAVEL

Walking is by far the easiest way to get around Melbourne, though it is far from being the most adventurous. That is, unless you happen to be walking over the tracks on the Bourke St. Mall when a tram ambles along. More than one tourist has been seen scrambling to get out of the way as the tram rattled through the heart of the city's busy shopping district.

## Getting from the Airport

The city's main airport, Tullamarine, is about 19 km (12 miles) from downtown. Cabs cost roughly $1 per mile, but a far less expensive means of transport (if you are not in a hurry), is the Skybus Coach Service, operated jointly by the country's two prime domestic airlines, Ansett and Australian. This service leaves every half hour from both the city and the airport and picks up at many downtown hotels. The fare is about $6. These large, white coaches can be seen outside the departure areas at the two airlines' terminals. The ride into town takes about 35 minutes once they've made stops at both departure areas. If heading out of town, passengers are advised to give about two hours notice for a Skybus shuttle to collect and deliver them to the Franklin St. terminal. Phone 663-1400.

# Using the Trams

If you can't beat them, ride them, because Melbourne is probably the only city in the world that still relies on the century-old cable cars as its primary means of metropolitan transport. Indeed, the tracks cover some 225 km (140 miles) criss-crossing throughout the city, even extending to the foot of the Dandenong Ranges to the east and around the western side of Port Phillip Bay. More than 640 of the green and gold (Australia's national colors) trams run daily, so if you miss one there'll be another along shortly.

The so-called City Loop stations include the Flagstaff Station at the corner of LaTrobe and William sts., Parliament Station on Spring St., and the Museum Station at the corner of LaTrobe and Swanston sts. Trams stop around midnight; begin around 6 A.M.

For maps and other details on tram rates, drop by the MTA stand at the Royal Arcade, located opposite the Myer Department Store on the Bourke St. Mall. An all-day pass purchased from conductors aboard any tram costs about $2.40 and allows the holder access to any MTA vehicle (including buses or trains) for that day. (It does not include entry to the Tourist Tram, though.) For further information, phone 617-0900.

# Taking Taxis

Melbourne also is well served by several taxi companies. Their major advantage over public transport, of course, being their ability to get you from one place to another more quickly. It will, however, cost considerably more. Tipping is not required in Australia. Many riders who believe they were given prompt service, however, generally leave behind any coins from the fare as a show of appreciation—or if it's been a much longer ride, 10 percent of the total charge. Cab etiquette is fairly standard throughout Australia: single men may sit in front with the driver, but single women are probably wiser to take a back seat.

You can hail cabs in the street; restaurants and clubs will call one for you, too, if you'd like.

# Driving

If these forms of city transport seem too restrictive and you choose to leave the driving to yourself, beware of Melbourne's other unique feature: right-hand turns in the city are generally made from the left lane. That's right, you must get left if you want to make a right-hand turn. Still want to drive? If so, here are the names of three major car-rental agencies, which for about $60 a day can get you a suitable vehicle. (They also have airport check-in counters.) Avis, 689-7777; Budget, 320-6333; and Hertz, 663-6244.

# TOURING

For those who prefer having the locals show the way, Melbourne has a handful of organized tour companies to contact. Most of them offer extremely personalized tours so don't expect them to jump for joy when you call up with a busload of convention delegates in tow.

One city tour that can handle a crowd, however, is the double-decker **City Explorer Bus.** Offered by the well-known local coach company, Australian Pacific, the bus departs Flinders St. Station on the hour 10 A.M.–4 P.M., daily except Mon. The charge is $10 per person and includes stops at Captain Cook's Cottage, Old Melbourne Gaol, Royal Melbourne Zoological Gardens, and the Victorian Arts Centre, to name a few. Passengers are able to leave or board the bus at any of these points, take a tour, and simply catch a later coach. For further information, call 650-1511.

A far less frenzied city tour is offered by **Cobb & Co. Horse-Drawn Carriages.** As the name implies, this tour's vehicles are outfitted with iron hooves instead of steel-belted radials. Americans may appreciate the fact that the company takes its name from the country's original commercial transport operation, set up by fellow Yank, Freeman Cobb, in 1853. The company's most popular tours are half-hour spins by such points of interest as Parliament House, Flinders St. Station, and down Little Bourke St.'s Chinatown. Cost of the trip is about $50 for the entire coach.

Cobb & Co. also offers a four-hour tour (minimum of 10 passengers), which, in addition to the sites mentioned above, passes by the Royal Botanic Gardens, Shrine of Remembrance, and Victorian Arts Centre complex and includes a picnic lunch along the Yarra River. Cost is $30 per person. For further information, call 338-7050.

At the extreme other end of the personalized tour spectrum is **Friends in Town,** which for a substantially higher fee ($151 per person), offers a day-long look at Melbourne. Their tour, which can handle between 2 and 22 people, focuses on fewer sites than other companies, but each one is certainly worth the visit. These include the National Gallery of Victoria, Como House, and the Royal Melbourne Zoological Gardens. For many, the highlight of the trip is lunch at a private home in the trendy suburb of Toorak, as well as high tea later in the afternoon.

Friends in Town also goes farther afield and offers day tours to such Victorian favorites as Phillip Island, site of the nightly fairy Penguin Parade, Sovereign Hill, a re-created gold-mining town in nearby Ballarat, and a look at some of the beautiful high mountain country in the northeastern corner of the state. Call 51-8877 for further information.

For the most detailed look at inner city buildings and monuments, as well as colorful historical commentary, though, book a tour with Maxine Wood's Melbourne—**Out & About Heritage Walks.** Maxine's love of the city (even though she originally hails from arch-rival Sydney), comes through easily and often during any one of her ninety-minute tours. Historical gems are Maxine's stock in trade. For example: Melbourne could have been founded thirty years earlier by Lt. David Collins in 1801, but he found it unworthy of settlement. Melbourne's forefathers exhibited much class by still naming one of the city's main boulevards, Collins St., after him.

Then, too, statues, which can leave most people cold, come to life with Maxine. Across the street from the Windsor Hotel is a statue of the Australian poet, Adam Lindsay Gordon (more notable elsewhere as Lord Byron's cousin). The statue won a British Society of Sculptors award in the 1930s, but was later revoked because the pencil held in the hand of Gordon was in fact a "modern" writing utensil. The wrong has since been righted.

Maxine's tours cost about $15 per person. Other city tours, as well as activities to meet the special needs of conference delegates and other large groups, can also be arranged. Tel. 241-1085 for further information.

---

# ❦ HOTELS

The first thing to remember about hotels in Australia (as in other British colonies), is that not every building with "hotel" on it necessarily offers overnight accommodation. Many, in fact, are not guesthouses at all but just the local pub.

When you do find a suitable place to rest your head, here are some other pointers about Australian overnight spots: tipping, as elsewhere mentioned, is not expected like it is in other parts of the world. Only if you were extremely impressed by the service.

All major hotels are air-conditioned, have modern conveniences such as color televisions, in-house movie channels, hair dryers, refrigerators, coffee and tea-making facilities, and mini-bars. (These alcoholic offerings, unlike all other services, are not free of charge.) Many medium- and lower-priced lodges mentioned here include most of the above except mini-bars and in rarer instances, televisions and air-conditioning.

Unless otherwise specified, all places listed accept every major credit card (AE—American Express, MC—MasterCard, V—Visa).

Room rates have been based on double occupancy and do not include top-of-the-range suites.

Hotels are keyed in to sections of the city and the color map using the same method followed in Priorities above.

## Top of the Line

At Melbourne's Top of the Line hotels, expect to pay about $185–$450 a night. In addition to the modern conveniences listed above, these properties often include extras such as swimming pools, saunas, spas, and gym facilities, 24-hour room service and business-related services like telex, fax, and photocopying.

The top seven hotels are listed here in alphabetical order.

### Hilton On the Park          EAST MELBOURNE, P. 19, E2
192 Wellington Pde., East Melbourne 3002; (03) 419-3311, telex HIMEL 33057, fax (03) 419-5630.

The first thing to understand about this hotel is that it is *not* a part of the U.S. Hilton chain, having long since dropped the connection. Rates for a double room run **$195–$215 per night.**

What the 406-room hotel may lack in flashy decor (though it is by no means cheap or old-fashioned), the Hilton more than makes up for with prompt, courteous service by everyone from the doorman to the house maid.

Though not in the downtown district, the Hilton is an easy ten-minute walk or tram ride away in the classy neighborhood of East Melbourne. (Note: if not in a hurry, just cross the road and walk to the city via the Fitzroy and Treasury gardens.)

Best room views are found at the front of the building, if you can overlook the ugly network of train lines found in the city's rail yard. The view includes the Melbourne Cricket Ground, National Tennis Centre, Government House, and the Royal Botanic Gardens.

The Hilton is particularly well suited for business clients, with an entire floor set aside for them. Facilities include telex, fax, photocopying, personal computer, stock market report, secretarial service, and use of board room if necessary.

The hotel includes a roof-top pool with barbecue facility, as well as several restaurants, the main dining area of which, The Cliveden Room, is listed in the restaurant section.

## Hyatt-on-Collins
MELBOURNE CENTER, P. 18, C2

123 Collins St., Melbourne 3000; (03) 657-1234, telex 38796, fax (03) 650-3491.

Like many members in this exclusive hotel chain, the Melbourne property emphasizes cascading waterfalls and marble floors in the main entrance area.

This Hyatt is located at the top, or so-called Paris End, of Collins Street, renowned for its trendy fashion boutiques, leather designers, and art galleries.

Its 580 rooms are well appointed and hotel staff members are proud of their express check-out service. (Patrons with vehicles should be advised that there is a $12 charge for overnight parking.) Rates for double rooms range **$165–$260** (with weekday rates being at the higher end).

Highlights include roof-top tennis court, aerobics studio, flotation tank, and other fitness facilities. You may need these services after indulging in the adjoining food court. (One highly recommended food stand is Bloom's Deli, where for about $12, two or more can feast on a platter of pastrami, corned beef, ham, turkey, swiss cheese, and the like.)

The hotel's main dining area, known as Max's Restaurant, is recognized as one of the city's finest (and most expensive) places to dine.

## Menzies at Rialto
MELBOURNE CENTER, P. 18, A3

495 Collins St., Melbourne 3000; (03) 620-9111, telex 136189, fax (03) 614-1219.

Located at the end of Collins Street opposite the Hyatt, in the Wall Street (financial) district, the Menzies at Rialto combines the opulence of the newer hotels with the charm of the older establishments. The feeling is achieved through the connecting of two neo-Gothic, 19th-century buildings with a glass roof above and cobblestones below.

Each of its 243 rooms is spacious and outfitted in dark-veneered, sturdy furnishings, mushroom-pink carpeting and wall covering. Rates: **$125–$215;** weekday rates are at the higher end. The Menzies is very popular with business travelers, tourists, and international cricketers, who when they are not at the cricket ground, can be found near one of the hotel's many watering holes. The Menzies has placed special emphasis on handling the needs of handicapped patrons, particularly on the lower levels of the hotel.

The Menzies has a marvelous atrium dining/bar area, which also leads to its only drawback—namely, crowd noise. This can sometimes be a concern to light sleepers, so request a room on one of the higher floors or on the outer part of the building.

The hotel's elegant Chandelier Room offers fine French cuisine and excellent service at about $40 per person for a three-course meal. (Add about $20 for a good bottle of Australian wine.)

## Parkroyal                    MELBOURNE CENTER
562 St. Kilda Rd., Melbourne 3004; (03) 529-8888, telex 152242, fax (03) 525-1242.

Visitors to this 220-room hotel, located on St. Kilda Road about seven minutes by tram from the most central area of the city, are first struck by the light, airy atmosphere best exemplified by the long front windows and bright marble floors. The decor is decidedly Asian with Colonial Oriental furnishings, including large screens in the foyers. Room color schemes are in various pastel shades of pink, green, blue, and orange.

The best views are found in the corner "king" rooms which look down St. Kilda Rd. to the city. Rates run **$106–$175** (weekdays on the higher end).

The hotel prides itself on personalized service for both holiday-makers and business clients alike. One nice touch is that all rooms come with iron and ironing board for those last-second suit and dress presses.

The hotel's bistro is perfect for breakfast or lunch as well as a New York–style Sunday brunch smorgasbord. The Parkroyal's formal dining room is recognized as probably the city's finest hotel French restaurant.

## The Regent              MELBOURNE CENTER, P. 19, D2
25 Collins St., Melbourne 3000; (03) 653-0000, telex 37724, fax (03) 650-4261.

This impressive fifty-floor facility thrilled Melburnians when it was built, as much for its grand scale (at least by Australian standards), as for its great city views—especially from the loos on the 35th floor!

Located just up the road from the Hyatt, The Regent is considered one of the city's best. Rooms are well equipped and decorated in light, soft colorings of peach, apricot, and blue. Marble dominates the bathrooms.

The 363 rooms do not begin until the 36th floor (offices and convention facilities are on 1–35), so views of the city abound from any unit. An open dining area on the 35th floor, though, should encourage guests to ask for rooms on the highest floor available. Rates for doubles run around **$170–$245.**

All of the restaurants are professionally run and well decorated; try high afternoon tea at the Green Room, which (like other such rooms around the world) isn't green at all. Other highlights include extensive services for business clients and a health club.

Staff members are also keen to point out the hotel's use of real wooden closet hangers and toasters in every room to ensure no one must spread their vegemite on a cold, hard piece of bread. One strike against The Regent, like its neighbor the Hyatt, is the parking garage charge for overnight guests.

## Rockman's Regency Hotel

MELBOURNE CENTER, P. 18, C1

Corner Exhibition and Lonsdale sts., Melbourne 3000; (03) 662-3900, telex 38890, fax (03) 663-4297.

This compact-sized hotel has long been considered the city's leader in service and personal attention to guests. Soon after walking in the front entrance, guests are made to feel more as if they were at home than at a hotel. Indeed, the reception area is filled with thick, dark carpeting, soft leather lounges, and lots of fresh flowers. While checking in, guests are served a glass of freshly squeezed orange juice.

Though there is nothing particularly notable about the hotel's location or the views from its 185 rooms, it is, more times than not, the overnight selection of many leading Australian businesspeople and international celebrities (just check the walls in the cozy Regency Bar for the hundreds of autographed black-and-white photos). Rates: **$150–$235.**

The basic units in the hotel are small but come with en suite dressing areas and separate sinks. The hotel prides itself on extras, including free morning paper (personalized with your name and weather forecast on the front); an umbrella for those less-sunny days in unpredictable Melbourne; and a wide range of toiletries.

Rockman's restaurants are of an equally high standard. It and the Hyatt and Regent hotels comprise the three most expensive properties in the city.

## The Windsor

MELBOURNE CENTER, P. 19, D2

103 Spring St., Melbourne 3000; (03) 653-0653, telex 30437, fax (03) 654-5183.

Long recognized as Melbourne's Grand Old Lady, The Windsor is the last remaining hotel property to recall the era in which Australia's ties to Mother England were far tighter, indeed. Located opposite the Parliament House and Treasury Building, The Windsor has always attracted many of the country's leading political and literary figures, both as a wonderful place to dine and to have a social drink or two.

The Windsor carries with it an Old World charm and dignity; many of its upper-priced suites include separate dining rooms and working fireplace. Rates on weekdays: **$245–$285; $170–$210** on weekends.

No visitor should leave Melbourne without experiencing high tea at The Windsor, served daily 2:30–6 P.M. Anglophiles should not miss the opportunity to stop by the Cricketer's Bar, long heralded as one of the city's most famous watering holes. It features several pieces of cricket memorabilia, including photographs from the 1884 English tour of Australia. The hosts' caption reads simply, "Australian," while the visitors are referred to as the "Gentlemen from England"—there were apparently no gentlemen on the Australian side!

The restaurants are all tastefully decorated, while the main area, the Grand Dining Room, is still considered one of the city's key places to be seen.

## Moderate

These hotels range $80–$170. The listings include all-suite hotels or serviced apartments as well as one elegant bed-and-breakfast–style property.

### Oakford Executive Apartments

32 Queens Road, Melbourne 3004; (03) 267-6511, telex 154492/Oakex.

Oakford is the leader in the rapid growth of all-suite hotels in Australia. Featuring three hundred rooms in several locations around the city, Oakford specializes in offering guests more than just a room to sleep in. The units are far more like furnished apartments than hotel rooms, including many standard features, such as color televisions and direct-dial telephone service. Many properties include pool, barbecue facilities, and tennis courts, too. Depending on which property you choose, rates run **$75–$180.**

About the only drawback is the weekly cleaning service, though daily service is available at additional charge.

### Sheraton                    MELBOURNE CENTER, P. 19, D2

13 Spring St., Melbourne 3000; (03) 650-5000, telex 31021, fax (03) 650-9622.

Like its sister across the gardens in East Melbourne, the Hilton, this property is not part of the well-known hotel chain its name implies.

Instead, it is a far more modest (in both price and appearance) hotel that recently had a major refurbishing of its 166 rooms, restaurant, cocktail lounge, and conference center. The rooms are spacious and outfitted with simple, comfortable furnishings. Doubles cost around **$190.**

Situated near the bottom of Spring St., the Sheraton offers great views of many city treasures, such as the Treasury Gardens and the Melbourne Cricket Ground. There is a brochure available detailing nearby jogging tracks. For a small charge, the kitchen crew will even send you packing to any of the nearby gardens with a picnic hamper of gourmet goodies.

### South Yarra Hill Suites            SOUTH YARRA

14 Murphy St., South Yarra 3141; (03) 268-8222, telex 136157, fax (03) 820-1724.

These serviced apartments are located just off Melbourne's trendiest boulevard, Toorak Rd. The area is well serviced by both train and tram lines for those who need to go downtown, but avid clothes shoppers should look no farther than around the corner for some of Australia's prime design houses.

The 107 rooms are well appointed with modern conveniences, including dishwashers, microwaves, and daily cleaning service. Deluxe rooms (and those more expensive) include spa baths. Continental breakfast included, too. Rates: **$95–$110.**

There are extensive facilities for business clients, including telex, fax, photocopying, secretarial services, and a meeting room for small conferences and social functions, as well as free use of limousine service. Heated salt-water pool and other exercise facilities are available, too.

## The Tilba                                       SOUTH YARRA
30 Toorak Rd. West, South Yarra 3141; (03) 267-8844, fax (03) 267-6567.

The Tilba is a gracious Victorian-era home that looks as though it could have been the backdrop for *Upstairs-Downstairs.* Each of its 14 rooms has been decorated individually, but most seem to have high ceilings, soothing color schemes, and lots of flowers, both fresh and dried, throughout the interior.

There are no television sets, but guests often find their way to the comfortable lounge area if they are in need of company. On retiring for the night, guests find a jug of iced water with a twist of lemon and delicate chocolates. Complimentary breakfast features freshly squeezed orange juice, croissants, brioches or bagels, and a hot cup of tea or freshly brewed coffee. Rates: **$90–$120.**

The Tilba is located near the corner of Toorak and St. Kilda roads, the main southern artery into the city. For joggers, there is a beautiful park located across the street.

# Budget
Despite the relatively cheaper price for a room in these hotels (most standard rooms cost no more than $80), neither Magnolia Court nor the Victoria Hotel should be considered unsuitable overnight spots. In fact, both have advantages in locations and amenities over some higher-priced properties.

## Magnolia Court                              EAST MELBOURNE
101 Powlett St., East Melbourne 3002; (03) 419-4222, telex MAGCRT 154435.

This is a stunning Victorian-era boutique hotel situated in historic East Melbourne. Many of its 25 rooms have been restored with period furnishings to the time the property was a ladies college in the 1860s.

Styled after the boutique-hotel concept in the United States, Magnolia Court is very long on personalized attention and details—like lots of bath towels! Rates run **$75–$80** per night.

Unlike those in some other smaller hotels, Magnolia Court's rooms come with color televisions, refrigerators, and hair dryers. The property also has an outdoor spa and a quaint breakfast nook.

## The Victoria Hotel

MELBOURNE CENTER, P. 18, C2

215 Little Collins St., Melbourne 3000; (03) 653-0441, toll-free reservations tel. (008) 33-1147, telex 31264.

Though far from seeing its best days, The Victoria Hotel offers visitors reasonably priced rooms in a central-city location. Just a charge card or two away, for instance, is Georges, Melbourne's most prestigious shopping store, as well as an equally pricey group of stores known, aptly enough, as the Shop of Shops.

For truly budget-conscious travelers (rates: **$44–83**), the hotel has rooms with shared bathroom facilities. For just a few dollars more, though, you can stay in a recently refurbished room (ask for a unit in the new wing). These rooms include air-conditioning and color television.

The other great thing about The Victoria is that with 520 rooms, you're bound to get a place to stay no matter how busy the city gets.

# Melbourne Center

Though a small struggling community soon after its founding in 1835 by a Tasmanian farmer named John Batman, the hub of Victoria soon developed an identity quite apart from its two older rivals, Sydney and Hobart.

For one thing, the town's founders refused convict ships, allowing only free citizens to come ashore. The most dramatic change in Melbourne's fortunes, however, occurred almost overnight in 1851 when gold was discovered at nearby Ballarat, boosting its population from about 225 in 1836 to 76,000 just 15 years later!

By 1860 Melbourne had a settled air. The city had been sensibly laid out on the banks of the Yarra River, with wide, straight streets lit by gaslight, and already there was a university, a public library, a Parliament House, a chain of trading banks, and public gardens filled with imported trees. At the Royal Theatre, which seated 4,000, one paid twelve guineas for a box when Catherine Hayes, the reigning prima donna, was singing, and there were half a dozen other theatres presenting Shakespeare, Sheridan and vaudeville—a great change from the days when the theatre was merely an annexe to the pub and no respectable woman could go there. The Cremorne Gardens (a model of those in London) provided another theatre, waxworks, a dance-hall, a menagerie and such entertainments as brass bands, balloon ascents and displays of fireworks. Horse-racing had a mass following, and the Melbourne Cup was about to be run for the first time. When an important game of cricket was being played at the Melbourne Cricket Ground Parliament suspended its sittings until the evening.

—Alan Moorehead
*Cooper's Creek,* 1963

While the streets may not have been paved with gold, many buildings such as **Parliament House,** located at the upper east side of the city on Spring Street, were decorated in thousands of dollars worth of gold leaf. Tours of the well-preserved statehouse are conducted daily at 11 A.M. and 2 P.M. while in session and more frequently other times. No admission is charged; for details call: 651-8911.

Many other historic Victorian-era buildings also are found at this end of the city, including the grand **Windsor Hotel,** which dates to 1883, the **Treasury Building** (1857), and the **Princess Theatre** (1887).

The old English ways and traditions are still maintained fairly rigorously at **The Windsor,** which is a top spot for a cup of tea and finger sandwiches. Afternoon tea is served daily 2:30–6 P.M.

After tea, head north along Spring Street until coming to Little Bourke Street. To your left will be Melbourne's **Chinatown,** a dizzying collection of Asian restaurants and shops that runs along the small, one-way road from Spring to Swanston streets.

Melbourne's prime **shopping and business districts** are found in the heart of the city, bordered by Flinders, Spring, Lonsdale, and Queen streets. The Southern Hemisphere's largest department store, **Myer,** is found in the middle of the pedestrians-only (except for trams!) segment of the **Bourke Street Mall.** Souvenir hunters may enjoy stopping by Myer's Australiana section, filled with everything from stuffed koalas to boomerangs. It is reached by entering Myer from the Little Bourke Street entrance.

Melbourne is also known for its wealth of shopping arcades, the two most notable being the **Block** and **Royal Arcades,** located between Collins and Bourke streets. These narrow walk-through areas are known, not only for their grand Victorian-style architecture, but for their quaint cafés, exclusive men's and women's boutiques, and old curiosity shops. Then, too, the arcades are great places to duck into when one of Melbourne's notorious rain showers passes overhead.

The city's most exclusive shopping area, however, is **Collins Street,** Melbourne's answer to New York's Fifth Avenue. Here, particularly from Swanston Street up to the so-called Paris End at Spring Street, are some of the city's priciest outlets, including **Georges** (162 Collins Street; 653-0411), which offers very fine clothing, fragrances, and jewelry, and across the way, **The Shop of Shops** (171 Collins Street; 650-5511), a collection of specialty and designer shops (such as Pierre Cardin), an imported men's shoe store, and an up-market Australiana shop called Thingummybob.

After dropping a bob or two at these shops, head for the nearby **Hyatt-On-Collins Hotel** (123 Collins St.) and stop by the marble-laden **food court** for a bite to eat or drink. It's one of Melbourne's most popular gathering places for weary shoppers, business lunches, and après-work meeting spots.

If time allows, two other open arcades worth a look are the shops along **Hardware Street,** a narrow thoroughfare between Lonsdale and Bourke streets, and **McKillop Street,** between Bourke and Little Collins streets. These two brick-paved alleyways are filled with little bookstores, outdoor shops, and bistros. One shop in particular to look for is **Craft Link,** the Arts & Crafts Society of Victoria's outlet at 37 Hardware Street. It features many fine pieces of pottery and hand-made clothing items, such as sweaters and kerchiefs.

For shoppers on the run, McKillop St. has a lovely collection of cuisines under one roof. Known as the **McKillop Food Hall,** diners may order everything from pastas to spring rolls, and either eat it there or take away.

Another mecca for shoppers is the nearby **Queen Victoria Market,** located at the northwestern edge of town. This is a great place to go for bargains on everything from kangaroo-leather wallets to Aussie wool hats. The marketplace is open every day but Mondays. Call 658-9800 for further information. Then, too, along the far northern side of the market, on Victoria Street, is a collection of brick-front shops that offer everything from Australian handcrafts to specialty gift shops and souvenirs. Antique lovers need not feel left out either; the nearby **Queen Victoria Antique Shop** at 114 Franklin Street (phone: 328-1461), sells everything from old books and Victorian-era furniture to second-hand clothing and Aboriginal tribal art. The cavernous shop is open daily from 9:30 A.M. to 5:30 P.M.

Another downtown shop to head for if it's Aboriginal artifacts you're after is the **Aboriginal Handcrafts** shop, located on the ninth floor of the Century Building at 125–133 Swanston Street. Open Monday through Friday, the tiny shop packs a wide variety of Aboriginal art and handcrafts, including boomerangs, bark paintings, bush-string bags, and didgeridoos, the traditional tribal woodwind instrument fashioned from a portion of a small tree trunk. For details call: 650-4717.

Just down from this building, at the corner of Swanston and Flinders streets, is the well-known **Flinders Street Station,** Melbourne's century-old French Renaissance-style railway building, with its copper dome and large clock faces. Here, thousands of commuters emerge from the tunnels each morning to make their way to work. The station is probably the city's most famous meeting place as many a Melbourne couple have met "under the clocks" to begin an evening on the town.

Just across the way is the city's venerable **Yarra River,** the southern border of the city center area, jokingly referred to as the waterway that flows upside down, or, by the even less kind, the river too thick to drink and too thin to walk on. It is not as filthy as its dark-brown, muddied waters suggest, and in recent years its shores have become a popular venue for picnics, joggers, and cyclists as well as for riverboat cruises and boat-launched barbecues.

Many visitors also enjoy stopping by the **Victorian Arts Centre** complex, located a few yards away from the Yarra.

In addition to guided tours of the complex, which includes the fabulous Melbourne Concert Hall and the Theatres building with its Eiffel Tower-like spire, the center features a marvelous eatery called **The Vic,** which is great for both light lunches and dinners. Several bars also are found at the Arts Centre, situated at 100 St. Kilda Rd.; 617-8211.

Culture lovers may also like stopping by the **National Gallery of Victoria,** located right next door to the Arts Centre. For details on current exhibitions, call 618-0222.

Finally, if these offerings seem too taxing or ambitious, Melbourne also is graced with many gardens and parks. One in every five acres of city soil, in fact, features displays of indigenous flowers, shrubs and trees, guaranteed to give you a life before returning to some guided tour, shopping spree, or restaurant.

One of the city's most popular garden spots is the 535-acre **King's Domain,** located on St. Kilda Road across from the Arts Centre complex. In addition to free open-air concerts at the Sidney Myer Music Bowl during the summer months, the finely groomed garden also is home to a large statue dedicated to the Garden State's namesake, Queen Victoria.

## Carlton

Though perhaps not as well defined as the Italian neighborhoods found in cities like New York or Boston, Melbourne's Little Italy is still well worth a visit.

In fact, Carlton represents one of the city's older settlements by European migrants, many of whom came here in the 1950s. In that relatively short period of time, the area's old Irish and English atmosphere has given way to exclusive Italian designer clothing boutiques, spaghetti bars, and gelati ice-cream shops.

Most of these establishments are found on Lygon Street (stop 12 on tram 15 as it heads north on Swanston Street from the city).

🏇 **Jimmy Watson's** (333 Lygon St., 347-3985) is one of the city's oldest and most colorful wine bars, specializing in luncheon buffets. It is a licensed restaurant open Mon.–Fri. 10 A.M.–6 P.M., and 10 A.M.–1 P.M. on Sat. (No credit cards are accepted.) The **Lygon Food Store** (263 Lygon St., 347-6279) is packed with more than seven hundred different types of cheeses and other gourmet food items. It is open every day but Sun.

The area also is filled with many good places to grab a table, order an espresso or cappuccino, and gaze at the passersby.

Points of interest to look for during the short tram ride from the city to Carlton are the **City Baths,** located at the corner of Swanston and Franklin streets, a colorful turn-of-the-century building that remains in use as a health and fitness center, and the **Carlton & United Brewery,** maker of Foster's beer.

## South Yarra/Toorak

By far the trendiest area in Melbourne and perhaps Australia, this is the place to head for if you like looking at Victorian-era terrace homes standing next to contemporary palatial estates.

All you need ask for is directions to **Toorak Road** (the 8 tram rattles right along it), which is lined with many of Australia's leading fashion designers' outlets like **Prue Acton, Carla Zampatti,** and **Adele Palmer.** (Tell the conductor you want to get off at stop 33, or Grange Road.)

Then, too, Toorak Road is filled with sidewalk cafés, coffee bars, and New York–style delis all vying to gain the number-one ranking as the "in" place to be seen.

For those in need of a cultural lift, don't pass up a tour of **Como House** (see Priorities listing), which is near stop 30 on Como Avenue. The Victorian-era home has period furnishing and pleasant gardens. Open daily 10 A.M. to 5 P.M.; there's an admission charge; telephone 241-2500.

## Armadale

Two things come to mind when Melburnians think of this southeastern suburb: High Street, its main thoroughfare, and antiques.

There are more than one hundred **antique dealers** in this region, covering every imaginable area of interest, ranging from antique jewelers and print galleries to two hundred-year-old colonial furniture dealers and ageless Persian rug merchants. If you're visiting Melbourne in early September, you may wish to make a special trip to Armadale; that is when the annual antique dealers' fair is held at the Malvern Town Hall (at the corner of High Street and Glenferrie Road).

**High Street** also is known for its abundance of sidewalk cafés, sushi bars, and high-style fashion designers. Look for **King's Arcade,** located near the corner of High Street and Kooyong Road, a superbly renovated 1893 building, housing a wide range of specialty shops.

High Street also is home to the **Australiana General Store** (1227 High Street, 20-2324), which offers shoppers many Aussie-made gifts, including Goanna Salve (an old-fashioned Aussie treatment for aches and pains; a "goanna" is a lizard—but there is no real lizard in the salve), Billy Tea (Billy Tea is what you drink over the fire in the Outback; a "billy" is a small tin bucket used for heating over the fire), and, of course, stuffed koalas.

To reach High Street in Armadale, simply board tram 6 in the city and get off either at stop 37 or 40. These two stops represent either end of the busiest stretch of High Street.

# St. Kilda

There's really no easy way to describe St. Kilda to newcomers. On the one hand, it caters to students, young professionals, and first-generation immigrants in much the same way the Greenwich Village area of New York does. On the other hand, its main drag, **Fitzroy Street,** is renowned for its 42nd Street–type atmosphere. Street-walkers and low-grade drug dealers can often be seen here after dusk amid all the brightly lit neon signs.

By day, though, Fitzroy Street is fairly quiet and leads toward some of Melbourne's more popular beaches and Luna Park, an eighty-year-old amusement park best known for its toothy-grinned façade.

On Sundays, some of the sidewalks are stacked with craftspeople selling wares such as fine leather garments and gumleaf necklaces. This weekly bazaar is known as the **Esplanade market** and is well worth the effort for browsers and buyers alike.

🐎 Walking along the footpaths is also a good way to work off the sumptuous cakes and other desserts found on nearby **Acland St.** Though these shops are open all week long, Sun. is when Melburnians flock to Acland St. to sample their favorite desserts and pastries. Some of the more famous Acland St. sweet-tooth havens are the **Creme Puff, Europa,** and **Acland cake shops.**

The main St. Kilda route by tram is the same one that goes to Carlton, number 15; only passengers should make sure they're heading south. The ride takes about thirty minutes and it's easiest to get off at stop 28, Fitzroy Street.

# SHOPPING

Whether you're looking for Aboriginal artifacts or Akubra hats, Ken Done T-shirts, or Billy Tea leaves, Melbourne's got them all in just as wide a variety of shops and department stores. In fact, Melbourne has long been considered Australia's mecca for shoppers—though Sydneysiders may debate this.

The prime downtown shopping area is along the **Bourke Street Mall,** a brick-paved, pedestrians-only collection of large retail stores like **Myer,** the largest department store in the southern hemisphere, and right next door, **David Jones,** another larger retail outlet. A few blocks away is **David Wang & Co.** (139 Little Bourke St; 663-2111), the city's largest Far Eastern emporium, offering everything from carpets and clothing to delicate jade jewelry and large pieces of furniture.

On nearby Collins Street, a stone's throw from the Hyatt and Regent hotels, are two of Melbourne's most exclusive shops, **Georges,** which would have to be considered the city's classiest retail store, beloved by both older, establishment and yuppie patrons alike (162 Collins Street, 653-0411). Across the street is a collection of the trendiest clothing and specialty stores, known as the **Shop of Shops** (171 Collins Street, 650-5511). For those still with a farthing or two to spend, the **Hyatt-on-Collins** and **Regent hotels** likewise feature very pricey leather and shoe shops and jewelry stores.

Another highlight of the Melbourne shopping scene is its vast number of walk-through arcades, brimming with smaller retail stores and old curiousity shops. Many of these sky-lit venues, such as the **Royal** and **Block arcades,** are found between Collins and Bourke streets.

Still another feature of Melbourne is its collection of unusual bazaars, ranging from the **St. Kilda Esplanade Art & Craft Market** every Sunday (for details, phone 536-1333), to the king of them all, the **Queen Victoria Market.** This huge, open-air marketplace is open every day but Monday (see Priorities for details), and offers everything from food produce to bargain-priced clothes and souvenirs.

Another crowd favorite is the **Meat Market Craft Centre,** found on Courtney Street in North Melbourne. Under timber-lined ceilings and next to name plates of long-since-retired butchers, some of Melbourne's finest craftsmen exhibit their wares. Open daily. For further details, phone 329-9966.

For those wishing to buy true-blue **Australian goods** such as pure wool sweaters (called jumpers in Australia), Akubra hats, or the unique bush raincoats, cheekily called Drizabones, there are several outlets, including the Australiana General Store in Armadale (see Armadale section for details), and Morrison's Australia at 462 Chapel St., South Yarra; 241-8255.

Two other specialties of great interest to tourists are Aboriginal arts and crafts and opals. Both markets are well served in Melbourne, though shoppers are encouraged to look around before buying. For **Aboriginal crafts** featuring contemporary and traditional arts and crafts go to Aboriginal Handcrafts, Century Building, 9th floor, 125 Swanston Street; 650-4717. Open most days.

**Opals** likewise are available from several sources. Two of the city's more well-known gem dealers are Altmann & Cherny and Gemtec, located next to each other on Exhibition Street (numbers 120 and 124). Both establishments offer in-depth information and background on the history of opals in Australia and can point out what makes some stones more precious than others. Don't expect any bargain deals, though. Contact numbers for these stores are: Altmann & Cherny, 650-9685; and Gemtec, 654-5733.

Serious shoppers will have to comb the outer suburbs for real **bargains** at shops like Rodos Souvenirs (583 Plenty Road in East Preston northeast of Melbourne; take the number 88 tram; 478-3388). This shop specializes in Australiana gifts such as sheepskin boots, tea towels, swagman dolls, and boomerangs.

More recently, several companies devoted to **shopping tours** have sprung up in Melbourne. Probably the best known is Pamm's Shopping Tours (telephone: 592-6911), which, for about $30, guarantees bargain hunters up to 50 percent discounts on merchandise. Day tours include lunch plus morning or afternoon tea. For those with limited time, the company's creator, American-born Pamm Durkin, even has a guide to discount shopping in Melbourne available at airports and certain bookshops.

## SPORTS

In a country that is renowned for being sports crazy, Melbourne may be the maddest place of all. Indeed, the Victorian capital is home to the country's answer to the Kentucky Derby—the Melbourne Cup—as well as boasting Australia's most celebrated cricket field, and more recently, the brand new National Tennis Centre, home of the Australian Open.

The city's most notable sporting venue would have to be the **Melbourne Cricket Ground,** more commonly referred to as the MCG, which is often the place for the Australian national cricket team's key match with sides from other countries in summertime, or the site for many lively games of Australian Rules Football during the autumn and winter months. It can reputedly hold up to 120,000, but for those visitors looking to find the more outrageous sports followers, head for the section called Bay 13, where the matches often take a back seat to the goings-on in the stands. For details on match times and prices, call 654-6066. The MCG is on Brunton Avenue, in the inner suburb of Jolimont, near East Melbourne.

The game Melbourne is probably receiving the most international interest for, however, is **Aussie Rules Football,** or "footy," a non-stop, hard-hitting game that makes American football look tame in comparison. Originally started in 1858 as a form of off-season exercise for cricketers, the game's last match of the year, known as the Grand Final, has a Super Bowl aura about it. Footy fever has even caught on in the United States, Europe, and Japan where several matches are now shown each season. Games are played between April and September while cricket runs from October to March.

Not far from the MCG is the country's most exciting new venue, the **National Tennis Centre,** which sports a retractable roof over center court as well as several adjoining tennis surfaces. This center, located in Flinders Park, also has usurped long-time home of the Australian Open, Kooyong, to become the permanent site of the prestigious Grand Slam event, held mid to late January. For details, phone 654-1234.

Both the National Tennis Centre and the MCG can be easily reached by taking tram 75 from the city down Flinders Street.

Melbourne is also home to some of the country's keenest horse racing at the **Flemington Racecourse,** located just 3½ kilometers (two miles) from the city. While punters (bettors) go there regularly during the year, the horse-racing season heats up during the Spring Racing Carnival, reaching its climax the first Tuesday in November. This is **Melbourne Cup** day, which for well over a century has attracted worldwide attention as much for the brilliant horses and riders as for the day-long champagne picnics and track-goers dressed in their finest finery.

## Melbourne Cup

All eyes are on Melbourne throughout the country on Melbourne Cup day, the first Tuesday in November, which has become such an event that wise politicos long ago decided to give everyone the day off—since little work would be accomplished anyway. The Cup has long enjoyed its notoriety as well, gaining early accolades from famous visitors like Mark Twain who dropped by in 1895 and could think of no other single event like it anywhere else in the world.

The track is reached by taking the Broadmeadow line from the Flinders Street station and getting off at Flemington Station. Phone 376-0441 for further information.

With more than fifty **golf** courses in a 40-kilometer (25-mile) radius of the city, the most difficult problem facing avid golfers is where to tee off from. Despite what you may have heard, kangaroos do not hop around the city's courses. (They do, however, leave their prints in sandtraps at courses like the one at Anglesea, a seaside resort located along the Great Ocean Road southwest of Melbourne.)

Several golf tours are available to help match up visiting golfers with the course best suited to them. Probably the best-known outfit is Koala Golf Day (telephone: 598-2574), which, for about $130, provides everything from clubs, shoes, and greens fees to lunch, hotel pick-up and return, and even a golfer's survival kit, the contents of which are known only to tourgoers!

For those visitors who like combining a bit of sightseeing with exercise, there are some **bicycle** rental companies located in the city as well. Several well-marked bike paths have been established in recent years, incorporating many of Melbourne's parks, rivers, and bayside regions. One of the most well-known rental companies is Hire-a-Bicycle, which has an office below the Princes Bridge on the bank of the Yarra River near the city (telephone: 288-5177). The company is open daily and offers hourly, half-day, and day rates. Hourly fees run about $5, half-day $12, and all day is about $15.

Local tourism promoters boast that you can be at any one of one hundred or more **beaches** within nine minutes in Melbourne. Seasoned beachcombers in other parts of Australia would snicker at this suggestion, but the fact remains that while the city's beaches won't threaten Sydney's, Perth's, or the many found in Queensland, they are not as bad as some people would have you believe. Indeed, residents in many other cities around the world would be thrilled to have Melbourne's beaches.

While surfers won't find many waves to their liking in nearby **Port Phillip Bay,** they can, farther down the stretch of land known as the Mornington Peninsula. This is a popular summer resort area, particularly at towns like **Sorrento** and **Portsea.** (At the very tip of the peninsula is Cheviot Beach, best known as the place where then Prime Minister Harold Holt went for a swim in 1967, and never came back.)

Closer to Melbourne, however, are **Elwood** and **St. Kilda** beaches which can be reached by tram from the city in about thirty minutes. (Take tram 15 to get to the beach.) Another popular spot is at the end of Kerferd Road in nearby **Albert**

**Park** where there is a pier and a lot of people peering as well! (Get to Albert Park via number 10 or 12 tram.)

In recent years, Victoria has even become a popular snow **ski resort** area. While the quality of slopes in the Swiss Alps or Colorado's Aspen will never be approached, many Melburnians swear they get a rocky mountain high from shooshing in the so-called Victorian Alps.

Due to the unpredictability of the snowfalls, visitors should not count on getting in a run or two, but for those who wish to try, remember the winter season is the exact opposite of the northern hemisphere's. Who knows, someone may get a charge out of saying they were skiing in July.

The most popular resort is **Mt. Buller,** located about 240 kilometers (150 miles) north of Melbourne near the town of Mansfield. It has more than fifty runs and claims to cater to nearly half-a-million skiers each season. Other popular resorts, though they are a good two-hour drive beyond Mt. Buller, are **Mounts Buffalo** and **Hotham** and **Falls Creek.** Further details can be obtained by calling either the Victorian Tourism Commission at 619-9444, or the Victorian Ski Association at 699-4655.

These resorts offer everything from rental equipment and lessons to all sorts of accommodations. Most trips are booked from the city at travel agents like the Allaround Travel Services, 200 Bourke Street; 663-4485. Specific information on other ski resorts can be obtained by calling the Mt. Buller Accommodation & Information Centre, 598-3011; Mt. Hotham Accommodation Information Centre, 240-8966; or the Falls Creek Information Centre, also on 240-8966.

Cross-country or nordic skiing has caught on in popularity recently, and is perhaps an even better way to combine a day on the slopes with checking out the scenery. For further details, contact the Victorian Ski Association at 699-4655.

If time allows, you may wish to rent your equipment in the city where salespeople will have more time to assist you and it will probably cost less as well. Some of the more well-known ski rental outfits include: Alpine Ski Centre, 17 Hardware Street (phone: 670-5869); and for cross-country ski buffs, Paddy Pallin, 360 Little Bourke Street (phone: 670-9485).

# 🐎 RESTAURANTS

Melbourne is arguably Australia's culinary capital, offering diners both the quality and range of cuisines they would expect to find in much larger cities around the world.

It is fitting, though, that the true flavor of the city's multicultural mix comes through in its restaurants, offering everything from French, Greek, and Italian to far more exotic Far Eastern eateries, featuring Malaysian, Indian, Vietnamese, and Cantonese fare.

Some Melbourne restaurants only have a BYOB license. This means alcoholic beverages are not sold, but you may bring your own wine or beer, which may be purchased at liquor stores or hotel bottle shops. (Note: Only 3 of the 15 restaurants listed here fall into this category—Ilios, Shark Fin Inn, and Vlado's Charcoal Grill.) You can expect to pay about $20 for a bottle of good Australian wine at a licensed restaurant. (The price will be at least $5 less if you buy from a liquor store before dining.)

Tipping is not obligatory, but for those who believe the service was exceptional, a 10–15 percent tip is considered generous. All restaurants mentioned below accept every major credit card (American Express, Visa, MasterCard, and Diner's Club).

Here is a list of 15 fine restaurants, found both in the city and surrounding suburbs, arranged alphabetically. When the location of a restaurant is on our color map, we have keyed it into the page number of the map insert and the appropriate map coordinates.

## Clichy's                                            COLLINGWOOD
9 Peel St., Collingwood; (03) 417-6700.

This former corner hotel has been turned into a cozy, elegant restaurant, more resembling someone's home than a public dining area.

Best known for having one of the city's most extensive wine lists (at least three hundred labels to choose from), the restaurant also features a charming, pint-size bar just beyond the front entrance offering beer and ale from all over the globe.

The menu is mainly French, but does offer other main courses such as poached ox tongue served with a shallot vinegar sauce and roasted loin of lamb. Only about six main courses are offered and are changed every six weeks or so.

Diners can expect to pay about $32 for a three-course meal and about $18 for a good bottle of Australian wine. (The restaurant also allows guests to BYOB if they so choose.)

Located in the nearby suburb of Collingwood, Clichy's is a short tram (numbers 86, 87, or 88 along Smith St.) or cab ride from the city. Open for lunch, Tues.–Fri. and dinner, Tues.–Sat.

## Cliveden Room                    EAST MELBOURNE, P. 19, E2
192 Wellington Pde., East Melbourne; (03) 419-3311.

Melbourne's four-and-five star hotels are well known for their fine restaurants, but the Hilton's Cliveden Room may be the crown jewel of them all. The first thing guests notice is the tasteful furnishings and attention to detail, such as the Florentine stained-glass windows and heavy oak paneling, also imported from Italy. One room resembles a 19th-century study, complete with bookshelves and fireplace, recalling many of the original features of the grand Cliveden estate which formerly stood on the hotel site.

The menu includes a fine range of Australian favorites, from appetizers (known as entrées in Australia) like Sydney rock oysters to grilled John Dory fillets and rack of lamb for main courses.

Three-course meals run about $44 per person, assuming you can make room for one of their delicious desserts, including hot berry sabayon or banana soufflé. In addition to an extensive list of Australian wines (expect to pay about $22 for a bottle), the restaurant also offers a wide range of after-dinner drinks.

Service is very swift and professional and women receive a small, fresh orchid soon after arriving.

Open for lunch Mon.–Fri., and dinner Mon.–Sat.

### Florentino's                    MELBOURNE CENTER, P. 18, C2
80 Bourke St., Melbourne; (03) 662-1811.

Florentino's has long been a favorite eating place for many leading political and business figures who rave equally about its French and Italian menus. There is always some fresh fish featured as well, like a baked fillet of trevally (an ocean fish) with pistachio nuts.

Though one of the pricier restaurants in town (three-course meals run about $45, plus close to $30 for a bottle of Australian wine), Florentino's has waiters who are very professional and knowledgable about the various offerings.

Another far less expensive way to sample Florentino's varied fare is to try its bistro grill, located on the first floor for lunch—or better still, the tiny adjoining bar known as the bistro cellar. Get there early, though, as it is usually mobbed by noontime. (See the Eating on the Run section for details.)

Main dining area open for lunch Mon.–Fri., and dinner Mon.–Sat.

### Flower Drum                    MELBOURNE CENTER, P. 18, C2
17 Market Lane, Melbourne; (03) 662-3655.

Found on a narrow side lane off the main Chinatown area of Little Bourke St. in the city, the Flower Drum delights locals and overseas visitors alike.

Proprietor Gilbert Lau has gone to great pains to decorate the restaurant in soothing color schemes, with elegant watercolors of traditional Oriental motifs lining the walls.

Flower Drum is probably one of the pricier Chinese restaurants in Melbourne (about $36 per person for three courses, plus special rice and soup), but it is also one of the best. Specialties include shredded duck soup with mushrooms and bamboo shoots for a starter, and boneless quail, surrounded by finely trimmed potatoes in the shape of a bird's nest, for a main course.

The restaurant also features seafood dishes, including fresh prawns (shrimp), lobster, and Queensland mud crab. (These items will cost substantially more than traditional dishes.) A bottle of Australian wine will run about $17.

Oriental food fans should note that reservations are a must, especially Thurs.–Sat. nights. If cramped for time, try the sumptuous *yum cha* luncheon buffet. Open Mon.–Sat. for lunch and every day for dinner. (See Eating on the Run section.)

### Gaylord's                    CHINATOWN, P. 18, B/C2
4 Tattersalls Lane, Melbourne; (03) 663-3980.

The restaurant's name may look familiar to avid lovers of Indian cuisine, and this is, in fact, one of the many such Gaylord's that have opened around the world since the original in the Indian pavilion in the 1964–65 New York World's Fair.

Long recognized as the only licensed Indian restaurant in the city, this Gaylord's maintains the chain's good reputation, especially with its northern Indian-style dishes. Highly recommended is the Tandoori mixed grill platter for a main course and for dessert, kulfi, or Indian ice cream flavored with saffron and nuts. (Several vegetarian dishes are available as well.)

Expect to pay about $28 per person for three courses, plus an order of special vegetable rice and soft bread. The restaurant has a small but adequate wine list that averages about $15 a bottle. Gaylord's also has a reasonably priced, all-inclusive buffet lunch.

Though located on a poorly lit lane along Chinatown on Little Bourke St., the interior is fit for a raja.

Open for lunch Mon.–Fri., and dinner Mon.–Sat.

---

## Eating on the Run

If eating on the run (and cheaply) is your style, here are five places Melburnians head for:

**Asian Food Plaza,** 196 Russell St., Melbourne; 663-3536. Specializes in many Southeast Asian cuisines.

**Fast Eddy's Café,** 32 Bourke St., Melbourne; 662-2551. An American-style establishment featuring hamburgers, fish-and-chips, sandwiches and other lunch-time favorites.

**Florentino's Bistro Cellar,** 80 Bourke St., Melbourne; 662-1811. Though sometimes difficult to find a seat (or place to stand), this restaurant serves up great pasta dishes at very reasonable prices.

**Xenia,** 191 Lonsdale St., Melbourne; 663-3532. One of the best spots to satisfy the urge for Greek specialties, situated in the heart of the Little Greece section of the city.

**Yum Cha.** This is not a restaurant's name, but the term used to describe the Cantonese version of a luncheon buffet. Many of the Chinese restaurants found on Little Bourke St. in the city, including the two mentioned in the restaurant section, feature *yum cha* daily.

---

## Gowings
EAST MELBOURNE, P. 19, E1

366 Albert St., East Melbourne; (03) 419-0366.

This elegant international restaurant blends in well with the Old World charm of East Melbourne. The main dining room has salmon-pink and gray-colored walls (with matching serviettes), covered by numerous oil paintings and fine prints.

Gowings offers diners the option of a set, three-course meal for about $36 or an à la carte menu that will cost a little more.

The menu offers a good deal of variety, due in large part to the background of the chefs. The head cook is from the island of Mauritius while the second is from Japan, so any dish such as the cold appetizer of sushi, sashimi, and raw beef or the Mauritian-style curried chicken breasts are always good bets. Other specialties include New Zealand venison and several seafood favorites: Atlantic salmon, grilled crayfish, and gumbo.

Gowings has an extensive wine list, featuring a broad selection of Aussie varieties that average about $20 a bottle, as well as several French, Italian, and German wines that will cost roughly three times the domestic selections.

Open for lunch Mon.–Fri., and dinner Mon.–Sat.

## Ilios                                          CARLTON
174 Lygon St., Carlton; (03) 663-6555.

While Greek restaurants traditionally are set in dark rooms with Hellenic-inspired decor and atmosphere, the Ilios extols the virtues of light and contemporary furnishings. Long panes of glass and modern stained-glass windows set the tone for the restaurant's menu which features some traditional Greek dishes, but also offers a wide range of local seafood platters such as prawns, calamari, and John Dory fillets.

Highly recommended is the Combination of Dips appetizer with crusty Greek bread and a special selection of hot and cold stuffed grape leaves—*mezethes.* Save room for a slice of *galaktobouriko,* a Greek custard pie that is sure to delight.

Meal prices vary greatly depending on your appetite, but will fall somewhere between $28–$43 per person. Though a BYOB restaurant, there is a hotel bottle shop just across the road.

Open for lunch Mon.–Fri. and dinner is served daily.

## Kenzan                        MELBOURNE CENTER, P. 19, D2
45 Collins St., Melbourne; (03) 654-8933.

Although its location within the mini shopping arcade surrounding The Regent hotel is not very alluring, once inside Kenzan you feel as though you have just stepped into a Japanese tea house.

Kenzan specializes in the style of Japanese cooking called *Kaiseki ryori* (tea ceremony cooking), considered by many to be Japan's true haute cuisine. Kenzan's *Kaiseki* menu comes as a banquet, featuring fresh seafoods, vegetables, and fruits. Cost is about $50.

The restaurant also features several other fixed dinners, including sukiyaki and sushi. Expect to pay about $40 for these meals. À la carte selections are also available, as is one of Melbourne's finest sushi bars. The restaurant has a fine short list of wines, with domestic as well as French varieties. An Australian bottle will cost about $21.

Open for lunch Mon.–Fri. and dinner Mon.–Sat.

## Masani's                                       CARLTON
313 Drummond St., Carlton; (03) 347-5610.

Located, appropriately enough, just around the corner from the Little Italy section of Lygon St., Masani's manages to cross the bridge between Australian and Italian cuisines.

While offering the traditional Italian dishes, owner and chief chef Richard Maisano emphasizes dishes featuring quail, duckling, and even charcoal-grilled porterhouse steaks.

During the chilly winter months, a large hearth in the main dining area is fired up and used for heating as well as for some cooking.

It's hard to go wrong with any selection, and the portions are filling, to say the least. Save some room for a slice of *tiramisu,* a cheesecake-like dessert with the consistency of angel's-food cake.

About $30 per person for three courses and the average price for any Australian wine is $14. Several Italian varieties are available as well and the menu features many specials each night.

Open daily for lunch and dinner.

---

## Lunchtime

For those with a little time, here are five lunch spots favored by locals and visitors alike:

**Lemon Tree Hotel,** 10 Grattan St., Carlton; 347-7514. One of the city's most popular converted old pubs, featuring plenty of informal French favorites.

**Lucattini's,** 22 Punch Lane, Melbourne; 662-2883. This classic Italian bistro is found in the heart of Melbourne's Chinatown section, and is a favorite noon-time haunt of businesspeople, politicians, and celebrities.

**Parlez,** 401 Little Bourke St., Melbourne; 670-6611. This popular restaurant is open for lunch only, so it prides itself on the food presentations and quality of service. Parlez also attracts a well-dressed crowd who delight in such offerings as vegetable curry, chicken bagel, or even water buffalo fillets! Daily specials available, too.

**Rosati,** 95 Flinders Lane, Melbourne; 654-7772. Considered by many natives we spoke to as the best place to be seen dining in town. Heavy emphasis on Italian ambience and cuisine, but don't spill any tomato sauce on the floor's lovely mosaic of multicolored tiles!

**The Vic Restaurant,** Victorian Arts Complex, St. Kilda Rd., Melbourne; 617-8180. Lovely recreation of a century-old English eatery, featuring sumptuous lunch and early dinner fare. Marvelous desserts, too.

---

## Mietta's
MELBOURNE CENTER, P. 18, C2

7 Alfred Place, Melbourne; (03) 654-2366.

Mietta's is one of Melbourne's most treasured restaurants, both for its Old World ambience and its five-star French food, served up by Burgundy-born chef Jacques Reymond. The restaurant is named after Mietta O'Donnell, who carries on a proud family tradition in the restaurant business in Melbourne.

Mietta and her business partner, Tony Knox, have spared no expense in refurbishing the century-old former German Club and turning it into a restaurant that would be the envy of any European restaurateur. The main dining room, in fact, had been the German Club's ballroom, with characteristically high ceilings and solid floors. Mietta has added lovely large pieces of Victoriana, including softly lit chandeliers, lavish floral arrangements, and balloon-backed mahogany chairs around tables set with fine damask and silver.

Three-course meals will run about $50, but this is not the place to worry about cost. You'll find many regional seafood specialties, such as a King Island (Tasmania) crab lasagne or gratin of yabbies (freshwater crayfish), with truffles for starters, as well as more traditional French-inspired main courses such as beef fillet à la bordelaise, chicken fricassée, and filet mignon.

The restaurant also features an extensive list of wines, ranging from the finest fruit in Victoria to the best from Bordeaux and Burgundy.

Mietta's has a marvelous gathering place downstairs for pre- or après-dinner drinks, while on Sun. afternoons, the lounge often is taken over with informal lectures by noted authors, choral groups, or classical recitals.

Open for lunch in the main dining room Mon.–Fri. and dinner every day.

## Nickleby's                                      CARLTON
71 Drummond St., Carlton; (03) 663-5100.

This lovely century-old terrace house was completed just three years after the death of its inspiration, Charles Dickens, whose character Nicholas Nickleby exemplified the pleasures of good food and drink.

Though the interior looks a little tired, Nickleby's does not disappoint either in its range of offerings, hospitality of the owners, or service by the staff.

Three-course meals run about $30 per person and change according to season. Thus, during the hotter summer months, the emphasis is on seafood and salad while the colder months are marked by more traditional game foods. (If just two are dining, request the romantic alcove area on the second floor.)

Try the escargot and button mushrooms for an appetizer and the lamb cutlets seasoned with dijon mustard and spicy bread crumbs for a main course. The chocolate and coffee mousse is a must, too. Open for lunch Mon.–Fri. and dinner Mon.–Sat.

The first floor features another restaurant known as Sketches (after the title of Dickens's first novel), open for dinner, but more often a lunch-time spot. Open for dinner every day but Sun.

## Shark Fin Inn                          CHINATOWN, P. 18, C2
50 Little Bourke St., Melbourne; (03) 662-2552.

What this popular Chinese restaurant lacks in atmosphere it makes up with consistently fine food and reasonable prices.

The Shark Fin Inn serves most of the traditional Cantonese dishes in addition to local favorites such as prawns, Queensland mud crabs, and lobsters. A typical three-course meal, including soup and an order of rice, will run about $25. Set banquets are also available for those who can't make up their minds from the sizable list of selections.

For lovers of spicy, hot dishes, there is a Szechuan-style chicken or beef fillet stir-fried with hot chili. The restaurant is BYOB.

*Yum cha* (buffet lunch) is served daily and is very popular among Melbourne executives. Reservations are generally required for this daily feast. Open daily for lunch and dinner.

## Stephanie's
405 Tooronga Rd., Hawthorn East; (03) 822-8944.

Though located several miles from the city in this eastern suburb, Stephanie's has become one of the most sought-after notches to put on anyone's gastronomic belt of Melbourne eateries.

Diners know they are in for a treat long before they sample the chef's creations. The restaurant is housed in a grand old Victorian mansion, with three separate dining rooms decorated with tapestries on both the chairbacks and walls.

---

## Tea Houses

If it's only a mid-morning or afternoon spot of tea you're after, here are five of Melbourne's more well-known tea houses:

**Café Tasma,** 2 Parliament Place, East Melbourne; 654-8262. This is a favorite among Victoria's political figures for both tea breaks and power breakfasts.

**Fairfield Park Boat House,** Panther Place, Fairfield (a few miles northeast of the city; take the number 546 bus from the corner of Victoria Pde. and Smith St.); 486-1501. A lovely river bank setting that highlights Devonshire teas (a cup of Earl Grey and scones topped with rich cream and strawberry jam).

**Hopetoun Tea Rooms,** 282 Collins St., Melbourne; 650-2777. This old establishment's proximity to downtown shopping areas makes it a natural for sitting down and cooling your heels (and charge cards) for a while.

**Royal Botanic Gardens Kiosk,** between Alexandra Ave. and Domain Rd., South Yarra; 63-9424. Many insiders say this is the best place for Devonshire tea in the city. Certainly, it suggests yet another reason for visiting these splendid gardens.

**The Windsor Hotel,** 103 Spring St., Melbourne; 653-0653. For our money, this is still the best place in town for experiencing high afternoon tea in Melbourne. Often attended by some of the city's most high-ranking political, theatrical, and business figures, it is a must for any visitor, 2:30–6 P.M. daily.

---

The staff is both courteous and well informed and take time to explain each and every item on the menu. Three-course meal prices are fixed at $65 per person and offer a constantly changing variety of dishes. Appetizers range from a buttery blini with smoked Tasmanian salmon and salmon caviar to snails on the grass, with sautéed mushrooms and puff pastry topping. (One waiter regaled customers with the tale of how the snails were not French bred, but the local garden variety—neighborhood children were paid $.05 apiece for them!)

Main courses run the gamut from steamed yabbies (freshwater crayfish) and rack of lamb to tenderly grilled quail.

Stephanie's offers an extensive selection of Australian wines as well as many French and German varieties. Several domestic and French champagnes are available, too (by both the bottle and the glass).

Guests are advised to reserve in advance and will need to take a taxi to reach the restaurant.

Open for lunch Fri., and dinner Tues.–Sat.

## Vlado's Charcoal Grill                    RICHMOND
61 Bridge Rd., Richmond; (03) 428-5833.

Make no mistake about this restaurant, it is simply the finest place for steak in Australia. There are no apologies made for those who'd like a piece of fish or prefer vegetarian, either. They need not enter this plainly decorated and cramped establishment in the working-class neighborhood of Richmond. Rest assured, their table will be turned over not once but twice each night, a rare event in Australian dining circles.

Red meat lovers come from all over to pay homage to Vlado Gregurek, the humble high priest of Vlado's Charcoal Grill. Indeed, ask Vlado what makes his steaks so delicious, and he'll tell you his main pleasure in life is gaining a complete knowledge of meat and proper aging techniques, and then producing the highest quality cuts of fillet, rump, or sirloin for his clients. (Some regulars say they are satisfied by just the delicious charcoal-grilled aromas that waft around the room, let alone the cuts themselves.)

Three-course meals are fixed at $45 per person and begin with freshly made sausage and some other delicacies like calves liver, pork necks, or tiny minced rolls, also made daily on the premises.

The main course is accompanied by a simple bowl of salad. Desserts are likewise kept simple, featuring strawberry pancakes with cream.

First-floor graziers are greeted as well by a wall-size photograph of well-fed beef cattle staring at them knowingly.

Reservations are practically mandatory but not honored more than two weeks in advance. Vlado's is reached either by taxi or by taking tram 28 or 29 and stepping off at the first stop after Hoddle St. in Richmond, a suburb east of the city. Vlado's is a BYOB restaurant.

Open for lunch Mon.–Fri. and dinner Mon.–Sat.

## Walnut Tree Restaurant          MELBOURNE CENTER,
                                            NEAR P. 18, A1
458 William St., Melbourne; (03) 328-4409.

The Walnut Tree offers guests more than just an evening meal. It offers an unusual mix of furnishings and atmosphere centered about the restaurant's namesake, a century-old walnut tree rooted firmly beneath the marble floor.

Three-course meals are reasonably priced (about $38 per person) and can accommodate nearly everyone's palate from vegetarians to lovers of veal. Seafood lovers need not fear, either, with main courses of Tasmanian Atlantic salmon (that's not a misprint, northern hemisphere salmon have been brought to Australia in recent years), and sea perch longfingers, which are rolled in shredded coconut and deep-fried with lime dressing.

Those looking for another out-of-this-world house specialty need look no further than the Flying Saucer, a highly combustible mixture of after-dinner liqueurs, including brandy and galliano, capped off by a thick coating of cream. Then, too, if there's still room, order a coffee and macadamia nut soufflé, Grand Marnier crêpe, or chocolate tart topped off by Baileys Irish Cream. Open for lunch Tues.–Fri. and dinner Tues.–Sat.

## ENTERTAINMENT

Melbourne has more than its fair share of after-hours offerings for everyone from classical music lovers to comedy-club-goers. For those who like a little faster beat, all-night discos are all the rage as well as the more traditional pastime known as pub crawls, which if done properly, make any other form of locomotion seem far too difficult.

The city also hosts a series of annual festivals that are well worth attending if you happen to be in Melbourne while they are in full swing.

Every spring (that's September to November Down Under), Melbourne presents the **Spoleto Arts Festival,** featuring opera, theater, dance, drama, films, and music. Melbourne represents the third jewel in the international festival's crown, along with Spoleto, Italy, and Charleston, South Carolina.

Every March, Melburnians pay their last respects to summer by celebrating **Moomba,** a two-week extravaganza perhaps best described as the city's more civilized answer to Rio's carnivale or New Orleans's Mardi Gras. Though many of the activities may be of interest only to natives, some events like the annual parade of floats up Swanston Street and the international water-skiing championship on the Yarra River can be enjoyed by all.

A recent addition to Moomba, and now a yearly event in its own right, is the **Comedy Festival.** Mirth-makers from around the world drop by to poke fun at everything from Melbourne's erratic weather (it is indeed possible to experience four seasons in one day!) to far more global topics. Recent headliners have included English funnymen Peter Cook and Graeme Chapman of Monty Python fame, as well as one of Australia's greatest entertainers, Barry Humphries, better known through his alter egos of Sir Les Patterson and Dame Edna Everage. (Dame Edna is not a drag queen—but the perfect example of a middle-aged, middle-income Australian woman.)

If it's a good time you're after, though, you needn't only come to town during the March joke fest. **Theater restau-**

**rants** like the Last Laugh are sure to get you smiling any time of year. Dinner and show costs between $30 and $35, depending on the night you attend, or just $15 for the entertainment segment. This comedy club is located at 64 Smith Street, in the suburb of Collingwood. Telephone: 419-8600.

For those who'd rather listen to live bands or dance the evening away at a **nightclub,** Melbourne has a number of offerings for both young and old(er) party animals. Two of these are located around the corner from the Menzies at Rialto Hotel on King Street, the Hippodrome (telephone: 614-5022) and the favorite of the stockbroker set, Inflation (at 60 King Street, 614-6122).

More recently, near the top of Bourke Street, the city's hottest night club opened, the Metro, which is housed in a vintage theater in its prime when Vaudevillian acts were all the rage. Tickets cost about $10. Doors open at 8 P.M. Telephone: 663-4288.

More traditional theater-goers will find plenty of choice as well, ranging from the three contemporary venues located at the Victorian Arts Centre, which in addition to **theatrical productions,** offer world-class **ballet, opera,** and **classical music** recitals, to the older downtown properties, including Her Majesty's Theatre, 219 Exhibition Street (telephone: 663-3211); Princess Theatre, 163 Spring Street (662-2911); and the Russell Street Theatre, 19 Russell Street (654-4000).

Tickets may be purchased at the theaters' box offices or Bass outlets located throughout the city. Half-priced tickets may be purchased on the day of the performance to many of these shows. The Halftix office is located opposite the Myer Department Store on the Bourke Street Mall.

Between November and April the city also offers many free **outdoor concerts** at the Sidney Myer Music Bowl in the King's Domain Garden on St. Kilda Road, as well as other venues.

For a bit of the **blues** or **jazz,** several pubs around town come to mind, including The Limerick Arms, at the corner of Park and Clarendon streets, South Melbourne (telephone: 690-2626); McCoppins, 166 Johnston Street, Fitzroy (417-3427); or the Troubadour Restaurant and Music House, 388 Brunswick Street, Fitzroy (419-4133).

Though less musical in nature, the city is also home to a number of **wine bars,** the patrons of which rarely are off-key, particularly at one of Melbourne's most popular establishments, Jimmy Watson's, 333 Lygon Street, Carlton (also see Carlton section).

For those looking to try their hand at a good ol' Australian pub crawl, here is a short list of popular **pubs:** The Loaded Dog Pub Brewery, 324 St. George's Road, North Fitzroy (telephone: 489-8222); Lord Jim's, 36 St. George's Road, North Fitzroy (481-0209); Mitre Tavern Hotel, 5 Bank Place,

Melbourne (670-5644); the Red Eagle Hotel, 111 Victoria Avenue, Albert Park (south of city, near St. Kilda and South Melbourne; take trams number 10 or 12; 699-4536); and for Sir Arthur Conan Doyle fans, the Sherlock Holmes Inn at 415 Collins Street, Melbourne (629-1849).

There's always Mietta's (see Restaurants, above) for a late-night drink or snack.

For full details on what's hot and what's not in the city, pick up a copy of the Friday *Age* daily newspaper and glance through the special "Good Weekend" section.

## SHORT TRIPS OUT OF MELBOURNE

There are a number of great day trips from Melbourne that range in scope from the nightly penguin parade at Phillip Island to the re-created gold-mining township called Sovereign Hill at Ballarat. All are well served by the large coach companies operating from Melbourne, both because of the comfort of the vehicles and because of the commentary offered by many of the bus drivers. Here are four five-star day trips listed in alphabetical order:

**Dandenong Ranges.** In less than an hour, visitors can be transported from the hustle and bustle of Melbourne to the overwhelming solitude of the Dandenongs, a low-lying mountain cluster covered in thick, fern-filled gullies and skyscraping eucalypt trees. These hills are often called the Blue Dandenongs, because of the blueish haze that results from the vapors of the gum trees' natural oils collecting in the higher elevations.

Perhaps the region's most popular venue is the ***Puffing Billy* steam train** that runs through some of the Dandenongs' lushest forest areas. The train operates most days and can be reached either by organized coach tour or by taking the Belgrave line train from the Flinders Street Station. The steam-train ride costs roughly $8. For more information, call 754-6800.

Another popular tourist attraction is the **William Ricketts Sanctuary** near the top of Mount Dandenong. This hilltop haven is filled with lovely wood carvings depicting various Aboriginal mythologies and wildlife. Nominal admission fee charged. For further information, call (03) 751-1300. If you're not traveling with a tour group, take the Lilydale Line train from the Flinders Street Station in Melbourne and get off at Croyden. There's hourly bus service from Croyden to the sanctuary.

**This bus service slows down considerably on Saturdays and Sundays.**

The Dandenongs also are filled with marvelous craft galleries in towns like **Olinda** and **Sassafras,** as well as wonderful places to enjoy morning or afternoon tea. AAT King's offers several day trips that include the Dandenongs as well as other nearby attractions. The cost of the day trip runs about $50 and this price includes lunch and entrance to venues such as *Puffing Billy.* For further details on the coach's tours, call (03) 650-1244. The other two main bus lines operating day tours are Australian Pacific (03-650-1511) and Ansett Pioneer (03-668-2422).

**Phillip Island.** This popular island getaway is only about 128 kilometers (80 miles) south of Melbourne at the entrance of Westernport Bay. (The bay was misnamed by early English navigators who first came to Melbourne via Sydney; thus from New South Wales, Victoria would have been in a westerly direction.) Though primarily a farming region, Phillip Island has long been known as the home of the **fairy penguins,** who each night at Summerland Beach waddle across the sand to their burrows.

These pint-size penguins, which are the smallest of 17 species, are Australia's only variety, and never disappoint the thousands of spectators who come to watch their nightly stroll.

All coach companies offer daily trips to Phillip Island, including one called the Express which leaves Melbourne late in the afternoon and returns directly following the penguin parade. This express runs only during the warmer months, or from November to March, and the AAT King's offering costs about $33.

For those with a little more time to spend, the coach companies and several smaller limousine services offer half- and whole-day trips to Phillip Island which take in other sites as well, including a large farm exhibit featuring sheep-shearing demonstrations and a stop at a dense eucalypt forest inhabited by a small colony of koalas.

For coach tour information, refer to the previous excursion listing. Some other tour companies, like Friends in Town, offer a day-long trip to Phillip Island for far fewer guests. The trip includes a gourmet three-course meal at a lovely Victorian-era cottage near the bayside resort of Cowes. This trip costs about $130 per person, all-inclusive. For details, call (03) 51-8877.

**Sovereign Hill.** This re-created gold-mining town recalls the 1850s when thousands of prospectors descended on Melbourne to find their fortunes in the nearby hills. Indeed, the town of Ballarat, among many others, sprang up overnight and for a while, was far larger than Melbourne. (Some of Ballarat's rich heritage is still visible during a drive along the town's main streets where marvelous examples of Victorian architecture stand proudly.)

Sovereign Hill may well be Australia's finest living museum, featuring many period shops, eateries, and an area for modern-day miners to try their hand at panning for nuggets. Costumed interpreters and horse-drawn vehicles add to the colonial-era flavor. Overnight guests may even stay at an 1850s-style guest lodge called Government Camp, which quite nicely re-creates the accommodation for English soldiers and officers who were stationed near the goldfields at Ballarat. If you want stay here, contact The Bookings Officer, Government Camp, Sovereign Hill Post Office, Ballarat Vic., 3350; (053) 31-1944.

It costs about $9 for entrance to Sovereign Hill. The village is open daily. For further details, call (053) 31-1944. Again, all major bus companies run trips to Sovereign Hill (see information under Dadenong Ranges) and there is daily V-Line rail service from Melbourne to Ballarat; (03) 619-1500 for details.

**Yarra Valley.** This fertile area is best known for producing some of the state's best wines and for **Healesville Sanctu-**

---

### Kangaroos

The first kangaroo many newcomers to Australia will see is the one on the tail of a Qantas jet at the airport. Although the 'roo might be rivaled these days by the koala as Australia's most famous animal, there's no contest over which one visitors have the best chance to spot in the wild.

Outside cities and towns, kangaroos are easy enough to encounter in the "bush." Of course as night-feeding marsupials, they aren't often found at mid-day but around dawn and dusk, they have a hop about. Nobody knows how many there are, because aerial counts are inadequate for a vast land which often conceals them well. Droughts, pest-control measures, and prolific breeding make for dramatic population swings.

There are 58 species in the kangaroo family (Macropodidae). The eastern gray, western gray, and red kangaroo are the human-size ones but there are also smaller wallabies, wallaroos, and tree-kangaroos. Even experts can be fooled when trying to identify the often-similar species, many of which overlap in habitat, especially forest grasslands.

Farmers consider all of them pests, with good cause. They eat crops, damage fences, and compete with stock for water and pastureland. Over the decades, they've been poisoned, gassed, snared, and shot by the millions. But they're survivors: kangaroo fossils have been dated at 14 million years old.

At some zoos and campgrounds, do hand-feed the wallabies. But if you drive on country roads at night, a "roo bar" fixed to the vehicle's front is the best collision insurance.

—Steve Bunk

## TOURS AND ACCOMMODATIONS

🦃 V-Line has hooked up with a local company called Mansfield Mountain Safaris to offer a weekend excursion into this region. For about $200, the trip includes four-wheel-drive adventures deep into untamed wilderness, scenic lookouts, cozy campfires, and lots of great bush tucker (that's food). For further details, drop by V-Line's Travel Centre at 589 Collins St., Melbourne, or call 62-0771.

A far different high-plains experience awaits those who prefer **horseback riding** through the bush by day, and relaxing in a **swimming pool** or **sauna** at night. For these people there is the **Sawpit Gully Lodge,** located about 16 kilometers (10 miles) beyond Mansfield. (V-Line offers regular bus service to Mansfield where guests are met and delivered to the lodge.)

For information, write: Sawpit Gully Lodge, Box 559, Mansfield 3722, or call (057) 769-562. The package costs about $100 a day, including meals. V-Line bus service is extra.

# RUTHERGLEN, VICTORIA

Yet a far different adventure greets those who travel to this quiet pastoral setting some 275 kilometers (170 miles) northeast of Melbourne.

Today, Rutherglen is known for its fine wines (especially fortified varieties like ports and muscats), but a century ago, the area was overrun by prospectors in search of gold. These veins soon dried up and a handful of settlers began planting grapevines in hopes of striking "liquid gold."

About a dozen **wineries** now are clustered in this region, most within a seven-mile radius of the hamlet of Rutherglen. Some of the more popular ones include All Saints Vineyard and Cellars, situated about five miles northwest of Rutherglen in Wahgunyah. Phone: (060) 33-1218. Just beyond All Saints is St. Leonard's Vineyard, another mainstay in this wine region. Phone: (060) 33-1004. Closer to Rutherglen is Campbell's Winery, only about one mile from town on the Murray Valley Highway. Phone: (060) 32-9458.

## TOURS AND TRAVEL

Many of the wineries are easily reached during a two-day **cycling trip** offered by Bogong Jack Adventures and V-Line. Unlike many cycling trips that require riders who are fit enough to enter the Tour de France, the Rutherglen region is so flat, even the most unfit cyclist can get from one port of call to another.

In addition to ample wine tasting, tour highlights include a sumptuous picnic lunch along Victoria's answer to the Mississippi River, the Murray, and dinner in one of Rutherglen's fine hotels or restaurants.

For further details, contact V-Line, or Bogong Jack Adventures at Box 221, Oxley 3678, or call (057) 27-3382. The trip costs about $200 and includes train fare, cycling equipment, accommodation, and most meals. It runs every spring and autumn.

main streets where marvelous examples of Victorian architecture stand proudly.)

Sovereign Hill may well be Australia's finest living museum, featuring many period shops, eateries, and an area for modern-day miners to try their hand at panning for nuggets. Costumed interpreters and horse-drawn vehicles add to the colonial-era flavor. Overnight guests may even stay at an 1850s-style guest lodge called Government Camp, which quite nicely re-creates the accommodation for English soldiers and officers who were stationed near the goldfields at Ballarat. If you want stay here, contact The Bookings Officer, Government Camp, Sovereign Hill Post Office, Ballarat Vic., 3350; (053) 31-1944.

It costs about $9 for entrance to Sovereign Hill. The village is open daily. For further details, call (053) 31-1944. Again, all major bus companies run trips to Sovereign Hill (see information under Dadenong Ranges) and there is daily V-Line rail service from Melbourne to Ballarat; (03) 619-1500 for details.

**Yarra Valley.** This fertile area is best known for producing some of the state's best wines and for **Healesville Sanctu-**

---

### Kangaroos

The first kangaroo many newcomers to Australia will see is the one on the tail of a Qantas jet at the airport. Although the 'roo might be rivaled these days by the koala as Australia's most famous animal, there's no contest over which one visitors have the best chance to spot in the wild.

Outside cities and towns, kangaroos are easy enough to encounter in the "bush." Of course as night-feeding marsupials, they aren't often found at mid-day but around dawn and dusk, they have a hop about. Nobody knows how many there are, because aerial counts are inadequate for a vast land which often conceals them well. Droughts, pest-control measures, and prolific breeding make for dramatic population swings.

There are 58 species in the kangaroo family (Macropodidae). The eastern gray, western gray, and red kangaroo are the human-size ones but there are also smaller wallabies, wallaroos, and tree-kangaroos. Even experts can be fooled when trying to identify the often-similar species, many of which overlap in habitat, especially forest grasslands.

Farmers consider all of them pests, with good cause. They eat crops, damage fences, and compete with stock for water and pastureland. Over the decades, they've been poisoned, gassed, snared, and shot by the millions. But they're survivors: kangaroo fossils have been dated at 14 million years old.

At some zoos and campgrounds, do hand-feed the wallabies. But if you drive on country roads at night, a "roo bar" fixed to the vehicle's front is the best collision insurance.

—Steve Bunk

**ary**—far and away the best place to see many of Australia's unique wildlife.

Located in the hamlet of Healesville, about 65 kilometers (40 miles) east of the city, this wildlife reserve presents many of its inhabitants in their natural surroundings. It features about 2,000 animals representing some two hundred species, including kangaroos, emus, koalas, platypuses, and wombats, as well as extensive numbers of colorful birds and reptiles. The park is open daily and costs about $6 to enter. For details, phone (059) 62-4022. To reach the Yarra Valley, take White-horse Road out of Melbourne; it becomes the Maroondah Highway and runs through the heart of the valley.

The region's other mainstay is its **wineries,** some of which, like Fergussons (just off Melba Highway in the Dixons Creek area), open their doors not only to wine buffs but to lunch and dinner guests most days as well. (Call ahead for booking at 059-65-2237.) Another popular winery is Yarra-burn, on Settlement Road, Yarra Junction, which features a lovely 1860s-vintage winery originally constructed by convicts. For information, call (059) 67-1428.

Again, these sites are often included on coach tours operated from Melbourne. AAT King's, for instance, has a marvelous Four-Tours-In-One excursion that takes in Healesville Sanctuary, Fergussons Winery, *Puffing Billy,* and the Dandenong Ranges for about $50. This price includes entrance fees and lunch at the winery. (See Dadenongs listing for AAT King's contact number.)

## CITY LISTINGS

Unless specified otherwise, area code is always (03). Each sight/establishment is keyed into its neighborhood and the color map of the city at the back of the book—both to the page number of the map insert and the appropriate map coordinates. Page numbers within the listings refer to the text pages on which the sight/establishment is discussed.

### Landmarks

**Captain Cook's Cottage** — FITZROY, P. 19, E2
In Fitzroy Gardens; 419-8742; daily 9 A.M.–5 P.M., p. 132

**Como House** — SOUTH YARRA
Como Ave.; 241-2500; daily 10 A.M.–5 P.M., pp. 132, 148

**Old Melbourne Gaol** — MELBOURNE CENTER, P. 18, B1
Russell St. (near Victoria St.); 663-7228; daily 10 A.M.–4 P.M., pp. 132–133

**Parliament House** — MELBOURNE CENTER, P. 19, D1
Spring St. (facing Bourke St.); 651-8911; tours Mon.–Fri. 11 A.M. and 2 P.M., pp. 133, 145

**Shrine of Remembrance** — MELBOURNE CENTER, P. 19, D5
Between Domain and St. Kilda rds.; 654-8415; daily 10 A.M.–5 P.M., p. 134

**Treasury Building**  MELBOURNE CENTER, P. 19, D2
Spring St., near Treasury Gardens, p. 145

**Victorian Arts Centre**  MELBOURNE CENTER, P. 18, C3
St. Kilda Rd.; 617-8211; daily 10:30 A.M.–4:30 P.M., pp. 134–135, 147

## Museums

**Museum of Chinese Australian History**  CHINATOWN, P. 18, C2
24 Cohen Place; 662-2888; Mon.–Thur., 10 A.M.–5 P.M.; Sat., Sun. noon–5 P.M.; closed Fri.; p. 128

**National Gallery of Victoria**  MELBOURNE CENTER, P. 18, C4
180 St. Kilda Rd.; 618-0222; Tues.–Sun. 10 A.M.–5 P.M., pp. 132, 147

## Parks and Gardens

**Fitzroy & Treasury Gardens**  FITZROY, P. 19, E2
Spring, Wellington, Clarendon, Albert, and Lansdowne sts.; 658-9800, for cottage tour call 419-8742, p. 132

**King's Domain**  MELBOURNE CENTER, P. 19, D4
St. Kilda Rd., across from Arts Centre, p. 147

**Royal Botanic Gardens**  SOUTH YARRA, P. 19, E5
Alexandra Ave. to Domain Rd.; 63-9424; daily 8 A.M.–dusk, p. 133

**Royal Melbourne Zoological Gardens**  PARKVILLE
Elliott Ave. in suburb of Parkville, north of city; 347-1522; daily 9 A.M.–5 P.M., pp. 133–134

## Shops

**Aboriginal Handcrafts**  MELBOURNE CENTER, P. 18, C2
Century Building, 9th floor, 125–133 Swanston St.; 650-4717, pp. 146, 151

**Adele Palmer**  SOUTH YARRA/TOORAK
459 Toorak Rd.; 241-2301, p. 148

**Altmann & Cherny**  MELBOURNE CENTER, P. 18, C2
120 Exhibition St.; 650-9685, p. 151

**Australiana General Store**  ARMADALE
1227 High St.; 20-2324, pp. 149, 151

**Carla Zampatti**  ARMADALE; SOUTH YARRA/TOORAK
1104 High St., Armadale; 509-3225, and 53 Toorak Rd.; 267-5606, p. 148

**Craft Link**  MELBOURNE CENTER, P. 18, B2
37 Hardware St.; 670-4063, p. 146

**David Jones**  MELBOURNE CENTER, P. 18, B2
Bourke Street Mall, 310 Bourke St.; 669-8200, p. 150

**David Wang & Co.**  MELBOURNE CENTER, P. 18 B/C2
139 Little Bourke St.; 663-2111, p. 150

**Gemtec**  MELBOURNE CENTER, P. 18, C2
124 Exhibition St.; 654-5733, p. 151

**Georges**  MELBOURNE CENTER, P. 18, C2
162 Collins St.; 653-0411, pp. 145, 150

**King's Arcade**  ARMADALE
High St. at Kooyong Rd., p. 149

**Meat Market Craft Centre**  NORTH MELBOURNE
Courtney St.; 329-9966, p. 150

**Morrison's Australia**  SOUTH YARRA
462 Chapel St.; 241-8255, p. 151

**Myer**  MELBOURNE CENTER, P. 18, B2
Bourke Street Mall, 314 Bourke St.; 6-6111, pp. 145, 150

**Prue Acton**  SOUTH YARRA/TOORAK
307 Toorak Rd.; 271-0283, p. 148

**Queen Victoria Antique Shop**  MELBOURNE CENTER,
P. 18, B1
114 Franklin St.; 328-1461, p. 146

**Queen Victoria Market**  MELBOURNE CENTER, P. 18, A1
Elizabeth and Victoria sts.; 658-9800; Tues.-Sun., hours vary, pp. 133, 146,
150

**Rodos Souvenirs**  EAST PRESTON
583 Plenty Rd., in suburb of East Preston northeast of Melbourne; 478-
3388, p. 151

**Shop of Shops**  MELBOURNE CENTER, P. 18, C2
171 Collins St.; 650-5511, pp. 145–146, 150

**St. Kilda Esplanade Art & Craft Market**  ST. KILDA
536–1333; Sun., p. 150

# Victoria Beyond Melbourne

Though mainland Australia's smallest state, Victoria manages to pack into its borders every possible natural setting from lush rainforests and dense eucalypt groves to sun-baked deserts and azure-blue waters.

Unlike other states, where visitors can spend a lot of time flying to and from various scenic spots, many of Victoria's attractions are within a two-to-three hour drive from Melbourne.

In addition to world-class national parks, the state also has other natural backdrops that are worth a look, particularly in the northeastern corner where a lovely wine region and high-plains, cattle-driving trails (and lore) dominate.

While it is possible to find your own way to these areas, many of them are best served by outdoor tour companies located in Melbourne. Their advantage, of course, is not only the professional guide service they can offer, but pick-up to and from the city.

Still, if you'd prefer renting a car and making your own way to one of Victoria's national parks, the first place to head for is the **Victorian Government Bookshop,** located at 318 Little Bourke Street, next to the Myer Department Store. In addition to all sorts of literature on Victoria, the shop includes a map section, containing detailed information on all national parks. (These brochures are free.) The bookshop is open Monday through Friday from 8:30 A.M. to 5:30 P.M. Another outlet for information on rural Victoria is the **Conservation, Forests, and Lands Department,** which includes the National Parks & Wildlife Division. Officials can be reached at 240 Victoria Parade, East Melbourne, or by calling (03) 412-4011.

Then, too, if a weekend cycling trip or trek across rugged terrain seems too demanding, there are other far less fatiguing ways to enjoy some of Victoria's prized outdoors— namely, farm holidays and a five-star resort in the Dandenongs called Burnham Beeches.

## PORT CAMPBELL NATIONAL PARK

The Northern Territory may be home to the Rock of Ages, Ayers Rock, but Victoria lays claim to a far more dazzling rock group known as the **Twelve Apostles.**

These towering pillars of limestone line the rugged southwestern shores of Victoria, but unlike their monolithic mate in the Northern Territory, they are not really rocks but the collected remains of millions of tiny sea creatures. The calcified offshore deposits date back thousands of years to a time, not only when the sea level was obviously much higher, but to a geologic era when Tasmania was connected to the mainland.

Four of the Apostles have succumbed to the ceaseless pounding of the surf in this region, but the survivors are no less willing to accept the "oohs" and "ahhs" of the many visitors who each day pay their respects.

Port Campbell National Park also features other unique rock formations such as London Bridge—a massive natural-rock crossing carved by constant wave action, and the Blowhole, where the ocean has tunneled several hundred yards into the cliff.

The region was long regarded by sailors as one of the most hazardous stretches of water to navigate in Australia. Of the many that went aground, none was more tragic than the *Loch Ard,* a three-masted iron clipper from England which wrecked in 1878, killing all but two of its fifty-four passengers. A small cemetery and memorial stand at the top of the cliff, not far from where the tragedy occurred.

## TRAVEL, TOURS, AND ACCOMMODATIONS

Many visitors tend to treat the park as a series of unique rock creations and little else. One Melbourne-based tour company, though, Walkabout Adventure Tours, offers a weekend excursion to the region, featuring everything from the national park to nearby treks through luxuriant rainforests and walks along huge sea swells near the so-called Great Ocean Rd.

Tour-goers are treated to sumptuous gourmet-style feasts at night in a cozy farmhouse not far from Port Campbell.

For further details, write: Walkabout Adventure Tours, Box 298, Heidelberg 3084, or call 459-2501. Cost of the trip is about $250 per person, all-inclusive, and trips run monthly Sept.–May.

For time-strapped visitors, the state's railway authority, V-Line, offers a day trip to the region, in conjunction with a local bus company. This tour costs about $60. For further details, contact either V-Line at 619-1542 or the Victorian Tourism Commission at 619-9444.

If you want to explore the park on your own, get maps from the Park Office, Tregea St., Port Campbell 3269; (055) 98-6382.

Camping is permitted at Port Campbell. Some sites include electricity, hot showers, and laundry facilities. Fees are charged. During the summer vacation period and major holiday weekends like Easter, sites must be booked in advance. Contact the park for details. Camping equipment may be rented from a number of downtown sporting-goods stores in Melbourne like Paddy Pallin, 360 Little Bourke (670-9485) and Kathmandu, 78 Hardware St. (642-1942). Accommodation outside the park is available at hotels and motels at Port Campbell and camping grounds at nearby Peterborough.

## GRAMPIANS NATIONAL PARK

Located north of Port Campbell National Park and about 250 kilometers (160 miles) west of Melbourne, Grampians National Park is a rugged stretch of terrain—a flora fanatic's delight with more than one thousand varieties on display, including about one hundred different types of orchids.

The Grampians likewise are famous among Australians for being the southwestern leg of the continent's Great Dividing Range, the name usually given to the eastern highlands that extend from the Cape York Peninsula in northern Queensland to western Victoria.

Australian Wilderness Expeditions, another Melbourne-based outdoor adventure group, makes regular weekend visits to the Grampians year round. In addition to wildflower watching (the best blooming time is between September and October), tour leaders offer a wide range of activities, including **horseback riding, abseiling, ballooning, canoeing,** and **water-skiing,** to name a few.

**Bushwalkers** love the Grampians, too, as much for its plethora of flora and fauna (including scores of kangaroos, wombats, and koalas), as for its reminders of the country's earliest settlers, the Aborigines. About forty rock shelters containing 20,000-year-old paintings have been discovered in the last few years, many of which are accessible to hikers.

Less-active outdoor types need not fret, either, as group organizers make it clear you may simply sit back at the lodge and sip champagne and chow down on gourmet specialties like pâté and smoked salmon, if you prefer.

## TOURS, TRAVEL, ACCOMMODATION DETAILS

For further details, write: Australian Wilderness Expeditions, 209 Toorak Rd., South Yarra 3141, or call 240-8188. The trip costs about $350 per person and includes all expenses.

Independent hikers should get maps from the park office at Halls Gap; (053) 56-4381, or contact the Department of Conservation, Forests, and Lands, 23 Patrick St., Stawell, Vic. 3380; (053) 58-1588. Camping is permitted in designated areas. There are motels and guesthouses at Halls Gap.

## MANSFIELD, VICTORIA

Mention Banjo Paterson's other famous work (yes, he wrote "Waltzing Matilda"), and Victorians will inevitably refer to the poem, "The Man from Snowy River." Now immortalized in two feature films, this picturesque high-plains region is best exemplified by the Mansfield–Mt. Buller area.

A three-hour ride northeast of Melbourne, the region is teeming with many of Australia's colorful birds, including everything from sulphur-crested cockatoos to lyrebirds—most unusual creatures with the ability to mimic all sorts of sounds.

It can get rather chilly in northeastern Victoria in wintertime (indeed, this region is at the foothills of the ski slopes), so most outdoor tours are confined to spring, summer, and fall.

## TOURS AND ACCOMMODATIONS

V-Line has hooked up with a local company called Mansfield Mountain Safaris to offer a weekend excursion into this region. For about $200, the trip includes four-wheel-drive adventures deep into untamed wilderness, scenic lookouts, cozy campfires, and lots of great bush tucker (that's food). For further details, drop by V-Line's Travel Centre at 589 Collins St., Melbourne, or call 62-0771.

A far different high-plains experience awaits those who prefer **horseback riding** through the bush by day, and relaxing in a **swimming pool** or **sauna** at night. For these people there is the **Sawpit Gully Lodge,** located about 16 kilometers (10 miles) beyond Mansfield. (V-Line offers regular bus service to Mansfield where guests are met and delivered to the lodge.)

For information, write: Sawpit Gully Lodge, Box 559, Mansfield 3722, or call (057) 769-562. The package costs about $100 a day, including meals. V-Line bus service is extra.

# RUTHERGLEN, VICTORIA

Yet a far different adventure greets those who travel to this quiet pastoral setting some 275 kilometers (170 miles) northeast of Melbourne.

Today, Rutherglen is known for its fine wines (especially fortified varieties like ports and muscats), but a century ago, the area was overrun by prospectors in search of gold. These veins soon dried up and a handful of settlers began planting grapevines in hopes of striking "liquid gold."

About a dozen **wineries** now are clustered in this region, most within a seven-mile radius of the hamlet of Rutherglen. Some of the more popular ones include All Saints Vineyard and Cellars, situated about five miles northwest of Rutherglen in Wahgunyah. Phone: (060) 33-1218. Just beyond All Saints is St. Leonard's Vineyard, another mainstay in this wine region. Phone: (060) 33-1004. Closer to Rutherglen is Campbell's Winery, only about one mile from town on the Murray Valley Highway. Phone: (060) 32-9458.

## TOURS AND TRAVEL

Many of the wineries are easily reached during a two-day **cycling trip** offered by Bogong Jack Adventures and V-Line. Unlike many cycling trips that require riders who are fit enough to enter the Tour de France, the Rutherglen region is so flat, even the most unfit cyclist can get from one port of call to another.

In addition to ample wine tasting, tour highlights include a sumptuous picnic lunch along Victoria's answer to the Mississippi River, the Murray, and dinner in one of Rutherglen's fine hotels or restaurants.

For further details, contact V-Line, or Bogong Jack Adventures at Box 221, Oxley 3678, or call (057) 27-3382. The trip costs about $200 and includes train fare, cycling equipment, accommodation, and most meals. It runs every spring and autumn.

The Hume Highway is the best road to Rutherglen; follow it to the northeast town of Wangaratta, 170 miles from Melbourne; the wine region is right next door.

# WILSONS PROMONTORY NATIONAL PARK

Perhaps Victoria's most prized natural wonders are found at this 120,000-acre national park in the South Gippsland region of the state.

Few Victorian **bushwalkers** have failed to trek across some of the park's well-marked trails or along its many kilometers of rugged coastline. While delightful day walks are available, a three-day trek of only 40 kilometers (25 miles) takes in everything from fern-rich gullies to the type of sandy white beaches many people associate only with Queensland. For trivia buffs, Wilsons Promontory also is home to the mainland's southernmost point, adorned by a simple, lonely lighthouse.

Then, too, the park is home to many of Australia's fauna favorites, including **kangaroos, wallabies, wombats,** and **koalas.** It's one thing to see a koala or wombat at the zoo, and quite another to run across one in the wild, a very common occurrence at Wilsons Promontory.

## 🐾 TRAVEL, TOURS, AND ACCOMMODATIONS

Walkabout Adventure Tours takes small groups into The Prom regularly during spring, summer, and fall. Unlike their Port Campbell trip, however, clients here must be able to carry a full pack and tent. Meals are far beyond the usual camp fare, though, and the trip is capped off by a classic Aussie barbie at the nearby settlement of Tidal River. The trip costs about $300, all-inclusive. For details, phone Walkabout Adventure Tours in Melbourne: 459-2501.

The Visitors Center in Tidal River will have maps for independent hikers; (056) 80-8358.

Many campsites are available in the large park. Permits, obtained from the Tidal River information office, are required for all overnight hikes. Low-budget cabins and lodges as well as caravan parks are located at Tidal River. Most of these units are booked out during the six-week period beginning at Christmas.

# BURNHAM BEECHES

If just reading about the previous more active getaways has given you a headache, then this Art Deco-inspired country house is guaranteed to soothe. Indeed, it was created in the 1930s by Alfred Nicholas, the man who was largely responsible for developing aspirin.

Set in the quiet surroundings of the Dandenong Ranges, just forty minutes or so from Melbourne, Burnham Beeches has long been recognized as one of Australia's leading **country estates.**

Though a popular spot for Melburnians to escape for Sunday afternoon tea or a quiet dinner, it is the overnight guests who truly come to appreciate the estate's Old World charm.

For starters, just a stone's throw away are the lovely **Nicholas Gardens** as well as **Sherbrooke Forest,** where even the bright Australian sun becomes lost amid the umbrella-like cover of towering gum trees and large, fan-tailed ferns. These woods are also filled with many of Australia's most colorful **birds,** such as crimson rosellas and lyrebirds, many of which are easily seen on the resort's grounds as well.

Burnham Beeches is a member of the prestigious European Country House Hotel Group, Relais and Chateaux, signifying not only a high standard of accommodation and service, but first-class cuisine as well. Other special amenities include picnic hampers for those who'd like to take a walk in the woods, two tennis courts, a small indoor swimming pool, sauna, and bicycles.

## ACCOMMODATION DETAILS

The estate has 50 bedrooms, 19 of which come with spa baths for about $200 a night, as well as 23 queen-size deluxe rooms at about $160 and several larger deluxe rooms and suites that range $230–$430. For further details, contact: **Burnham Beeches Country House,** Sherbrooke Rd., Sherbrooke 3789, or call (03) 755-1903.

# FARM HOLIDAYS

One of the best ways to meet true-blue Aussies, of course, is to sign up for a weekend or more at a farm property in Victoria. From the sun-drenched Murray district in the far northwestern part of the state to the beautiful coastal and alpine settings of the southeast, there's a slice of life of Australia's cockies (farmers) waiting for you.

In addition to helping (or simply observing) the family with farm chores, many properties offer all sorts of activities, including **horseback riding, bushwalking, swimming, fishing,** and **golf.**

**For fishing on inland waterways, you'll need a license; a 28-day license costs around $5 ($10 for one-year). You can obtain one at major sporting goods shops and at the Victorian Tourism Commission's office in Melbourne, 230 Collins Street.**

Meals are spent sitting around the dinner table discussing the day's events and swapping stories with the hosts.

If visitors sign up through the Victorian Farm Holidays program, which has more than one hundred listings, they need only make their own transportation arrangements to the closest railway, bus stop, or airport and the host will meet them.

## ACCOMMODATION DETAILS

For specifics, contact the Victour at 230 Collins St., Melbourne, or call 619-9444. The cost for these stays varies greatly, but averages about $80 a day, including meals. (Recently, some farms have also begun offering bed-and-breakfast-style packages.)

V-Line as well offers all-inclusive, four-day farm holidays to several properties, ranging in price from about $300–$377. For details, call V-Line in Melbourne at 619-1215.

# 7

# TASMANIA

Dangling like a heart-shaped locket beneath Australia's mainland is Tasmania, an island of natural beauty and rich historic ties to the colony's notorious past.

Though by far the country's smallest state (it is about the same size as Ireland), Tassie, as locals call it, has developed a personality distinct from the rest of the continent.

For starters, natives like to be called Tasmanians, not Australians, whom they rather cheekily refer to as residents of the North Island. Even the animals are different here—the best-known being the nasty Tasmanian devil.

Tasmanians have every right to relish their island hideaway because of its varied, and in places quite un-Australian landscape, ranging from rugged mountains and dense, impenetrable scrub on the wild western side to long deserted beaches, open moorland, and blossom-filled fruit orchards over much of the central and eastern portions.

More recently, the island has earned a well-deserved reputation for fine produce, including everything from apples and game birds to trout and salmon, as well as dairy products and cuts of beef from neighboring King Island.

Tasmania has often been called more English in appearance than England, with its plethora of century-old cottages surrounded by meandering stone walls near villages with names like Sheffield, Evandale, Dover, and Devonport. Indeed, English author Anthony Trollope was so smitten by Tasmania following an extended journey Down Under in 1875, that he considered it the only place he'd live if he ever moved to Australia.

The romantic image of cozy English hamlets, however, is only half of the island's colonial heritage. It is also home to the harsh realities of the country's founding as a penal colony for unsavory British subjects following America's successful struggle for independence in 1776.

Tassie's first European settlers were convicts and their military guards near the turn of the 19th century. Reminders of the state's horrific past can best be seen at Port Arthur National Park, site of Australia's most infamous colonial penitentiary, located on a jagged stretch of land along the southeastern corner of the isle known as the Tasman Peninsula.

Long before the English settled there, however, French and Dutch explorers had cruised along the rocky coasts. Indeed, the island was originally discovered by Dutch navigator Abel Tasman in 1642, who promptly called it Van Diemen's Land, after the then governor-general of the Dutch East Indies. Holland never followed up on Tasman's landing, though, and no further attempts to colonize the island ever occurred.

By the 1870s, Tasmania had more paupers, lunatics, orphans and invalids than South Australia and Queensland combined, concentrated in a population less than half of theirs. Despite the labor shortage, most ex-convicts were discriminated against, usually with a sullen reflexive viciousness, by the freeborn. They were regarded as lazy, improvident, unworthy to own land; and as the Victorian animus against homosexuals grew ever stronger in Australia after 1850, so did the belief that most convicts were sexually tainted. "The growing dread of the frightful practices to which it is well known many of them are addicted," remarked a Parliamentary committee in 1860, "render[s] their search for employment often tedious and difficult." In contrast to the ex-convicts of New South Wales, the felonry of Tasmania was so fettered by social prejudice that it could never rise. Moreover, the laws governing their work and their relations to their employers retained, dilute but unmistakable, the iron and gall of the System. Thus, under the 1856 Master and Servants Act, masters had the power to arrest their servants, and it was quite legal for an employer (or any member of his family) to put a hired hand in custody on suspicion of an offense and keep him confined for a week without trial. The extraordinary fact was that this law remained on the statute books of Tasmania for more than a generation; in 1882, the Legislative Council rejected efforts to repeal the employer's right of arrest.

—Robert Hughes
*The Fatal Shore*, 1986

Modern-day voyages to Tasmania are far easier to make and generally start from one of its two largest communities, the capital city of Hobart or Launceston.

Hobart, which is Australia's second-oldest capital (after Sydney), was founded in 1804. It is picturesquely situated at the southeastern end of the island near the mouth of the Derwent River and backed by Mount Wellington, which provides fine views of the city and is often dusted with snow in winter.

Many locals finger the Wrest Point Federal Hotel-Casino as the city's most prominent man-made landmark, but this says more about the way natives like to spend their idle hours than it does for their taste in architecture. As grand as the casino's towering cylindrical shape is, it can in no way compare to the wealth of well-preserved Georgian-era buildings housed downtown and along the waterfront, or even the mighty Tasman Bridge that links the city to its eastern suburbs.

Launceston, located about 200 kilometers (125 miles) due north of Hobart, is probably best known as the birthplace of Melbourne, Victoria. In 1835 English explorer John Batman sailed from Launceston and landed on the banks of the Yarra River (Melbourne's present-day site), where he promptly pulled off the second-most-lopsided land deal of all time (after the great Manhattan Island transfer). Indeed, Batman bought more than half-a-million acres from the local Aborigines for a few blankets, knives, and other mundane implements.

Launceston's roots pale in comparison to this un-real estate deal, but visitors are encouraged to spend at least two days in the northeastern gateway. Though home to only 65,000 people, Launceston offers several natural and man-made attractions many cities several times its size would long to have, including a stunning rocky ravine known as Cataract Gorge and a well-preserved colonial homestead called Franklin House.

## Dining Out in Tasmania

As elsewhere in Australia, Tasmanian restaurants cover a wide spectrum of cuisines and price ranges. In general, however, the island state's eateries, particularly in its two largest tourist centers, will not only rival their mainland counterparts for quality and presentation, but cost substantially less.

While seafood dishes are probably Tassie's best-known offerings, don't overlook other items such as King Island cheeses or cuts of beef, fresh fruit from some of its prosperous orchards, or succulent game birds. Tassie's wine growers are likewise earning a well-deserved reputation with many of the vineyards located just north of Launceston along the Tamar Valley. Popular wines include European-style varieties such as chardonnay, pinot noir, and cabernet sauvignon.

Finally, as noted on the mainland, some Tassie restaurants are licensed and others prefer you BYOB. We will mention those requiring you to provide your own grog where appropriate.

Specific restaurants are recommended under the appropriate towns, below. By major credit cards we mean American Express, Diners Club, Visa, and MasterCard.

# TRAVEL

The first thing to realize, of course, is that you'll have to leave the mainland to reach Tassie.

## Flying

It is a short flight from either Sydney or Melbourne, the two main cities with regular connecting service. Both major domestic airlines, Ansett and Australian, have daily flights from both mainland capitals to Hobart and Launceston. Return fares to Launceston from Melbourne are about $280 and from Sydney $480. Return air fares to Hobart from Melbourne go for about $320 while Sydney is about $520. Ansett can be reached at (002) 38-1111 in Hobart or (003) 31-7711 in Launceston. Australian's phone numbers are (002) 38-3333 in Hobart and (003) 31-4411 in Launceston.

A regular shuttle bus service operated by Tasmanian Redline Coaches operates between the airport and Hobart, a trip of about 20 kilometers (13 miles). The ride costs about $4. For details, call (002) 34-4577.

## Packages

One way to combine a quick jaunt to Tassie while at the same time taking in some of its best spots is to sign up for a package like the one offered by Australian Airlines called "Tastes of Tasmania." These three-day deals include accommodations which range from Hobart's lovely Sheraton Hotel to some of its finer colonial-era accommodations, and can include unrestricted à la carte selections from the city's best restaurants. Another package takes in a top-class trout-fishing resort in the central highlands, while yet another option takes you to lovely Flinders Island, located off the northeastern corner of the island state. Packages do not include airfare, but are a fine way to experience some of the state's best food, tours, and accommodation at reduced rates. For details, contact Australian Airlines in Melbourne or Sydney, or the Tasmanian Travel Centre (Tasbureau) in any state capital city.

## Taking the Ferry

A far slower (and less expensive) way to reach Tassie is via the *Abel Tasman* ferry which leaves from Melbourne's Station Pier at 6 P.M. every Mon., Wed., and Fri. to the northern coast town of Devonport. The trip takes some 12 hours to cross the often-troubled waters of Bass Strait. One-way fares run about $160–$230, depending on the standard of accommodation. For details, call (003) 645-2766. A connecting bus service links Hobart with Devonport.

## Taking the Bus

Motorcoach services operate from Hobart to all the main towns in Tassie and this service is run by Tasmanian Redline Coaches. What these buses lack in comfort, they make up in low prices.

Indeed, visitors can buy a Tassie Pass with 14 days unlimited travel for under $90. Call (002) 34-4577 in Hobart or (003) 31-2744 in Launceston for details or a Tasbureau in any state capital city.

## Car Rentals

To really see Tasmania, however, you'll need a car. Major car-rental agencies available in Hobart include: Avis Tasmania, (002) 34-4222; Auto Rent-Hertz, (002) 34-5555; Budget Rent-A-Car, (002) 34-5222; and Thrifty Rent-A-Car, (002) 23-3577.

Launceston is serviced by many of the same companies and likewise has car-rental outlets both at the airport and in the city. Some numbers to remember are: Tasmanian Redline Coaches, (003) 31-2744; Central Cabs, (003) 31-3555; Taxis Combined, (003) 31-4466; Avis, (003) 91-8314; Budget Rent-A-Car, (003) 91-8566; Auto Rent-Hertz, (003) 31-2099; and Thrifty Rent-A-Car, (003) 91-8105.

For further details on which companies are offering special packages, pick up a copy of the state department of tourism's bimonthly newspaper called *Tasmanian Travelways,* which is available at any local Tasbureau office (that's the travel information office) or island airport.

---

# ❧ ACCOMMODATIONS

Tasmania offers a wide range of guesthouses ranging from large four-star hotels to five-room bed-and-breakfasts. A short list of these varying styles of accommodations are described here for both Hobart and Launceston, where we recommend you base yourself for exploring the island's southeast and northeast points respectively (excursions from each city are detailed below). We're also recommending a few other great spots—accommodations that are destinations in themselves, including a "chain" of 25 privately owned and operated establishments around the state known as Tasmanian Colonial Accommodation. By major credit cards we mean American Express, Diner's Club, Visa, and MasterCard.

## Hobart

In Hobart, there are two major hotels in the top price range: the Sheraton Hobart and Wrest Point Federal Hotel-Casino.

**The Sheraton Hobart,** 1 Davey St., 7000; (002) 35-4535, telex: 58037. Has 234 rooms and is situated on a prime waterfront location. The hotel's features include concierge service for all travel, ticketing, and entertainment needs; business center facilities, including secretarial services, telex, and fax; health club and heated indoor pool; and several eating and drinking areas. A typical rate for a double will be about $150. All major credit cards accepted.

**The Wrest Point Federal Hotel-Casino,** 410 Sandy Bay Rd., 7000; (002) 25-0112, telex: 58115 RESOTEL; fax (002) 25-1481. Best known as the country's first legal gambling venue—

established in the mid-1970s. It is also home to some of the city's best views (and great food) at its Revolving Restaurant; there is also the Asian Restaurant, and for late-night snacks, a 24-hour coffeeshop.

In addition to the casino, the hotel also features regular performances by local and overseas talent as well as a disco and piano bar. Extensive business services are available as well as sports facilities. Its 197 rooms are well equipped and cost about $150 for a double. An 81-room motor inn sits next door to the column-like casino hotel and its rates cost about 50 percent less than the casino's. All major credit cards accepted.

**Hadleys Orient Hotel,** 34 Murray St., 7000; (002) 23-4355, telex: 58355, fax (002) 24-0303. Offers far less upmarket trimmings, but lots of atmosphere. Indeed, the 63-room hotel, built in 1848 by convicts, once was the city's premier overnight spot and lays claim to handling the country's first royal visitors as well as being the site from which polar explorer Amunsden revealed his exploits to the waiting world.

Situated in the heart of the business district, Hadleys has a lovely café for breakfast, lunch, or tea, as well as a more formal dining room. Doubles start from about $95. All major cards accepted.

Perhaps the city's most unique overnight spot is **Islington House,** 321 Davey St., 7000; (002) 23-3900. An 1850s-vintage manse outfitted with lovely period furnishings. Though it contains only eight suites, each one is a jewel, with beautiful imported chintz and curtains and matching spreads.

Islington also offers breathtaking views of nearby Mt. Wellington and each morning a lovely continental breakfast of freshly squeezed orange juice, freshly brewed coffee or tea, and croissants, brioches, or bagels. Suites cost about $110.

# Launceston

By far the city's most popular overnight spot is the **Launceston Federal Country Club Hotel-Casino,** Country Club Ave., 7250; (003) 44-8855, telex: 58600 FEDLAN. Opened shortly after its sister operation in Hobart—Wrest Point—the Launceston property combines fast-paced entertainment and gambling venues with a very relaxed atmosphere.

A full array of sporting facilities are available, including a nice 18-hole golf course.

The room decor is a little behind-the-times, but the hotel's staff makes up for it with prompt and courteous service. Several dining options are available as well as entertainment attractions, ranging from nightly floor shows to blackjack video machines, poker, and keno.

The country club is located a few miles from the city, but is well serviced by local cab companies. A typical charge for one of its 104 rooms is about $140. All major cards accepted.

One of the city's more popular smaller hotels is the **Old Bakery Inn,** corner York and Margaret sts., 7250; (003) 31-7900. Built about 1870, its 16 rooms are well appointed. The hotel includes a lovely restaurant called The Folly and its proximity to major attractions like the Cataract Gorge and Penny Royal World makes it very popular with tourists.

Typical room rates run about $62 for a double. All major cards accepted.

A far more intimate experience, however, awaits those who check into **Kilmarnock House,** 66 Elphin Rd., 7250; (003) 34-1514. A lovely turn-of-the-century Edwardian manse. Its nine rooms are filled with period antiques, but guests are not left wanting any modern conveniences, ranging from private bathrooms and color televisions to refrigerators and continental breakfast. It costs about $60 for two people and the staff is very helpful in pointing out local sites and restaurants.

(*Note:* At time of publication, a 176-room Sheraton was being built in the city's central business district and was expected to be open by January 1989.)

## In the Country

**Cradle Mountain Lodge,** via Wilmot, 7310; (004) 92-1303, telex 58761; fax (004) 92-1309. Postal address is Box 153, Sheffield 7306. This may be the most exciting hotel in Tasmania, as much for its splendid bush setting as for the lodge itself. Located about 84 km (53 miles) inland from Devonport, Cradle Mountain Lodge has very quickly gained a reputation for offering fine bush tracks, fishing holes, canoeing, and other day-time activities, while also offering guests hearty meals and a chance to come face to face with some of the state's unique wildlife. Indeed, following dessert each evening, floodlights are turned on outside so guests can see everything from possums and wallabies to the famous Tasmanian devils come to dine.

Guests may stay either in rooms at the lodge or in separate cabins. Rates run about $60 for two.

Located at the northern end of the rugged Cradle Mountain-Lake St. Clair National Park, the lodge is a one-hour drive from Devonport or about two hours from Launceston. Regular bus service also is available from both towns.

The island state is a trout-fishing enthusiast's paradise, particularly in the central highlands area where countless idyllic lakes and ponds abound. The state's most famous fishing hole is **London Lakes,** tel. (002) 89-1159, reputed to be Australia's only privately owned, fly-fishing resort. About ten fly-fishing fanatics can be accommodated in a stone and log lodge of international standard. London Lakes is located about 152 km (95 miles) from both Hobart and Launceston and the tariff of $315 per person a day include all meals, accommodation, fishing tackle, licenses, professional guide, and transport to angling spots. Write to London Lakes, Fly Fishing Resort, c/o Post Office, Bronte Park, Tas. 7140.

**Strathmore,** Main Rd., Nile; (003) 98-6213. A lovely estate dating back to 1826, found near the tiny hamlets of Nile and Evandale, just outside of Launceston. Housed on a working sheep farm, your hosts, Lorna and Allister Cowdery, go out of their way to ensure your every whim is met. They will pack you a lunch and send you off for a day trip, give you a fishing pole if you'd like to try catching a trout, or even provide rackets and balls for a brisk set of tennis.

The charge is about $65 for two which includes a full breakfast. For about $17, don't pass up the opportunity of sitting down to dinner with the Cowderys. Everything is homemade from the soup starter to the luscious fruit cake.

The property also is next door to Clarendon House (see Excursions from Launceston for details).

Because of the state's compact size and rolling English-like countryside (at least along its eastern and central regions), a group of century-old bed-and-breakfast inns fit in perfectly.

Twenty-five properties—calling themselves Tasmanian Colonial Accommodation—range in location from Hobart and Launceston to lovely settings near Port Arthur on the Tasman Peninsula and Richmond, a twenty-minute drive from Hobart.

One of the group's most sought-after overnight spots is **Prospect House** in Richmond, tel. (002) 62-2207, an 1830-style manse where guests stay in a refurbished barn built by convicts. About the only thing better than the setting is the property's dinner menu, featuring local produce, game, and seafood.

Other backdrops for this unique overnight group include a former convict out-station near Port Arthur called **Cascades** (002-50-3121) and a two-story farm cottage built solely from local stone in the east coast town of Swansea called **Wagner's Cottage** (002-57-7576).

Rates range about $55–$75 a night, including breakfast, though at some properties such as Wagner's Cottage, guests prepare it themselves.

Bookings may be made through your travel agent, Tasbureau, or directly with the property. For further details, contact **Tasbureau** in any mainland capital city or in Hobart at 80 Elizabeth St.; (002) 30-0211; in Launceston at (003) 32-2484.

# Hobart

Most visitors' introduction to Tasmania will be through its waterfront capital of Hobart. Located on the western bank of the Derwent River, the best way to explore the city is on foot.

(However, buses do operate daily from downtown to the suburbs, between 6 A.M. and midnight. Special all-day Rover fares are available. For details call 71-3223.)

Taxis can be found at designated ranks or in front of major hotels. They may be difficult to get during morning and evening rush hours, so it is advisable to book by phone: City Cabs, 34-3633; Silver Top Cabs, 23-7711; Taxis Combined, 34-8444.

In addition to lovely formal gardens, Hobart features countless examples of well-preserved Georgian-style buildings both inland and along its historic foreshore. Major sights are described below.

Built in 1834, the **Penitentiary Chapel/Old Criminal Court** is one of Tassie's oldest and most historic buildings, recalling as well some of the state's early roots as a convict colony. The criminal court opened in 1860 and was also used until very recently as the state's Supreme Court building. The chapel is one of the few colonial Georgian ecclesiastical buildings in Tasmania and was used for convict services. A nominal fee is charged and tours are offered daily from 10 A.M. to 4 P.M. Call 31-0911 for details.

Though the smallest of the country's royal gardens, the **Royal Tasmanian Botanic Gardens** rarely disappoints visitors. Located near the Tasman Bridge and next to Government House (about a mile from the chapel; it's best to drive there), the garden features many exotic species, including a few like the towering huon pine, which is indigenous to the island. One of its most popular areas is the Japanese Garden, which includes azaleas, camellias, conifers, Oriental flowering cherries, as well as a large collection of Japanese maples. The garden includes a lovely tea room and admission is free. Open daily from about 8 A.M. to 5 P.M. Call 34-6299.

Drive along the waterfront to Salamanca Place and Battery Point. **Salamanca Place** is a row of attractively restored sandstone warehouses on the harborfront, filled with arts and crafts shops, furniture and antique stores, as well as food and grog establishments with colorful names like the Ball and Chain and Sloppy's Waterfront Inn. The area, located just below Battery Point, truly comes alive every Saturday morning with its weekly open-air bazaar.

Located less than 1½ kilometers (a mile) from downtown, the historic **Battery Point** area was named after a battery of guns set up there in 1818. The region has changed very little in the past 150 years and features many cozy bed-and-breakfast establishments and quaint shops. The National Trust offers a marvelous walking tour of the area every Saturday for about $3, including morning tea. Allow about two hours for the tour. For further details, call 23-6236.

Like much of Tasmania, Hobart features some fine **golf courses.** Local clubs welcome overseas visitors as long as they have a letter of introduction from their home course. For further information, contact the Tasmanian Golf Council, 2 Queen Street, Bellerive, or call 44-3600.

The city's best shops are located near the waterfront at Battery Point and Salamanca Place. Then, too, the downtown district is home to both fine arts and crafts shops as well as more traditional stores like the ones found in the **Cat & Fiddle Arcade,** located in Hobart's main shopping block, bordered by Elizabeth, Murray, Liverpool, and Collins streets.

This arcade contains about seventy small shops, two department stores, a large gift shop, and a bank.

## ❦ RESTAURANTS

**The Astor Grill,** 157 Macquarie St.; (002) 34-8333. This is perhaps the city's most popular spot for a cut of prime Tassie beef. Though seafood and poultry offerings abound as well, it's hard to go wrong with an eye fillet, porterhouse, or rump for a main course. The restaurant also features a wide range of hot and cold appetizers, but meat lovers will enjoy the Yugoslavian Chevapchichi—small skinless sausages liberally spiced and garnished with finely chopped onions and tomatoes.

Three-course meals will cost about $30. Open for lunch Mon.–Fri. and dinner daily. All major cards accepted.

**Dear Friends,** 8 Brook St.; (002) 23-2646. This is considered by many Tassies to be the island's finest restaurant. Situated in an elegantly restored, 19th-century flour mill not far from the waterfront, the restaurant's menu can best be described as international, and the service is both prompt and professional.

Main course favorites include everything from Tasmanian Atlantic salmon to fresh game meats while opening courses vary from venison fettuccine to barbecued boned quail.

Because of its intimate size and immense popularity, reservations are recommended. Expect to pay about $40 for three courses. Open for lunch Tues.–Fri. and dinner Mon.–Sat. All major cards accepted.

**Mures Fish House,** 5 Knopwood St.; (002) 23-6917. A long-standing favorite in Hobart, Mures specializes in the very best of local seafood delicacies. The restaurant is a delight as well, located in a cozy, old house in the historic Battery Point part of town. Expect to pay about $26 for three courses.

Owners George and Jill Mure have recently opened another winner, the **Mures Fish Centre,** located on the wharf overlooking Constitution Dock. This complex includes everything from a sashimi bar to a take-out shop for tourists on the go. The older restaurant is open for lunch Mon.–Fri. and dinner daily. Most major cards accepted.

**Prosser's on the Beach;** Sandy Bay Regatta Pavilion, Beach Rd.; (002) 25-2276. Prosser's likewise emphasizes the wealth of local seafood offerings, but manages to provide good beef and poultry alternatives for landlubbers as well. Save room for one of their delicious desserts!

Situated along Beach Rd., in the Sandy Bay area of town, on the top floor of the Sandy Bay Regatta Pavilion, the restaurant has great waterfront views and a relaxed atmosphere. Open for lunch Tues.–Fri. and Sun.; dinner Mon.–Sat. Most major cards.

**Sisco's,** 121 Macquarie St.; (002) 23-2059. This lovely restaurant, tucked away in a laneway near Hadleys Orient Hotel, features Spanish Mediterranean dishes, a rarity in Australian eateries.

Specialties include paella and dishes like *mariscada* (local shellfish dipped in a chili sauce) and *zarzuela* (a selection of seafoods served in a brandy almond sauce). Three-course meals will cost about $24. Open for lunch Tues.–Fri. and dinner Tues.–Sat. All major cards.

## NIGHTLIFE

While there are a variety of late-night spots in Hobart, the center of evening entertainment here would have to be the **Wrest Point Hotel-Casino.** You'll find a nonstop assortment of activities, ranging from gaming tables to slot machines to a cabaret room with a dinner show most evenings, and a disco open every night of the week.

Men are asked to wear jackets after 7 P.M., and jeans, sneakers, and sandals are taboo. Still, the place is pretty relaxed for a casino—less frantic than the Las Vegas/Atlantic City world American visitors may be used to; it's surprisingly quiet and the staff is friendly. For details, call (002) 25-0112.

## EXCURSIONS FROM HOBART

**Devil Jet Tours.** This aptly named thirty-minute rapid river run will leave visitors either breathless or howling like the island's ferocious Tasmanian devil. It's not so much a joy ride along twenty kilometers (13 miles) of the mighty Derwent River as it is a supersonic powerboat trip that guarantees satisfaction to the thrill-seeking crowd. Fares run about $28 per person. City pick-up available as well as day-long tours of the area. Call (002) 61-3460.

**Derwent River/Harbor Cruises.** Several larger vessels offer regular tours of the city's waterfront and Derwent River. These tours range in time from two hours to all-day affairs. Luncheon and twilight cruises are also available. One of the more popular trips offered by the *Derwent Explorer* is a four-hour cruise stopping at the mouthwatering Cadbury chocolate factory in Claremont. This trip costs about $15 per person and leaves twice a week. For further information, contact the *Derwent Explorer* at (002) 34-4032. Other operators include: Commodore Cruises, (002) 34-9294; M.V. Emmalisa, (002) 23-5893; and "Carmel D" Leisure Cruises, (002) 25-2725.

**Hastings Cave State Reserve.** This huge limestone cavern is located near Southport about seventy minutes southwest of Hobart (take the Huon Highway). Daily tours are offered by local park rangers into the largest of the many caves in the region, Newdegate Cave. Geologists estimate it to be more than forty million years old with ceiling and floor formations going back at least ten million years. At a nearby lush grove of rainforest-type bush is a thermal pool where the water temperature rarely varies from about 26° C (81.5° F). Admission to the cave is about $4.

A day-tour taking in Newdegate Cave, the thermal pool, and the neighboring rich fruit orchards in the Huon Valley is offered through Tasbureau. Cost of the trip is about $35. For information, call (002) 30-0211.

**Mt. Field National Park.** This marvelous national park is located about an hour north of Hobart in the Derwent Valley. It features both stunning forest hideaways, including the unusual two-tiered set of waterfalls known as Russell Falls, and splendid vistas from atop peaks like mounts Mawson and Field. Its hills and vales are alive with myriad exotic plants and birdlife. In addition to a day tour run through Tasbureau, two private operators drop by the park. While these tours offered by Bushventures 4WD Tours (002-29-4291) and Open Spaces (002-31-0977), will cost substantially more than the $35 charged by Tasbureau, they are far more informative and leisurely paced.

**Mt. Wellington.** Many would consider their stay in Hobart incomplete without a trip to the top of nearby Mt. Wellington, which often is snow-capped during the colder months of the year. Beautiful views of Hobart as well as the rest of southeastern Tasmania are possible from this vantage point. Regular trips are offered through Tasbureau, as is a tour designed for fitness buffs. Brake Out Cycling Tours takes you to the top via coach and lets you coast down from the mountain on a multi-geared bike. Cost is about $48 and includes transport, lunch, and cycling gear. Call (002) 23-7020.

**Port Arthur National Park.** This bucolic setting, located about 100 kilometers (63 miles) southeast of Hobart on the Tasman Peninsula, belies its founding as the home to some 13,000 convicts between 1830 and 1877. Visitors today roam among the ruins of the once-teeming convict colony in structures such as the church, "model prison," and hospital, all of which were built by the inmates, but have long since fallen into disrepair due to brush fires. It was commonly referred to as "hell on earth" among the convicts, a nickname enhanced by jail guards armed with guns and vicious dogs, as well as by tall tales of shark-infested waters. Highly informative tours of the penal settlement are conducted hourly, and if time permits, make the short cruise to the nearby Isle of the Dead, where nearly 2,000 people, mostly convicts, were buried. Admission charge to the park is about $5. For more information, call (002) 50-2363.

Plan on spending a day at the site as well as other points of interest along the peninsula such as the **Tasmanian Devil Park** and **Bush Mill.** The former exhibit, of course, features the island's most notorious critter, the Tasmanian devil, which, true to its name, is rarely in anything but a foul mood. Though a hard-core carnivore, the devil, which resembles a large skunk, rarely hunts down its own game, preferring instead to feast on carrion. They are worth a look-see, but cute and cuddly they are not! Call (002) 50-3230 for details.

Bush Mill offers visitors everything from a lovely ride on a miniature steam-driven train to a walk back in time through a well-conceived turn-of-the-century steam sawmill village. The complex also includes a souvenir shop and tea room. For details, call (002) 50-2221.

Tasbureau operates a day trip taking in all these sites for about $50. Call (002) 30-0211 for details.

**Scenic Flights.** Several smaller air carriers offer flights ranging from a half-hour bird's-eye view of Hobart to full-day trips over the island. Half-hour trips cost about $25 while half-day trips cost about $100 and full-day excursions about $180. Two of the more well-known carriers are Par Avion Air Tours, (002) 48-5390 and Tas Air, (002) 48-5088.

# Richmond and the Midlands Highway

The so-called Midlands Highway between Hobart and Launceston is a fairly straight and flat road through fertile sheep and cattle grazing land. Many historic towns dot the roadside, though, and are worth a look if time permits.

The first place to head for if going from Hobart northward, though not actually on the highway, is the historic hamlet of Richmond. In addition to featuring the oldest bridge in Australia (a convict-built beauty dating to 1823), many of Richmond's shops have retained their colonial look and atmosphere. Delicious sweets and Devonshire teas are available, too.

After leaving Richmond, a short drive will get you to the Midlands Highway where historic towns such as Kempton and Oatlands will first appear and then Ross, perhaps the loveliest spot of them all. Though a small community, **Ross** exudes colonial charm as evidenced by the four corners of its Town Square, featuring "Temptation"—the Man-O-Ross Hotel which was set up in 1831 and was well patronized during the early days; "Salvation"—the Roman Catholic Church which was converted from a store in 1920; "Recreation"—represented by the town hall; and "Damnation"—home of the town's early jail. It is a great place to walk about, shop, take tea or lunch at one of its fine establishments.

Finally, farther up the road and just a few miles from Launceston is **Evandale,** long known for its wealth of historic buildings and rich grazing land. You can find locally made goods here that make unusual souvenirs.

Like Hobart, Launceston owes much of its European founding to its waterfront location. Along the upper reaches of the Tamar River, the town has a number of historic homes and garden settings.

**Franklin House,** for instance, is a historic home dating to 1838, built for a local innkeeper and brewer. Later, it was turned into a boys school. It has been dutifully restored and furnished by the National Trust. Morning and afternoon tea available. Located about 6½ kilometers (four miles) from town, it can be reached by regular city bus service. Allow about an hour for the visit. Open daily from 9 A.M. to 5 P.M. (it closes an hour earlier in wintertime). Call 44-7824.

**Cataract Gorge** is one of Tasmania's most spectacular sights—a 400-acre state reserve offering a wide range of scenic walks and places to relax for a cup of tea or lunch. While the gorge was created more than forty million years ago during violent volcanic eruptions, the park today offers breathtaking cliff walks and bird's-eye views of the steep ravine from a chairlift. Locals also enjoy stopping by at night when the gorge is floodlit. Call ahead to find out lighting times. There is no charge for entering the park. Chairlift ride costs about $3. Allow a couple of hours to enjoy the views. Call 37-1288.

An attractive theme park, **Penny Royal World,** located near Cataract Gorge, houses several popular attractions, including a gunpowder mill and watermill complex, a restored tram car, and a paddle boat named *Lady Stelfox,* which cruises the Cataract Gorge and upper Tamar River. Open daily; separate fees charged for individual attractions or about $12 for everything. Call 31-6699.

For combining exercise with an introduction to native fauna try a round of **golf** at the 18-hole course at the Launceston hotel-casino. Despite being slowly surrounded by a suburban sprawl of homes, a recent game was interrupted by a mob of cuddly wallabies in search of greener pastures as well as by the turtle-paced stroll of an echidna, a porcupine-like creature that slowly ambled across several fairways.

Two of Launceston's best-known stores feature woolen products made from the thousands of sheep that graze in the northeastern and central districts of the state. **Waverley Woolen Mills** is open every day from 9 A.M. to 5 P.M. and in addition to a well-stocked showroom of woolen goods, features a tour through the century-old mill, a coffee/tea shop, and the National Automobile Museum of Tasmania. There is a minimal charge for museum tours. All major credit cards accepted. For details, call 39-1106.

The **Tamar Knitting Mills** likewise feature fine garments made from local lambswool. Visitors can see yarn being knitted into cloth on both new and old machinery, as well as a number of other exhibits. Open daily with nominal entrance fee. Call 44-8255.

Launceston's downtown area meanwhile is home to several quaint crafts stores like the Old Umbrella Shop and Emma's Arts, both found on George Street. Built in the 1860s, the **Old Umbrella Shop** not only features a display of parasols used during the past century, but modern samples, souvenirs, and gift baskets. Call 31-9248. **Emma's Arts,** 31-5630, specializes in crafts carved from indigenous woods like huon pine and myrtle, while a third store, the **Design Centre of Tasmania,** in Tamar Street, combines timeless works of wood with a gallery of glass, ceramics, weaving, water colors, and oil paintings. Call 31-5506.

Just around the corner from these stores is **Yorktown Square,** a marvelous re-creation of a colonial shopping village of fashion, gifts, and fine foods. This collection of old-fashioned-looking stores, which opened in 1984, is just right for either serious buyers or window shoppers.

❧ When in Yorktown Sq., don't pass up one of the mouthwatering cakes or pastries at **The Gateau,** or, for true sweet-tooths, a single scoop of freshly made ice cream from the **Great Australian Ice Creamery;** call 31-4002.

## ❧ RESTAURANTS

**Burgundy's,** 124 George St.; (003) 31-5422. "We're a pub that happens to have a nice restaurant, too," is how one waiter describes Burgundy's. Indeed, the restaurant shares space with a raucous bar known as O'Keefe's Pub, but you'd hardly know it from the lovely Victorian decor of the main dining room.

Burgundy's offers an international range of dishes, including braised pheasant breast with diced Tasmanian fruit, porterhouse steaks, chicken breasts filled with brie and coated in breadcrumbs and served with a mustard seed sauce, as well as various local fish favorites.

The wine list is extensive but no half bottles are available—however, waiters have been known to split fine bottles.

Expect to pay about $35 for three courses. Open for dinner Tues.–Sat. Most major cards accepted.

**Calabrisella,** 56 Wellington St.; (003) 31-1958. Make no mistake about this place, it is just an unpretentious restaurant specializing in great pastas and pizzas. It has a very informal atmosphere and is one of the few places open Sun. nights. For about $8 you can get a plate of spaghetti, covered with mushrooms and tiny prawns, big enough to fill two people. Although the toppings are not fresh ingredients, the sauce is first rate. BYOB. Open Fri. for lunch and Wed.–Mon. for dinner. Most cards accepted.

**Shrimps,** corner of George and Paterson sts.; (003) 34-0584. If it's seafood you want, then head for Shrimps when in Launceston. Try the garlic prawns with bean sprouts for an appetizer (locals also rave about the cold-smoked sea trout), and the huge cast-iron kettle serving of mussels marinara for a main course. It's hard to go wrong with any of their offerings, though, and non-seafood dishes are available, too. The restaurant has a small but high standard of Australian wines in stock and half bottles are available.

Housed in a classic Georgian-style building dating back to 1824, the restaurant has been painstakingly decorated—there are even a couple of blue-masked lovebirds in the lower dining area. Open for lunch Mon.–Fri. and dinner Mon.–Sat. All major cards accepted.

**Woofie's,** Macquarie House, Civic Square; (003) 34-0695. This casual eatery is housed in the historic Macquarie House building in the heart of the city. Although a lovely spot for dinner, Woofie's is perhaps an even better place to visit for lunch. Its extensive blackboard menu of daily specials concentrates on local produce, but insiders highly recommend one of the pasta dishes or crêpes for lunch. King Island products are also emphasized and save room for an American-style hot caramel fudge sundae. The restaurant is licensed. Open for lunch Mon.–Fri. and dinner Mon.–Sat. Most cards accepted.

## NIGHTLIFE

Again, it's the casino that is the town's hottest nightspot, although the **Launceston Federal Country Club Hotel-Casino** is somewhat smaller and younger than its Hobart counterpart. The sprawling setting is quite attractive—even if gambling isn't your thing; you'll also find a disco here, eight bars, and a cabaret.

## EXCURSIONS FROM LAUNCESTON

**Central Highlands.** This lush rolling bushland is studded with picturesque waterfalls, fern-lined walking trails, and thousands of lakes and mountain tarns. A local tour outfit called Tas-Trek picks you up at your hotel and has you drinking morning tea following a leisurely hike at the beautiful Liffey Falls State Reserve. Then, too, the day away also includes a long look at the so-called Great Lake and even a stop for a beer at the Compleat Angler, a true-blue Tassie pub that comes complete with its own pet wombat (a cuddly cousin to the koala), that snuggles up close to the fireplace on colder days. Cost of the trip is about $60. For details, call (003) 31-1000.

**Clarendon House.** This grand Georgian mansion rises out of the flat sheep-grazing land just outside the village of Evandale like a re-incarnation of Scarlet O'Hara's precious Tara. Built in 1838 for a wealthy sheep grazier, the home took twenty years to complete and used many materials sent from England. Visitors may make their own way to the historic homestead or sign up for a tour by a local outfit such as Scenic Travel Tasmania, which offers a half-day tour of Clarendon for about $20 (003-26-5306), or Classic Coach Tours' one-day trip that costs about $25 and takes in some other historic settings as well as Clarendon. Call (003) 31-5833.

**Mole Creek Caves/Wildlife Park.** An easy 45-minute drive west of Launceston brings you to **Deloraine,** an attractive town that has restored many of its Victorian and Georgian-era buildings dating back to the 1840s. Not far beyond Deloraine is Mole Creek, home to some of the state's tasty leatherwood honey and two underground addresses worth dropping by.

One is Marakoopa Cave, a huge limestone cavern that in addition to its many formations, features rare insects known as glow-worms that light up the ceiling on one of the walls like a natural planetarium.

**Get to the cave before the first tour at 10 A.M. and you're sure to see flocks of colorful green parrots roosting in the trees near the gatehouse.**

Nearby is King Solomon's Cave, a good deal smaller than Marakoopa, but offering an equal number of geologic wonders. Admission charge to either cave is $4.

Back toward town is the marvelous Mole Creek Wildlife Park (just look for the place with the huge Tasmanian devil replica in front). Open from 9 A.M. to 5 P.M., this well-kept park features most of Australia's fauna favorites like kangaroos, wallabies, koalas, and wombats, many of which roam freely about the grounds. Park staff also invite visitors to take part in regular feeding sessions with many of these cuddly creatures. Admission charge is about $5.

Classic Coach Tours offers a day-long trip taking in these spots as well as some others for about $25. Call (003) 31-5833.

**Tamar Valley.** This beautiful valley located to the north of Launceston figures prominently in the city's early founding due to the Tamar River which unites it with the ocean port of Bell Bay.

A half-hour drive north of the city along the East Tamar Highway, for instance, brings you near the **Bridestowe Lavender Farm,** one of the world's largest producers of perfumery lavender oil. Only open to the public for a few weeks during the flowering season in December and January, the farm is a must if you happen to be there during this time of year. Farther north along the eastern highway is the **Pilot Station,** at Low Head, dating back to the early 1800s, and including a small but informative maritime museum. Just down the road is the **Low Head Lighthouse** where some visitors may wish to climb up and gaze out across Bass Strait.

Not far back along the eastern highway is a turn-off to the Batman Bridge, the only riverbank link between Low Head and Launceston. Once on the other side, turn right and head for **Beaconsfield,** at one time a booming gold-mining town. At the **Grubb Shaft Museum Complex,** you'll see how the town's gold-mining operations extracted nearly thirty tons of the precious mineral from the ground from 1877 to 1914. Nominal charge for the tour.

Farther south, only a 15-minute drive from Launceston, is **St. Matthias Vineyard,** a popular spot for sampling (and buying) some of Tassie's award-winning vintages. Open daily from September to May and by arrangement from June to August; call (003) 30-1700 for details.

A far different experience awaits those who make their way to the **Notley Fern Gorge** outside of Exeter. A one-hour loop track takes hikers deep into the heart of dense bush, huge ferns, and towering eucalypt trees. Good barbecue facilities make it a great place for a picnic lunch.

Both Classic Coach Tours (003-31-5833) and Scenic Travel Tasmania (003-26-5306) offer tours of the Tamar Valley. Call for details.

# Extended Touring: East and West

For those with more time to spare than just two or three days, Tassie offers a wide variety of other options. For starters, self-drive tourists may like traveling along the East Coast which is filled with excellent **fishing, skin diving,** and **surfing** sites near towns like St. Helens and Scamander.

You can rent fishing equipment in Hobart at Bridges Brothers—Compleat Angler, 142 Elizabeth Street (002-34-3791) or at The Fishing Connection, 77 Harrington Street (002-34-8800); in the Launceston area, at Jet Fly, 78 Main Street, Cressy (003-97-6272), or Terry Charlton's Sports Store, 155 Brisbane Street, in Launceston (003-31-8322).

Diving enthusiasts can be outfitted in Hobart at Sport and Dive, 109 Elizabeth Street (002-34-3798).

**Bushwalkers** may like tackling some of the island's rugged national parkland found on the wild western side of Tassie. Week-long treks into World Heritage–listed real estate such as Cradle Mountain–Lake St. Clair, South West, and Franklin/Lower Gordon Wild Rivers national parks can be arranged through several tour operators such as World Expeditions and Craclair Guided Tours. Guides are especially recommended for trips lasting more than one day. (Contact Tasbureau offices on the mainland for details on tours, as well as maps if you're planning to do it on your own. Camping areas will be designated in the national parks.)

Less adventurous but no less rewarding extended tours into these regions are offered by many of the **four-wheel-drive operators** such as Bushventures 4WD Tours (002-29-4291), Open Spaces (002-31-0977), and Tas Trek (003-97-6340). These companies often offer other sorts of trips as well like **kayaking, canoeing,** or **river rafting.**

**Note:** Drastic weather changes are common occurrences in Tassie, especially in the higher elevations, so take some warm clothing and rain gear if planning long trips. Remember, the next major landfall south of the island is Antarctica!

Extended island tours are also offered as well by leading mainland coach companies such as AAT King's, Australian Pacific, and Ansett Pioneer. Further information may be obtained from any mainland branch or Tasbureau office.

# 8

# QUEENSLAND

Queensland encapsulates Australia's environmental diversity. From the Great Barrier Reef and coastal rainforests to the plains and desert of the Outback, Queensland is the great outdoors. It may be tasted at luxury level, but the visitor prepared to "rough it" a little will be rewarded with an intriguing insight into its many complex characters—animal, geological, vegetable, and human.

The state covers more than 1.7 million square kilometers, almost a quarter of the continent, an area twice the size of Texas. Distances between towns are vast and, "out west," are sometimes measured by locals in "stubbies"—the number of bottles of beer that will be consumed on the journey. (Even a "three-stubbie drive," however, is not recommended as the roads are often rough and the legal blood alcohol limit is .08.) Unless you're satisfied sipping cocktails in a tropical resort, be prepared to travel, even without venturing beyond the coastal strip. From Brisbane, the capital in the southeast, to Cairns, gateway to Far North Queensland, is over 1,300 kilometers (over 800), a two-hour direct flight, or 25 hours by express coach.

For most people, air travel is the only option, but visitors planning an extended trip will cut costs by renting a car or campervan. It's possible to base yourself in Brisbane, explore some of the state's most rugged rainforest, take a charter flight by amphibious plane to the southernmost part of the Great Barrier Reef, and even stay overnight on a working cattle station. But the benefits of traveling farther north are many. Not least, the chance to sample life in the slow lane where people are far removed from city preoccupations and have more time for a yarn (you'll notice they drawl) and to show you their country.

Queensland's east is a rich, narrow coastal plain, containing most of the state's 2.4 million people and secondary industry, and fringed, from Cape York at the top to Bundaberg (378 kilometers, 235 miles, north of Brisbane), by the Great Barrier

Reef. West of the aptly named Great Dividing Range are vast dry plains rising in the northwest to rugged uplands which then slope to the marshlands of the southern Gulf of Carpentaria. Here, sheep and cattle graze on stations measured by their owners—who steadfastly refuse to convert like the rest of Australia to metric—in copious square miles.

First settled as a penal colony in 1824, Queensland became a brand new state in 1859. Squatters seeking land for their sheep and cattle pioneered the Outback and were followed by the hardy optimists of the gold rushes. The towns grew in their wake. There are remnants of the convict days around Brisbane, though much colonial architecture has been sacrificed to progress. The farther north you travel the more survivors of the pioneering era you'll see, like the rambling weatherboard houses known as Queenslanders, perched on stilts and encircled with verandas to capture any relieving cool breezes.

The climate is sub-tropical to tropical and winter is normally the best time to visit. Daily temperatures in the south of the state range from the high 20°s C (high 70°s F) to a minimum of around 20° C in summer, and from the low 20°s C to around 10° C (50° F) in winter. In the far north, the daily range is low 30°s C (90°s F) to low 20°s C in summer, the "wet" season, and mid 20°s C to between 16° and 20° C in winter. The Outback is harsher, with a summer variation from mid/high 30°s C to low 20°s C and winter from mid 20°s C to below 10° C. Remember, averages disguise extremes. In the north and west summer temperatures can be uncomfortably high, tolerably less so in the west where the humidity is low.

## Slip, Slop, Slap . . .

. . . goes the Queensland Cancer Council's warning ditty. Slip on a shirt, slop on some sunscreen, and slap on a hat. The necessity for taking precautions against the sun cannot be overemphasized. Summer temperatures will often reach the 30°s C (90° F), even 40°s C (about 110° F). If you're planning any water-based excursions, the risk of sunburn is multiplied. Wear a hat, the Mick Dundee style is fashionable with locals. A slouch hat of the kind worn by Aussie sporting teams will mark you as a tourist, and one with corks bobbing from the brim, though a semi-effective fly deterrent, will cause mirth. It's no coincidence Queensland medical researchers pioneered ultra-violet sunscreen—the incidence of sun-induced skin cancer is high in this state. Lotions are graded according to a Skin Protection Factor (SPF) from 4 (light, for tanned skin) to 15 (maximum, for pale skin). Even if the product claims water resistance, it's advisable to re-apply after swimming. If you're still burning, cover up (slip on a shirt, wrap a towel around your legs) and seek shade.

Visitors should not feel underdressed without ties or stockings. In summer, shorts and short-sleeved shirts and sundresses are regular office attire in most cities (Brisbane slightly more formal). Take your cue from the locals. Sandals or loafers are acceptable, with sandshoes obligatory for reef walking and boots for venturing into the bush. For winter, a light jacket is all you'll need in the north. In the south and west, long pants and a medium-weight jacket will be necessary. Don't forget a swimsuit.

---

### Organizing

Most visitors will find they have to leave many fascinating areas of the state off their itineraries. To make hard decisions easier, this chapter has been divided into regional sections with the emphasis on the popular coastal belt. The sections cover the state from south to north, beginning with Brisbane and its nearby Gold and Sunshine Coasts. Then there is Central Queensland, with side trips to the Outback, the Far North, and, to its west, the Gulf Savannah country. The Great Barrier Reef and coastal islands complete this sketch of the Sunshine State.

---

## TRAVEL

## Flying

If coming from another country, you could begin your Australian visit by flying to one of Queensland's international airports. They're in the capital, Brisbane, in Townsville, 1,460 km (over 900 miles) to its north, and Cairns, 800 km (about 500 miles) farther north. Most foreign travelers, however, elect to fly first to the southern capitals of Sydney or Melbourne.

The domestic airlines, Ansett Airlines, 733 Ann St., Brisbane, (07) 854-2222, and Australian Airlines, 247 Adelaide St., Brisbane, (07) 223-3333, have daily services between Brisbane, Townsville, Cairns, and other major centers. Direct flights also operate from the southern capitals to resorts such as the Gold and Sunshine Coasts and Whitsunday Islands.

Smaller operators within Queensland service lesser centers and remote parts. Sunstate Airlines, 247 Adelaide St., Brisbane, (07) 223-3333, and Lloyd Aviation, 733 Ann St., Brisbane, (07) 854-2222, fly to the minor coastal ports while Flight West, 1st Floor, 55 McLachlan St., Fortitude Valley, (07) 252-1152, services the Outback.

## Taking the Train

Air-conditioned trains link Perth, Adelaide, Alice Springs, Melbourne, Sydney (and centers between) with Brisbane. There is no rail link to Darwin. Queensland's most traveled route is between Brisbane and Cairns, serviced by the *Sunlander* and *Queenslander*. Other long-distance passenger trains are the *Ca-*

*pricornian* (Brisbane to Rockhampton in central Queensland), the *Westlander* (Brisbane to Quilpie in the southwest), the *Midlander* (Rockhampton to Winton in the central west), and the *Inlander* (Townsville in the north to Mount Isa in the northwest). All these trains have sleeping berths and dining cars (you won't write home about the food). Further information available from Queensland Railways, 208 Adelaide St., Brisbane, (07) 225-0211.

## Taking the Bus

Coach companies provide economical, express services into and within Queensland. Discounted passes for unlimited travel are available. Major long-distance operators in Queensland include Greyhound, Brisbane Transit Centre, Brisbane, (07) 240-9333; Skennars, 22 Barry Pde., Fortitude Valley, Brisbane, (07) 832-1148; Ansett Pioneer, Brisbane Transit Centre, (07) 228-8003; and Deluxe, 114 Elizabeth St., Brisbane, (07) 229-7655.

**The Brisbane Transit Centre on Roma St. is a pivotal point for all inter- and intra-state and local trains and coaches. On the Rail, Coach, and Mall levels computerized video information is available and there is a tourist information center on the Mall level.**

## Driving

Highways link Brisbane and other state capitals. From Adelaide, Brisbane is approximately 2,000 km (over 1,200 miles), from Melbourne, about 1,800 km (under 1,200 miles), and from Sydney, about 1,010 km (625 miles).

Petrol prices fluctuate enormously, but you can expect to pay around $.60 per liter and $.80 in remote areas. (In isolated parts it is sometimes advisable to carry extra fuel and water; take local advice before setting out.) Speed limits are 60 km.p.h. in built-up areas and 100 km.p.h. on the open road unless otherwise indicated. Seat belts are compulsory and in some resorts (Airlie Beach in the Whitsundays for example) police are known for their aggressive "revenue raising" on this infringement.

## Rentals

Given limited time, you'll probably choose to fly to Queensland and hire a car in one of the major cities. The leading companies in Brisbane include Hertz, (07) 268-6133; Avis, (07) 268-5322; Budget, (07) 268-6444; and Thrifty, (07) 268-7377. Most rentals allow unlimited km, but if you're renting a car in one area and returning it in another a drop-off fee occasionally applies. To rent a car you must be over 21 and have a current driver's licence (International Driving Permits accepted).

The car-rental companies also rent campervans (two to three berths) and motor homes (four to six berths) which bring even more independence to a holiday on the road. Most vehicles have a refrigerator, sink, gas stove, wardrobe, convertible beds, and a water tank, and some have a shower and toilet. There are more than 250 roadside rest areas in Queensland—safe areas where vehicles can stop, with fireplaces, picnic tables and shelters, water, and toilets. Overnight stops or camping are permitted in most of these, but their appeal is limited, as they are generally located beside highways. There are unfortunately few places where it is legal to park your car and camp wild in Queensland—in most places you will have to park your campervan in a caravan park. Consolation is that the parks are frequently in prime positions in terms of views, proximity to beaches and town facilities.

Amenities at caravan parks vary. Most offer communal shower/toilet/laundry blocks and barbecues. The majority have electricity at each van site, a shop for food, gas refills, and ice. Some have a swimming pool, TV lounge, and restaurants. Prices vary accordingly, but expect to pay $10 per night for a van site for campervan and $5–$10 per night to pitch a tent. Most caravan parks also have on-site vans which are equipped with basic crockery, cutlery, and bedding and cost around $10–$20 a night.

Further information on touring Queensland is available from the **Queensland Government Travel Centre,** 196 Adelaide St., Brisbane 4000, (07) 833-5300.

# Brisbane

Brisbane, with a population of slightly more than one million, is a sprawling city which grew around the Brisbane River. The central business district is a triangle formed by a loop in the river with the sub-tropical Botanic Gardens at its apex. Best way to explore the city center is on foot—the streets run on a grid pattern with those parallel to Queen, the main street, named after queens of England and intersecting streets after kings.

Most of the city's historic buildings are within walking distance of the center, so base yourself as close as possible. With the exceptions of South Brisbane and Paddington, the suburbs are primarily residential, although some have attractions worth visiting.

Inner-city Paddington is a speciality shopping precinct set among colonial cottages and shops, a good place to pick up Australian-made craft and clothing—not souvenirs in the strictest sense, but quality gifts. South Brisbane, across the river from the city center, underwent a massive redevelopment for World Expo '88. A fortunate by-product was a range of accommodation near the city, but at lower prices.

## TRAVEL

Council buses operate 6:30 A.M.–11:15 P.M. on weekdays with reduced services on weekends and holidays. A $4 Rover ticket for an unlimited day of travel is available. Timetables and route information are available from the Public Transport Information

Centre, at the corner of George and Ann sts. in the city, (07) 225-4444, where suburban train information is also available.

Ferries between the city and the south side of the river run every 10 minutes during the day and every 15 minutes after 6:30 P.M. Wharfs are at the end of Edward St. and Customs House at the top of Queen St. Phone (07) 399-4768 for more information. The major taxi company is B&W Cabs Ltd., (07) 229-1000. To rent bikes contact Brisbane Bicycle Sales and Hire, 214 Margaret St., (07) 229-2592.

For further information: **Tourism Brisbane,** City Hall, King George Sq., Brisbane 4000, (07) 221-8411, or the Queensland Government Travel Centre (see Queensland Travel, above).

# ORGANIZED TOURS

Coach (bus) tours are convenient and provide a good overview, though you must move with the group. Reputable companies include Aladdin's Tours, with head office at Brisbane Transit Centre, 3rd Floor, Roma St., (07) 229-9477, or tours departing from the Queensland Government Travel Centre, at the corner of Adelaide and Edward sts., (07) 226-5400. Boomerang Tours, 3rd Floor, Brisbane Transit Centre, Roma St., (07) 221-9922, also have day and half-day tours of the city and will pick up from inner-city accommodation.

City Walkabout Tours, c/o Portway Meet and Greet, 123 Anzac Ave., Redcliffe, (07) 283-1681, take leisurely strolls through the city center. They leave from the statue in King George Square at 1:30 P.M. Mon.–Fri.

The city can also be seen from the water on the paddle wheeler *Kookaburra Queen.* Head office is at 247 St. Paul's Terr., Fortitude Valley, (07) 252-1400. Morning tea, lunch and dinner cruises are available. Koala Cruises also provide the opportunity to see some suburbs from the river, en route to one of Brisbane's oldest attractions, **Lone Pine Koala Sanctuary.** They leave the Riverside Centre at 12:50 and North Quay at 1:10 daily. Entry to the sanctuary is reduced from $8 to $6.50 for passengers and the three-hour return trip costs $10. Alternatively, you can visit Lone Pine by catching Council bus 518 which departs from opposite the Mayfair Crest Hotel on Roma St., hourly from 7:35 A.M. At the sanctuary you can feed kangaroos, watch platypus, see a Tasmanian devil, and cuddle a koala. Lone Pine, open 9.30 A.M.–5 P.M. daily, is on Jesmond Rd., Fig Tree Pocket.

# ❦ ACCOMMODATIONS

Best advice is to stay as close as possible to the center. Unless otherwise noted, the hotels in this section accept all major credit cards (American Express, Diners Club, Visa, and MasterCard) and have air-conditioning. Brisbane has not outgrown its "big country town" reputation and at least in the center you'll have a chance of a meal after 9 P.M. or on Sun.

At the premium level the **Brisbane City Travelodge,** where prices range from $145 a room, is conveniently located above the Transit Centre on Roma St., Brisbane 4000. The hotel has a pool, the usual catering facilities, plus a bar much favored by jazz enthusiasts for its live shows every night. Tel. (07) 238-2222.

When the **Hilton International** first opened, Brisbanites used to go there just to ride in the exterior glass elevator that services the rooms around its internal atrium. The novelty has worn off now, so you won't have to fight for space. Accommodation is Hilton at its best, overlooking the Queen St. Mall and with the major department stores at the doorstep. There's also a swimming pool and gym. The Atrium Café is renowned for its banquet breakfasts, while Victoria's Restaurant is one of the city's most elegant dining venues. Single rooms begin at $170 a night, doubles from $190. The address is 190 Elizabeth St., Brisbane 4000; (07) 231-3131, fax (07) 231-3199.

The **Sheraton Brisbane Hotel** complex incorporates the Central Railway Station (no problems with train noise, however) and you can walk out of the hotel and drink on a platform bar with commuters on their way home from work. Inside, guests are cosseted from the daily grind. There's a pool, as well as a health club. The hotel's signature restaurant, Denisons, on the top level, provides excellent city views and formal dining. The Sheraton is at 249 Turbot St., Brisbane 4000, (07) 835-3535, fax (07) 835-4960, and room prices start at $190.

The **Brisbane Parkroyal** is a few blocks from the heart of the city but has the advantage of being across the road from the Botanic Gardens, a great spot for a walk or jog. On the premises, you'll find a health club and a pool. If you'd rather exercise by pedal, Brisbane Bicycle Sales and Hire is next door to arrange a bike (there are cycle paths in the gardens). The Parkroyal is at the corner of Alice and Albert sts., Brisbane 4000; (07) 221-3411. Room rates are $132–$165.

In the moderate price category the **Albert Park Motor Inn,** 551 Wickham Terr., Spring Hill 4000, (07) 831-3111, offers comfortable accommodation for around $65 single and $69 double. The **Tower Mill Motor Inn** is also on the city fringes (less than 2 km from the post office). It's at 239 Wickham Terr., (07) 832-1421, with single rooms for around $70 and doubles $80. While neither hotel has a pool, the Centenary Pool (see below) is a short walk away. If you prefer the space of an apartment, **Cliffside** at 25 Ellis St., Kangaroo Point 4169, (07) 345-5534, is a ferry ride across the river from the city. Two-bedroom units begin at $80 a night and weekly rates are available. The hotel has no pool. The **Embassy Hotel,** at the corner of Elizabeth and Edward sts., Brisbane 4000, (07) 221-7616, is right in the city heart, though the accommodation is pub-style (shared bathroom facilities). Rates are around $70 for single and $80 double. Counter meals are available in the downstairs bar.

At budget level (not air-conditioned) **Annie's Shandon Inn,** 405 Upper Edward St., (07) 831-8684, is just 2 km from the post office and offers bed-and-breakfast for $30 single and $40 double. A little farther afield (4 km from the GPO), the **Brisbane International Backpackers Hostel** (836 Brunswick St., New Farm 4005, (07) 358-3777), has dormitory accommodation in a renovated colonial house for around $10 a night, and a courtesy coach from the Transit Centre.

Be sure to see Brisbane's only two remaining convict buildings, the **Commissariat Stores** at 115 William Street in the city and the **Old Windmill** on Wickham Terrace on the city fringe. The windmill was intended to grind grain but because of a design error, failed and was converted to a convict-operated treadmill. It later became a signal post and then a meteorological observatory. Some of the world's first TV broadcasts were beamed from here in the 1930s.

For a glimpse of a gentler time, head for **Early Street Historical Village,** 75 McIlwraith Avenue, Norman Park, where a number of colonial buildings have been preserved in 2 hectares of gardens. Take the Carina-Seven Hills buses 8 A, B, C, D, or E from the Ann Street side of King George Square. Admission is $6 and it's open every day. Light meals are available. For further information phone (07) 398-6866.

**Mt. Coot-tha Forest Park,** (07) 377-5896, encompasses the new botanic gardens with a comprehensive tropical display dome and arid zone collection and Australia's largest planetarium (see how the stars look from the bottom of the world). Open 9:30 A.M.–4:30 P.M.; take a Toowong bus 39 from the Ann Street side of King George Square and, if you want to continue to the mountain-top lookout (see Restaurant listings) connect with a 10C bus.

The **Queensland Art Gallery and Museum** are in the Cultural Centre on the South Bank, South Brisbane. At the museum you can see relics of Queensland's aviation history, fossilized dinosaur remains, and the iron tank in which Mrs. Watson made her fateful escape from Lizard Island. Phone (07) 840-7200 for hours. Admission is free, but a tour of the Cultural Centre's Performing Arts complex costs $2.50. Nearby on Stanley Street, South Brisbane, is the **Queensland Maritime Museum,** a dry dock which is home to steam tug *Forceful,* WW2 frigate *Diamantina,* and an authoritative display of maritime matters. Admission is $2 and it's open on weekends from 10 A.M. to 4:30 P.M. and Wednesdays from 10 A.M. to 3:30 P.M.

### Mary Watson

Mary Watson lived on Lizard Island with her fisherman husband and infant son. In 1881 Aborigines attacked, and Mrs. Watson, her baby, and Chinese servant attempted to escape in an iron boiler tank. Alas, they never made it: her body and that of her son and servant were found on number 5 Howick Island, where they had died of thirst.

The Gold and Sunshine Coasts, Moreton Bay islands and rainforest areas of Mt. Tamborine, and the Gold Coast Hinterland are within day-tripping distance of Brisbane. Boomerang Tours (see Brisbane Organized Tours, above) offer a variety of programs to these destinations.

## SHOPPING

Head for the Paddington circle for locally designed **clothes and resort wear.** Take the Bardon bus 144 from Adelaide or George streets. The driver will sell a Rover ticket for unlimited travel that day. Boutiques to visit for women's wear include Chally and Jane, Shop 121, 261 Given Terrace; Joonz, 47 Arthur Terrace, and Lyn Hadley Clothes, Shop 46, 283 Given Terrace. In the city center, Shepherd's has evening wear made from riotously mismatched printed and floral silk. They're in Rowes Arcade. At the opposite end of the spectrum, Settlers & Company, on the second floor in the new Myer City Store, sells colonial clothing and small items of furniture in much the same way that Banana Republic covers the safari market in the States. Boundary riders' jackets, sundowners' pouches (shoulder bags), and shearers' singlets are popular items here.

The Mansions, a set of terraces on the corner of George and Margaret streets, houses **gift and antique shops,** a **print gallery,** and the National Trust shop—with **Australiana** as the theme for its wares. Paddy's Market, for **bric-a-brac,** is open daily on the corner of Florence and Macquarie streets in New Farm, an inner city suburb just north of the central business district. To reach New Farm take any 160 airport bus from Adelaide and Edward streets and get off at Fortitude Valley. New Farm is a short walk east. For **handcrafted goods** wait for Sunday and head for Cat's Tango Markets in the Riverside Centre in the city. The stalls feature work by local weavers, potters, glass artists, and leather workers, in a colorful setting.

## RECREATION

**Golfers** can head for Indooroopilly Golf Club, (07) 870-2012, or Royal Queensland at Hamilton, (07) 268-3134. Both are a $6 to $10 taxi ride from the city, and have equipment for rent. The Indooroopilly welcomes visitors with 18-hole fees of $8.50 on weekdays, $10 on weekends; the Royal Queensland has reciprocal rights with other golf clubs.

Public **swimming pools** close to the city are the Centenary Pool, 400 Gregory Terrace, (07) 831-8259, open daily from September to April, and the Valley Pool (heated) at 432 Wickham Street, Fortitude Valley, (07) 852-1231, open all year. Entry is $1.10. Phone for opening hours.

Tennis courts and equipment can be hired five minutes by car from the city at the Queensland Lawn Tennis Association, Milton Road, Milton, (07) 368-2433, for around $15 an hour for a grass court and $5 to $7 an hour for a hard court.

For something completely different, a **hot-air balloon flight** over the city followed by a champagne picnic in the field; phone Lovely Balloon Flights at (07) 844-6671. Flights are early in the morning, and a half hour costs around $150.

## ❧ RESTAURANTS

Make the most of the tropical fruit, seafood, and quality beef while you're in Brisbane. Don't miss the chance to sample the prized barramundi and coral trout, Queensland mud crabs, and Moreton Bay bugs (a.k.a. Balmain bugs in Sydney, a slipper lobster). Pineapple is practically the state's fruit emblem and passionfruit, starfruit, rambutan, lychees, mangoes, papaya, and bananas are also in abundance. Queensland's wine-producing region is small, so you'll be lucky to find any on restaurant lists. Robinson's is a label to look for. Unless otherwise noted, all listings have full liquor licenses. Best to book.

**The Breakfast Creek Hotel** is at 2 Kingsford Smith Dr., Breakfast Creek, (07) 262-5988, but the address is unnecessary—just ask any cab driver for the Brekky Creek. It's a Brisbane legend for its beer drawn from wooden kegs in the public bar and the steaks served in the Spanish Garden Steakhouse at the back. For around $10 you get to choose your own piece of rib or eye fillet, rump, or T-bone and have it char-grilled to your liking. The Brekky Creek is open seven days a week for lunch and dinner. Across the creek from the hotel is the **Breakfast Creek Wharf Restaurant** at 192 Breakfast Creek Rd., Newstead; (07) 252-2421. It has a good reputation for seafood in a casual outdoor setting and is open daily for lunch and dinner. Two courses without liquor will cost around $25 and major credit cards are accepted. These two establishments are a short cab ride north of the city, or take a 160 Council bus.

If you're planning a visit to Lone Pine (see Organized Tours, above), consider ending the day with dinner at **Cat's Tango** at 242 Hawken Dr., in the university suburb of St. Lucia; (07) 371-1452. This eclectic restaurant mixes food from all corners of the globe—start with a Creole entrée, have a classic French main course, and finish with a Caribbean dessert—in an original setting with entertainment provided by belly dancers, minstrels, and palm readers. Three courses will cost around $25 per person without wine and it's open for lunch Tues.–Fri. and dinner Tues.–Sat. Major cards are accepted. Downstairs is **Pasta Pasta** for a cheap carbohydrate fix and reputedly the best ice cream in Brisbane. Worth a trip to the inner-west in their own right.

The Paddington circle (Bardon bus 144 from Adelaide or George sts.) is the spot for brasseries and some are open 24 hours on weekends. **The Caxton Hotel,** 38 Caxton St., Petrie Terr., (07) 369-5971, has a casual outdoor area offering carvery and grill selection for around $10. It's open for lunch daily and dinner with live jazz Tues.–Fri. No credit cards. **The Caxton St. Brasserie** is open till late every night for cheap ($8–$10) bistro fare with bands playing. It's at 111 Caxton St., Paddington, (07) 858-2737. All major cards accepted.

A Brisbane institution in this area is **Gambaro Seafood Restaurant,** 33 Caxton St., Petrie Terr., (07) 369-9500. The seafood platters here are a cook's tour of Queensland's best. It's open for lunch Mon.–Fri. and dinner Mon.–Sat. Dinner for two without liquor will cost around $70. Major cards accepted. More modestly, take away (fish 'n chips or fresh shellfish) from their outlet next door.

If you're visiting Mt. Coot-tha Botanic Gardens or the summit lookout, allow time for a devonshire morning or afternoon tea in the colonial building of the **Mt. Coot-tha Summit Restaurant,** Sir Samuel Griffith Dr., Mt. Coot-tha, (07) 369-9922. This moderately priced restaurant, serving steaks, grilled fish, and veal scaloppine (main courses around the $8 mark), is also open for lunch and dinner and frequently wins awards, though panoramic views of Brisbane and Moreton Bay probably have more to do with this than the "international" food. All major credit cards.

**Possums Australian Food** at 681 Brunswick St., in the inner-city suburb of New Farm, (07) 358-1442, offers home-style fare with an innovative twist. Dine on roast lamb or shepherd's pie surrounded by potted gums and gladdies (the favored flowers of Aussie anti-hero Dame Edna Everage) in this BYOB restaurant for around $10 for "big tucker" (main courses) and $6 for "little tucker" (entrées; "appetizers" in the States). Don't miss the drunken wombats—a calorie-laden chocolate confection. It's open for lunch and dinner Mon.–Sat. and takes all major cards.

(For non-Australians: Dame Edna, played by Barry Humphries, is the queen of Australian housewives—an exaggerated "average" woman, who favors blue-rinsed bouffant hairdos and opera-house framed spectacles. Unfortunately she's made gladdies very unpopular.)

**The Roseville Restaurant** is set in an 1881 colonial residence surrounded by beautiful gardens and serves French-influenced Australian cuisine—Moreton Bay Bug (a sea-going crustacean) salad with dill and avocado dressing, as one example. It's at 56 Chester St., in the near-northern suburb of Newstead, and is open for lunch Tues.–Fri. and dinner Tues.–Sat. Entrées are around $10 and main courses $15. Tel. (07) 358-1377. All major cards.

The current trend in Australian cuisine uses a mix of French and Asian cooking methods and **Rumpoles Restaurant,** at the corner of North Quay and Turbot sts. in the heart of the city, (07) 229-5922, has the style down to a fine art. Dine on several entrée-size portions for around $10 each under the sun sails of their courtyard setting. Crocodile is on the menu here and the designer pizzas are highly recommended. Open for lunch weekdays and dinner Mon.–Sat. All major cards.

## Light Meals

For a great cup of coffee, light meals (bagels with trimmings), and Swiss chocolates, head for **Aroma's** in the city center at the Hoyt's Cinema Complex foyer and the Wintergarden Centre under the Hilton Hotel. Both can be reached from the Queen St. Mall. If it's a snack, or a full meal you need at any time of the night or day, **Jimmy's** on the (Queen St.) Mall is a handy place to sit outdoors and watch the passing parade. It's open 24 hours, for cocktails, seafood platters, Chinese dishes, bacon and eggs, or croissants, and amazingly manages to do them all well. Tel. (07) 229-9468.

# ENTERTAINMENT

All tastes are catered to with Brisbane's night scene, though for professionals the definition of a night out usually means dinner in a restaurant or a visit to the theater. The younger set are less concerned with formal dining and can be found at live music venues in pubs or clubs, or at concerts by visiting music stars. The newspapers are the best way to find out about current attractions.

Greater Union and Hoyt's both have **cinema complexes** on the Queen Street Mall—check the newspapers for current movies and screening times. The Performing Arts Complex in the Cultural Centre on the South Bank, South Brisbane, caters **opera, music, and ballet** buffs. Performances are advertised in the newspapers, or phone the box office at (07) 844-0201. The **Queensland Theatre Company's** base is in the Suncorp Theatre, Turbot Street, in the city. Check the paper or phone the box office at (07) 221-3861.

**Nightclubs** in the major hotels include Her Majesty's and the Red Parrot at the Hilton and Reflections in the Sheraton. They attract a fairly sophisticated clientele drawn from both in-house guests and Brisbanites prolonging a night out after dinner. Friday's, in the Riverside Centre, 125 Eagle Street, is the place to be seen by the yuppie legal and business types from the nearby offices. It has a variety of dining facilities from buffet to à la carte, but if you don't want to eat there's a cover charge of $6 after 8:30 P.M.

There's a **disco** behind Buzzard's on Mary Street—go down the alley behind the bistro, or phone them at (07) 221-1511 for more precise directions. It's open Friday and Saturday until 5 A.M. and weekdays until 3 A.M. In the upstairs bar you can order from a range of imported beers, wines by the glass, or coffee, while meals are available in the restaurant below.

The Brisbane Underground, at the corner of Caxton and Hale sts., Paddington, (07) 369-2633, is a young people's venue in an old boot factory. You can buy snacks in the disco, but more substantial meals are available from the Caxton St. Brasserie (see Restaurants) in the same building.

# Gold Coast

The Gold Coast is Queensland's traditional tourist capital. For fifty years visitors have flocked to holiday in one of its twenty villages stretching along a 42-kilometer (about 26-mile) beach frontage in the south of the state. These days it's difficult to tell where one ends and another begins as they form a string of development from the twin towns of Coolangatta and Tweed Heads on the Queensland/New South Wales border north to the commercial center of Southport. But each claims its own identity. Burleigh Heads plays host to the Stubbies Surf Classic, one of the largest surfing carnivals in Australia. Surfers Paradise claims to be the entertainment and accommodation capital, while the $400 million residential resort of Sanctuary Cove bills itself as the exclusive retreat for anybody with an interest in water-based (and money-based) activities.

Brash and a trifle vulgar, the Gold Coast illustrates what developers can do with a prime location, but it also demonstrates the difficulty of upstaging nature. It's not the high-rise, the restaurants, night clubs, and amusement parks that bring the visitors back, but the beaches and surf. And if frantically relaxing becomes a bit much, you can always retreat to the "green behind the gold"—the mountain hinterland to the west of the coast, with walking trails for exploring the Lamington National Park, with reputedly more than 500 waterfalls to admire, and possibly the world's oldest rainforest trees.

## TRAVEL

The Gold Coast can be a day trip from Brisbane, though many prefer the reverse, treating the capital as an excursion from their surfside base. Ansett and Australian Airlines have daily direct flights to Coolangatta airport from the southern capitals and coach services operate from both northern and southern centers.

By car, take the Gold Coast Freeway from Brisbane—Coolangatta is 106 km (about 66 miles) to the south—or, once on the coast, use the orange and white buses of the Surfside Bus Line, (075) 36-2524, which leave Coolangatta for Southport every twenty minutes. The major taxi company is Regent Taxis, (075) 32-8000. Chauffeur-driven limousines are popular, often comparable to taxi costs for a group. Companies include Budget, (07) 92-0000, and ABC Limousines, (07) 38-8422.

For greater flexibility, hire a car. Most companies have representation at the airport and will deliver to hotels. Leading firms include Budget, at the corner of Gold Coast Hwy. and Enderley St., Surfers Paradise, (075) 92-0000; Avis, at the corner of Ferny and Cypress aves., Surfers Paradise, (075) 39-9388; Hertz, 3108 Gold Coast Hwy., Surfers Paradise, (075) 38-5366. Top-less Car Rentals, 15 Ferny Ave., Surfers Paradise, (075) 39-8490, rents soft-top convertible Volkswagen Beetles.

For further information contact **The Gold Coast Visitors & Convention Bureau,** 115 Scarborough St., Southport 4215, (075) 91-1988. There's also an information center in Cavill Mall, Surfers Paradise, (075) 38-4419.

---

# ❦ ACCOMMODATIONS

Accommodation on the Gold Coast ranges from international hotels and luxury high-rise apartments to family motels, caravan parks, and camping grounds. For most of the year, you'll have no trouble finding somewhere to suit your budget. Exceptions are the peak holiday periods in Dec. and Jan. and at Easter, when reservations are essential.

Where you base yourself is a question of style. Surfers Paradise is unquestionably the most central location, but your accommodation will most likely be high-rise. Southport has a more residential flavor, while Burleigh Heads and the settlements farther south such as Palm Beach and Currumbin have managed to retain some of the sleepy seaside village character. The following accept major credit cards (American Express, Diners Club, MasterCard, and Visa).

Top of the range is the new **Sheraton Mirage Resort,** Main Beach; Surfers Paradise 4217; (075) 91-1488. It's set in a palm-studded landscape with lagoon and ocean views and has all the facilities you'd expect of five-star accommodation. Rooms range from $150 per person per night.

**The Sands Motel,** 40 The Esplanade, Surfers Paradise 4217, (075) 38-8433, offers both budget and moderate accommodation for $60 double or $80 double respectively. It's handy to the beach, has a swimming pool, and is central to shops and restaurants.

If you're planning to escape to the hinterland for a night or two, consider sampling the hospitality the O'Reilly family has been dispensing for three generations at their **guesthouse** in the Lamington National Park. The Lamington Plateau is about 30 km inland from the coast; O'Reilly's is about 65 km (40 miles) from the coast by road. This spot catapulted into the headlines in the 1930s when Bernard O'Reilly was responsible for locating and coordinating the rescue of the survivors of a Stinson aircraft which had crashed in the wilderness of the McPherson Ranges. The family share their bush knowledge by taking visitors on four-wheel-drive excursions and guided walks to observe wildlife and explain rainforest botany. The ambience is distinctly old-fashioned, with hearty country-style meals and sing-alongs at night (participation optional). Accommodation ranges from basic rooms with communal facilities for around $65 per person to fully self-contained units for around $90 per person (no air-conditioning, however), all meals and activities included. O'Reilly's Guesthouse is at Green Mountains, via Canungra 4275; (075) 45-1611.

Another hinterland institution is **Binna Burra Mountain Lodge,** located about 40 km by road from the coast. The rustic wooden cabins sit atop a knoll overlooking the Coomera and Numimbah valleys, with spectacular scenery and national park all around. Here again the emphasis is on the outdoors with activities ranging from leisurely bushwalking to more strenuous abseiling (descending from mountains by rope; qualified instructors on the staff). Highlights include barbecue breakfasts in the forest on Sun., night walks, and bush dances. Accommodation ranges from $66 per person for basic room with communal facilities to $95 per person for self-contained units with private facilities, but no air-conditioning. All meals are included. Binna Burra Mountain Lodge, Beechmont, via Nerang 4211; (075) 33-3536.

Another rural retreat, 90 km (about 55 miles) from both the Gold Coast and Brisbane, is **Kooralbyn Valley Resort.** A sporting person's equivalent of paradise, this complex is set in 4,000 hectares and boasts a championship 18-hole **golf** course voted the best resort course in Australia by *Australian Golf Digest*. Other facilities include a social nine-hole golf course, four swimming pools, ten all-weather tennis courts, horse trail riding, two lawn bowls greens, three dining facilities from budget (hamburgers, minute steaks, and fisherman's basket for $8–$10 each) to à la carte in The Aviary ($25–$30 for three courses). Accommodation ranges from $156 per night for a self-contained villa which can sleep four adults and two children to $86 per room for a motel-style, serviced unit for two adults. Length-of-stay discounts apply. The resort is at Kooralbyn Valley, via Beaudesert 4285; (075) 44-6100.

## ✾ RESTAURANTS

The Gold Coast has a fast-food outlet for every whim and almost as many restaurants. You'll find seafood on almost every menu, but one spot not to be missed is the garden setting of **Oskars,** Elkhorn Ave., Surfers Paradise, (075) 38-5244, for lunch except Mon. and dinner seven days. Three courses without wine will cost around $30.

You can **surf** at every beach but Flagstaff Beach (which the locals persist in calling by its former name, Duranbah). All beaches are divided by flags into body surfing (swimming) areas and board-riding areas. Greenmount, Kirra Point, Burleigh Point, Surfers Paradise, and Broadbeach have the most consistent conditions. The Brothers Neilsen operate a chain of shops where surf and boogie boards can be hired, and tuition can be arranged. They're in the following shopping centers: Scarborough Fair, Southport, (075) 32-5763; Centre Arcade, Orchid Avenue, Surfers Paradise, (075) 39-0176; Paradise Centre, Cavill Avenue, Surfers Paradise, (075) 50-1186; Pacific Fair, Broadbeach, (075) 38-1897; Burleigh West, Burleigh Heads, (075) 35-9270, and Tweed Mall, Tweed Heads, (075) 36-4615. Surf boards rent for around $15 a day and boogie boards about $10. A deposit of the value of the board—American Express or Visa accepted—is required. Tuition is $25 for an hour-long lesson and novices usually need three or four. The shops post a daily surf report and radio 4GG updates this information regularly.

If you prefer **still water** to rolling waves, head for the Broadwater, north of Surfers Paradise, a shallow stretch of water protected from the ocean by The Spit and South Stradbroke Island. It's ideal for swimming and fishing for whiting, flathead, and bream. The calm waters also provide ideal conditions for sailboarding. Max Brown Watersports rent sailboards and provide lessons. You'll find them on Broadwater Beach next to the Gold Coast Bridge; (075) 32-7722.

For the heart-stopping experience of being harnessed into a parachute and towed airborne behind a speedboat, drop into Gold Coast **Parasailing** based at the Southport Broadwater Carpark, off the Gold Coast Highway; (075) 91-4466.

Gold Coast promoters emphasize their man-made attractions and if you're traveling with children it will probably be difficult to avoid a visit to one of them. **Sea World** on The Spit at Main Beach combines hair-raising rides with marine shows. Brave the corkscrew (a three-loop roller coaster), take a spin on the Viking's revenge, a flume ride, and see dolphin, whale, sea lion, water skiing, and shark-feeding shows for a $19 admission fee for adults and $13 for children. The venue is open every day except Christmas from 10 A.M. to 5 P.M.

**Helicopter joy flights** over the Gold Coast are available, beginning at $25 per person. For further information telephone (075) 32-1055. Other **bird's-eye views** of the coastline are provided by Tigermoth Open Cockpit Charters which takes off from Raceway Park on the Broadbeach/Nerang Road, (075) 38-9083, and Ken Keane's Air Adventure, (075) 36-3877, from Coolangatta Airport. Prices are around $40.

**Dreamworld,** 15-minutes' drive north of the Gold Coast at Coomera on the highway to Brisbane, is a Disney-style theme park boasting the world's longest double loop roller coaster and the Imax theater with a terror-inducing screen as tall as a six-story building. It's open every day except Christmas from 10 A.M. to 5 P.M. and admission charges are $22 for adults and $15 for children; (075) 53-1133.

You might find your time better spent exploring the waterways and canal systems around the Gold Coast on a **cruise boat.** Reputable operators include *Chevron Princess* with offices at Ferny Avenue, Surfers Paradise, (075) 39-9833; *Shangri-La* at Fisherman's Wharf, Main Beach, (075) 91-1800; and *Sir Bruce* at Ferny Avenue, Surfers Paradise, (075) 32-5031.

**Fishing** enthusiasts have a host of day and half-day trips to choose from, and amateur fishermen don't need a license to fish in Queensland. The Broadwater is a popular ground for the leisurely pursuit of dinner, though game fishermen can head for deep-sea destinations where marlin, tuna, snapper, and red emperor abound. Charter operators include Surfers Paradise Charters, which has a fleet of twenty vessels for fishing on the Broadwater and off-shore. Prices range from $750 a day; (075) 50-2705. Janosea Charters can take a maximum of six people to fish on the Broadwater for $300 for a full day and $170 for a half day; (075) 96-3686.

In the unlikely event of an empty-handed return, stop at Queensland Prawn and Ice, the **seafood market** at Fisherman's Wharf, Main Beach, where fish straight from the trawlers is sold. Cooked prawns, sand and mud crabs, and lobsters are also available.

## The Hinterland

Unless you're planning to stay in the Gold Coast hinterland, it's probably best to hire a car and explore it at leisure. Scenic points to visit include **Natural Arch,** on Numimbah Valley Road, where a rock archway has been carved by centuries of cascading water, the **Lamington National Park** with 140 kilometers (about 87 miles) of walking tracks through rainforest to waterfalls and 3,000-year-old Antarctic beech tree stands, and **Mt. Tamborine,** where craft and art galleries compete with rainforest and 15,000-year-old Macrozamia palms (said to be the oldest living things in the world) for visitors' attention. Ranger offices are located in both Binna Burra, (075) 33-3584, and O'Reilly's, (075) 45-1734, and can provide maps and walking information. There are also camping grounds at both locations.

# Sunshine Coast

The Sunshine Coast, Brisbane's beach playground to the north, lacks the brashness of its southern counterpart, the Gold Coast, and that's why its devotees wouldn't spend their holidays elsewhere. It's not that this resort area—a 115-kilometer (about 71-mile) stretch of beaches and villages from Caloundra to Rainbow Beach—wants for sophistication. The restaurants and accommodations equal those of Brisbane or the southern capitals. But its appeal is an attitude, a mood of cosmopolitan informality for the cognoscenti who place natural before artifical attractions.

Surf, sun, and sand aside, the Sunshine Coast also provides the opportunity to explore untamed wilderness in the Noosa and Cooloola national parks, to cruise, fish, or paddle on the Noosa River and lake system, four-wheel-drive up the forty-kilometer (25-mile) undeveloped Teewah Beach to marvel at the 72 hues in the colored sand cliffs, and, possibly, venture farther by taking a barge to the world's largest sand island,

Fraser. The region's hinterland is a complete contrast—lush, rolling hills where the air is crisp, the views panoramic, and the communities made up of creative city folk and alternative lifestylers who came for a day and stayed for good.

Noosa, a conglomeration of settlements, including beach-side Noosa Heads, commercial Noosa Junction, and river-fronting Noosaville, makes a central base for exploring the region.

## TRAVEL

The Sunshine Coast begins at Caloundra, a two-hour, 105-km (65-mile) drive north of Brisbane. Take the Bruce Hwy. from Brisbane past the volcanic plugs of the Glasshouse Mts. and turn off 9 km (5½ miles) north of Landsborough. A 45-km (30-mile) coast road links Caloundra with the resort towns of Alexandra Headland, Maroochydore, Peregian and Sunshine beaches, and Noosa. Traveling directly to Noosa, stay on the Bruce Hwy. through Nambour and Yandina and take the turnoff via Eumundi. Skennars Coachlines run 13 services daily from Brisbane to Noosa and points between.

If you choose to base yourself on the Sunshine Coast and make Brisbane a day trip, East-West Airlines and Air New South Wales fly direct to Maroochydore airport from Sydney in 1 hour 20 minutes. Both provide shuttle buses for connections with Noosa. The Sunshine Coast Coach Company, (071) 43-4555, also plies up and down the coast road hourly.

### Car Rentals

Car-rental firms have airport representation, or you can pick up a car from their coastal offices. Companies include Hertz, 10 Aerodrome Rd., Maroochydore, (071) 43-6422; Budget, 16 Hastings St., Noosa, (071) 47-4588; and Avis, Ocean Court, Ocean St., Maroochydore, (071) 43-5055. If you like the breeze in your hair, Konomy Kar Rental's mini mokes, (071) 47-3368, should satisfy. You can also hire a four-wheel-drive vehicle to visit Teewah Beach and Fraser Island. Sunshine 4WD Hire, (071) 47-3702, will help. Both companies are at 42 Hastings St., Noosa Heads. Sunshine Chauffeured Limousines, (071) 46-1691, will do the driving for you.

For further information on the Sunshine Coast contact **Sunshine Coast Tourism & Development Board,** Alexandra Pde., Alexandra Headlands, 4572; (071) 43-2411.

## ❧ ACCOMMODATIONS

School holidays, Christmas and Easter aside, you should have no trouble finding accommodation without booking ahead. Unless otherwise noted, hotels in this section accept major credit cards.

At the premium level, **Netanya,** 75 Hastings St., Noosa Heads 4567, (071) 47-4722, telex 44476, has absolute beach frontage overlooking Laguna Bay, a heated pool, sauna, 24-hour room service, and all suites have air-conditioning, kitchen facilities, and indoor spa baths. Beachfront room rates are $250 (peak season), $170 (off-peak). An added attraction is Michelle's Licensed Restaurant, open for breakfast, lunch, and dinner, with a reputation for local seafood prepared in the French style. A table on the sundeck overlooking the beach is prized for Sunday brunch.

For moderately priced accommodation with a difference, take to the Noosa waterways with a **houseboat** from **Sunshine Riverboats,** Gympie Terrace, Noosaville, 4566 (071) 49-8044. They have a range of boats with two to eight berths. The galleys are equipped with all utensils, gas stoves, and small refrigerators. Showers with hot and cold water, flush toilets in separate compartments, battery-powered lighting, and black-and-white TVs are also provided. Blankets and pillows are on board, linen rental can be arranged. The houseboats have dinghys and crabpots are available.

**Lake Cooroibah Holiday Park** on Noosa's North Shore (Box 220, Tewantin 4565), (071) 47-1225, has both budget ($30 per night for a four-berth cabin, bring your own linen) and moderate ($100 per night for a fully equipped timber cottage which sleeps four comfortably) accommodation. Cook for yourself (barbecues are provided) or have family-style meals in the park's Sundowner Lounge. The park is set in 120 hectares of wilderness, with Lake Cooroibah on one side and the surf of North Shore and Teewah Beaches a walk away on the other. Canoes are available, there's an all-weather tennis court (rackets for hire), and horse rides including beach treks are popular (lessons available). The owners also have a six-wheel-drive vehicle to take visitors to the colored sands and Rainbow Beach. Access is via the car ferry at Tewantin ($6 round-trip).

## ❦ RESTAURANTS

Seafood is understandably popular—it's fresh, available all year round, and presented in innovative tropical style. The restaurants mentioned accept major credit cards and are open for dinner Tues.–Sun. Average price for main courses is around $15, though if you order lobster or mud crab this can reach around $20. While all of the restaurants below specialize in seafood, they will have a few veal, chicken, and beef dishes for hardened carnivores.

**Annabelle's,** Hastings St., Noosa, (071) 47-3204, has a prime beachfront location and a reputation to match for imaginatively presented local fare. If you're visiting any of the southern beaches, **Charades,** (071) 44-2017, and **Fronds,** (071) 44-1573, both on The Esplanade at Mooloolaba, are worth the trip. In the hinterland, **Misty's Mountain,** (071) 42-9264, and **Pottingers,** (071) 42-9407, both on Main Rd., Montville, share a reputation that draws diners from Brisbane.

Most Sunshine Coast beaches provide good **surfing**—Radio 4SS broadcasts a report on conditions at 6:30 A.M. on weekdays and 7 A.M. on weekends—but Sunshine and Peregian, south of Noosa, are the most consistent. Noosa Heads beach is patrolled by lifeguards but can become crowded. Walk through the Noosa National Park (see below) to the less populated but unpatrolled, though safe, **swimming spots** of Ti Tree, Granite Bay, and Alexandria Bay (the last for an all-over tan).

**Bicycles and fishing** rods can be hired from the Noosa Bicycle Shop, at the corner of Quamby Place and Noosa Parade; (071) 47-3062. Beach fishing will yield tailor, bream, whiting, and flathead, while the upper reaches of the Noosa River are good bass grounds.

A few minutes' walk from the boutiques of Noosa's Hastings Street and you're at the entrance to the 477-hectare **Noosa National Park.** Walking tracks through the rainforest of the park are a cool alternative to the beach and you can drop down to a secluded beach for a dip. While there is no camping at the park, feel free to walk around—the ranger office, (07) 41-3243, at the entrance has maps and walking info.

The Noosa River tidaly connects a series of lakes (Como, Cootharaba, Cooroibah, Doonella, and Weyba) as it wends its way to the ocean and discharges into Laguna Bay. The northernmost lake, Cootharaba, is bordered by the 23,000-hectare **Cooloola National Park.** Both the ranger office and the camp ground are at Boreer Point, (071) 497364. Options for exploring this watery haven include driving yourself to Booreen Point, 21 kilometers (13 miles) north from Tewantin, car ferry across the Noosa River, then travel by gravel road or by paved road via Pomona just off the Bruce Highway.

If **canoeing** around Lake Cootharabra appeals, head for Booreen Point and Fred's Fleet Hire, (071) 85-3174. Fred also rents **dinghies** with outboard motors, **sailing cats, wave skis,** and **sail boards.** Escorted Noosa River safaris, camping equipment provided, arranges for groups of four to six who want to experience Lake Cootharaba, the upper Noosa River, and Everglades of Cooloola National Park at their best—after the day-trippers have gone.

🐝 Make time for a lunch stop at **The Jetty,** Boreen Pde., Boreen Point, (071) 85-3167. It's justly famous for its waterfront location and tropical fare.

There are a number of day tours available for those who'd prefer to see the lake system from the water. Cooloola **Cruises,** (071) 49-7884, depart from Apex Park at Noosaville and offer full-day trips on the leisurely *Cooloola Queen,* or half-day excursions on the jet boat *Everglades Express.* The *Kookaburra Jet* provides similar excursions. Telephone (071) 47-3798 for further information.

Noosa's **North Shore** is one of the few remaining areas of untouched wilderness on Australia's eastern seaboard. The forty-kilometer (25-mile) beach is a designated road, though access is limited to four-wheel-drives (via the Tewantin car ferry). At the northern end of the beach are multi-hued cliffs which stretch for several kilometers. Farther north of Rainbow Beach is Inskip Point, for departure to **Fraser Island.** It's accessible by paved road by taking the Tin Can Bay turnoff from the Bruce Highway at Gympie. You can hire four-wheel-drives at the Mikado Motor Inn, Cooloola Drive, Rainbow Beach, (071) 86-3211, for trips to the colored sands or Fraser Island. (They also provide an excellent barbecue lunch.) If you plan to drive to Fraser, it's advisable to book for the ferry, the *Rainbow Venture.* Phone Fraser Island Ferry Service & Tours, (071) 86-3120. More Fraser Island details in the Central Queensland section.

Day trips from Noosa combining the colored sands and Fraser Island are available. Recommended operators include The Fraser Bus, (071) 47-3127, and Fraser Explorer Day Tours, (071) 49-8647. Costs are around $55 per person including lunch. The latter is run by island personality Sid Melksham, and provides guests with the option of extended stays on the island at Eurong Beach Resort and return to the mainland at Hervey Bay, to avoid backtracking to Noosa. The transport sector for this option costs $40. Contact the resort on (071) 27-9122.

The hinterland region of the **Blackall Ranges** can be toured by a circuit drive. From Nambour on the Bruce Highway take the turnoff for Mapleton, go on to Flaxton and Montville, and rejoin the highway at Landsborough. Return to Noosa via Caloundra or Eumundi. Take time to see the waterfalls at Mapleton and Kondalilla Falls 6 kilometers (under 4 miles) north of Montville.

**Camphor Cottage,** a craft shop selling local artists' clothing, woodwork, pottery, and children's toys, is set in a Queenslander building and incorporates the **Verandah Café,** a good spot for lunch or morning or afternoon tea. It's in Main St., Montville, (071) 42-9300, and is open every day.

The Mapleton Pottery, Flaxton Road, Mapleton, (071) 45-7477, and Bainbridge Island Pottery, Noosa Road, Eumundi, (071) 42-8048, are showcases for local clay and earthenware.

# Central Queensland

Central Queensland symbolizes the Big Country. Beginning at Maryborough, 264 kilometers (about 165 miles) north of Brisbane, it continues for another 1,100 km (680 miles) north through the coastal centers of Gladstone, Rockhampton, and

Mackay to Townsville, and as far again inland. The coast is punctuated by resorts, access points for the Great Barrier Reef, and splendid spots for getting away from it all, like the rainforested sand island of Fraser, or the outdoor enthusiasts' resort Susan River Homestead.

If you plan to divert to outback Queensland on the way, the center of Longreach is 684 kilometers (424 miles) west of Rockhampton. Don't even contemplate driving if time is limited. It's a day's motoring or more without sightseeing. A tight schedule need not deny an Outback experience—for example, from Brisbane you can fly to Rockhampton, transfer to Planet Downs Resort, spend a few days with their mustering teams (or watching them), then head back to Rockhampton to continue north. Alternatively, fly from Brisbane to Longreach, visit the Outback pioneer memorial, the Stockman's Hall of Fame, and sheep or cattle station, then fly to Townsville or Cairns.

### Buzz Words

The great Aussie salute—a constant waving motion across the face to brush flies away—is no joke, particularly when you're also coping with the heat and dust of the Outback. Flies seem particularly attracted to white, so colorful clothing is preferable. You can wear a fly veil which gathers around the brim of the hat and loosely around the neck—these are available at army disposal stores and camping shops in most major cities. Carry insect repellent. This is also effective against mosquitoes, the cause of many a sleepless night in the tropics. Most accommodation will be screened against insects, beds equipped with mosquito nets or slow-burning insect coils provided.

## TRAVEL

The Bruce Hwy. links the coastal ports and this route is serviced by Greyhound, Deluxe, and Ansett Pioneer coaches. The *Sunlander* and *Queenslander* trains follow the coast, Lloyd Aviation and Sunstate Airlines service the smaller ports, and Ansett and Australian Airlines connect the major centers. (See Queensland: Travel for tel. numbers.)

The Capricorn Hwy., serviced by Greyhound, links Rockhampton and Longreach, or you can take the Midlander train. Flight West flies from Brisbane to Longreach with connections to Townsville and Cairns.

Cars or campervans hired in Brisbane can be dropped in Rockhampton, Townsville, or Cairns without drop-off fees. (Booking offices for these services in Queensland Travel.)

## ❦ ACCOMMODATIONS AND RESTAURANTS

Because of its size there is no feasible base for exploring the whole area, so this section moves with the traveler from Brisbane to Cairns. Motel, hotel, and caravan park accommodation is available in all of the centers discussed and there are resort and home-stay facilities close to the major attractions.

In most cases dining will be a matter of eating in-house— many places mentioned include all meals in the tariff. Elsewhere, options include counter meals in hotels, the local Chinese restaurant (even small country towns have one), or café. These places are early closers, so plan to dine by 7 P.M. Exceptions are the larger centers and resort towns such as Rockhampton, Mackay, Airlie Beach, and Townsville with metropolitan-standard restaurants.

### ON THE WAY TO FRASER ISLAND

For most, Maryborough is a refueling point on the route north, but if you're planning a visit to Fraser Island, this is the turn-off for Hervey Bay, 33 km (about 20 miles) northeast. Hervey Bay is also the nearest center to **Susan River Homestead Resort,** a cattle station 16 km (9 miles) away. At the homestead guests are accommodated in motel units. Activities include parasailing or water skiing on the lake, horse riding, tennis, and swimming; instruction is provided for beginners. Rates are $90 per person per day, or $600 per week including all activities and healthy, family-style meals. Day trips to Fraser Island can be arranged. Write to Susan River Homestead, via Maryborough 4650, or phone (071) 21-6846.

Before heading for Fraser Island you can stay in the coastal town of Hervey Bay. The **Melanesia Village Resort,** Elizabeth St., Urangan 4658, (071) 28-9702, has air-conditioned motel units and cabins with cooking facilities. Set in a tropical garden with a 2-hectare waterbird sanctuary lake, it has bars, a bistro, and a restaurant. Rates are $55 per double for units and $70 for cabins. All major credit cards.

### FRASER

Most of Fraser, the world's largest sand island, is National Park. Features include more than 100 kilometers (over 62 miles) of white, sandy beaches, colored sands (the most famous are the Cathedrals), more than forty perched dune and window lakes, natural rock swimming pools, wildlife, including dingoes and herds of brumbies, wildflower heaths, and rainforest. There is only one road on the island and elsewhere— the beaches are designated roads—four-wheel-drives are essential.

To explore Fraser independently, rent a four-wheel-drive at Shed 3A, Industrial Estate, Boat Harbour, Pialba. Write to Peter Raymond, Box 648, Pialba 4655, or phone (071) 28-4788 for further information. You can also rent four-wheel-drives on the island—see Orchid Beach Resort, below. You'll need to book it on the ferry, $25 round-trip, which makes two daily trips from Mary River Heads near Hervey Bay. Phone (071) 28-1900 for details.

## 🦐 TRAVEL AND ACCOMMODATIONS

Unless you're an experienced beach driver, let someone else take care of your transport. The owners of **Eurong Beach Resort,** (071) 27-9122, operate day tours from Hervey Bay and the Sunshine Coast and you can use these vehicles for transfer to the island. They also provide day ($16) and half-day ($9) tours to the island's scenic points. The resort incorporates a hotel, bistro, dining room, swimming pool, tennis court, and general store and offers air-conditioned motel units or family flats with kitchen facilities. Rates are $60 a day for the units, $70 for the flats, or $50 per person per day with all meals. All major credit cards.

The resort at **Orchid Beach** is slightly more up-market with air-conditioned bungalow units decorated in tropical style with cane furniture and Ken Done prints. Their tariff includes meals (barbecue or buffet lunches, à la carte dinners) and ranges from $95 per person per night. Credit cards are accepted. The resort offers $6 tours to the island's attractions, but unless you have your own four-wheel-drive, the only way to get there is to fly from Brisbane, Maroochydore, Hervey Bay, or Maryborough with Sungold Airlines, (071) 48-7000. For more information contact the resort by writing to P.M.B. 4, Maryborough 4650, or by phoning (071) 27-9185. They also have a Brisbane office, (07) 221-6399.

# BUNDABERG

Bundaberg, 114 kilometers (70 miles) north of Maryborough, is the departure point for Lady Musgrave and Lady Elliot Islands (see Great Barrier Reef). It's also home to one of Australia's most popular beverages, Bundaberg rum. "Bundy," as it is affectionately known, is throughout Australia a generic for rum—ask for a Bundy and Coke and you might not get either. There are tours of the distillery at 10 A.M., 12:30 and 2:30 P.M. every weekday. Follow the main street through town over the bridge and turn off at Avenue Street.

Be sure not to miss the fascinating show on nearby **Mon Repos beach** if you're there between November and February. This is the only mainland nesting ground for green and loggerhead turtles and at night National Parks officers will guide you to spots where you can watch them laying their eggs and, later, hatching. Mon Repos is also a good swimming beach.

## 🦐 ACCOMMODATIONS AND RESTAURANTS

**Turtle Sands Caravan Park,** Mon Repos Beach, (071) 79-2340, has on-site vans for around $25 a night, or Bundaberg township is only about 15 km (10 miles) away and accommodation here is competitive with motels advertising units for $35 double.

On Fri. and Sat. night, the seafood smorgasbord at **Lump-A-Rump,** 251 Bourbong St., (071) 72-5262, is excellent value at $25. Other nights it has an à la carte menu featuring steak and seafood. **Alexandra's Seafood Restaurant,** 66 Quay St., (071) 72-7255, in a renovated Queenslander overlooking the river, is slightly more formal. Open seven nights, three courses will cost around $30 without wine. For cheaper, home-style fare, such as prawn and seafood cocktails and roast of the day, **Millaquin House Family Restaurant,** also set in an older-style building, which once belonged to one of the district's sugar mills, at 169 Bargara Rd., (071) 71-6716. Open Wed.–Sat. night; three courses about $15. All three accept major credit cards.

# GLADSTONE

Gladstone, the nearest port to Heron Island (see Great Barrier Reef), is 172 kilometers (107 miles) north of Bundaberg, and Rockhampton, gateway to the Outback, 90 kilometers (56 miles) farther north. Choose from the motels lining the highway into these towns.

## ❧ ACCOMMODATIONS

You can be picked up for a taste of the Outback, albeit a fairly classy one, at **Planet Downs Resort,** near Rolleston in the central-west. It's a working property with more than ten thousand head of cattle on its 104,000 hectares. There are two caves with aboriginal paintings to explore, horse riding, and four-wheel-drive treks to watch the mustering gangs at work. Accommodation is in the Tasmanian cedar Gunyah, or hut, with ten units. Bedrooms have private facilities, king-size beds, pot-belly stoves for winter, and air-conditioning for summer. The complex includes a licensed restaurant, swimming pool, tennis court, spa, and sauna. Rates: $225 per person per day including all meals and activities. Drinks and transfers are extra. Bookings and further information from the resort's Brisbane office, Box 420, Zillmere 4034, (07) 265-5022, fax (07) 265-3978. You can also fly from Brisbane to Thangool and be transported to Planet Downs. Independent travelers can drive to the property from Gladstone on the Dawson Hwy., or arrange for pick-ups from Emerald on the Capricorn Hwy.

If Planet Downs doesn't fit your budget, consider a diversion to **Carnarvon Gorge Oasis Lodge,** reached by traveling 142 km (88 miles) south from Emerald (270 km, 160 miles, west of Rockhampton) to Springsure and Rolleston, then an additional 94 km (58 miles) on an unpaved road. The Lodge is at the entrance to the 200,000-hectare Carnarvon Gorge National Park, an area of rough ranges, deep rock swimming pools, rare ferns and palms, and cave galleries of Aboriginal art. To explore these sites you'll have to walk and climb, so this is not a destination for the unfit. Accommodation is in safari tents for $86 per person per day or cabins for $106 per day. All meals, including pack lunches, are covered in the tariff as well as ranger-guided walks, and night entertainment such as wildlife slide shows and bush dances. Phone (079) 84-4503.

# LONGREACH

Longreach, 410 kilometers (250 miles) west of Emerald, earned its place in history as the site of the first board meeting of the fledgling Queensland and Northern Territory Aerial Services (now better known as Qantas) in 1922. The hangar where its first aircraft were built is still in use at the airport. A dominant feature on the stark landscape of the town outskirts is the **Stockman's Hall of Fame,** a museum memorial to the Outback pioneers. As well as static exhibits recording bush ingenuity and stoicism, there are working displays of horse-shoeing, shearing, and whip cracking, and audio-visual shows. It's open every day except Christmas and entry cost is $6.

Day trips to outlying **sheep and cattle properties** can be arranged through Transwest Tours, on Eagle Street, (074) 58-2599, as can tours to **Starlight's Lookout,** a hillock where bushranger Harry Redford kept watch for troopers after his audacious cattle theft from the property "Bowen Downs." Read more about the man dubbed Captain Starlight in Rolf Boldrewood's novel, *Robbery under Arms.*

## 🌿 ACCOMMODATIONS

In Longreach, the **Jumbuck Motel,** Ilfracombe Rd. (Longreach 4730), (074) 58-1799, and the **Longreach Motor Inn,** Galah St. (Longreach 4730), (074) 58-2322, are recommended places to stay. Room rates are around $55 double and both have good licensed restaurants, air-conditioning, and pool, a welcome reprieve from the meat and three-veg standard in the bush. Both accept credit cards.

For a more in-depth view of property life, stay with the Robinson family on the 31,000-hectare **Lorraine Station,** 126 km (78 miles) north of Longreach on the road to Winton. (The address is Winton 4735; tel. 074-57-1693.) Pick-ups can be arranged from Longreach. Accommodation is $55 per person including meals in converted shearers' quarters (fairly basic with shared bathroom facilities) and meals are taken with the family and any other station workers and visitors. Apart from participating in farm life and $4 tours of the property, day trips to some of the district's attractions can be arranged, including the ghost town of Opalton, still an opal fossicker's delight, the Combo waterhole, where Banjo Paterson found the inspiration to write Australia's unofficial national anthem, "Waltzing Matilda," and the wildlife sanctuary of Carisbroke Station, where there are also Aboriginal paintings and bora rings. The dinosaur trackway is at nearby **Lark Quarry Environmental Park.** The fossilized footprints record in stone a stampede of about two hundred small dinosaurs escaping from a predator some 100 million years ago.

# MACKAY AND AIRLIE BEACH

Back on the Bruce Highway the sugar town of Mackay is a boring 341 kilometers (212 miles) north of Rockhampton. The only punctuations on this road are a few petrol stations, the tiny township of Marlborough (you even have to divert to go into it, but the hamburgers at the service station are worth the extra minutes), and Sarina, just before Mackay. **Mackay** is a bustling sugar town, quickly developing its tourist potential and motels are readily available. At the present time, there is no reason to make a special trip to Mackay. However, it's a pleasant tropical town and a good place to break the journey up the coast.

## Caution

From October to May venomous sea wasps known as box jelly fish infest coastal waters north of Mackay. They have a 12-centimeter-wide head and trailing tentacles, are transparent, and are virtually impossible to see. At best their sting is excruciatingly painful, at worst lethal. Believed to breed in estuaries, they are usually found close to the mainland coast, and aren't a problem at island resorts or on the reef. Beaches usually have warning signs. Some have netted enclosures but protection is not guaranteed as stingers can wash over the nets. You may see bottles of vinegar along the foreshores, a mitigating treatment only. Medical help should be sought immediately. There are "stinger suits"—lightweight, all-over wetsuits—and some locals wear pantyhose. But unless you cover your body—face and neck included—you're taking a risk. Stay out of the sea and check out the pool.

Most visitors push 126 kilometers (78 miles) north to Proserpine and the turnoff for the 30-kilometer (19-mile) drive to Airlie Beach. This is the mainland resort of the Whitsunday Passage, 74 islands in azure waters. Two of the resort islands—Hayman and Hamilton—are covered in the Great Barrier Reef section, but many visitors prefer to base themselves on the coast and take day trips to the resort and uninhabited islands such as South Molle, Lindeman, Long, and Palm. The islands have good fringing reefs and most day-tripping boats allow time for **snorkeling** as well as **boom netting** (riding in a net towed by the boat), **catamaraning,** and **tunnel diving.** This exhilarating sport involves jumping off the front of the boat and being washed between the hulls to the back, where (hopefully) you grab a rope and drag yourself back on board. Day trips range from $35 to $55 a day depending on the boat—you'll pay more to sail on the retired America's Cup contender *Gretel.* Barbecue or picnic lunches are included and you can book them at any of the travel agents in the main street of Airlie.

## ✦ ACCOMMODATIONS AND RESTAURANTS

Accommodation ranges from hostels with dormitory accommodations through the mini village of **Whitsunday Wanderer's,** Airlie Beach 4802, (079) 46-6466, $90 for an air-conditioned, double motel-style unit with kitchenette. The hotel has a pool and accepts credit cards. The more secluded apartments of **Tropicana Heights,** 37 Airlie Crescent, Airlie Beach 4802, (079) 46-6820, are about $70 per night, including tropical breakfast and sweeping views of the Whitsunday Passage. There is no air-conditioning but the hotel has a pool. Credit cards accepted. Outside the main hotels, dining leans toward fast food but two worthwhile exceptions are **KC's Chargrill** (steaks and fish for about $10) on the main street, (079) 46-6320, and **Seagulls** in nearby Cannonvale, (079) 46-6741, whose European owners offer veal, home-made sausage with sauerkraut and black bread, and grilled vegetables with chili pickle to complement the seafood menu. Be sure to book.

Airlie may be a resort town, but the nightlife is decidedly Aussie ocker. Highlights include **cane toad racing** at the Airlie Beach Hotel and **crab race meetings** at the Whitsunday Village. You're not likely to run into anybody you know, so you could find yourself enjoying these exercises in troppo madness.

## TOWNSVILLE

The port of Townsville is 265 kilometers (165 miles) north of Proserpine, and it's the departure point for Orpheus Island and the Four Seasons floating hotel (see Great Barrier Reef). Townsville boasts the **Sheraton Breakwater Casino Hotel** and the **Great Barrier Reef Wonderland,** a walk-through live coral aquarium, open daily except Good Friday and Christmas Day, admission $15. There's plenty of choice for accommodation but it's a still, sticky city and you might prefer to continue 350 km (218 miles) north to Cairns, the gateway to Far North Queensland, which somehow seems to cope with the tropics with much more style.

# Cairns and Far North Queensland

In Far North Queensland (F.N.Q.) two of Australia's major attractions, the reef and the rainforest, are separated only by a few kilometers. Yet the region is vast, covering an area twice the size of the state of Victoria—from the finger of Cape York Peninsula, north from Cairns to Thursday Island, west to the "Outback by the sea," the savannah lands around the Gulf of Carpentaria and Northern Territory border.

At press time, the international airport at its gateway city, Cairns, had three flights a week from the United States, making it a popular starting point for visitors to Australia. For others it's a logical stop-over when traveling to or from the Top End of the Northern Territory.

Cairns is a pretty, sprawling city with some splendid examples of colonial architecture. Modern development has also been sympathetic with new buildings incorporating verandas, iron-lace work, and bull-nosed awnings. While there is no beach in the city area, there are water views everywhere and palm trees add to the tropical feel.

The region has spectacular unpopulated beaches (beware of crocs and stingers), World Heritage listed rainforest that meets the sea at Cape Tribulation, fertile tableland, hinterland with volcanic crater lakes and waterfalls, and safari and fishing country in the western Outback. Here, the Great Barrier Reef hugs the coastline—it's only 14 kilometers (9 miles) from Cooktown, 16 kilometers (10 miles) from Port Douglas and 24 kilometers (15 miles) from Cairns as opposed to 55 kilometers (34 miles) from Townsville, 75 kilometers (46 miles) from the Whitsunday area, and 80 kilometers (50 miles) from Gladstone. The marlin fishing grounds lure visitors from all over the world from September to December.

## China Shop Syndrome

Look but don't touch is the best motto when exploring the reef and rainforest. Sandshoes are essential for reef walking as many of its inhabitants don't take kindly to being stood on. Don't put your hands into holes you can't see into, or pick up shells or creatures that could sting or bite. Coral scratches easily become infected. If you do graze yourself, the resort or tour operators will provide immediate first aid, though it's advisable to seek medical attention when you reach the shore. The rainforest is also home to some malevolent creatures. Of the plant variety these include the stinging tree which causes great pain and requires medical attention, and the "wait-a-while" which is a climbing palm studded with curved thorns. Should you brush against its canes, the process of extricating yourself makes the name self-explanatory. Wear protective clothing, sturdy boots, and socks. Experienced bushwalkers recommend a liberal coating over the body and socks with an insect repellent called Rid as a safeguard against that other rainforest nasty—the leech. While these little bloodsuckers won't cause serious injury and can generally be brushed off, or removed by applying salt, they don't add to your enjoyment.

F.N.Q. doesn't really have a winter but it does have a rainy season, from December to April, when humidity is high, travel to remote areas can be impossible and ocean swimming is prohibited because of the box jelly fish, or stingers. Best to avoid the area, and the top end of Australia during these months.

---

### Warning

Far North Queensland is crocodile territory. There are two species of croc—the docile freshwater which inhabits inland gorges, rivers, and waterholes and the larger and more dangerous saltwater which can be found in salt or fresh water of the coast, swamps, rivers, and waterholes. They are the rulers of their domain, no respecters of man or beast and just because you can't see them doesn't mean they're not there. Observe the warning signs—don't stand in rivers to fish, don't swim, don't canoe or camp near the water's edge. Take a conducted boat tour to see crocs basking on the shores, but treat them with the respect their prehistoric survival deserves.

---

## TRAVEL

Ansett and Australian Airlines have daily service to Cairns from southern capitals, as well as Alice Springs and Darwin. Ansett Pioneer, Deluxe, and Greyhound coaches travel the coastal highway north from Brisbane every day while the *Queenslander* and *Sunlander* provide daily train service from Brisbane. (See Queensland: Travel for details.)

If you choose to tour from Cairns by coach, White Car Coaches, 25 Spence St., (070) 51-9511, services Kuranda and the Atherton Tableland while Coral Coaches has daily service to Port Douglas and Mossman and three-times-a-week service via Bloomfield to Cooktown. It's an arduous journey—the coach takes eight hours to cover the 158 km (98 miles). Book at Tropical Paradise Travel, 25 Spence St., (070) 98-1611, or (070) 51-9533.

Car-rental firms include Avis, 135 Lake St., (070) 51-5911; Hertz, 141 Lake St., (070) 51-6399; Tad's, 239 Lake St., (070) 51-9183, and Budget, 153 Lake St., (070) 53-4222. It's a condition of hire that you don't take conventional two-wheel-drive sedans north of the Daintree River, but Budget hires four-wheel-drives for this purpose. They also have campervan hire at 436 Sheridan St., (070) 53-4222.

The taxi company in Cairns is Black & White, (070) 51-1333, or hire a chauffeur-driven car from Budget Chauffeur Drive, (070) 31-2444.

---

## ORGANIZED TOURS

Cairns makes a good base for exploring F.N.Q., which is well serviced with tours ranging from half-day Cairns sights bus trips to extended tours of the Cape and Gulf in four-wheel-drives. Most operators pick up from hotels and their tour prices include morning and afternoon tea and lunch. Ansett Trailways, 58 Shields St., (070) 51-8966, and Australian Pacific Tours, 12 Shields St., (070) 51-9299, offer almost identical programs including city sights, around $18; full days to Kuranda and the Atherton Tableland (one way on the scenic railway), around $40; Cape Tribulation, about $60; Daintree River (with boat cruise), approximately $30; three-day Cooktown/Quinkan Aboriginal art sites expeditions for about $270 including accommodation and meals.

Specialist operators to the Daintree rainforest region include Daintree Wildlife Safari who combines a guided rainforest walk-and-river cruise for $64. Travel to Daintree independently and the nearly three-hour river cruise is $25. Phone (070) 98-6125 or fax (070) 98-6192. Tropical Walkabouts run four-wheel-drive excursions for small groups (maximum seven people). You'll be accompanied by a botanist; $90 for the day. Phone (070) 31-1113 (Cairns) or (070) 98-5899 (Port Douglas).

As well as cruises to Agincourt Reef (see Great Barrier Reef) Quicksilver Connections, Marina, Mirage Resort, Port Douglas (76 km north of Cairns), (070) 98-5373, has day trips with marine biologists aboard to the coral cays of the Low Isles and historic Cooktown. A guided snorkeling tour is $20.

Trezise Bush Guide Service, (070) 60-3236, operates out of Cairns and takes visitors to the Quinkan rock art sites in the center of Cape York with the Peninsula mail-run operators, Cape York Air Services. Cost of the day trip is about $250.

# ✤ ACCOMMODATIONS

Cairns is well equipped with five-star hotels and budget accommodation—there are more than fifteen hundred backpacker beds in the city—but moderately priced accommodation is harder to find. Remember also that you're in a holiday center—accommodation prices may increase in the high season from May to Oct. Unless otherwise noted, hotels in Cairns will accept major credit cards. Hotels and resorts in the other centers will be mentioned as the destinations are discussed.

At the premium level, the **Hilton International,** The Esplanade, Cairns 4870, (070) 52-1599, telex 48292, and **Tradewinds Esplanade,** 137 The Esplanade, Cairns 4870, (070) 52-1111, telex 48316, provide luxury amenities in close to city locations. About 15 minutes from the city is the **Kewarra Beach Resort,** a smaller complex (23 motel units, 36 self-contained apartments) right on the beach which, at $140 double, is slightly cheaper than city counterparts with premium facilities. All of the above are air-conditioned and have pools. It's also recommended for its restaurants, the silver service **Lagoon's** and bistro **Island Kings**. Tel. (070) 57-6666 or telex 48340.

**The Cairns Colonial Resort,** a 200-room motel at 18–26 Cannon St., Cairns 4870, (070) 53-5111, telex 48221, has air-conditioned rooms ranging from $60 double. For a little more space, **The Reef Gateway Apartments,** 239 Lake St., Cairns 4870, (070) 52-1411, telex 48443, has 24 self-contained, air-conditioned two-bedroom apartments for around $90 a night. They have a barbecue area around the pool and provide "starter" packs containing breakfast ingredients for $20.

At budget, though not backpacker, level, **Inn the Tropics,** 141 Sheridan St., Cairns 4870, (070) 31-1088, and **UpTop Down Under Holiday Lodge,** 164–170 Spence St., Cairns 4870, (070) 51-3636, both have rooms with shared bathroom facilities for around $30 double. Neither has air-conditioning nor pool.

## ☞ RESTAURANTS

Cairns has more than one hundred restaurants and once again seafood is the speciality—coral trout, barramundi, king prawns, and Torres Strait crayfish are plentiful. Crocodile is relatively new on Australian menus and in Cairns you can sample it at (where else?) **Dundee's Licensed Grill,** at the corner of Sheridan and Aplin sts., (070) 51-0399. It also has spare ribs, grain-fed beef, and seafood for around $10 for main courses. It's licensed, and open every night. Major credit cards.

**Fathom's** is a pretty restaurant with lots of greenery. The emphasis is on seafood presented with French overtones and three courses without liquor will cost around $30. It's at the corner of Grove and Digger sts.; (070) 51-2305. Major credit cards.

For a spicy change, **Jungles** restaurant in the Bay Village Tropical Resort, 227 Lake St., (070) 51-4622, prepares Asian stir-fries and curries for around $10 a dish. It has a tastefully tropical decor, with potted palms and cane and bamboo furnishings. Licensed, open seven days; major credit cards.

**Tawny's** is the long-established mecca for seafood on the Marlin Jetty in the center of town. With main courses around the $15 mark, it's not cheap. It's licensed; tel. (070) 51-1722. Major credit cards.

Although Cairns is on the coast it has no beach—head for the Marlin Coast, 15 to 30 kilometers (9 to 18 miles) north, to swim in the ocean. **Popular beaches** include Trinity, Holloway's, Yorkey's, and Kewarra and these have stinger-free enclosures for the summer months. (Swim in them at your own risk—they're not 100 percent safe.) There's no surf on this coast as the Great Barrier Reef acts as a buffer for the waves. However, there are **surfing trips** organized beyond the outer reef. The Brothers Neilsen Surf Shop in the Palm Court shopping complex on Lake Street can provide information.

There are countless opportunities for **fishing** enthusiasts to try their luck. The Shell Marlin Jetty Tour Services office provides a list of fishing and boat charter operators; telephone (070) 51-9566. With a group it will cost about $100 for the day, or $800 to charter a private trip. All equipment provided.

You can also learn to **dive** in Cairns. Reputable companies include Deep Sea Divers Den, 319 Draper Street, (070) 51-1404, and Pro Diving Services, Marlin Parade, (070) 51-9915. Dive courses cost from $300 upwards and generally include two days' pool instruction and lectures followed by three days and two nights on a boat on the outer reef with night dives.

If **horse-riding** is your fancy, Peter and Lyn Gargan will take you to their cattle property, Springmount Station, 100 kilometers (62 miles) west of Cairns, for the day. They have mounts for all riding standards. The trip costs around $50 and includes morning tea and lunch; (070) 93-4445.

Koala Kraft, 17a Aplin Street, (070) 51-1259, sells a range of quality **local arts and crafts** including pottery from Yarrabah Aboriginal Mission, hand-painted, and screen-printed resort wear and appliquéd hand knits. For **Aussie clothing** such as oilskin coats and B.C. leather bush hats, a visit to Kangaroo Blue, at the corner of Lake and Spence streets, (070) 31-2388, is recommended. The Kuranda market, popular for **arts, crafts, and local** produce, is on Wednesday and Sunday mornings. Local tour operators run special services.

## TOURING OUT OF CAIRNS

## KURANDA

A trip to the Atherton Tableland township of Kuranda is a high priority. It takes about twenty minutes to drive there, but it's worth investing an extra hour and taking the **Scenic Railway** for the 300-meter ascent through 15 tunnels with a stop at Barron Falls. The 34 kilometer (21 miles) of railway took hundreds of men armed only with picks, shovels, and determination from 1884 to 1888 to build. The quaint Kuranda Railway Station has a magnificent display of tropical fernery. The trains leave Cairns railway station, McLeod Street, daily at 8:30 and 9 A.M. and depart Kuranda at 12 noon and 3:15 P.M. The Great Northern Railroad Company, (070) 55-2222, services the line with commentary cars for $22 round-trip and Queensland Railways, (070) 51-0531, charges about $15 round-trip. They also have a cheap rail motor for commuters, not promoted as a tourist option. (The term "rail motor" dates from the steam age. Rail motors had petrol or diesel engines whereas trains were coal fire powered. Now all trains are diesel or electrically powered.)

In Kuranda you can visit the **Australian Butterfly Sanctuary** at 8 Kennedy Highway. Said to be the world's largest, this enclosure features many rare species including the elusive vivid blue Ulysses butterfly. Telephone (070) 93-7575 for opening times and admission prices. The **Tjapukai (rainforest) Aboriginal Dance Theatre** is in the Kuranda Village Centre, (070) 93-7544, and there are performances daily at 10:45 A.M. and 1:30 P.M. for $9.

## ❦ ACCOMMODATIONS

You can stay on the edge of the Atherton Tableland on the cattle property **Gunnawarra.** The Atkinson family collect guests for the two-hour journey from Cairns, show them over the station, and accommodate them in the Heritage Commission–classified slab and shingle homestead. Meals here tend to rely on old-fashioned bush favorites such as corned beef and damper and they're included in the daily tariff of $200 per person which includes three meals a day, all alcohol, and trips around and about in comfortable vehicles. Phone (070) 97-9155 or fax (070) 97-9242.

# PORT DOUGLAS AND MOSSMAN

Port Douglas, or Port as the locals call it as if there were no other in the world, is 76 kilometers (almost 50 miles) north of Cairns along the coast-clinging Captain Cook Highway.

## ❦ ACCOMMODATIONS AND RESTAURANTS

Port Douglas has recently been jolted out of its tropical/alternative lifestyle torpor with the opening of the **Sheraton Mirage Resort,** where no expense has been spared to create the ultimate in luxury. In spite of the importation of 1,300 fully grown oil palms, the complex still looked like a giant construction site in mid-1988. Fortunately, in the tropics things grow quickly. The resort boasts three hundred air-conditioned rooms, a golf course, seven tennis courts, three restaurants, and a 3-hectare saltwater lagoon. Room rates begin at $200 per person per night; write Port Douglas 4871; (070) 98-5888, telex 48888. All major credit cards accepted. Hover-Mirage operates a daily hovercraft connection to the resort from Cairns airport for $66 one way; (070) 53-7000.

Apart from the resort, the main reasons for visiting Port seem to be to take one of the cruises run by Quicksilver Connections and sample Mocka pies, which have a reputation far greater than the modest shopfront in the town's main street would suggest—just look for the queue.

## ❦ ACCOMMODATIONS AND RESTAURANTS

If really getting away from it all is your aim, you'd be better off heading 27 km (17 miles) farther north to **Silky Oaks Colonial Lodge** overlooking the Mossman River Gorge. Take bush walks, go horse-riding or swimming, or just sit on the veranda of one of ten timber cabins and listen to the birds and water cascading over the rapids. Then return to the 20th-century with fresh tropical fare in the licensed restaurant. The Lodge's address is Finlayville Rd., Mossman 4873, (070) 98-1666, and its all-inclusive tariff is $125 per person per day. Four-wheel-drive safaris to the Daintree, Cape Tribulation, and Cooktown can be organized.

## DAINTREE AND CAPE TRIBULATION

At the township of Daintree, 50 kilometers (over 30 miles) north of Port Douglas, the paved road ends and the **wilderness rainforest** begins. Go croc-spotting on a river cruise (see Organized Tours, above), or visit the **Daintree Coffee Plantation,** where freshly roasted coffee is served from 10 A.M. to noon and 2 to 4 P.M. daily. Or cross the Daintree River on the car ferry which operates from 6 A.M. to 6 P.M. daily and push on to the **Cape Tribulation National Park,** 34 kilometers (over 20 miles) to the north. This road is for four-wheel-drives only, can be impassable in wet weather, and is rough going at the best of times.

There is a National Parks camping ground at Noah's Beach about 9 kilometers (5 miles or so) south of Cape Tribulation. The ranger will provide maps. You can also pick up maps and information in Cairns at the National Parks and Wildlife Office, 41 The Esplanade (opposite the Hilton Hotel); (070) 51-9811.

Fortify yourself before you set out with a break at **Floravilla Art Gallery Tea Gardens,** 11 km (about 6 miles) north of the ferry. It's run by artist/photographer team Betty and Bill Hinton and samples of their work and other local craft are on sale. So are wholemeal scones and locally grown tea for $3. The Hintons can also help with local information.

Heading for the park, next stop is **Thornton Beach Kiosk,** (070-51-3088), in what must be one of Australia's most remote locations for a licensed restaurant specializing in barbecues.

Cape Tribulation is where the rainforest literally meets the beach and figuratively meets the reef; it's about 15 kilometers (over 9 miles) off shore. Swim at your own risk and *not* during stinger season; the coastline is also inhabited by salt-water crocodiles.

### ACCOMMODATIONS AND RESTAURANTS

Cape Trib. is well supplied with backpacker accommodation including **The Village,** which has a two-night package including four-wheel-drive coach transfers from Cairns for $55. Accommodation is in log cabins and the complex has a licensed restaurant, **Clambango's,** with meals around the $6 mark. Book through Tropical Paradise Travel, 25 Spence St., Cairns 4870, (070) 31-2125. For more creature comforts **Bloomfield Wilderness Lodge,** just north of Cape Trib. has a poolside restaurant, catamarans, sailboards, four-wheel-drive tours, fishing expeditions on a 30-foot power cat, and accommodation for a maximum of thirty guests in rooms with en suites. Rates are $195 per person per day, inclusive of all meals and air transfer to and from Cairns. Book by phoning (070) 51-9687.

# COOKTOWN

Cooktown, 158 kilometers (about 100 miles) north of Cairns, can claim to be the first site of European settlement in Australia. In 1770 Captain Cook, charting the east coast of the country, spent six weeks there repairing his vessel, the *Endeavour,* after it was holed by a reef. A gold rush in the late 1800s made Cooktown Queensland's second largest town, with 65 hotels. Today it's a shadow of its former self, but an interesting spot to visit for anyone with an interest in Australian history. Choose between the Cape Tribulation/Bloomfield track or the inland route which leaves the highway just north of Mossman. Either way, it will take at least four hours, with good road conditions, from Cairns in a four-wheel-drive.

Alternatively take the Quicksilver Connection three-hour cruise from Port Douglas and arrive the way the original settlers did.

## ❦ ACCOMMODATIONS AND RESTAURANTS

Stay overnight at either the **Sovereign Hotel,** on the main street, Cooktown 4871, (070) 69-5400 (motel units $90 double; resort units with separate sitting rooms for $110 double), or **The River of Gold Motel,** Cooktown 4871, (070) 69-5222, with en suite units for $60 double. Both are air-conditioned, take credit cards, and have licensed restaurants.

Visit the **James Cook Historical Museum** (open daily from 9:30 A.M. to noon and 2 to 4 P.M.), the **Cooktown Cemetery** with its Chinese Shrine and grave of Mrs. Mary Watson (see Lizard Island, Great Barrier Reef), and set aside a morning or afternoon to go to **Ossie Walker's Cooktown Sea Museum.** Apart from having a large collection of maritime and Aboriginal artifacts, Ossie is a fountain of local information. It's open daily from 9 A.M. to 4 P.M., or whenever you knock on the door. You can also buy moderately priced **black coral jewelry** here.

Keen anglers shouldn't miss the opportunity to go **barramundi fishing** while in F.N.Q. This can be arranged by flying from Cairns to the Gulf of Carpenteria.

## ❦ FISHING ACCOMMODATIONS AND RESTAURANTS

Near Burketown is **Escott Lodge** (radio telephone (077) 43-7887 and ask for Escott or call 011 and ask for Burketown 45-

5108) where as well as fish you can horse-ride, clay target shoot, or take a helicopter flight to the gorge country of Lawn Hill National Park. Accommodation is in fairly basic units (you go there to fish) and there's a licensed restaurant. You can also game and sport fish at **Birri Fishing Resort** on Mornington Island, (077) 44-1711. It closes from December to March for the wet season.

At press time, the airline that services Burketown and Mornington Island was in the process of takeover—up-to-date information on both spots is available from the F.N.Q. Promotion Bureau.

# Great Barrier Reef

The Great Barrier Reef is Queensland's major attraction. Only a world-weary visitor would not be impressed by its vast splendor—more than 2,500 individual coral reefs stretching 2,000 kilometers (1,260 miles) along the coast from the top of the state to just north of Bundaberg. With more than twenty island resorts and countless charter and day trip boats, the opportunities to explore are boundless.

## TRAVEL

The *Quicksilver Connection* operates daily from Port Douglas (with bus connections to and from Cairns) to Agincourt Reef. The trip includes lunch and costs around $75, (070) 98-5373.

The *Reef Link* heads for John Brewer Reef from Townsville daily (with pick-ups at Magnetic Island). The trip with lunch costs $75, (077) 72-5399.

At Airlie Beach a recommended operator to the outer reef is the Hamilton Island 2000 Wave Piercer, which goes via Hamilton Island on Tues. and Fri. Cost including lunch is $70, (079) 46-9444.

From Bundaberg aim for Lady Musgrave Island on the vessel of the same name on Tues., Thurs., and weekends. Cost is $70 including lunch. Alternatively, fly to the island for $150 round-trip per person for a minimum of four passengers. Catch a connecting flight from Brisbane to Bundaberg and the cost of the day trip will be around $400 per person. For more details about Lady Musgrave Island call (071) 72-9011.

The off-shore resorts scattered along the coast give a better chance to experience the Reef at leisure and this selection covers the possibilities, north to south, from luxury accommodation to budget bring your own, including food and water.

Some words of warning. With the exception of the facilities on the coral cays of Heron, Lady Elliot, and Lady Musgrave islands, and the Four Seasons floating hotel (floatel), most resorts are located on continental or land islands which were separated from the mainland after the last ice age. While these islands have fringing reefs, their coral is at best a support act for the star turn, the outer reef, generally about an hour away by speed boat.

---

### Great Barrier Reef

The *Beagle* turned south from Sydney, which meant Charles Darwin never did see the Great Barrier Reef. Yet, his 1838 theory sparked debates which went on for more than a century, finally proving him right, about how coral reefs are formed.

In 1770, the first scientists to encounter the Reef (a party under the command of Capt. James Cook) was more concerned about the danger they posed to the ship than their natural wonder. The coral was "dreadful," the group's prospects "melancholy."

Darwin was more eloquent. After sighting Pacific coral, he wrote: "We feel surprise when travellers tell us of the vast dimensions of the Pyramids and other ruins, but how utterly insignificant are the greatest of these, when compared to these mountains of stone accumulated by the agency of various minute and tender animals!"

Covering 230,000 square kilometers, the Barrier Reef is the world's largest living thing. Theories about how reefs formed had to do with the lowering of the sea level during glacial ages or the growth of coral on the rims of submerged volcanos.

It was known that coral forms in shallow water and yet, many reefs rise from great depths. Darwin solved the riddle by deducing that coral grows just offshore from land which is slowly sinking. As the land subsides, the coral builds on top of its own skeleton, so the living reef remains near the sea's surface. The Great Barrier Reef thus marks the edge, millennia ago, of Australia's land mass.

—Steve Bunk

---

## LIZARD ISLAND

To take it from the top (both geographically and in price structure) Lizard, 240 kilometers (149 miles) north of Cairns, is one of the closest land islands to the outer reef. (Bank's Bank is about twenty minutes by boat.) The resort is exclusive with 32 bungalow-style suites and has a reputation for hosting the rich and famous. There are 24 secluded beaches and, just off shore, hectares of giant clam gardens to delight the snorkeler. (Don't put your feet down.)

Visit the remains of the Watsons' cottage and learn of Mary Watson's desperate attempt to flee the island in an iron *beche de mer* boiling tank after attack from Aborigines in 1881. When her fisherman husband returned from a trip, her body and that of her infant son and Chinese servant were found on number 5 Howick Island, where they had perished from thirst. The tank and diary recording the tragedy can be seen at the Queensland Museum (see Brisbane, above). No such fate is in store for the modern visitor to Lizard as the dining room menu offers a choice of tropical fare and full bar service.

## ❦ ACCOMMODATIONS
**Lizard Island Resort** is owned and operated by Australian Airlines with daily flights from Cairns. Tariff inclusive of meals is $270 per person per night for suites and $320 per person per night for deluxe suites with separate living area. The resort's address is Box 1381, Cairns, Queensland 4870; (070) 50-4305, telex: 48448.

## ORPHEUS ISLAND

Like Lizard, Orpheus Island has no nightclubs, no discos, no TV, and no "packdrill" (organized activities). The emphasis is on total relaxation for a pampered few—there are 23 studio units, two bungalows, and six privately owned villas, managed by the resort's Italian consortium owners. Orpheus does have seven sandy beaches, two charter boats for the ninety-minute trip to the outer reef, and full water-sports facilities. The island is 80 kilometers (about 50 miles) north of Townsville and transport from there is by seaplane (regular service) or chartered helicopter.

## ❦ ACCOMMODATIONS
Rates at **Orpheus Island Resort** are inclusive of meals—(the restaurant has a buffet and à la carte selections, specializing in seafood and tropical fruit)—$230 per person per night for studio units, or $250 for bungalows (larger units). The villas have two bedrooms and cost $800 per night, accommodation only. All major credit cards accepted. The resort's address is Private Mailbag, Ingham, Queensland, 4850; (077) 77-7377 or phone toll free (008) 22-1837.

You can't get much closer to the outer reef than the **Four Seasons Barrier Reef Resort.** Just dive off one of the hotel's pontoons and you'll be swimming around on John Brewer Reef, 70 km (43 miles) northeast of Townsville. Among the many claims the owners can make for this 200-room hotel is that it is the world's first floating hotel, has the world's first floating tennis court, pharmacy, newsagency, post office. . . . Access is by chartered helicopter or regular high-speed catamaran from Townsville. Rates range from $190 per person per night, twin share to $700 for an executive suite for one to four people. Meals and drinks extra. There is a formal restaurant, as well as a coffee lounge and outdoor snack bar. The address is The Barrier Reef, via Townsville, Qld. 4810; (077) 70-9111. All major credit cards accepted.

## WHITSUNDAY ISLANDS

The Whitsunday group of islands boasts a host of resorts including the Ansett Airlines–owned Hayman Resort and Hamilton Island Resort owned by entrepreneur Keith Williams. Hamilton has a jet airstrip and Ansett flies directly to the island every day from Sydney and Melbourne (with a 30-minute, or two glasses of champagne, boat connection for Hayman guests). **Hayman** is aimed at the sophisticate, the stressed executive, or world-weary traveler. It's an oasis of marble and sandstone in a man-made jungle of more than 660,000 plants shipped from the mainland. Even the inevitability of tidal fluctuation has been countered—the developers dredged a channel through a facing reef, took away the coral, crushed it into sand for a beach where the tide never goes right out.

## ❦ ACCOMMODATIONS AND RESTAURANTS

The **Hayman Island Resort** has 190 rooms and 33 suites, a freshwater lagoon with a capacity equivalent to five Olympic swimming pools, French, Italian, Oriental, and Polynesian restaurants and a Japanese tea garden. Rates range from $220 per room per night to $745 per night for a suite. All rooms are air-conditioned. Meals extra. The address is Hayman Island, Great Barrier Reef, Queensland, 4801; (079) 46-9410 or toll-free (008) 07-5110, telex 48163. All major credit cards accepted.

By contrast, **Hamilton Island** resort caters for the young and the restless with non-stop activity ranging from boat trips to the outer reef and scenic helicopter flights to sailboarding, parasailing, and bingo in the guest lounges. It's almost a self-contained city with four hundred air-conditioned hotel rooms and apartments catering to about thirteen hundred guests. There are five styles of accommodation ranging from high-rise apartment to bare (more on the drawing board), restaurants, bars, discos, and shopping arcades. As well, the resort has a 200-berth marina, fast-food outlets, and bare-boat charter base. The island hosts a number of yachting series during the year but it never really has a quiet moment.

## ❦ ACCOMMODATIONS

Rates at **Hamilton Island Resort** range from $170 per person per night to $1,250 a night for a four-bedroom penthouse. All major credit cards. The address is Private Mailbag, Mackay, Queensland, 4740; (079) 46-9144, telex 48516.

## HERON ISLAND

If getting back to nature is more your style, Heron Island should appeal. In fact you might find it's a bit close for comfort as Heron is a wildlife haven and avoiding the bird droppings is something of an island hazard. The island is a 17-hectare coral cay, right in the middle of the outer reef, ninety minutes by high-speed catamaran or thirty minutes by charter helicopter from Gladstone.

The resort here is operated by P&O shipping so meals are liner-style with running sittings, but any inconvenience this incurs is far outweighed by the bonuses—the coral at your doorstep, moderately priced dive courses ($220 for seven days tuition), the chance to see loggerhead and green turtles nesting from October to March and hatching from December to March, and crested shearwaters (mutton birds) unceremoniously crash landing on their runways during the mating season. (Keep out of their way, they can't change their flight paths.)

## ❦ ACCOMMODATIONS

The accommodations at **Heron Island Resort** range from lodge-style units for $90 per person per night to beach houses for $360 per night. None of the rooms have air-conditioning. Children are welcome. Heron's booking office is c/o P&O Resorts, 482 Kingsford Smith Dr., Brisbane, Queensland, 4007, or phone the resort direct at (079) 78-1488 or toll-free (008) 77-7243, telex 49455. Accepts major credit cards.

## LADY MUSGRAVE

If you fancy staying on an uninhabited coral island, Lady Musgrave will fill the bill. Mind you, there's no resort and you have to take your own camping gear, food and water. The vessel *Lady Musgrave* takes day trippers out to the cay and will drop you on the island. If you make arrangements with the skipper in advance, the boat will also replenish your supplies while you're staying on the island. They charge $140 per person return from Bundaberg for campers and $120 for backpackers. (The rate depends on the amount of gear you're carrying and includes lunch on the catamaran on arrival and departure days.) You'll need permission from the National Parks and Wildlife Service in Gladstone, (079) 76-1621, to stay there. There's no charge; this is a precautionary measure to keep campers to less than fifty at any one time. Mid-week in winter you could be lucky enough to have the place to yourself. The island is also a turtle nesting ground, migrating bird pit stop, and snorkeling and scuba diving paradise. For further information call (071) 72-9011.

## LADY ELLIOT ISLAND

Lady Elliot Island is similarly back to basics, though not quite as minimalist as Lady Musgrave. To walk around this coral island takes just over half an hour, to get there about the same time in a light plane from Bundaberg. Again, fishing and coral viewing are the main attractions. For nightlife? Maybe a night dive or watching the turtles lay their eggs on the beach. The resort offers moderately priced dive instruction (introductory dives $50 including lectures, $30 a day for up to four shore dives). Lady Elliot is on the southernmost tip of the Great Barrier Reef.

## ✿ ACCOMMODATIONS

The low-key **Lady Elliot Island Resort** offers cabin accommodation with en suite bathrooms for $100 per person, per night; cabins with shared bathrooms for $85; and safari-style tents for $75. The rooms are not air-conditioned. All meals are included in these prices. For further information, tel. (071) 72-2322 or toll free (008) 07-2200. All major credit cards accepted.

# 9

# SOUTH AUSTRALIA

South Australia bills itself as the festival state—even the car license plates proclaim it as such. Indeed, the state has much of the good life to celebrate. It's home to some of Australia's premier wine regions, best opal fields, protected wildlife, and two events that attract hordes of both domestic and international visitors—the Australian Formula One Grand Prix held in October or November each year and the biennial Adelaide Festival, a three-week cultural feast held in March of even-numbered years.

The state's area of nearly one million square kilometers easily swallows its meager population of only 1.4 million people. Slightly less than one million of these live in the capital, Adelaide, in the southeast corner. Less than 1 percent of the total live north of the 32nd parallel which crosses the state just above Port Augusta at the apex of Spencer Gulf. The population is concentrated in the southeast because the country to the north, the bulk of the state's area, is extremely harsh desert, the Simpson Desert and Sturt's Stony Desert—endless expanses of sand dunes and salt-bush studded plains where the summer temperatures can burst thermometers. At Oodnadatta, for example, temperatures of 51° C (over 130° F) are not uncommon. The nearby Lake Eyre, ranked number 16 in size of the great lakes of the world, spends most of its life as a massive pan of salt.

By Australian distance reckoning, Adelaide is close to many of the state's attractions and therefore makes a good base for sampling the wine-producing regions of the Barossa and Clare valleys and the Adelaide Hills in the near north, and for exploring the mighty Murray, Australia's largest river, which reaches the coast less than an hour's drive from the capital. Here you can fish, swim, or water ski and play Tom Sawyer to your heart's content from the deck of a paddlewheeler, houseboat, or cruise boat.

About 300 kilometers (190 miles), four hour's drive, farther south and east and you'll be in Mount Gambier with its volcanic crater lakes, the most famous of which is the mysterious Blue Lake which has a startling color change in spring. Nearby are limestone caves and the historic fishing ports of Robe, Kingston, and Port MacDonnell.

Kangaroo Island, site of the state's first official European settlement, in 1836, had in fact been providing shelter to shipwrecked sailors, sealers, and whalers for previous decades. Today it's a relaxed holiday destination, a thirty-minute flight from Adelaide to a protected environment where kangaroos, seals, sea lions, fairy penguins, and rare birds can be observed in their natural habitat.

Tours to the Outback can be arranged from Adelaide, or if you're traveling through to Ayers Rock and Alice Springs in the Northern Territory you'll pass through it on the Stuart Highway. Visiting the Flinders Ranges involves a diversion from this route of about 150 kilometers (almost 100 miles) north from Port Augusta (300 kilometers—over 180 miles— north of Adelaide) but you'll be rewarded with rugged ranges, and deep gorges that closet rich fossil remains. You can take anything from a two-hour to a two-week bush walk and explore the natural amphitheater of Wilpena Pound.

Back on the Stuart Highway, 535 kilometers (over 300 miles) northwest of Port Augusta and a similar distance from Alice Springs, is the opal city of Coober Pedy. Its fields yield more than half the world's production of the fiery gem. In pursuit of it and in refuge from the heat, many of the locals live underground in elaborate dugouts. There are also a subterranean church and motel.

The southeast corner of South Australia has a temperate, Mediterranean-style climate with a short, wet winter and long, dry summer. Summer (December to February) has an average maximum of 29° C (around 90° F) with low humidity. Winter (June to August) has an average maximum of 17° C (around 60° F) and rainy periods. In the southernmost part the climate is cooler and moister, in the arid north rainfall is erratic and summer daytime temperatures frequently reach the high 30s C (high 90s F). Best to avoid the Outback from November to March.

Casual clothes will best serve the visitor—light weight in summer and medium weight for winter. (This includes the Outback, where low night temperatures can come as a shock after the day's warmth.) If you're planning any formal dining or a visit to the casino in Adelaide, men should include a coat and tie, and women a semiformal dress. For the Outback don't forget a hat, sunscreen, and sturdy walking shoes.

South Australia was founded as a convict settlement. While sealers had based themselves on Kangaroo Island from the early 1800s, the creation of an official colony didn't occur until

1836 when Captain John Hindmarsh was proclaimed governor. The settlement was based on Edward Gibbon Wakefield's theories for opening up the "waste lands" of the British Empire and creating new opportunities for English laborers who wanted to migrate. The site for the capital city (named for Queen Adelaide) was laid out by Surveyor General Colonel William Light, with a central business district area of one square mile (miles being used rather than kilometers in those Imperial days) farsightedly surrounded by a belt of parkland. Partly because of these gentrified beginnings and design, Adelaide was shackled with a staid image which has only been cast off in the past twenty years, largely due to the Festival of Arts, recognized as Australia's major regular cultural event. However, visitors will still find Adelaide's pace gentler than the eastern capitals of Sydney and Melbourne.

The state's economy is predominantly agricultural, based on cereal grains, sheep, wine, and fishing. Secondary industries include car manufacturing and ship building. Yet the state's public image is clearly projected as the place to sample the finer side of life—wine and song counterbalanced by the simpler pleasures of getting back to a unique form of nature in the Outback.

## TRAVEL

### Flying

As South Australia is sandwiched in the center of the country, it's unlikely that, if you're coming from North America or Europe, you'll begin your visit to Australia by flying directly to its capital, Adelaide, which has the state's only international airport. If you're arriving in Australia with Qantas, you can arrange with them to fly on to Adelaide from the other capitals, but most visitors arrive with the domestic carriers.

Both Ansett and Australian Airlines have daily flights from the interstate capitals with connecting services to the major centers. Ansett offices in Adelaide are at 205 Greenhill Rd., Eastwood (08) 233-3322. Australian Airlines is at 144 North Terr., Adelaide, (08) 217-3333. Kendell Airlines, 1st floor, 94 Hindley St., Adelaide (08) 231-9567 provides extensive regional services. Lloyd Aviation, which flies to Kangaroo Island, is at 101 Grenfell St., Adelaide; (08) 224-5722. Airtransit also flies to Kangaroo Island (Adelaide Airport, West Beach; 352-3177).

### Taking the Train

Air-conditioned trains link Adelaide with Alice Springs, Perth, Melbourne, and Sydney. There is no rail link to Darwin. The major interstate services are the *Indian-Pacific*, which passes through South Australia from Sydney to Perth, the *Ghan*, which links Adelaide with Alice Springs, and the *Overland*, which provides an overnight service to Melbourne. Country and interstate trains operate from the Passenger Rail Terminal at Keswick, just a few minutes from the city center; (08) 217-4444.

## Taking the Bus

Major interstate and country coach operators include Ansett Pioneer, 101 Franklin St., Adelaide, (08) 233-2700; Greyhound, 111 Franklin St., Adelaide, (08) 212-1777, and Deluxe Coachlines, 101 Franklin St., Adelaide, (08) 212-2077. Bus Australia, Shops, 130 Gawler Pl., Adelaide (08) 212-7344, run a number of tours including the Flinders Ranges and Kangaroo Island.

## Driving

The other states are linked by a network of highways. Adelaide is approximately 870 km (540 miles) from Melbourne, 1,700 km (1,050 miles) from Alice Springs and 3,220 km (almost 2,000 miles) from Darwin, 2,815 km (1,750 miles) from Perth. The shortest route to Sydney is the Barrier Hwy. via Broken Hill, a distance of 1,540 km (over 950 miles).

### RENTALS

While South Australia is well serviced by tour operators, the independent traveler may prefer the flexibility of a rental car. The major national companies are represented in Adelaide. Avis is located at 108–114 Burbridge Rd., Hilton, (08) 354-0444; Budget at 274 North Terr., (08) 223-1400; Hertz at 233 Morphett St., (08) 231-2856; and Thrifty at 100 Franklin St., (08) 211-8788. Seat belts are mandatory and speed limits are 60 km.p.h. in built-up areas and 110 km.p.h. on the open road, unless otherwise indicated.

Campervans and motor homes provide an economical way to explore the state as your accommodation costs are included in your travel costs. The only extras will be food and caravan park or campsite fees, usually around $10 per night. Touralong Travel Homes, 344 North East Rd. Klemzig, (08) 261-8833, and Autohansa, 250 Richmond Rd., Marleston, (08) 234-1463, are reliable operators.

For further information on touring in South Australia, contact the **S.A. Government Travel Centre,** 18 King William St., Adelaide 5000, (08) 212-1644. Tours out of Adelaide are discussed below.

# Adelaide

The fathers of the city of Adelaide were farsighted indeed when they designated one square mile for the central business district and enclosed it with parkland. Today this design is a major contributor to Adelaide's image as an attractive city, one which is reinforced by the fact that many of its older-style buildings have been recycled, rather than pulled down. Hence you'll find the casino in a handsome railway station, a nightclub complex in an old church, and an arts center in a former factory.

The city center streets run on a grid pattern, enclosed by North, South, East, and West terraces and bisected by the office-lined King William Road. Rundle Street, part of which is a mall with a maze of arcades opening off it, and is the main shopping street. Best way to get around the city center is on foot—if you tire of that, hail a cab or book one from Amalgamated at (08) 223-3333 or United Yellow at (08) 223-3111. Alternatively, hop on a free Beeline or City Loop bus, which circle the main shopping area from 8 A.M. to 6 P.M. weekdays and from 8 A.M. to noon on Saturdays.

The State Transport Authority (STA) runs the buses, trains, and trams which service the city and suburbs. For routes and timetable information visit the city office on the corner of King William and Currie streets, or telephone at (08) 210-1000. Tickets are valid for any tram, train, or bus travel for two hours. You can purchase a day-trip ticket for $5, valid for all Greater Adelaide travel. Suburban trains run from the railway station on North Terrace (under the casino). Adelaide's only electric tram, to the seaside suburb of Glenelg, leaves from Victoria Square every 15 minutes. The journey takes about 25 minutes.

Bus Australia's **Adelaide Sightseeing Explorer Bus** makes stops at eight major attractions on its 34-kilometer (21-mile) circuit. Passengers may alight and rejoin at any stop and the ticket cost is $10. Telephone (08) 212-7344 for details. Briscoes offices are at 101 Franklin Street, and they also conduct day and half-day coach tours of the city's outlying sights. (Rental cars are discussed in the South Australia Travel section, above.) For information on river tours from Adelaide see S.A.'s Southeast.

---

## ❧ ACCOMMODATIONS

These accommodations in Adelaide, in a range of prices, were chosen for their proximity to the city center. As with most cities of its size, Adelaide's public transportation system is fine during the day, but not so good at night. It's best to stay close to center, where the major concentration of facilities, attractions, and restaurants can be found. Expect air-conditioning, unless otherwise noted. All the hotels and motels accept credit cards.

Adelaide's premium hotel is the new **Hyatt Regency** on North Terr. next to the casino, Adelaide 5000, (08) 231-1234, telex 88582, fax (08) 231-1120. It incorporates 369 rooms, 20 suites, and all five-star facilities—swimming pool, sauna, restaurants, bars, nightclub, even Scoops licensed ice-cream parlor. Rooms have TVs and in-house movies. 24-hour room service is available. Room rates begin at $200 a night.

The **Hilton International Adelaide,** 233 Victoria Sq., Adelaide 5000, (08) 217-0711, is a few blocks from the commercial center, but any inconvenience is outweighed by its peaceful view over the square. Room rates begin at $170 and the hotel has the usual five-star amenities—pool, sauna, nightclub, and the highly recommended Grange Restaurant. All rooms have TVs and room service is available 24 hours.

If you have your own transport, consider getting right away from the city bustle (well, 14 km—8 miles—at least) in the Adelaide Hills at the country estate of **Mt. Lofty House,** 74 Summit Rd., Crafers, (08) 339-6777. This elegant colonial establishment has Relais and Chateaux status and standard room rates are $150 or $190 for a suite with spa, breakfast included. On Sun. you can take high tea there and enjoy cucumber and smoked-salmon sandwiches, petit fours, and cakes for $15 a head. Sun. brunch is the same price and fare includes fresh fruit compote, poached eggs with smoked turkey and chive hollandaise on croutons, and champagne. Dinner is à la carte in the restaurant, Hardy's.

More moderately priced accommodation is available in the center of town at the **Festival Lodge Motel,** 140 North Terr., Adelaide 5000, (08) 212-7877, and the **Grosvenor Hotel,** 125 North Terr., Adelaide 5000, (08) 231-2961. The former has room-only accommodations starting at $45 single and $55 double. Room service breakfast only. The Grosvenor rates begin at $50 single and $60 double. Rooms are compact, but have en suite (private) bathrooms, TVs, phones, and the basic modern conveniences. There's a dining room for moderately priced meals (main courses around $8) and a more up-market restaurant which is patronized by locals as well as guests.

The **Parkway Motor Inn,** 204 Greenhill Rd., Eastwood 5063, (08) 271-0451, is about 2 km (1¼ miles) from the city and has motel facilities, including a pool and restaurant, for $50 single and $55 double. The **Earl of Zetland Hotel,** corner of Gawler Place and Flinders St., Adelaide 5000, (08) 223-5500, has a rather unprepossessing exterior, but inside are comfortable rooms with en suite bathrooms for $40 single and $50 double: more than you'd usually expect in a pub. They prepare inexpensive buffet lunches ($6) and counter meals, and one bar specializes in an extensive range of single malt whiskies. Presumably the rationale is you can drink what you save on accommodation prices.

A walk along the tree-lined North Terrace will take you to many of Adelaide's attractions and provide glimpses of the city's colonial buildings. Start at the western end with the **Living Arts Centre** on the corner of Morphett Street. This complex in an old factory contains performance spaces, galleries, artists' workshops, and retail outlets. Toward King William Road is the **casino** in the old railway station (see Entertainment, below), then side by side, the old and new parliament houses. **Old Parliament House** is now a constitutional museum, open weekdays from 10 A.M. to 5 P.M. and weekends from 11:30 A.M. to 5 P.M. Admission is charged for various exhibitions.

Continue past the State Library to the **South Australia Museum,** open every day except Christmas and Good Friday from 10 A.M. to 5 P.M., Wednesday from 1 P.M. to 5 P.M. (223-8911). Admission is free and the museum shop has a selection of quality Australiana—books and artifacts. The museum has one of the most extensive collections of Aboriginal anthropology in the country. Unfortunately it lacks display place, so until it is extended, the exhibits are rotated.

Turn left down Frome Road for the **Zoological Gardens,** open every day except Christmas from 9:30 A.M. to 5 P.M. (267-3255). Admission is $6, and the zoo is landscaped with moat enclosures rather than cages for animals that include Australian natives. There's a thriving colony of yellow-footed rock wallabies—seldom-seen inhabitants of the Flinders Ranges.

**Ayers House,** 288 North Terrace (223-1196), the residence of a long-term premier of South Australia, is now the headquarters of the National Trust. The house is furnished in the grand style of the late 19th century and for $2 admission you can look over it from 10 A.M. to 4 P.M. Tuesday through Friday and weekends from 2 to 4 P.M.

Across the street from Ayers House is the **Adelaide Botanic Garden** open weekdays from 7 A.M. to sunset and weekends from 9 A.M. to sunset. Admission is free and tours set out from the kiosk (open from 10 A.M. to 4:30 P.M.) Tuesday and Friday at 10:30 A.M. (228-2311). Be sure to see the giant water lily house and Australia's only museum of economic botany.

**Cleland Conservation Park** is a native fauna reserve set in natural bushland on the slopes of Mt. Lofty, 19 kilometers (about 12 miles) southeast of Adelaide. Admission is $2 and the park is open every day from 9:30 A.M. to 5 P.M. (Telephone 339-2572.) Koala viewing and handling is from 2 to 4 P.M. If you don't have your own transport, Briscoes' day tours (see the introduction to the Adelaide section, above) take in this spot. Otherwise from Adelaide take Glen Osmond Road which becomes Mt. Barker Road.

## SHOPPING

South Australia is famous for its **opals** from the fields of Coober Pedy and Andamooka. Reputable opal dealers in Adelaide include Opal Field Gems, 29 King William Road, (08) 212-5300, and Olympic Jewelers, 5 Rundle Mall, (08) 211-7440. The Adelaide Gem Trading Company, 26–28 Currie Street, (08) 212-3600, also has a wide range of opals and jewelry and incorporates a contemporary and traditional Aboriginal art and craft gallery.

Quality 5 Crafts, Shop 47, City Cross Arcade, (08) 212-3340, has a good selection of **Australian crafts** and will pack and ship your purchases. Head for the **bush outfitter,** R.M. Williams, for Drizabones (riding coats for wet weather), moleskin trousers, and Akubra hats. The factory is at 5 Percy Street, Prospect, and they have a retail outlet in the city at The Gallery, Gawler Place, (08) 344-8191.

## RECREATION

Adelaide is well equipped with parklands, and the beaches at St. Vincent Gulf are a twenty-minute drive from the city center. Locals make good use of these natural facilities and head for the great outdoors.

The City of **Adelaide Golf Links,** Memorial Drive, North Adelaide, (08) 51-2359, welcomes guests, and equipment can be hired by phoning (08) 267-2171. **Grass and hard tennis courts** are available for hire at the Memorial Drive Courts (near Torrens River), War Memorial Drive, North Adelaide, (08) 51-4371.

You can cycle on tracks in the Adelaide parklands and **bikes** may be hired from Super Elliot, Rundle Mall, during business hours. The **Adelaide Swimming Centre** is in the north parkland near Fitzroy Terrace, (08) 218-7312, or you can take the twenty-minute drive via Anzac Highway to Glenelg to the **beaches and calm waters** of St. Vincent's Gulf—Grange, Henley, Glenelg, Brighton, and Seacliff.

At the Bay World Tourist Information Centre on Glenelg Beach (100 meters from the tram stop) you can hire **bikes, wave skis,** beach chairs, umbrellas, **snorkels,** masks, fins, and wetsuits (although the best diving is on Kangaroo Island; see below). Next door is the Magic Mountain complex which incorporates a huge **water slide.**

## ❧ RESTAURANTS

Perhaps it's due to the surrounding wine country, or maybe it's because Adelaide is such a civilized place, but the city has a fine dining scene. South Australia is the only state where it's legal to sell kangaroo meat for human consumption, so try it while you're here, if you must. Seafood is abundant—discard any preconceived notions about whiting and try the King George variety. Lobster (crayfish actually) is also available locally and high in quality. On the beverage side, some of Australia's finest wines come from this state—be sure to taste Cabernet Sauvignon from the Coonawarra, Rhine Reisling from the Barossa and Clare valleys, and if your budget extends to them, Australia's most famous drops—Penfold's Grange Hermitage and Seppelt's 100-year-old Para Port. The locally brewed beer, Cooper's Sparkling Ale, is famous all over Australia.

Credit cards are widely accepted. Major cards are considered AE—American Express, V—Visa, MC—MasterCard, DC—Diner's Club.

If Thai food takes your fancy, the place to go is **Bangkok,** 1st floor, 217 Rundle St., City, (08) 223-5406. It's open for lunch Mon.–Fri. and dinner Mon.–Sat. and is licensed. Main courses are around $10. All major cards.

In the Adelaide Hills (about 25 minutes southeast from the center of town), the Bridgewater Mill complex, Mt. Barker Rd., Bridgewater, (08) 339-4227, contains (in addition to the production facility for the premium sparkling wine, Croser) the **Granary** bistro for lunches and the starkly elegant **Petaluma** restaurant, open for lunch Fri. and Sun. and dinner Thurs.–Sat. Food is innovative Australian (with Asian influences—Thai-style prawn and lemon-grass soup; King George whiting with coriander and lemon sauce), and if you're having dessert, try their splendid Petaluma Botrytis Essence wine. Three courses without wine will be around $45 and major credit cards are accepted. The best route to the Hills is the Montacute Scenic Route; get directions from the S.A. Travel Centre (see above and Vital Information).

French cuisine moderne is available at **Chloe's,** 36 College Rd., Kent Town, (08) 42-2574. It's set in a restored villa, about 2 km (that's about a mile) east of the city, and is open for lunch Mon.–Fri. and dinner Mon.–Sat. Its extensive wine list is one of Adelaide's best. All cards accepted and the bill, without wine, will come to about $45 a head. Take Rundle St. from the center of town.

**The description "cuisine moderne" is used where the chef is trying particularly hard to make use of local ingredients. Much of the hallmarks of what Americans know as "California cuisine" are here: char-grilling, simple sauces, smoking.**

For Australian fare with flair, head for **Duthy's** at 19 Duthy St., Malvern, (08) 272-0465. Malvern is an inner-city suburb just south of Adelaide's center; Unley Rd. will take you there. It's licensed and BYOB, accepts all credit cards, and is open for dinner Tues.–Sat. Main courses are around the $15 mark. Try grilled tuna steaks with balsamic vinegar sauce, loin of lamb with Thai curry sauce, tuna tartare with wasabi.

**Jarmers,** 297 Kensington Rd., Kensington Park (east of central Adelaide), (08) 332-2080, is open for dinner Mon.–Sat. and presents creative Australian food. It takes all cards and will cost about $50 a head without liquor. On the first Mon. each month this elegant establishment holds a gourmet night, with a set menu with matched wines. Features may include crayfish with mango and lime mayonnaise or rare roasted kangaroo fillet with a reduction sauce. Reach the restaurant via Rundle St., which becomes The Parade through the suburbs of Kent Town and Norwood.

**Jasmin Indian Restaurant,** 31 Hindmarsh Sq., City, (08) 223-7837, has a national reputation for fine North Indian food. Not as spicy as Southern Indian, food here may be marinated in yogurt; the rice dishes biryani are popular; as is the tandoori oven. It's licensed, open for lunch Tues.–Fri. and dinner Tues.–Sat.; main courses are around $12. Credit cards accepted.

If you fancy what Australians call "a good feed of fish 'n chips," try any of the **cafés on Gouger St.**, City, in particular, **Paul's** at 79, (08) 231-9778. It's BYOB, and main course will cost about $10. Open for lunch Mon.–Fri. and dinner Mon.–Sat.

**Reilly's** at 138 King William Rd., Hyde Park (south of city: take Unley Rd.), (08) 272-0873, specializes in char-grilled steaks and is open for lunch Mon.–Fri. and dinner Mon.–Sat. It accepts all cards and three courses will cost around $25.

**Sarah's Café** is vegetarian, but even meat eaters will be satisfied with the imaginative food served: vegetable pâtés and terrines; noodle dishes and stir fries; spaghetti squash with vegetable sauces. It's licensed, located at 199 Hutt St., City, (08) 223-3533, and dinner without wine will come to about $20.

**Windy Point Restaurant,** Belair Rd., Belair (take Unley Rd. south of city; it becomes Belair Rd.), (08) 278-8255, earns a mention more for the night lights view than the food (veal steaks, beef steaks, and roasts, among the standard fare). It's licensed, open for dinner Mon.–Sat., accepts major credit cards, and three courses will cost about $30.

Hardly a gourmet delight, but none the less a true Adelaide dining experience, is the **floater**—a meat pie served floating in a bowl of split green pea soup topped with tomato sauce (ketchup). You can buy these at night from the pie carts that set up in Victoria Square and outside the Railway Station and you eat them standing at the service bar. There's no recommended time for eating a floater, though most people seem to find the courage late at night.

# ENTERTAINMENT

Adelaide is not New York, but for its population it boasts a large number of performing arts venues, well patronized by the locals. Fringe theater is also alive and well. The city enjoys a cultural feast during its biennial Festival of the Arts.

The **Adelaide Casino** on North Terrace, (08) 212-2811, is located in the classic sandstone Railway Station building and has two floors of gaming tables for blackjack and roulette as well as the Aussie favorite, two-up. (Two-up is a gambling game involving the tossing of two coins; players bet against the spinner's throwing two of a kind—heads or tails.) There are five bars and the Pullman Restaurant and the complex is open from 11 A.M. to 4 A.M. weekdays and 24 hours on weekends.

The Adelaide Festival Centre, behind the casino on King William Road, (08) 213-4600, is the main venue for the **performing arts,** though of course during the Adelaide Festival (in March of even-numbered years) music, opera, dance, and drama groups take over halls and theaters throughout the city and suburbs. For current shows see the entertainment pages of the morning newspaper, *The Advertiser,* or phone Bass Booking Agency at (08) 213-4777. There are several cinema complexes along Rundle Mall and Hindley Street; check the papers for current movies.

St. Paul's Entertainment Centre, formerly a church on the corner of Pulteney and Flinders streets, (08) 223-4255, contains a number of **restaurants and bars with live entertainment.**

**Nightclubs** in the major hotels featuring visiting artists include Juliana's, in the Hilton, and Waves, in the Hyatt Regency. The crowds here are fairly sophisticated; young ragers prefer the live music in the pubs.

During October, the streets of Adelaide are taken over by hoardes of people wearing flashy overalls and baseball caps. **Grand Prix** is an exciting time to be in the city and even people who couldn't care less about Formula One racing say they become caught up in the spirit of the event. Accommodation is at a premium during this period, so be sure to book well in advance.

# S.A. Wine Country

South Australians are fortunate in that their capital is virtually surrounded by wine districts (except to the west—vines don't do too well in the sea). The most famous is the Barossa Valley (named and mis-spelt by Colonel Light in 1837 because it reminded him of the Barrosa ranges in Spain). The Barossa is about 65 kilometers (about 40 miles) to the north of Adelaide, and an additional 75 kilometers (47 miles) north is another premium wine producing area, the Clare Valley. Take North Road from Adelaide; at Gawler turn right into the Barossa. Both can be visited in a day trip from Adelaide with Briscoes (see Adelaide introduction), but to soak up the rustic charm of these districts properly, and fit in a few tastings as well, it's advisable to spend a couple of days there.

The locals love to party—they do it formally in the Clare with a vintage festival during Easter of even-numbered years and a gourmet weekend every May. The Barossa Vintage Festival is held during Easter of odd-numbered years and their gourmet weekend is in August. On these occasions, restaurateurs from Adelaide and the eastern capitals pack up their kitchens and team up with vignerons to serve complimentary food and wine to hundreds of visitors who ostensibly call to taste that year's infant wines. Informally, the party continues year-round as the area offers hospitality unrivaled by other wine districts. They have splendid restaurants, charming guesthouses, and a genuine welcome for visitors who are treated as the lifeblood of their industry rather than a necessary evil.

The Barossa Valley was established as a wine region in the 1840s when the area was settled by Silesian refugees. Today it is still a German enclave, probably the only region in Australia where the pub counter meal menus nonchalantly list kassler and sauerkraut alongside the standard bangers and mash and steak with three veg. The German influence is also present in the Clare—Aloysius Kranewitter, a Catholic priest, joined his countrymen in South Australia in 1848, established Sevenhill monastery, and planted vines for the production of altar wine. Sevenhill is still a monastery, but also a winery producing quality table wines.

## ❦ ACCOMMODATIONS

The Barossa is closely settled and the major towns (none are very big) of Tanunda, Angaston, and Nuriootpa all have motels. This style of accommodation is also available in the Clare Valley township of Clare. But this entire region specializes in small rural retreats—so why not pamper yourself and book into one of them? No air-conditioning in these; all accept credit cards.

**The Landhaus,** Bethany Rd., Bethany, via Tanunda 5352, (085) 63-2191, bills itself as Australia's smallest motel—but that is as misleading as describing the Savoy as a pub in London. A former shepherd's cottage, this white-washed mud and straw inn has accommodation for just one couple and can seat a maximum of 12 guests in its dining room. Antique furnishings, silver and crystal, a private spa, lace and subtly printed fabrics testify to its present role as a place for self-indulgence. Host Frans Kroser is also the chef and his set dinner menus reflect his European training. Accommodation with a cooked breakfast is $80 a couple and dinner will cost around $35 without wine.

**Lawley Farm,** Krondorf Rd., Tanunda 5352, (085) 63-2141, has four suites in a renovated stone cottage and converted barn. They're furnished in colonial style, but no comforts are sacrificed. Refrigerators in each unit are supplied with breakfast ingredients so guests can prepare their own, and picnic and barbecue packs are available for lunch and dinner (tables and fireplaces on the grounds). Tariff is $75 double.

If you've seen the Australian movie, *Picnic at Hanging Rock,* then **Martindale Hall,** 2 km (1¼ miles) from Mintaro in the Clare Valley, will be familiar. It served as the girls' boarding school on that occasion, though in real life the gracious Georgian mansion was built for a wealthy Adelaide landowner. Its stone masonry, parquet flooring, and imposing staircase are a tribute to the English craftsmen who were brought out for the job, and today visitors can sample the high life as it was lived in the 19th century by staying in one of its six guest rooms. A fixed menu dinner of expertly prepared country fare (soups, roasts, and old-fashioned puddings), accommodation, and cooked breakfast will cost around $100 per person. Bathroom facilities are unisex and shared. The building is also open 1–4 P.M. daily for inspection, (088) 43-9011 for more information.

The **Old Stanley Grammar School,** Commercial Rd., Watervale 5452, also in the Clare, (088) 43-0013, has more humble accommodation in four guest rooms in the converted dormitories of this former boarding school. The retreat has a rich collection of Australiana in its furniture and decorations and as signatures scrawled on the walls of the Three Roses Restaurant prove, it was once a classroom. The restaurant is open for dinner Fri.–Sun. and Sun. lunch. It's BYOB and the menu is innovative Australian. Bathroom facilities are shared. Bed-and-breakfast will cost $70 a double, dinner around $35 a head without wine.

## ❦ RESTAURANTS

A meal in the Barossa can be as simple as smoked sausage from one of the butchers with kibble bread from the Apex or Linke's bakeries. But for more elaborate fare head for the **Pheasant Farm,** Samuel Rd., Nuriootpa, (085) 62-1286. It's licensed, specializes in game, and is open for lunch Wed.–Sun. and dinner on Sat. All major cards accepted. **Die Gallerie** on Murray St., Tanunda, (085) 63-2788, is European in influence with German overtones. It's open for dinner Mon.–Sat. and lunch Fri.–Sun. All major cards. Both restaurants will cost around $30 a head without liquor.

In the Clare, **Mintaro Mews,** Burra St., in the historic town of Mintaro, (088) 43-9001, provides an imaginative dinner menu Tues.–Sun. and lunch on weekends. (Try the beef on a string, cooked in a rich vegetable stock.) Dinner will cost around $35 and cards are welcome. The Mews also has accommodation upstairs and in converted stables, for around $80 double including breakfast.

## TOURING THE WINERIES

Most wineries have tasting rooms and visitors are welcomed from 10 A.M. to 5 P.M. Signposts to look out for include **Seppeltsfield,** where the 100-year-old Para port is blended, **Yalumba** and **Peter Lehmann** at Angaston, **Orlando** at Rowland Flat, and **Henschke** at Keyneton. In the Clare, drop in on Tim Knappstein at the **Enterprise Winery** on the outskirts of Clare. **Mount Horrocks, Jeffrey Grosset, Jim Barry,** and of course, **Sevenhill,** are other names on quality labels.

The S.A. Government Travel Center (see the beginning of this chapter, or Vital Information in the back of this book) can provide maps and touring information. Ask for their publication, *The Name Droppers' Guide to South Australian Wine.*

## RECREATION

For an early morning bird's-eye view of the Barossa vineyards contact **Balloon Adventures** for a one-hour hot-air balloon flight followed by a champagne celebration. They can be reached at (085) 24-4383 and the fare is $160 per person.

If you'd like to work off the excess of all that eating and drinking head for **Stockport Stables,** Main Road, Stockport; (085) 28-2132. They have horse trail rides for about $10 an hour or full-day rides including barbecue lunch for $45. Phone in advance.

# S.A.'s Southeast

To visit the Southeast corner is to step back in time. While you take in river sights as the pioneers did from the decks of paddlesteamers, marvel at stalactites in a limestone cave or fossils more than ten thousand years old, it's hard not to be impressed by the evolutionary forces that have shaped this ancient land and the mere heartbeat in time that has been European man's attempt to conquer it.

The region takes in the lower reaches of the massive Murray River which joins the sea at Lake Alexandrina, 150 kilometers (93 miles) from Adelaide. From here you can follow the Princes Highway an additional 300 kilometers (186 miles) south, past the Coorong National Park and through the historic fishing ports of Robe, Kingston, and Port MacDonnell to Mt. Gambier with its volcanic crater lakes. About a half an hour's drive north of Mt. Gambier is the Coonawarra wine district, producer of premium Australian reds. At Naracoorte there are remarkable fossil deposits in the caves. From here, you can complete the circuit back to Adelaide by following the Duke's Highway to Tailem Bend, where the Princes Highway will take you back to Adelaide.

## TRAVEL

It's a rewarding area to explore by car, but if you don't have your own transport, you can still enjoy some of the attractions by day tour from Mt. Gambier or by cruising the Murray. The *Overland* train leaves Adelaide for Mt. Gambier every day except Saturday, and Murray cruise boats can arrange transfers from the capital to their departure points.

Recommended **Murray River cruise operators** include Murray River Cruises, 151 Franklin St., Adelaide, (08) 211-8333, and Proud Mary Cruises, 33 Pirie St., Adelaide, (08) 231-9472. The former offers six-night cruises on the 44-cabin *Murray River Queen* departing from Goolwa, the first major shipping port in the state, where paddlesteamers of the past unloaded their produce from the inland for transportation overseas. Cost of the cruise is around $625 per person including all meals. Proud Australia has two- and five-day cruises on the 18-cabin *Proud Mary* departing from Murray Bridge. To reach Murray Bridge, take the Princes Hwy. southeast from Adelaide for about 83 km (about 50 miles). Cost for the short cruise is around $225 per person including meals, $635 for the longer one.

If you prefer to go it alone, the South Australian Government Travel Centre (see South Australia Travel Vital Information) has a list of **houseboats for hire.** Costs are around $800 for a week and $500 for a weekend but vary enormously depending on the number of berths each vessel has. Houseboats are equipped with gas stoves, refrigerators, hot water service, showers and toilets, and a 12-volt electric lighting system. Bed linen can be hired. A boat operator's license isn't required but you will need to show a car driver's license.

## ❧ ACCOMMODATIONS AND RESTAURANTS

The accommodations described below were selected with an eye to giving the traveler a place to stay in each likely overnight stopover. Standard motels are available in major towns, but here, whenever possible, we have tried to find places where visitors will have a chance to absorb local color. Credit cards are generally accepted. The ivy-covered **Caledonian Inn,** Main St., Robe 5276, (087) 68-2029, was built as a "public house" in 1859 and has been dispensing hospitality ever since. Some of the timber used to build this charming hostelry came from shipwrecks in Guichen Bay on whose shores it is situated. There are six rooms available in the original pub (shared bathroom facilities) or self-contained accommodation in a row of four new cottages. Pub rooms cost around $45 double. There's a dining room and room service is available. Be sure to sample the local crayfish. (No air-conditioning.)

Mt. Gambier has a range of motel accommodations and the **Presidential Motor Inn,** Jubilee Hwy. West, Mt. Gambier 5290, (087) 24-9966, is recommended. Air-conditioned units are around $50 single and $60 double, and the motel has a swimming pool, spa, sauna, and licensed restaurant.

**Padthaway Estate** homestead, at Padthaway 5271, (087) 65-5039, just north of the Coonawarra district, welcomes visitors with a glass of the house wine—a champagne made from chardonnay and pinot noir grapes grown on the property. The gracious homestead built in 1882 for a wealthy grazing family now has eight guest rooms individually furnished in colonial style, though guests must share bathrooms. Breakfast is served in the rooms, or on the balcony with views of the red gum–studded countryside. The house contains a licensed restaurant, featuring local produce, seafood from the port at Kingston, and an excellent selection of regional wines. Its formal English gardens include tennis and croquet courts. Dinner, bed, and breakfast is $250 per person. (No air-conditioning.)

Through the **Coorong National Park** bush trails reveal an unspoiled stretch of wilderness scrub, dunes, salt pans and lakes, and a range of wildlife including colonies of pelican.

Camping in the park is wild—there are no designated areas. Call at the National Parks and Wildlife Service office in Salt Creek (085-75-7014) and a ranger will direct you to good spots. (If there's no answer at the office, just pitch your tent and eventually a ranger will find you.)

The village of **Robe** has countless reminders of its early settlers—whalers and sealers took refuge there, and during the 1850s 17,000 Chinese miners on their way to the Victorian gold fields came through the port to avoid that state's landing taxes. Markers of their passage today are numerous historic houses and cottages. Wilson's, a craft shop, is housed in one of them on the main street.

Australia's youngest intact volcanic crater is **Mount Schank** and there's a spectacular view in store for those who climb to the rim. It's an easy climb: park your car at the base and follow the signs. Nearby **Port MacDonnell's coast** has an unusual rock formation and a petrified forest. The **lakes of Mount Gambier** are part of one of the world's largest volcanic plains. If you're there between November and March, you'll see the azure water which earned the Blue Lake its name.

The ceiling of **Tantanoola Cave** is changing all the time as the limestone formations of straws, columns, and stalactites imperceptably grow. The cave is off the Princes Highway about 40 kilometers (25 miles) north of Mount Gambier. Tours are held daily in summer (in cooler months) only on weekends. Phone (087) 34-4153.

**Naracoorte Caves** also contain limestone formations and in the Victoria Fossil Cave is the evidence of an era when giant kangaroos, marsupial lions, and hippo-size wallabies roamed the ridges. Naracoorte is also a fine-wool producing center and in the town you can buy **woolen crafts** at the Sheep's Back, or take home a **souvenir sheep** from the Mini Jumbuck in Smith Street. Naracoorte Caves are about 100 kilometers, 60 miles, north of Mount Gambier on the road that leads through the Coonawarra to the Dukes Highway. Three caves are open for inspection; tours are conducted daily. Adventure tours for minimum-sized groups of four (maximum eight) are also held; helmuts, overalls, and flashlights provided. Telephone (087) 62-2340.

# Kangaroo Island

Kangaroo Island's isolation has meant that the flora and fauna have never been ravaged by dingoes, foxes, and rabbits, so wildlife flourishes here. Seals, sea lions, fairy penguins, rare birds, and of course, kangaroos, can be seen in their natural environment and between August and November the wildflowers add a burst of color. You'll find native fuchsia, orchids, blue aster, purple fringe lilies, and Australia's national flower, the golden wattle, in abundance.

## TRAVEL

This tranquil spot, 110 km (68 miles) southwest of Adelaide, is a half hour's flight from the city with Lloyd Aviation (see S.A. Travel, above). Alternatively, you can visit it on a boat and coach day trip for $70 with Philanderer Ferries, (0848) 3-1122. However, most of your time will be spent traveling and you'll have a better experience if you allow a couple of days to explore this 150-km-long (almost 100-mile-long) island at leisure.

The Kangaroo Island Connection provides a coach service from Adelaide to the ferry at Cape Jervis. One-way fares are $7, and it departs twice daily from the Bus Australia terminal, 101 Franklin St., Adelaide. Phone (08) 272-6680 for reservations; pay fares to the driver. One-way tickets on the ferry, the *Philanderer III,* are $22 per person, or $50 if you take your car. Book on (0848) 3-1112. You can leave your car at Cape Jervis, about 1½ hours' drive from Adelaide; phone (085) 98-0276 to arrange for supervised parking.

On the island a bus and taxi service operates on demand between Kingscote, American River, and Penneshaw (where the ferry stops). Phone (0848) 2-2640 to book. Or you can explore the island by conducted tour from the hotels. If you're driving yourself, remember the ironstone gravel roads tend to corrugate, so take it easy.

# ❦ ACCOMMODATIONS AND RESTAURANTS

The resorts recommended here all have air-conditioning, pools, spas, and are on the waterfront. Major credit cards accepted. Though the farm houses don't boast such amenities, they make up for it in personality.

Resort accommodation is available at the island's largest town, Kingscote, at the **Ozone Seafront Hotel,** Kingscote 5223, (0848) 2-2011. They have motel-style units for $70 double, a pool, a bistro, coffeeshop, and à la carte **Terrace Restaurant** which concentrates on local seafood. They'll arrange a rental car, book coach tours, and pack picnic lunches for day trips.

At the fairy penguin beach of Penneshaw the **Sorrento Resort,** Penneshaw 5222, (0848) 3-1028, offers motel rooms, or chalets and cottages if you want to cook for yourself. Motel units are around $60 double, chalets $50 double, and two or three bedroom cottages $60 double and $5 per extra person. Coach tours and car and bike hire can be arranged at the resort which also has a licensed restaurant.

More moderately priced accommodation is available by renting **farm houses** scattered around the island. These average around $30 a night and can be arranged through Australian Odysseys, Box 144, Kensington Park, Adelaide 5068, (08) 31-5321. Amenities vary; most are equipped with all kitchen utensils but some require you to bring your own bed linen.

Fairy penguins promenade the foreshore at **Penneshaw** at night between Christmas Cove and Hog Bay, while birdwatchers head for **Murray's Lagoon** where swan, duck, and rare waterfowl congregate. The island's star attraction is **Seal Bay** where sea lions and New Zealand fur seals and leopard seals share the beach and frolic in the surf. **Flinders Chase** is a sanctuary for all wildlife—you'll see kangaroos, emus, Cape Barren geese, koalas, wallabies, and goannas (lizards), as well as black cockatoo and lorikeets. In winter, albatross ride the coastal winds along with white-breasted sea eagles and ospreys. The extremely fortunate might catch a glimpse of whales which occasionally pass the island.

The island juxtaposes spectacularly rugged scenery with long white beaches and protected swimming areas. The east coast contains the sweeping beach of **Antechamber Bay** and **Chapman River** for safe **swimming** and good **fishing**. (Transcontinental Safaris, see Travel, above, can provide fishing equipment. You can buy it in Kingscote, but it will probably be cheaper in Adelaide.) Just to the south stands **Cape Willoughby Lighthouse** which overlooks the cliffs and a devil's kitchen of boiling surf. The south coast has **D'Estrees Bay** for fishing and an old whaling station at **Port Tinline.** At **Little Sahara,** near Seal Bay, you can play Lawrence of Arabia amid tall sand dunes, while the dunes at **Kelly Hill** cover a series of limestone sinkholes and caves. The largest cave is lit and open for guided inspection during the day.

The west coast is dominated by **Flinders Chase National Park** (headquarters at Rocky River, reached via the South Coast Road), but two geological features vie for visitors' attention. **Remarkable Rocks** are weirdly shaped granite boulders on a promontory that plunges to the sea. **Admiral's Arch** has been weathered into a wave shape and is fringed with stalactites. At **Cape Borda Lighthouse,** which watches over the treacherous coast of the north, you can take in the views from the highest cliffs in the state. **Stokes Bay** is reached by a narrow path through giant boulders and there are rock pools for swimming. You can safely swim in the ocean at **Emu Bay,** and there's a pool on **Nepean Bay** at Kingscote.

# The S.A. Outback

The South Australian Outback is inhospitable country, yet that is precisely why visitors are lured there. Relentless sun, precious little water, and an arid landscape combine to make it a high priority for anyone with a sense of adventure.

The Outback stretches west to the Great Victoria Desert, northeast through Sturt's Stony Desert to Innamincka, on the Queensland border, and northwest through the Simpson Desert along the Stuart Highway to Coober Pedy (690 kilometers, 428 miles, from Adelaide) and eventually to Alice Springs in the Northern Territory. On its fringe, about 350 kilometers (217 miles) north of Adelaide, are the Flinders Ranges, rugged terrain with razor-backed quartzite ridges, granite peaks, deep gorges, and rock enclosures where Aboriginal paintings can be seen. Wilpena is an Aboriginal word meaning "bent fingers," which is how this natural amphitheater got its name.

But what was new in Australia in 1860 was that the settlers had as yet failed to take possession of or even explore the land they were so confidently governing. . . .

The coastline of the continent had been charted from the sea, but as yet very few adventurers had penetrated far into the interior. All that was known was that the further one advanced into that vast empty space the hotter and drier it became, and it was perhaps because of this aridity that the colonists dreamed that one day they would discover an inland sea, a 'new Mediterranean' in the centre of the continent. It was like the legendary Atlantis or the land of Prester John; the more serious geographers scouted the idea, yet it had the persistence of a mystery. After all, no one had actually been in the centre, no one could say with finality exactly what there was to be found there, and the fact that half a dozen expeditions had already set out to resolve the matter and had returned defeated seemed, irrationally, to suggest that some great prize was awaiting the first explorer who succeeded in breaking through.

There is a good deal about these early journeys that reminds one of the re-discovery of the Sahara in the nineteenth century. Here in Australia, as in Africa, the travellers speak of the dry antiseptic air, the cold nights, the incredibly high temperatures by day, the dreadful thirst, the mirages, the impression of empty land stretching away silently into infinity. Human beings are reduced to tiny atoms in these desolate wastes, cyclonic thunderstorms burst upon them out of a clear sky, and there is no shade or shelter anywhere.

—Alan Moorehead
*Cooper's Creek*, 1963

## TRAVEL

You can travel the 430 kms (267 miles) from Adelaide to Wilpena on paved roads by heading north through Quorn and Hawker. To continue on to the Arkaroola Sanctuary in the northern ranges is an additional 200 kms (124 miles), much of it on unpaved roads. However, the roads are quite accessible to sedans, and if you don't want to overtax your vehicle you can always take tours once you get there.

Briscoes, 101 Franklin St., (08) 212-7344, conducts coach tours from Adelaide, or you can join a smaller group for a four-wheel-drive safari with Trekabout Safaris, 30 Berryman Dr., Modbury; (08) 264-3770.

You can see the Flinders Ranges as the early explorers did—from the saddle of a horse from Stockport Stables. Transport from Adelaide or their Gawler base can be arranged for the three- to nine-day rides. They rent swags (sleeping rolls) for $30 and accommodation is either in a communal room or, on longer rides, in tents. Costs range from $350 and include all meals. For more details, phone (085) 28-2132.

## ❦ ACCOMMODATIONS

The accommodations below are the only ones available in the S.A. Outback. Unfortunately lack of competition means that standards aren't as high as elsewhere in the state—so be prepared to put up with occasionally indifferent service and food. Credit cards are generally accepted.

The **Wilpena Pound Resort,** (086) 48-0004, Wilpena, has 34 motel-style rooms, a dining room, lounge, and bar, and swimming pool. They run day tours ($35) and half-day tours ($20) from the resort and can arrange scenic flights and will provide picnic hampers for day trippers. Room rates are $60 single and $70 double inclusive of a light breakfast; rooms are air-conditioned. Bookings can be made at 32 Whitmore Sq. Adelaide 5000, (08) 212-6386, fax (08) 231-5327.

**Greenwood and Mawson lodges** at Arkaroola each have twenty motel suites, a licensed restaurant, lounge bar, and swimming pool (swimming in waterholes is prohibited). They run four-wheel-drive tours from the resort and can arrange flights over the surrounding countryside. Rooms are around $65 a double, though they have budget accommodation with shared bathroom facilities for around $30 a night. Only some rooms are air-conditioned. Bookings must be made through the Adelaide office at 50 Pirie St., Adelaide 5000, (08) 212-1366, telex: 82248.

In Coober Pedy, do as the locals—stay underground at the **Desert Cave Motel,** Hutchison St., Coober Pedy 5723, (086) 72-5688. Rooms are about $60 single and $70 double. Or you can base yourself aboveground at the **Opal Inn Hotel Motel,** Hutchison St., Coober Pedy 5723, (086) 72-5054, which has rooms for around $20 single and $30 double. (No pools at either of these last two.)

One of the most interesting features of the **Flinders Ranges** is that the rugged terrain entombs extensive fossils, many from sea creatures. The mountains were once seabeds and have been pushed up through the millennia. The fossils are haunting proof of the great inland sea which, several million years too late, early Australian explorers died searching for.

You'll see fossils near Wilpena Pound, at Brachina, and Bunyeroo gorges. These are also havens for modern wildlife—heron and dotterel can be spotted among the reeds. Nearby are parallel ranges so jagged they're called the ABC Range—there are as many peaks as letters in the alphabet. Aboriginal paintings can be found at Arkaroo Rock and carvings at Sacred Canyon.

There are two ranger offices in the Flinders Range National Park; campgrounds are at both. In the north, in Oraparinna: (086) 48-0017, and near Wilpena Pound in the South: (086) 48-0048. Maps are available from both.

At Balcanoona Creek, in the **Gammon Ranges National Park,** not far from Arkaroola, the wild orange or iga grows and you'll spot euros and yellow-footed rock wallabies. Chambers Gorge is filled with sparkling pools and adorned with Aboriginal carvings. Another spot to visit is Paralana Hot Springs, the last vestige of active volcanism in Australia, where near-boiling water flows from the ground.

The ranger office for Gammon Ranges is at Balcanoona (near Arkaroola, the privately owned tourist area just outside the park). There's a campground here (maps available, too). As with all national park campgrounds, except during holiday periods, reservations aren't necessary.

The name **Coober Pedy** comes from the Aboriginal description of the first opal miners there—it means "white man in a hole." In addition to the mines, shops, museums, and churches are built underground, for citizens to find refuge from the heat and dust. There's a new language to be learned, that of the opal miners. "Potch" is uncolored opal, "mullock" means the waste mining material, and "noodling" means hunting in the mullock for missed opal. Cabochon are solid opals and the most expensive; doublets are a sandwich of precious and common opal; and a triplet is a sliver of opal with a clear quartz cap. You can buy opals at countless shops in Coober Pedy and every miner has a "bargain" to sell kept in a matchbox in his hip pocket.

Coober Pedy Tours show visitors through the **opal fields,** demonstrate opal cutting, visit a dugout home, and allow time for fossicking. They leave from the winch called the Miner's Pit every morning at 10 A.M. For bookings phone (086) 72-5333.

# 10

# NORTHERN TERRITORY

The Northern Territory was probably the entry point for Australia's original inhabitants, possibly the world's oldest surviving race. During the last ice age, the fall in the sea level meant that although there wasn't a complete land bridge, travel from Indonesia to New Guinea to Australia became feasible and migration followed. There is firm evidence that the first Australians, the Aborigines, have lived in the land that is Kakadu for 25,000 years and possibly for 40,000 to 50,000 years.

## The Dreaming

All peoples have their stories of creation—the ancient Greek and Roman civilizations created the myths surrounding a panoply of gods and goddesses, responsible for the vices and virtues found in man and nature. Ancient peoples in North and South America did this in similar ways—as did the peoples of Asia and Africa. And so did the indigenous peoples of the Australian continent, the Aboriginal people.

For the Aborigines, the time before man walked the earth was The Dreamtime. In this Dreamtime, man was created, began to make use of his given land—Australia, or that part of it which each individual tribe understood as his country—and to interact with the other forms of creation with which he shared this land.

Each account of the Dreaming differs among the various tribes that make up the Aboriginal people; some concur with each other, others take up a tale where another tribe left off, many are completely at variance with the others. What is common to all is a profound spirituality and reverence for nature. Aboriginal people are completely at one with nature, joined in a brotherhood with all forms of life in their experience.

Like many other ancient peoples, the traditions, laws, ceremonies, and secrets of their participation in the Dreaming were—and are—handed down via stories and songs which form song cycles. These are passed on from the elders of each tribe to younger members once they are initiated into full participation in the life of the tribe.

Like the native American people, each tribe and each individual adopts or is given a totem, usually drawn from some aspect of nature such as an animal—goanna (a lizard), crocodile, kangaroo, etc. This creature is indigenous to the region in which the tribe resides, signifying a oneness with their surroundings. These totems represented more than just local fauna, because it is part of Aboriginal lore that the beings responsible for creation were animals of all descriptions, not just human-like.

Unlike most other "religions," there seems to be no concept of a god, or superior being which demands worship. Rather, the sense of kinship with all aspects of nature is stressed in the legends and myths associated with the Dreaming. The kangaroo is honored because of its place in the structure of things, ordained since the Dreaming, and so is every man, animal, plant, and bird.

Associate spirits also run through the pantheon, spirits of a non-living nature: water, rock, earth, fire. Some of these are playful, some timid; others are powerful, capable of causing great havoc in the lives of men. The way to deal with them is simply to leave them be, avoid disturbing them by declaring the places that are deemed to be theirs off limits to men. When they are inadvertently disturbed, ceremonies of appeasement must be performed.

The stories of the Dreamtime are the Aboriginal peoples' explanation of their appearance on this continent 40,000 years ago. Throughout the millenia that intervened between that time and this, these stories have solidified into a solid core of belief that is intrinsic to every Aboriginal person, as real and compelling today as it was when the first Europeans arrived here to settle two hundred years ago.

—Mary Ellen Dyster

White Australia's record of its treatment of the Aborigines is not something of which it can be proud—tribes were herded off their traditional lands, and the subsequent problems of dispossession decimated the race. In the past ten years much has been done to redress this situation and it's appropriate that the greatest advances have occurred in the Northern Territory. Land rights have been granted and sacred sites returned to the traditional owners. After two hundred years the Aborigines once more have control of at least some of the land that was theirs. They are involved in joint ventures with private and public enterprise and share their knowledge with visitors. Still, the problems are far from eradicated. You'll doubtless encounter racism, see victims of the white man's evils—alcohol and drugs—and pass shanty towns where living conditions are squalid.

The Northern Territory is sandwiched between Western Australia and Queensland, covering a quarter of a million square kilometers (around 155,000 square miles), about one sixth of the Australian mass. With 145,000 people, 65,000 of whom live in the northern capital of Darwin, it's home to about 1 percent of the nation's population. The climatic variation between the top and bottom, 1,600 kilometers (1,000 miles) south, is immense.

Territorians divide the region into the "green"—the crocodile-infested swamps, rainforests, and wetlands of the Top End, and the "red"—the vast arid expanses of the center of Australia, home of Ayers Rock and The Olgas and A Town Like Alice (Springs, that is). This chapter also covers the points of interest along the corridor that links the two, the Stuart Highway, known locally as "the track."

The year is similarly divided by the Wet in summer (October to April) and the Dry in winter. In the Top End, monsoonal rain, high humidity, and daily temperature fluctuations from the mid-20's C (that's mid-70's F) to the mid-30's C (mid-90's F) can make The Wet rather uncomfortable. Unsealed roads, in Kakadu for example, can be closed and large areas cut off by floods. Most rain falls from December to March when, unless mudlarking in a natural sauna is the objective, it's advisable to avoid the Top End.

Most visitors prefer the Dry when daily temperatures range from about 20° to 30° C (about 72° to 92° F). Even in the Center, while rain is unlikely to mar a summer visit, the heat can be prohibitive. Temperatures average from the low 20's C (low 70's F) at night to the high 30's C (90's F), with maximum in the 40's C (over 100° F). In winter, averages are around 20° C (70° F) in the day dropping to about 5° C (low 40's F) at night.

Territorians dress casually. Coolness is the essence, but pack a jacket even for summer nights when a temperature drop of 15° C can seem icy. For winter in the Center, you'll need heavier clothing. It's advisable to dress in layers because you'll appreciate being able to shed them as the day warms up. Sturdy walking shoes, a hat, sunscreen, and insect repellant are other musts.

The Northern Territory's economy is predominantly agricultural supplemented at times by gold, bauxite, and uranium mining. Vast tracts of the land are devoted to cattle stations and there are opportunities to stay on these properties and sample a way of life that's a constant battle against the elements and isolation. But, even more enticing is the chance to learn from the people who know how to live in harmony with this environment. On Bathurst and Melville islands, north of Darwin, you can stay with the Tiwi people and gather and prepare bush tucker; from Alice Springs you can "go bush" with the Aborigines and learn about the Dreamtime, the mythology, medicines, music, and entertainment of this ancient race.

# TRAVEL

## Flying

Unless you're flying direct from Asia, it's unlikely that non-Australians will begin a trip at the Northern Territory's international airport in Darwin. Air travel is, however, the fastest way of seeing this region and Australian and Ansett Airlines have regular services connecting Darwin and Alice Springs with Cairns in Far North Queensland and the state capitals. Ansett is at 46 Smith St. Mall, Darwin, (089) 80-3333, and at the corner of Todd Mall and Parsons St., Alice Springs, (089) 52-4455; Australian Airlines at Shop 90, Casaurina Sq., Darwin, (089) 82-3311, and also at the corner of Todd Mall and Parsons St., Alice Springs, (089) 50-5211.

## Taking the Train

The major train line in the Territory is the *Ghan,* linking Adelaide, in South Australia, with Alice Springs. This train features sleeping berths, dining and lounge cars, and now an entertainment car with poker machines, video movies and games, and a hairdressing salon. With four paying passengers an automobile will be carried free of charge. The trip takes 24 hours and bookings can be made at the Alice Springs Railway Station, George Cres., Alice Springs; (089) 52-1011. There is no rail link to Darwin.

## Taking the Bus

Coach companies provide economical services to and within the Northern Territory. Discounted passes for unlimited travel allow you to set your own schedule. Major operators include Deluxe at 50 Mitchell St., Darwin, (089) 81-8788, and Ford Plaza Coach Terminal, Hartley St., Alice Springs, (089) 52-4444; Ansett Trailways, 63 Smith St., Darwin, (089) 81-6433, and Ford Plaza Coach Terminal, Hartley St., Alice Springs, (089) 52-2422; Greyhound, 67–69 Mitchell St., Darwin, (089) 81-8055, and Todd Mall, Alice Springs, (089) 52-7888.

## Driving

The major highway in the Territory is the Stuart, which bisects Australia, linking Adelaide, through Alice Springs, to Darwin, a distance of 3,261 km (2,038 miles). The Barkly Hwy. joins the Stuart just north of Tennant Creek and heads to Mt. Isa in Queensland. The Victoria Hwy. leaves the Stuart at Katherine and heads west to Kununurra and connects with the Great Northern Hwy., which leads eventually to Perth. From Darwin to Kununurra is 880 km (550 miles) and Perth is a further 3,326 km (2,078 miles). Darwin is 1,700 km (1,062 miles) from Alice Springs and Ayers Rock is a further 446 km (279 miles) south and west. All these roads are paved.

## On the Road

There is no maximum speed limit on the open road in the Northern Territory. Unfortunately, the long flat highways encourage speeding and this is particularly dangerous as many are unfenced. Care should be taken to avoid hitting wandering stock and wild buffalo, especially at night when livestock can become mesmerized by car headlights. Take extra care when approaching, passing, or overtaking road trains. These multi-trailer vehicles can be up to 50 meters in length and, even when the road is two-lane and sealed, they create great clouds of dust making visibility difficult.

## Car and Campervan Rentals

The major car-rental companies provide one-way rentals if you want to drive between Alice and Darwin or vice versa. They include Avis at 145 Stuart Hwy., Darwin, (089) 81-9922, and 78 Todd St., Alice Springs, (089) 52-4366; Budget at 1427 Stuart Hwy., Winnellie, Darwin, (089) 84-4388, and 64 Hartley St., Alice Springs, (089) 52-4133; Hertz, corner of Woods and Daly sts., Darwin, (089) 41-0944, and 105 Todd St., Alice Springs, (089) 52-2644. Motor homes or campervans are a convenient option if you'd rather be self-catering. Recommended companies include Koala Camper Rentals at 90 Mitchell St., Darwin, (089) 41-0877, and Melanka Lodge, 94 Todd St., Alice Springs, (089) 52-2233; Touralong Travel Homes, 344 North-East Rd., Klemzig, Adelaide, (08) 261-8833, and c/o Econorent, 84 Todd St., Alice Springs, (089) 52-9633.

## Touring

Pioneering adventure tour operator Bill King, through his Destination Australia company, has a number of packages which enable the visitor to see the Territory "off the beaten track"—by four-wheel drive, bus, canoe, even camel. The head office is at 3/418 St. Kilda Rd., Melbourne, (03) 820-0700, or toll free in Australia (008) 33-1373. Tours of specific areas are discussed in the appropriate sections, below.

Further information on touring in the Northern Territory is available from the **Northern Territory Government Tourist Bureau,** 31 Smith St. Mall, Darwin 0800, (089) 81-6611, Ford Plaza Building, Todd Mall, Alice Springs 0800, (089) 52-1299, and at its offices in other state capitals.

# Darwin and the Top End

To fly into Darwin from the temperate southern cities of Sydney or Melbourne is to land in the tropics. If the temperature doesn't immediately tell you, then the palm trees, heavy scent of frangipani, mango trees dropping their fruit, and bursts of red and purple from the flowering bougainvillea will.

The city center straddles a peninsula which juts into Darwin harbor and is bounded on either side by the picturesque beaches of Fannie and Frances bays. Most of the residential suburbs are in the sister settlement of Palmerston, about 10 kilometers (6 miles) away, designed to avoid urban sprawl.

Darwin township was named Palmerston when it was settled in 1869, following the epic journey of John McDouall Stuart who was the first European to cross the continent from south to north. The highway which follows this route is named in his honor. Several unsuccessful attempts to establish a strategic port, a "new Singapore," in the Top End had been made previously, including Fort Dundas on Melville Island. Just as those efforts foundered due to isolation, the modern city of Darwin, named after evolutionist Charles who called there while sailing the world in the *Beagle,* has something of a frontier image, a reputation for surviving the odds; the city was, in fact, devastated twice this century. The first cause was Japanese bombers during WW2 and the second, was Cyclone Tracy, which flattened the city on Christmas Day, 1974.

Consequently, with the exception of public buildings and large hotels, the city has been rebuilt with an eye to durability and what's referred to as the cyclone code, rather than aesthetics. Hardy survivors of the colonial days such as the Darwin Hotel—the Raffles of the N.T.—with its bar fanned by punkahs (very large ceiling fans), and the seven-gabled Government House contrast handsomely with the modern brick architecture. Darwin's population also reflects the ethnic diversity of its battling pioneers—the Chinese who came for gold, the Japanese who came for pearls, southern Europeans escaping post-war oppression and, more recently, refugees from Southeast Asia. It's all to the visitor's advantage suggesting, especially in Darwin's dining and shopping scene, the cosmopolitan sophistication of a city with a far greater population than its present 65,000.

The city center runs on a grid pattern with Smith, the main street being the end of the Stuart Highway as it reaches the sea. It's a small area, easy to explore on foot.

## TRAVEL

Should you tire of walking, ring Radio **Taxis** at (089) 81-8777. Public transport is provided by **buses,** which service the city and suburbs adequately during business hours but poorly at other times. Rte. 6 takes in most of the city sights, and timetables and route information are available from the city terminal on Harry Chan Ave., (089) 89-7513. For a more formal overview of the city, join a morning or afternoon **tour** with Darwin Day Tours, (089) 81-8696.

# ❦ ACCOMMODATIONS

Darwin center has no shortage of accommodation, from backpacker hostel to luxury hotel. Most of the five stars are on The Esplanade, with ocean views just a few blocks from the main street. Darwin hotels will usually accept American Express, Diners Club, MasterCard, and Visa. (Expect air-conditioning unless otherwise noted.) They include the **Darwin Travelodge,** at 122 The Esplanade, Darwin 0800, (089) 81-5388, telex 85273, with a palm-studded forecourt and 120 rooms ranging from $120. The hotel has a pool, a restaurant, and bar. Rooms have TVs, mini bars, and 24-hour room service. (If these matters concern you, this was the only one of the high-rise grand hotels that was built before, and survived, Cyclone Tracy.)

The 235-room **Beaufort Hotel,** also on The Esplanade, Darwin 0800, (089) 82-9911, telex 85818, is a modern architect's vision in desert colors and incorporates the city's performing arts complex. Also on the premises: restaurant, bar, spa, and pool. Rooms range from $130.

The **Sheraton Darwin Hotel,** 32 Mitchell St., Darwin 0800, (089) 82-0000, telex 85991, also overlooks The Esplanade and Port Darwin and has 233 rooms starting at $150. There is a swimming pool here, too, as well as a restaurant, spa, and sauna.

About a kilometer from the city center is the futuristic **Diamond Beach Hotel Casino,** which as the name explains, includes blackjack, baccarat, and roulette tables in its guest facilities. The 96 rooms have stunning sunset views over Fannie Bay and begin at $110 single and $130 double. A pool is also here, as well as dining and drinking facilities. Address is Gilruth Ave., Darwin 0800; (089) 46-2666, telex 85214.

More moderately priced accommodation is available close to the center of town at the colonial **Hotel Darwin,** 10 Herbert St., Darwin 0800; (089) 81-9211, telex 85194. Modern amenities here, including a swimming pool. Motel-style rooms range from $80. The **Asti Motel,** corner of Smith and Packard sts., Darwin 0800, (089) 81-8200, telex 85103, has single units for $60 and doubles for $65. There's a pool. If you prefer a bit more space, **City Garden Apartments,** 93 Woods St., Darwin 0800, (089) 89-1913, telex 85718, has 15 self-contained units for $75 single and $80 double. Each has a separate balcony overlooking the pool, though not every one has a phone.

At budget level, **Sherwood Lodge,** 15 Peel St., Darwin 0800, (089) 41-0427, offers single rooms from $12 a night. Kitchen and bathroom facilities are shared and there is a communal laundry and TV lounge. This accommodation isn't air-conditioned, though the rooms have ceiling fans. **Darwin Capricornia Motel,** 3 Kellaway St., Fannie Bay 0820, (089) 81-4055, has more motel-style frills in its 24 rooms and a restaurant on the premises. It's about 3 km from the center of town, but close to the beach. Tariff is $40 single and $45 double.

The reminders of the relatively recent days when Darwin was an outpost of the British Empire are everywhere in the center of the city and you can see many of them by taking a circuit walk beginning with **Lyons Cottage** on the corner of Knuckley Street and The Esplanade. Better known as the BAT (British Australian Telegraph company) house, this 1925 bungalow is built of local stone and is now a museum relating to the history of telecommunications in Australia. Open seven days from 10 A.M. to 5 P.M., telephone (089) 41-0607. Across the road is the former **Admiralty House,** until recently the residence of the naval officer commanding Northern Australia. This typical example of pre–air-conditioning tropical architecture has some ingenious features—it's built on stilts and surrounded by verandas to encourage air circulation and capture any breezes.

On the corner of The Esplanade and Herbert Street is the "Raffles of the N.T.," the **Hotel Darwin,** with another early air-conditioning device in its main bar—electrically operated punkahs which constantly fan the patrons. Farther down The Esplanade you'll pass the **old Post Office,** built in 1872 and bombed during WW2, killing ten occupants. Part of the original stone wall is now incorporated in the Legislative Assembly building and other stone is used in the present GPO on Knuckey Street. On the turn in The Esplanade is **Government House** (residence of the governor of the Northern Territory), called the "Seven Gables," obviously because of its roof, and farther down, on the corner of Smith Street, the police station and old court house, built in 1884 and now renovated for use as offices of the Administrator of the N.T. Across the road is **Christ Church Cathedral,** a modern church which incorporates a section of the 1902 building devastated by Cyclone Tracy. Another block down Smith Street are **Brown's Mart,** originally a mining exchange, later a fruit and vegetable market, and now a theater, and the old **Town Hall,** another distinguished stone building wrecked by Tracy. Continue down the Smith Street Mall to Star Village, Darwin's first motion picture house, with an open-air design. Across the road is **The Vic (Victoria Hotel),** designed and built in 1894, and the survivor of three cyclones.

The balcony of The Vic, overlooking the Mall, is a good spot to take a cooling drink at the end of a hot walk.

Darwin's place in Australian history as the site of the first mainland attack by an enemy force during WW2 is recorded at the **Artillery Museum,** East Point, (089) 81-9702. Gun emplacements are among the more obvious reminders of Darwin under seige, as is the former military airstrip, Ross Smith Drive, to which you'll travel to see them. The museum has a collection of war memorabilia and shows black and white movie footage of the bombings. It's open daily from 9:30 A.M. to 5 P.M.

You'll see Darwin weathering another attack at the **Fannie Bay Gaol Museum,** East Point Road, Fannie Bay, (089) 82-4211. This time it's the devastation of Cyclone Tracy on Christmas Day, 1974, when winds registering up to 280 km.p.h. took only four hours to destroy 5,000 homes. It's open daily from 10 A.M. to 5 P.M. and visitors can also inspect the former maximum security prison buildings and, for the ghoulish, the gallows where the Territory's last execution was held in 1952.

If you want to see crocodiles at close range, head for the **Darwin Crocodile Farm,** 40 kilometers (25 miles) from the city along the Stuart Highway (between the Arnhem Highway turnoff and Elizabeth River). The farm has the largest collection of crocs in Australia including Bert, the largest in captivity. It's open every day, but feedings are held on Wednesday and Sunday at 3 P.M. and Friday at 11 A.M.—sometimes more frequently during the high season. Telephone (089) 88-1450 for more information or visit with **Darwin Day Tours,** (089) 81-8696.

**If seeing crocs is a high priority the farm is definitely worth a visit during The Wet when you're unlikely to see them in the wild.**

You are, however, likely to see crocs year round if you take the **Adelaide River Queen cruise.** Crocs are fed from the deck of the boat. It departs twice daily from the Adelaide River bridge on the Arnhem Highway, 64 kilometers (40 miles) from Darwin. The 2½-hour cruise costs $22 or $45, with hotel pickup and sightseeing on the way. Telephone (089) 32-2631.

If you'd rather your crocs safely stuffed, you can see the five-meter body of the scourge of Darwin, Sweetheart, lying in state at the **Museum of Arts and Sciences,** Conacher Street, Bullocky Point, Fannie Bay, (089) 82-4211. (Sweetheart didn't kill anyone, but was feared by Darwin fishermen because he was known to eat the outboard motors of their boats.) The museum also has an excellent Gallery of Aboriginal Man, and a Natural Sciences collection of snakes, spiders, and other nasties which will leave you wondering why Australians ever venture into the bush. It's open weekdays from 9 A.M. to 5 P.M. and weekends from 10 A.M. to 6 P.M.

Check the paper for high tide times if you're planning a visit to **Aquascene** at Doctor's Gully at the end of The Esplanade. The daily fish-feeding ritual has been going on there since a resident threw bread scraps to a few small mullet more than twenty years ago. These days you'll see hundreds of milkfish, catfish, bream, and batfish, as well as big mullet, come to shore for a few hours. Admission is $2.50; (089) 81-7837.

## SHOPPING

Darwin has plenty of souvenir shops selling such "interesting" items as croc catcher's T-shirts (torn and blood-spattered)—you'll find a number of them on Smith Street Mall. Most sell some Aboriginal arts and crafts, but if you're seriously interested, head for the government-sponsored **Aboriginal Artists' Galleries,** 153 Mitchell Street, (089) 81-1394, which sells bark paintings, weavings, didgeridoos, and modern sand paintings on canvas. It also has a good range of books including many for children about Aboriginal legends. The **Raintree Gallery,** 29 Knuckey Street, (089) 81-2732, also sells Aboriginal art and specializes in the work of the Tiwi people of Bathurst and Melville islands. Traditional items include carvings and burial poles while more modern work features pottery and screen-printed fabric and clothing.

The workshop and retail center of **Opal House Creations by Nature** are at M24 Paspalis Centrepoint (in city center), (089) 81-4602. They produce silver and gold jewelry based on the Territory's wildlife and the Aborigines' X-ray technique of painting. The range includes earrings, pendants, rings, cuff links, and stick pins.

 Darwin's **markets** are difficult to categorize as either a shopping or dining experience, for they are both. At the Parap Market in the tree-shaded center square, vendors of dim sum, Thai soup, and rice cakes vie for your dollars with exotic fruit and vegetable stalls and bric-a-brac merchants Sat. mornings. On Thurs. nights during The Dry, Darwinians make a night out of the **Mindil Beach market** beside the Diamond Beach Casino, bringing their own wine and picnicking on the multicultural fare that is on sale.

## RECREATION

**Golfers** can head for the Municipal Golf Course, in Palmerston Park beside the Botanic Gardens and opposite the Diamond Beach Hotel Casino, where equipment can be hired. Telephone (089) 32-1324. **Tennis courts** are available on the Mindil Beach side of Gilruth Avenue, outside the casino, for $4 an hour during the day and $8 an hour at night. Rackets are also available for hire. Phone (089) 81-2181 or (089) 41-0410 after hours to book. There's a **public swimming pool** on Ross Smith Avenue, Fannie Bay. Entry is $1. Phone (089) 81-2662 for hours.

Photography enthusiasts can join Top End Wildlife **Photographic Safaris** for an early morning (4:30 A.M. pick-up) or evening (4 P.M. pick-up) expedition with shots of birds and animals in the wild as your catch. Camera equipment and film are supplied and dinner or breakfast with champagne are included in the $100 per person fee. Phone (089) 27-2716 for details.

In June each year Darwinians organize a regatta-with-a-difference at Mindil Beach. Vessels of varying seaworthiness are made from empty beer cans and raced for charity. It's difficult to say whether the participants enjoy the preparation or the **beer-can regatta,** itself, more, but it generally draws an enthusiastic crowd.

---

### Water Warnings

From October to May, Northern Territory coastal waters are infested by the deadly box jelly fish or stingers. And if they don't get you, chances are the crocs will. Observe all warning signs. Locals swim in Fannie Bay waters, but visitors might be well advised to stay away. More details on these menaces in the Queensland chapter.

---

## ✿ RESTAURANTS

Eating out in Darwin is a matter of mastering the abbreviations—buff, croc, and barra. If you haven't sampled them, according to the locals, you've no sense of adventure. For cautious adventurers: buffalo well-aged is barely distinguishable from beef, crocodile is similar to chicken and tends to take on the flavor of its sauce, and barramundi is a large fish prized for its firm flesh and fighting qualities. The barra season is closed to professional fishermen from Oct.–Jan., so if you see it on restaurant menus at that time, chances are it's been frozen.

Darwinians pride themselves on their thirst—witness the "Darwin stubbie" which holds two liters of beer compared with the 375-milliliter bottles known as "stubbies" elsewhere in Australia. If beer isn't your fancy, you'll have no trouble finding wines from other parts of Australia and sometimes from the Territory's only and Australia's least likely winery, Chateau Hornsby, near arid Alice Springs.

Major cards mentioned in this chapter are AE—American Express, DC—Diner's Club, V—Visa, MC—MasterCard.

**The Beagle Restaurant** is in the Museum and Art Gallery complex, Bullocky Point, Fannie Bay, (089) 81-7791. It serves a smorgasbord lunch Sun.–Fri. for $15 a head and à la carte dinners Mon.–Sat. Croc, barra, and buff are on the menu here and if you're going to be there at sunset, ask for a table on the terrace. Three courses without wine will cost around $27. It's licensed and major cards are accepted.

**Holtze Cottage Restaurant** in the Botanical Gardens, (089) 81-7455, is open for lunch and dinner Mon.–Fri. and has indoor and outdoor seating. The menu concentrates on regional produce with barramundi and buffalo steaks among the features; three courses will cost about $40 without drinks. Major cards are welcome.

With its large Chinese population Darwin boasts some fine Chinese restaurants and the **Jade Garden,** 30 Smith St. Mall, (089) 81-5261, is one of the better moderately priced establishments. The food is Cantonese. It's open every day for $10 banquet lunches and à la carte dinners. Three courses (without drinks) will cost around $15. It's licensed. Major cards welcome.

The **Lee Dynasty** in the Workers Club Complex, Cavenagh St., (089) 81-7808, enjoys a reputation as Darwin's best Chinese restaurant and is open for lunch Mon.–Fri. and dinner Mon.–Sat. Three Cantonese courses without drinks will cost around $30.

If you're in need of a curry fix, head for **Maharaja,** Knuckey St., (089) 81-6728, which should cure the need without breaking the budget (main courses are around $7). It's licensed and BYOB, open Mon.–Sat. for dinner and accepts major cards.

**Le Breugheul,** 6 Dashwood Cres., (089) 81-2025, offers French provincial fare from its blackboard menu, with features such as escargots, pepper steaks, crepes, and creme caramel. It's open for dinner seven nights and the bill without wine will come to around $30 a head. Cards accepted.

**Peppi's,** 84 Mitchell St., (089) 81-3762, serves classic French cuisine in elegant surroundings and wins awards for its extensive wine list. The menu will offer lobster Thermidor, entrecôte of beef, crème brûlée. Right in the center of town, it's open seven nights and accepts major cards. Three courses will cost about $40.

All the five-star hotels have good signature restaurants, but **Siggi's** in the Beaufort Hotel, (089) 82-9911, deserves a special mention for its silver-service cuisine moderne. Try barramundi fillets with avocado mousseline. Open for dinner Mon.–Sat.; major cards welcome and dinner without wine will cost around $45.

---

The big hotels also have brasseries for light meals and lunches. Head for The **Café Esplanade** in the Beaufort and **Mitchell's** in the Sheraton, which also has the **Pub Bar** serving counter lunches. For even more casual snacks, the **Darwin Plaza,** off the Smith St. Mall, has take-away stalls selling Mexican, Thai, Middle Eastern, and vegetarian food. You can sit in the Mall and watch the passing parade.

---

## ENTERTAINMENT

Much of the entertainment enjoyed by Darwinians centers around pubs—they have a reputation for drinking enormous quantities of beer. However, the visitor will find that more sedate tastes are well catered to—most touring performers include Darwin on their national itineraries.

The **Diamond Beach Hotel Casino,** Gilruth Avenue, (089) 81-7755, features visiting artists as well as the gaming tables. The casino is open every day from noon, but it's very strict about its "dress regulations." It doesn't matter how up-market your jeans are, you won't be allowed in. Denim is not acceptable, nor are shorts, thongs, or running shoes. So leave the Reeboks in your room.

The **Darwin Performing Arts Centre,** Mitchell Street, (089) 81-1222, is in the same building as, though not associated with, the Beaufort Hotel. For current performances check the afternoon paper, *The Territory News.*

On Sunday evenings from 8 P.M. the **Top End Folk Club** holds sessions on the East Point Gun Turret for $2. Expecting to see an authentic corroboree is about as optimistic as a woman hoping to be invited to join the Freemasons for a night—the Aborigines simply don't perform such deeply spiritual ceremonies for an unknown audience. You can, however, see Aborigines doing traditional dances by taking the **Billy J Cruises sunset boat trip** to Mandorah. In addition to the entertainment, you'll be served a feast of barramundi and mud crab cooked in the coals. More information at (089) 81-6744.

# THE TOP END OUTSIDE DARWIN

The Territory's Top End is the home of killer crocs, Mick Dundee—who the movies would have us believe can tame them—and Aborigine-owned lands such as Kakadu National Park and the Tiwi Islands. It takes in some of Australia's roughest country, including spectacular gorges and waterways and a rich array of wildlife. Parts can be explored from a Darwin base, while others such as Kakadu and Katherine Gorge, are a logical diversion from the Stuart Highway on the way to or from Alice Springs. Accommodation will be discussed as each destination is covered.

# KAKADU NATIONAL PARK

It's said that if you visit Kakadu in the Wet and return in the Dry, you'll swear you've never been there before. To put it in figures, the average rainfall in January is 338 millimeters (around 13 inches), while in June it's a mere 2 millimeters (that's a lot less than an inch). In the Wet you'll see vast green marshlands and water lilies in bloom; at this time, you can cruise on a meter of water, where, later in the year, you can park your car. Crocs find the water temperature quite appealing in the Wet, so you'll be lucky to spot any. Come the Dry, they find the bathwater too cool for comfort and conspicuously sun themselves on the banks. The birds are here all year round, but you'll see more in both numbers and variety as the summer sea shrinks and they congregate around the few permanent winter puddles. Four-wheel-drives are the best transport at any time and are essential during the Wet. Be wary, though, because even with off-road capability some roads will be impassable.

Kakadu National Park, 220 kilometers (over 135 miles) east of Darwin, is approximately 19,000 square kilometers of woodlands, forests, waterways, and floodplains, containing a wealth of wildlife, Aboriginal history, and rock art. Bounded by the 500-kilometer Arnhem escarpment, the park covers the catchment area of the East, South, and West Alligator and Wildman rivers, and is probably best known around the world as the location for much of the movie *"Crocodile" Dundee.* On the U.N. World Heritage List, it's reached by a paved road from Darwin—head south along the Stuart Highway and turn off to the Arnhem Highway. Headquarters are near the township of Jabiru. To visit in a day trip, even if you fly both ways, is to scratch the surface. For those planning a more in-depth visit, there are many tours, with accommodations ranging from safari tent to motel resort.

## Water Buffalo

Paul Hogan's two movies could just as well have been called *"Buffalo" Dundee.* Yet in real life, the crocodile flourishes after a concerted conservation campaign, while the water buffalo is in rapid decline.

Although both beasts are commercially harvested in the tropical Top End, the crocs are cultivated on farms and almost all buffalo meat is wild game. That was the way most buffalo-catchers and shooters liked it but times are a-changin', due to a government brucellosis and tuberculosis eradication campaign scheduled for completion by 1990. Most of the country's cattle have been declared "clean" but tests show that some water buffalo are TB carriers, and they can spread it to other stock.

The government has determined that the only sure way to curb the disease in the swampy forests of places like Kakadu National Park is by aerial shoot-outs. Some animals are being domesticated for breeding and meat production, while others will still be allowed to roam free in remote parts of the Northern Territory, where no disease has been found. However, the vast majority of the approximately 300,000 buffalo is being slaughtered from helicopters.

Proponents of the kills note that the buffalo is an introduced species anyway, from Indonesia. Ranchers complain about economic waste, animal rights' activists talk about cruelty, and ecologists debate over environmental damage caused by wallowing buffalo. For the tourist, it means see wild water buffalo soon, before it's too late.

—Steve Bunk

Croc spotting may be a high priority for most visitors, but in fact they take up little space on the park's list of 51 native mammals, 75 reptiles—including giant monitors (goannas) and frill-neck lizards—and 22 frog species. Kakadu, however, really belongs to the birds—nearly half of all Australian bird species live here. You'll see brolga, jabiru (black-necked stork), pelicans, sea eagles, kingfishers, pygmy geese, wood sand pipers, and kookaburras to name a few. Birdwatchers can join one of six daily **cruises** on the Yellow Waters billabong; they leave from the Four Seasons Cooinda Motel (see Accommodations, below). The two-hour cruise is conducted by National Parks rangers and costs $20. You'll also see crocs (in the Wet) and learn of the Aboriginal plant and animal food sources of the region.

If that whets the appetite, you can expand your knowledge by joining traditional Aboriginal owner Mick Alderson for his full day **Wild Goose Tour,** which leaves from the Cooinda motel every day except Monday. For $80 Mick will take you to the bird breeding ground of Bamurru Djadjam, share his people's food-gathering and fire-making techniques, and show you an old buffalo shooter's camp, where as a young boy he worked with his father. For more information on both tours, telephone the Four Seasons Cooinda Motel, (089) 79-0145.

### Photography

The Northern Territory is a photographer's paradise. Feel free to take pictures of its splendid landscapes and wildlife, but remember, the Aborigines are not a tourist attraction. They feel pretty much as you would if someone walked into your home and started snapping away. Respect their privacy.

The major **Aboriginal art sites** are at Obiri (Ubirr) and Nourlangie Rock. Both have clearly marked walking tracks to the major paintings and you'll see examples from the three main periods—pre-estuarine, estuarine, and contact. The main subjects of the pre-estuarine period (before the sea level rose after the last ice age) reflect man the hunter, with stone axes, spears, and boomerangs. At Obiri, there's a painting of the thylacine or Tasmanian tiger which became extinct on the mainland some 4,000 years ago. The estuarine era shows the arrival of fish, in particular the barramundi, and the emergence of X-ray art, so called because it depicts the internal organs and skeletons of the subjects. Contact art came after the arrival of Europeans and illustrates their rifles and steel axes.

### TRAVEL

To fully absorb the ecological contrasts of the park, Kakadu Air conducts hour-long **flights** which leave from the Jabiru airstrip several times a day, depending on demand. You'll see the Arnhem escarpment and Jim Jim and Twin Falls, which plummet more than 200 meters to gorges below. Flights cost around $60 and the company also has day tours from Darwin. Tel. (089) 79-2031.

During The Dry, four-wheel-drives can get to within a kilometer of Jim Jim Falls. From there you walk through the forest and have the option of taking an air mattress paddle to Twin Falls. (You'll have to carry your own unless you're traveling with an operator.)

Maps and further details are available from the Park Information Centre, which is about 5 km (3 miles) from Jabiru. It's open daily from 8 A.M. to 5 P.M.; tel. (089) 79-2101.

One of the most experienced Kakadu tour operators is Tom Winter of Terra Safari Tours, 5 Moil Cres., Moil. During the past twenty years he's built his family business to its present fleet of four-wheel-drives, which take a maximum of ten passengers for day trips and longer jaunts. Accommodation is in safari tents and, weather permitting, camp sites are chosen to take you as far from the madding crowd as possible. Terra guides are well-versed in the park's points of interest and will accompany you to its few safe swimming holes. One tour incorporates Mick Alderson's Wild Goose expedition.

Tom Winter is also the only operator who can take you beyond the Border Store—that is, across the East Alligator River and into the Aboriginal-owned country of Arnhem Land. He has a special arrangement with the Gummulkbun people who act as tour guides for visitors to their land. The guides take you fishing for barramundi and mud crabs, using spears, and cook the catch in the traditional way in the coals. They'll also show you spots few Europeans have been privileged to see, such as rock art sites and food-rich wetlands. (Access to this area otherwise is by Lands Council permit only.) Arnhem Land tours can be taken as an extension of Kakadu trips and one provides the option of return to Darwin across Van Dieman Gulf on the 23-meter (75-foot) schooner, *Algerias*. Terra Tours can be contacted at (089) 45-0863, telex 85925.

## ACCOMMODATIONS

**The Four Seasons Cooinda,** (089) 79-0145, telex 85463, has 48 rooms ranging from $60 in the Dry and $120 in the Wet, and is the closest accommodation to all the park's attractions. The motel is air-conditioned and has a small swimming pool, a restaurant, and a bar; many tours leave from here. Major credit cards are accepted. At press time a new motel, also to be managed by Four Seasons, was being constructed in the township of Jabiru. The designers apparently were overtaken by a fit of Oz kitsch, for this building, which is to be the park's premium accommodation, is in the shape of a crocodile. Alternatively, you can stay on the outskirts of the park at the **Kakadu Holiday Village** at South Alligator, (089) 79-0166, telex 85732. Set in 7 hectares (about 15 acres) of bushland, this complex has motel units for $66 single and $98 double, or more modest safari cabins for $35 single and $50 double (no phone). There's air-conditioning, a licensed restaurant, and an attractive swimming pool covered with a cloth canopy shade. While the Holiday Village is about 40 km (25 miles) from the park's major attractions, most tour operators pick up from there or you can take the shuttle bus to Jabiru and the park headquarters for $15 round-trip. Major credit cards accepted.

There are about twenty campsites in the park area, which range from tent-only areas with pit toilets to sections with provisions for caravans, with flush toilets, showers, and hot water. Powered caravan sites are available at Kakadu Holiday Village and Four Seasons Cooinda Hotel. For most of the year, it's not necessary to reserve campsites; but it is advisable during school holidays in the Dry.

**There are so many safari operators offering tented accommodations, unless you are planning to camp all the way through Australia, it's easier to use their facilities and itineraries.**

# THE TIWI ISLANDS

A visit to the Tiwi Islands will provide contact with a completely different Aboriginal culture. Although they're only about 80 kilometers (50 miles) from Darwin, the Bathurst and Melville islanders had little contact with mainland Aborigines until the late 1800s. Unlike the mainlanders their heritage has no Dreaming and their art is purely abstract.

## TRAVEL

Access to these islands is by Lands Council permit only, or with several limited-group tour operators. **Tiwi Tours,** 27 Temira Crescent, Darwin, (089) 81-5115, telex 84115, operates day tours from Darwin that include a DC-3 flight to Bathurst Island, visits to a mission school, screen printing and pottery workshops, then a transfer across the Apsley Strait by small boat to Melville Island. Visitors are taken to Turacumbie Falls for a swim in a natural spa, then served a picnic lunch before continuing on to see a pukamani burial site. Here the Tiwis' artistic talent is evident in the elaborately carved logs placed around the grave as tokens of remembrance and to keep the spirits of the dead from straying back to the camp at night. These days most Tiwis have a Christian burial as well, and you'll see the cultures meet on the traditionally covered graves which are also adorned by crosses. You fly back to Darwin from the Milikapiti, or Snake Bay, airport. Cost of the tour is around $200.

## ☙ ACCOMMODATIONS

If you fancy trying your hand at hunting and gathering, you can join the Tiwi people at the **Putjamirra safari camp** on Melville Island. They'll take you fishing, foraging on the foreshore for mangrove worms (shut your eyes, swallow them whole, and they're said to resemble oysters), and crab catching. Accommodation is in screened two-person tents and European-style fare supplements the "bush tucker." The cost begins at $500 for two days, including air transfers, and further information is available from Australian Kakadu Tours, Box 1397, Darwin 0801, (089) 81-5144, telex 85586.

## Aboriginal Lands

Most Aboriginal art sites are extremely vulnerable to damage. The pigments used in these paintings are water based and are susceptible to moisture, such as sweat from human hands. Don't touch, scratch, or interfere with them in any way. Stay behind the protective fencing.

There are a number of spots in the Northern Territory that are of special significance to the traditional owners. Known as sacred sites and signposted as such, entry to them is prohibited. To ignore these signs is not only to transgress the ancient law of your hosts, but also to face the jurisdiction of the Northern Territory and Commonwealth governments.

In the tourist areas, permission for visitors to come and go is part of a permanent agreement between the government and the traditional owners. If you want to enter Aboriginal land outside these areas, you must first obtain permission from the Aboriginal community. Curiosity is not a valid reason, anthropological research sometimes is. You must apply in writing and allow at least two weeks for processing. Write to the Permits Officer for the appropriate Lands Council: Darwin, Nhulunbuy, and Katherine—Northern Land Council, Box 39843, Winnellie 0820; Alice Springs and Tennant Creek—Central Land Council, Box 3321, Alice Springs 0870; Melville and Bathurst islands—Tiwi Land Council, Nguiu, Bathurst Island, via Darwin 0801. If you're visiting these places with a tour such as Terra Safaris (Arnhem Land) or Tiwi Tours (Bathurst and Melville islands) the operators will have taken care of the permits for you.

It must be said that the emphasis of a stay at a safari camp is to join the Tiwi people in their traditional lifestyle; they don't alter their time-honored patterns to satisfy tourists. Be prepared to fit in with their loosely structured food-gathering habits and innate sense of timing—for example, the best time to go fishing.

If you'd rather fish all day long, perhaps the **Barra Base Lodge** on Bathurst Island is your ideal destination. For $225 a day (including air fares from Darwin) you'll stay in air-conditioned twin rooms, have all meals and equipment provided, and the services of professional fishing guides. More details are available from North Australian Tourist Services, Shop 4/109 Smith St., Darwin, (089) 45-0966, or the Lodge direct on (089) 81-1486.

# KATHERINE

When the tourist brochures describe the Top End, they talk of the "magic triangle"—Darwin and the Tiwi Islands to the north, Kakadu to the east, and the Never Never to the south. This area derives its name from the local saying that those who live there can "never never" leave it. Certainly in the pioneer days the area was so isolated that the chances of getting there, let alone getting out, were pretty remote. These days, however, it's a fast 300-kilometer (about 185-mile) drive south of Darwin on the Stuart Highway, or a short hop with Ansett N.T. to the center of Katherine.

About 30 kilometers (18 miles) east of the small town Katherine is one of the region's most famous attractions, the 180,000-hectare **Katherine Gorge National Park.** The park covers 13 canyons gouged in the earth through the millennium as the Katherine River winds its way towards the Timor Sea southwest of Darwin. The best way to see the 10-kilometer (6-mile) system is by cruise and clamber, boarding a boat at the first gorge, traveling up it, climbing over the rocks to the next, and so on. Highlights of the trip include the Hanging Gardens, where rock springs and shade create an ideal environment for masses of delicate ferns, the (self-explanatory) Butterfly Gorge, and Swallows' Cave, in which fairy martins' mud nests line the roof. The 60-meter (180 feet) sheer sandstone walls of Jedda's Leap were the inspiration for Australia's first color movie—Charles Chavel's *Jedda,* the tale of a young Aboriginal woman who escaped abduction by plunging to her death from the rock face. There is a daily bus from Katherine to the Gorge. Gorge tours can be booked through Travel North, 6 Katherine Terrace, Katherine 0850, (089) 72-1044, telex 85425; a full day will cost around $50. Access may be limited during The Wet. (Courtesy coach picks up tour members from Katherine accommodations and the BP Roadhouse on Katherine Terrace three times a day.)

There are a number of **Aboriginal art sites** in the park, which, with more than 100 kilometers (60 miles) of bush trails, visitors can explore at leisure. **Canoes** can also be hired for independent or guided tours of the gorges. Contact Kookaburra Canoe Hire at the park headquarters, (089) 72-3301.

The park headquarters is about 3 kilometers (2 miles or so) inside the park. Park headquarters is open daily from 9 A.M. to 5 P.M.; (089) 72-1886.

The **Cutta Cutta Caves** contain fascinating limestone formations and can be inspected during the day. They're 27 kilometers (16 miles) south of Katherine and Travel North conducts guided coach tours from the town for around $20. Other destinations for this tour operator include **Springvale Station,** the oldest surviving homestead in this region, and **Elsey Station.**

Elsey is a familiar name to most Australians, having been the subject of the books *We of the Never Never* and *Little Black Princess,* written by an early manager's wife, Mrs. Aeneas Gunn. In them she records the austerities of being one of few European women in the Outback in the early 1900s. Typical of her generation, she never called herself Jeannie, preferring the formal address of her husband's name. Their graves and a replica homestead are about 7 kilometers (4 miles) from the

Stuart Highway, 112 kilometers (70 miles) south of Katherine.

## ❦ ACCOMMODATIONS AND RESTAURANTS

Katherine is well equipped with motel accommodations and in most cases you'll dine in their in-house restaurants where char-grilled buffalo and beef steaks feature. (Major credit cards usually accepted.) If you tire of that, **Alexander's,** Banksia Arcade, Katherine Terr., Katherine, (089) 72-2182, aims further up-market with nouvelle-cuisine based main courses for around $12. Open for dinner only Tues.–Sat.

Recommended motels include the air-conditioned **Katherine Frontier Motor Inn,** Stuart Hwy., Katherine 5780, (089) 72-1722, telex: 85359. It has fifty units for $60 single and $75 double, a swimming pool, and tennis court.

At the **Mataranka Homestead Tourist Park,** 120 km (72 miles) south of Katherine, Mataranka 5780, (089) 75-4544, telex 85425, there is a palm-fringed thermal pool which, while its therapeutic powers may be a matter for conjecture, has revived many a weary traveler's spirits. The Homestead has a bistro with Aboriginal dance entertainment at night, and its 41 air-conditioned rooms range from $43 single and $56 double. Alternatively, there is the 26-unit **Territory Manor,** Martin Rd., Mataranka 5780, (089) 75-4516, telex: 85599, set in attractive bushland with rates from $60 single and $75 double. Air-conditioning and pool here, too.

Near park headquarters, a few miles within the park, you can hire permanently erected tents, which can hold up to six people. Book in advance. Camping elsewhere in the park is not permitted.

# Alice and the Center

Ask most Australians to name their country's greatest landmark and the unhesitating response will be Ayers Rock (Uluru). Its significance as the world's largest monolith is secondary to its symbolic role as the beacon of the Outback, set in the splendid isolation and raw beauty of the country's Red Center. More than 200,000 tourists annually make the pilgrimage to watch the Rock light up in the sunset.

But as a visitor to the Territory's Center quickly learns, the region has much more to offer than a great lump of rock in the middle of the desert. Among them: the Olgas (Kata Tjuta)—36 huge rock domes within sight of Uluru—and the Territory's second city, Alice Springs (population 26,000), 440 kilometers (over 250 miles) to the northeast of Uluru.

The Alice's relics of the pioneer days and the gorges of the surrounding MacDonnell Ranges are worthy of several days' investigation. Beyond Alice, the Stuart Highway leads 500 kilometers (over 300 miles) north to the gold-mining center of Tennant Creek (population 3,500). From there, it's a mere

948 kilometers (under 600 miles) on to Darwin, gateway to the Top End.

While the independent traveler will pass through many of the Center's attractions when driving across Australia from Adelaide to Darwin, most can be visited by day or extended tour from Alice Springs.

The Alice, as it is called by all, was established in 1871 as a repeater station for the Overland Telegraph Line between Adelaide and Darwin, which was to make possible communication, other than by sea, between Australia and the rest of the world. South Australia's Superintendent of Telegraphs, Charles Todd, was responsible for the 3,200-kilometer (2,000-mile) link which was frequently out of order in the early days because Aborigines found the insulators made useful weapons. The settlement was named after Todd's wife, Alice, and the river that occasionally flows through it (in the annual regatta boats are carried along the dry bed; see Entertainment, below) was called the Todd. Originally a support center for the telegraph, the surrounding properties, and Aboriginal communities, Alice Springs has been changed dramatically in recent years by the U.S. satellite monitoring base at nearby Pine Gap and an ever-increasing flow of tourists which stretches the airport's facilities to their limit.

However, Alice Springs has always been an oasis and, with copious artesian water to nourish parks, gardens, and even a turfed golf course, it still is a welcome sight for eyes grown accustomed to the seemingly endless ochers of the Center.

# ❦ ACCOMMODATIONS

Alice Springs' luxury accommodations are clustered 4 kilometers (2½ miles) from the center of town on Barrett Dr. Expect air-conditioning in the accommodations here, unless otherwise stated. Major credit cards generally accepted. They include the new **Sheraton Alice Springs Hotel,** Alice Springs 0870, (089) 52-8000, telex 81091, with 250 rooms, ranging from $145 single and $165 double and the **Four Seasons Alice Springs,** Alice Springs 0870, (089) 56-2100, telex 81367, with 142 rooms for $95 single and $110 double. Both are low-set buildings, to conform with the local building code limit of three stories, and provide panoramic views of the MacDonnell Ranges. They have pools (the Sheraton also has a spa) and are both within walking distance of the golf course; tel. (089) 52-5440. However, unless you have a car, you'll need to take a taxi (089-52-1877), to get to town. This is probably no great disadvantage to most guests as tour operators pick up from the hotels and each has a variety of in-house dining options.

The **Desert Rose Inn,** Railway Terr., Alice Springs 0870, (089) 52-1411, telex 81144, is right in the town center and offers budget (single rooms $40, doubles $50) and moderately priced accommodations (with sitting areas; single $60, double $70). It has a licensed char-grill, private (guests only) and public bars, a pool, squash courts next door, and tennis courts opposite.

The **Diplomat Motor Inn,** at the corner of Gregory Terr. and Hartley St., Alice Springs 0870, (089) 52-8977, telex 81044, is another centrally located motel with 91 rooms for $90 single and $100 double. Its licensed Italian restaurant, **Puccini's,** (089) 53-0935, is highly recommended. The motor inn has a pool, spa, and sauna.

## ✤ RESTAURANTS

You can dine on barbecued steaks and barramundi accompanied by Aussie damper and the house wine at **Chateau Hornsby,** the Northern Territory's only winery. It's 11 kilometers (7 miles) from town on Petrick Rd., (089) 52-5771, and is open for lunch and dinner every day. Major credit cards accepted. If you don't have your own transport, Pete's Aussie Tours, (089) 52-1011, take visitors from The Alice for tastings and country music nights. Alternatively, ride a camel to lunch or dinner there with Frontier Tours, (089) 53-0444. The outing costs $45 and includes your steed, meal, wine tasting, and coach return and is available Sun., Tues., and Fri.

At **The Legend,** 4 Traeger Ave., (089) 52-1588, you can dine on barra, buff, and croc surrounded by photographs and memorabilia of the pioneering days. It's licensed, open for dinner Mon.–Sat., and accepts major credit cards. Three courses will run around $30.

**Mr. Pickwick's,** 20 Undoolya Rd., (089) 52-9400, offers elegant dining in the cuisine moderne mode for lunch every day and dinner Mon.–Sat. The menu changes as seasonal produce does; selections range from lamb with light fruit sauces to fillet of beef and barramundi with lemon mousse. Major cards welcome.

Most city dwellers take facilities such as telephone, education, and medicine for granted, but they've been hard earned in the Outback. In and around Alice you can visit a number of sites that honor the pioneers who brought these "luxuries" to the region. At the **Aviation Museum,** Memorial Drive, there are a number of aircraft used by the early Royal Flying Doctor Service. The museum is open every day; telephone (089) 52-4241 for hours. The grave of the service's founder, John Flynn, is 7 kilometers (2½ miles) west of town. You can see the modern **flying doctor at work** by visiting the base on Stuart Terrace. It's open Monday through Saturday from 9 A.M. to 3 P.M. and Sunday from 1 to 4 P.M. Admission $1.50; (089) 52-1129.

Radio communications brought education to children on far-flung properties, and you can watch a teacher instructing students as far as 1,000 kilometers (630 miles) away at the **School of the Air** on Head St., (089) 52-2122. Open Monday to Friday from 1:30 to 3:30 P.M. The **Old Telegraph Station** is 3 kilometers (2 miles) north of Alice on the Stuart Highway. The buildings and equipment have been restored and there's a pictorial record of the mammoth task of building the line that connected Australia, through The Alice, to the outside world.

---

### The Royal Flying Doctor Service

The Royal Flying Doctor Service has for many years provided the only medical service to people in remote settlements. It operates on a radio network covering pastoral stations, bush communities, and mining towns. Patients have radio consultations with doctors at the base in Alice Springs and at regular intervals the doctor flies to remote centers to conduct clinics. The Flying Doctor also acts as an aerial ambulance in emergencies.

---

The **MacDonnell Ranges** running to the east and west of Alice Springs surround spectacular gorges and geological formations within day-tripping distance. To the east are Emily and Jessie gaps (10 and 18 kilometers, 6 and 11 miles, from Alice, respectively) and the road continues on to the ghost town of Arltunga, which pulsed to the beat of the goldminer's pick in the 1890s. The most famous gorge country is to the west, along Namatjira Drive. Here are Simpson's Gap, 23 kilometers (about 15 miles) from Alice, and Standley Chasm, 50 kilometers (about 30 miles) from Alice. Farther afield are the ancient formations of Serpentine (100 kilometers, about 60 miles, from Alice), Ormiston, and Glen Helen gorges (both about 132 kilometers, 83 miles away).

**Swimming holes surrounded by tall ghost gums make ideal picnic spots in these locations, or you can stay overnight at Glen Helen Lodge, radio telephone: 137. It has motel units for $45 single and $55 double or smaller rooms for $24 single and $34 double. There's a licensed restaurant.**

**Finke Gorge National Park** is 138 kilometers (about 85 miles) southwest of Alice, accessible only by four-wheel-drive and reached by turning off Namajira Drive, 48 kilometers (about 30 miles) from town and onto Larapinta Drive.

**It's also possible to get there by four-wheel-drive from Glen Helen Gorge by traveling down the Finke River bed, but this exercise is recommended only for experienced off-road drivers with complete confidence in their vehicles and the equipment and ability to handle repairs.**

The park contains Palm Valley, a relic of the age when Central Australia was covered by lush vegetation. It's home to more than thirty rare plants including the *Livistona Mariae* palm, unique to this valley.

## SHOPPING

Alice Springs is the major distribution point for the **sand paintings** of the Aboriginal artists of the western desert. As well, you can buy **batik** from the Utopia settlement northeast of the town, **bark paintings, weavings,** and **carvings.** A recommended gallery is the government-sponsored Aboriginal Art Gallery, 86 Todd Street, (089) 52-3408. The Arunta Art Gallery is in the same block, (089) 52-1544, and it also has an extensive range of books on Outback flora, fauna, and Aboriginal culture. Art Mart, 54 Todd Mall, (089) 52-5552, specializes in local pottery, screen prints, and paintings. The Alice is also a good spot to buy **opals** from the mines at Coober Pedy and Andamooka. The Gem Cave, 85 Todd Mall, (089) 52-1079, sells cut and set opals as well as other precious and semi-precious stones.

## RECREATION

Most accommodations have swimming pools, but if you fancy a **water-slide ride** or **aquarobics class,** head for the Alice Springs Swimming Centre, Speed Street, open every day from 10 A.M. from September to May. Phone (089) 52-3757 for class times.

Watch the sun rise as you drift over the MacDonnell Ranges with **Aussie Balloons,** (089) 53-0544. The $100 fee includes transfer to the launch site, half-hour flight, and chicken and champagne brunch afterwards. Available only from April to October and subject to weather conditions.

As discussed above under Accommodations, there's a **golf** course near the hotels on Barrett Drive; rentals are available. Telephone: (089) 52-5440.

Glenrowan Trail Rides, (089) 52-6447, conducts a number of **horseback treks** through the near bush for around $15 an hour.

## ENTERTAINMENT

**Lassiters Casino,** Barrett Drive, (089) 52-5066, opens its gaming tables Sunday through Thursday from 7 P.M. to 3 A.M. and until 4 A.M. on Friday and Saturday. The Old Alice Inn, at the corner of Todd Street and Wills Terrace, (089) 52-1255, has a **piano bar** with live entertainment Thursday through Saturday from 8 P.M. to 1 A.M., **disco** Thursday through Saturday from 8 P.M. to 2 A.M., and **folk nights** on Sunday from 8 P.M. The Araluen Arts Centre, Larapinta Drive, (089) 52-5022, contains **cinemas, performing arts** theaters, and two **art galleries.** Phone for current shows. The galleries are closed on Monday. Interesting features of the complex include a large mural by western desert artist Clifford Possum Tjapaltjarri and stained-glass windows designed by local Aboriginal school children.

On a less esoteric level, The Alice hosts two annual events which draw crowds of locals and tourists. The **Henley-on-Todd Regatta** is held at the end of September or beginning of October. Essential ingredients are a dry river bed, bottomless boats, and a sense of the ridiculous. Competitors pick up their boats and run. Not for the boater brigade.

The **Camel Cup** is also run on the Todd River bed at the end of April or early in May. Although this event is organized to raise money for charity, it recalls the days when camel trains run by Afghan masters were the primary mode of transport in the Territory.

## ORGANIZED TOURS FROM ALICE

All the destinations discussed below are serviced by tour operators from The Alice. Recommended companies include Ansett Trailways, 2 George Cres., Alice Springs, (089) 56-2066, telex 81254, and the family-owned Spinifex Tours, Box 2433, Alice Springs, (089) 52-2203, telex 81098.

There are also a number of special-interest tours available. They include Desert Tracks' 10- and 14-day expeditions to stay with the Pitjantjatjara people of the western desert, participating in the collection and preparation of bush food, sleeping in swags under the stars, joining in their singing and dancing, and learning about their country and spirituality. The tour prices begin at $1,000 and further information is available from the company, Box 8706, Alice Springs 0870, (089) 52-4422. This is Aboriginal land and it's otherwise necessary to obtain a Lands Council permit before visiting.

Dedicated fossil enthusiasts can join Penny van Oosterzee of Desert Discovery on a month-long swoop through the fossil fields of the Northern Territory and Queensland. If your time is more limited, she also does more localized tours from Alice Springs concentrating on subjects such as ornithology, herpetology (the study of lizards), anthropology, and ethnobotany. For more details, write to Box 3839, Alice Springs 0870, (089) 52-8308.

You can also "take a camel to bed" or, more accurately, go camping on camelback with Frontier Tours, (089) 53-0444. The $150 fee includes transfers to the camel farm, camping equipment, and a guided bush trek.

## THE CENTER OUTSIDE ALICE

To reach Ayers Rock, take the Stuart Highway 202 kilometers (about 127 miles) south to Erldunda and turn on to the Lasseter Highway for another 247 kilometers (156 miles).

## SIDETRIP

There are numerous geological wonders to break the journey, though most involve diversions from the main road. The **Ewaninga Carvings** (34 km, 20 miles, south of Alice), more correctly called petroglyphs, are considered to be the work of a culture older than the Aborigines, since the Aborigines don't understand the petroglyphs' significance. The 50-meter sandstone tower of **Chambers Pillar** is 160 km (100 miles) from Alice (four-wheel-drive only), while the 13 craters gouged by meteorites at **Henbury** (147 km, about 93 miles, south) and **Goose Bluff** (155 km, about 97 miles, south), formed by a comet hitting the earth more than 130 million years ago, might cause a few anxious glances at the sky.

You can also visit **Kings Canyon,** a mighty cleft with sheer walls of striking color and immensity, en route to the Rock without having to backtrack. Although this detour is open to sedans, the roads are not paved. Turn off Stuart Hwy. just south of the Henbury craters (132 km, about 83 miles, from Alice) and head west for 199 km (about 125 miles). The only accommodation in this area is at **Wallara Ranch** on Angus Downs station, 64 km (about 40 miles) from King's Canyon National Park. It has 32 motel-style units for $60 single and $80 double. Less-spacious rooms are $30 single and $50 double; it's air-conditioned and there's a licensed restaurant. Tel. (089) 56-2901. The road south to the Rock leaves from this point and it's 70 km (about 44 miles) till you join the Lasseter Hwy., 138 km (about 86 miles) from the Yulara complex.

# ULURU NATIONAL PARK AND AYERS ROCK

The Uluru National Park which encompasses Ayers Rock (Uluru) and the Olgas (Kata Tjuta, meaning many heads) is of enormous spiritual significance to the Aborigines and in 1985, ownership of the area was returned to them by the Australian government. It is now leased to and managed by the National Parks and Wildlife Service. To protect the park, all accommodation is concentrated in the Yulara complex about 20 kilometers (12 miles) from the Rock. Essential services and worker residences are included in the settlement (winner of a string of national architectural awards), which curves around a long sand dune and is designed for minimal intrusion on the environment. Buses operate from the complex to Ayers Rock and the Olgas. The Aboriginal Mutitjulu community is within the park confines and is not open to the public. You will, however, have opportunities to meet Aboriginal people on patrols, ranger guided walks, at the Ranger Station and at the **Maruku Arts Centre** behind the entry station, where traditional arts and crafts are sold against a backdrop of Aboriginal dwellings.

## ❦ ACCOMMODATIONS AND RESTAURANTS

The following will generally accept all major credit cards. Top-of-the-range accommodation is the 234-room **Sheraton Ayers Rock Hotel,** (089) 22-2229, telex 81108. Room rates begin at $175. The **Four Seasons Ayers Rock Hotel,** (089) 56-2100, telex 81367, has single rooms from $140 and doubles from $160. **The Ayers Rock Lodge,** (089) 56-2170, telex 81089, offers budget accommodation in buildings which housed the resort's construction workers. Rooms are $62 plus $15.50 for each extra person, or $15.50 per person in dormitories. All have air-conditioning, and pools.

Dining at Yulara ranges from the **Old Oak Tree Coffee Shop and Takeaway** (open 7:30 A.M. daily until late into the night) for burgers, pizzas, and fries, to the Sheraton's signature restaurant, the **Kunia Room** (tel. 089-56-2200). Homestyle cooking and snacks are also available from the **Ayers Rock Lodge Food Bar.** The **Stuart Room** in the Four Seasons has buffets as well as an à la carte menu.; (089) 56-2100.

---

**Ayers Rock** is estimated to be about 600 million years old and was formed when major earth movements forced up a mountain chain, which has through the years weathered to leave only the 3.3-square-kilometer mass of the Rock, the 36 domes of the Olgas, and Mt. Conner—the flat-topped landmark seen from the road about halfway between Erdunda and Yulara.

You can climb the 1.6 kilometer (1 mile) to the Rock's 348-meter (1,110-foot) summit and sign your name in the visitors book, or take the marked 10.4-kilometer (6½-mile) walk around the base.

**The Olgas** are scattered over an area of 36 square kilometers, and there are a number of walking tracks for exploring. Maps showing designated trails are available, as are maps for Ayers Rock, at the **Visitors Centre** which is within the Yulara complex. But Uluru National Park is not just about fascinating geology—about 480 plant species, 159 birds, at least 70 reptile species, and 42 mammals also call the area home. They include Australia's largest lizard, the perentie, which can grow to 2½ meters in length (that's over 8 feet long); the ferocious-in-appearance-though-harmless-in-reality Thorny Devil; and the shield shrimp, which miraculously appears in rock pools on top of Ayers Rock after rain.

Ranger-guided walks will give the visitor a better appreciation of the park's diversity. They include the "edible desert" ($5) which explains the natural foods and medicines used by the Aborigines; the "secrets of the dunes" ($5), which takes a close look at the flora and fauna; and a night walk (free), where you'll be shown the constellations of the southern skies and their stories. Numbers are limited and bookings must be made at the Yulara Visitors Centre, (089) 56-2122, between 8 and 10 P.M.

## Ayers Rock

Does the spiritual presence of Ayers Rock, which is evident to almost every visitor, have anything to do with its extreme age? That question can neither be answered nor escaped. This large monolith dates to perhaps 600 million years ago, when the earth's crust was still forming.

Back then, part of Central Australia was a giant, inland sea. One theory is that over the eons, a mountain range crumbled into the water. The sandy sediment eventually hardened into sandstone which erupted to the earth's surface during a powerful upheaval about 450 million years ago. As it rose, the sandstone strata was tilted on edge, which is why the Rock's faces are steep. More than half of it is probably still underground.

Today, Ayers Rock is slowly flaking away, an erosion caused by moisture and air interacting with minerals. This process continues upward and inward, causing the caves at the base.

For the Aborigines, parts of the Rock represent sacred events from the Dreamtime, when the creation beings made all the geographical features and life on earth. The nearby Olgas appeared at about the same time and also are eroding. Their problem is "off-loading," when internal stress in the main body of rock causes large slabs to break loose and either slide or fall to the ground.

Don't worry, these sites won't be gone overnight. In fact, if the time it took to form Ayers Rock were compressed into a 365-day scale, the first Aboriginal visitor (say, 42,000 B.C.) would have arrived roughly a half hour ago.

—Steve Bunk

## The Climb

There are no prizes for climbing Ayers Rock (Uluru). In fact there is probably more status attached to T-shirts that proclaim "I didn't climb the Rock." Sections of the climb are very steep and it shouldn't be attempted by anyone who suffers from heart conditions such as high blood pressure or angina, asthma, fear of heights, or vertigo. There are memorials at the bottom to people who ignored this advice. At the top, strong gusts of wind can remove hats, bags, or anything not securely fastened. (There have been cases of people actually being blown off.) If there's a strong wind at the base, it will be stronger at the summit.

Allow several hours for the climb, carry water, and set out in the cool of the morning. Stick to the chain and the painted white lines. There is an alarm at the base which will contact a ranger immediately should an emergency occur. Having said all that, you'll no doubt still want to join the line of ant-like figures that wends its way up the Rock every day. Take your time. It isn't a race.

If you fancy watching the sunset in style, VIP Chauffeur Tours, (089) 56-2283, can provide the limo, the champagne, and "gourmet tailgate cuisine" to accompany the show nature turns on every night at The Rock. Or you can opt for a bird's-eye view from a number of charter aircraft which operate from the airport. Tillair, (089) 56-2280, has daily scenic flights and picks up from your accommodation.

It is very hard for a European not to sense some of the sacredness and complex mystery of the Rock. For much of the day the great red inselberg seems lit from within. Its crevices and caves are marked with ancient naïve but disturbing art. It is becoming a place of pilgrimage for European Australians, its astounding unity and indifference drawing tourists up its flank, specifically at the point known as Webo, the place where the kangaroo-rat men of antiquity crouched, ancestors with both human and animal natures, the fall of their tails creating a slope quite awesome to the European who stands at the bottom and considers the ascent. Giles himself, standing at this point and wondering whether he should make an attempt on the great rock, wrote, 'Its appearance and outline is most imposing, for it is simply a mammoth monolith that rises out of the sandy desert soil around, and stands with a perpendicular and totally inaccessible face at all points, except one slope near the northwest end, and that at least is but a precarious climbing ground . . . Mount Olga is the more wonderful and grotesque; Mount Ayers the more ancient and sublime.'

—Thomas Keneally
*Outback,* 1983

# 11

# WESTERN AUSTRALIA

To most Australians the state of Western Australia is the last frontier—one third of the continent which few have visited. And of those who have ventured into the unknown most know only the capital, Perth, or the fertile southwest corner.

Slightly more than 1 million of the state's total population of 1.44 million live in the capital. The remaining third have 2.5 million square kilometers, an area greater than the combined surfaces of Texas, Japan, New Zealand, and the United Kingdom, to call their home. They're miners—gold from the Kalgoorlie fields east of Perth, iron ore from the Pilbara to the north, and diamonds from even farther north in the Kimberleys—or cattle and wheat farmers on properties that sprawl across sandy semi-arid plains and salt-pan desert.

This harsh, hostile environment, however, contains some of the nation's most spectacular geological formations. To see them you'll need determination, for this is country where distance has a different meaning. To fly from Perth to Broome, in the north, takes three hours by jet. From Sydney it's a 4½-hour flight to the capital. Even the people who've always lived in the West, as the state is commonly called, have a keen sense of its isolation. Locked between the Indian Ocean and the inhospitable deserts of Central Australia, they refer to the rest of Australia as the "eastern seaboard" or the "eastern states" as if it were another country. Viewed from the east, Western Australia might as well be another country. Perth is closer to Jakarta in Indonesia than it is to Sydney.

Covering more than 3,000 kilometers (almost 2,000 miles) from south to north, Western Australia (never West Australia) spans a temperate zone in the south, through subtropical and tropical belts to the subequatorial far north. Perth and the southwest corner enjoy a Mediterranean climate, with a summer average maximum of 30° C (around 90° F) and low humidity and a winter average maximum of 18° C (around 60° F), with most rain falling in June and July. From August to November is the West's celebrated wildflower season, when more than 8,000 flowering natives give the state a fresh coat of paint. In the north, they abandon the seasons altogether and refer simply to the Wet and the Dry. The best time to visit is from April to October when humidity and rainfall are low and average temperatures range from 16° C to 24° C (around 60–80° F).

Such climatic extremes obviously call for a variety of clothing, but Western Australians essentially dress casually. Medium-weight garments (and a raincoat) are all you'll need for winter, but in the far north in the Wet (October to April) take your cue from the locals, wear as little as possible, and treat the rain as a refreshing wash. Hats, swimsuits, and insect repellent are other packing essentials.

As many place names along the coast testify, Western Australia was first charted by Dutch explorers in the 17th century. It remained unannexed by Europeans until the activities of French explorers and American whalers provoked the British into forming a settlement in 1826 at King George Sound, near the present township of Albany. Their exploration of the region led to the establishment of a colony on the Swan River in 1829, near the present site of the capital Perth. Convict labor was imported—the last convicts to be transported to Australia arrived in Western Australia in 1868—but the handicap of isolation thwarted the development of the region until the first gold rushes in the 1880s. Wheat farming, timber milling, and pearling at Broome, in the far northwest, quickly followed as major industries, and the state was finally linked by rail to the rest of Australia in 1917. The state's economy remained primarily agricultural until the 1960s when minerals—iron ore, nickel, and bauxite—boomed, and more recently diamonds in the Kimberleys and a rebirth of gold mines at Kalgoorlie have added to the state's coffers.

A number of individuals profited from these developments and Perth is dubbed by Australians as "millionaire city." The wealthy include Alan Bond, financier of the much-publicized America's Cup victory in 1983. The subsequent (unsuccessful, for Australia) rematch in 1987 was held off Perth's port of Fremantle and was largely responsible for earning the city its present reputation as a sophisticated, cosmopolitan center.

The southwest corner, with its wineries, forests of massive karri and jarrah trees, cliffs riddled with caves and splendid surfing beaches, and the "wild west" goldfields 500 kilometers (over 300 miles) east of Perth feasibly can be visited by touring from the capital. But if you plan to venture north to see the midwest with its fascinating geology such as the petrified forest of the Pinnacles, the world's largest monocline of Mount Augustus, or the gorge country of the Kimberleys, it's best to do so without having to backtrack. The most logical way to see the north is as part of a journey to or from the Top End of the Northern Territory.

# TRAVEL

## Flying

Unless coming from Southeast Asia, it's unlikely that non-Australians will begin an Australian visit by flying into Western Australia's international airport in Perth. Most foreign travelers fly in from the eastern capitals of Sydney, Melbourne, or Adelaide, and the domestic carriers service these routes daily. In planning an itinerary it's worth remembering that you can fly to Perth from Cairns and the Barrier Reef via Alice Springs and Ayers Rock.

From Perth, Ansett Airlines, 26 St. George's Terr., (09) 323-1111, and Australian Airlines, 55 St. George's Terr., (09) 323-8444, have regular connections to major centers in the state. Smaller towns are serviced by Skywest, Perth Airport, (09) 478-9999, and East West Airlines, 140 St. George's Terr., (09) 321-9232.

## Taking the Train

The major rail line links Perth with Sydney, 4,000 km (about 2,500 miles) to the east. The journey takes 65 hours and is run by the Indian Pacific, departing Perth every Sun., Mon., and Thurs., and Sydney on Thurs., Sat. and Sun. The *Trans Australian* also follows this route across the Nullarbor Plain to Adelaide with connections to Melbourne. It leaves on Wed. and Sat. The first section of this line—east of Perth to Kalgoorlie—is serviced by the *Prospector* every day except Sun. The *Australind* serves the line from Perth south to Bunbury. All inter- and intra-state trains leave from the terminal at West Parade, East Perth. Telephone (09) 326-2222 for fares and bookings.

## Taking the Bus

The major coach companies have express services into and within the West. Short of walking or hitching, this is probably the most economical way of covering this vast state. The coaches are air-conditioned, have toilet facilities on board, and screen videos to pass the time, but long hauls will still be something of an endurance test. From Perth north to Broome, the gateway to the Kimberleys, is 2,312 km (about 1,500 miles). Kununurra near the Northern Territory border is an additional 1,000 km (630 miles), and Darwin another 880 km (554 miles). The long-distance operators from Perth include Ansett Pioneer, 26 St. George's Terr., (09) 325-8855; Deluxe, 762 Hay St., (09) 322-7877; and Greyhound, 26 St. George's Terr., (09) 478-1122.

## Driving

You might choose to hire a car to explore Perth and its environs, the southwest corner, and the goldfields, which are about six hours' drive to the east. Because of huge drop-off fees, it's inadvisable to hire a car for a trip to the far north or Northern Territory (unless, of course, you plan to return to Perth). Car-rental firms in Perth include Avis, 46 Hill St., (09) 325-7677; Budget, 960 Hay St., (09) 322-1100; Thrifty, 33 Milligan St., (09) 481-1999; and Hertz, 39 Milligan St., (09) 321-7777. They're also represented at the airport. To hire a car you must be over 21 and have a current driver's licence (international driving permits accepted). Speed limits in W.A. are 60 km.p.h. in built-up areas and 110 km.p.h. on the open road unless otherwise signposted.

If there are, for example, four people traveling together, consider taking your accommodation with you by hiring a campervan or motor home. This is only cost effective if shared with a group because the fees are considerably higher than sedan rental. Westland Travel, 708 Canning Hwy., Applecross, (09) 364-5529, is one Perth agent.

Major highways in W.A. are the Albany Hwy., which leads to the southwest corner, and the Great Eastern Hwy. west to Kalgoorlie, eventually connecting with the Eyre Hwy., passing across the Nullarbor Plain and into the eastern states. To travel north, you can take the North West Coastal Hwy. or head inland and north on the Great Northern Hwy., which rejoins the coast just north of Port Hedland. The Great Northern continues up the coast to Broome and Derby, west through Fitzroy Crossing and Halls Creek, then north to Wyndham and Kununurra. From the latter you can join the Victoria Hwy. to Katherine in the Northern Territory and head up the Stuart Hwy. to Darwin.

**Don't even consider this trip to the Northern Territory if time is at a premium. Some experienced Outback drivers allow twice the time the journey should take because breakdowns can mean delays of days. If there are two or more drivers a useful tip in traveling long distances is to change every 50 or 100 kilometers (30 to 60 miles). Taking frequent breaks, stretching the legs, and being able to take your eyes off the road can add hours to a safe driving day.**

## Organized Tours

If you'd rather someone else did the organizing and driving, a number of safari tour operators combine the highlights of the far north of W.A. and the Northern Territory's Top End. They include Bill King's Destination Australia, 3/148 St. Kilda Rd., Melbourne, Victoria 3004, (03) 820-0700, telex 152369, and Amesz Adventure Charters, 223 Collier Rd., Bayswater, W.A. 6053, (09) 271-2696, telex 92212. Some tours have tent accommodation options for those who want to rough it a little.

For further information on touring in the West contact the **Western Australian Tourist Centre,** 772 Hay St., Perth, W.A. 6000, (09) 322-2999, telex 93030.

# Perth

With the Indian Ocean on one side, and the Swan River mean-dering through it, the water seems to intrude on Perth more than any other Australian city. As the brochures frequently proclaim, Perth also has more hours of sunshine than any other capital, so for most of the year it's appealing to head outdoors. They don't tell you that Perth can also be windy, not so pleasant in winter, but a welcome relief at the end of a 40° C (around 100° F) summer day in the form of a breeze known as the Fremantle Doctor.

Perth's port of Fremantle, or Freo as it is called by most, is 19 kilometers (12 miles) from the city center—though it's hard to tell where Perth ends and Fremantle begins. Fremantle has another alias—Bond City—a reference to the developmental facelift the city underwent preceding the defense of the America's Cup in 1987, and the role of Alan Bond in financing the exercise. These days, the reminders of those heady five months are evident in the marinas and the concentration of hotels, restaurants, and tourist facilities. Most of Fremantle's historic buildings, from the days when it was the first Australian port for most travelers from Europe, have been restored, which adds a village atmosphere.

If the surf at your doorstep appeals, consider staying in Freo or in one of the beach suburbs, such as Scarborough, to the north and exploring the region from there. With a combined population of slightly more than one million, traffic jams are almost unknown, so it's a short taxi, bus, or train ride between the two centers.

Perth's central business district is compact and easy to explore on foot. The major shopping area centers on Hay and Murray streets. St. George's Terrace is the main street, lined with office towers and historic buildings.

## TRAVEL

There are **taxi stands** throughout the city or you can book one by phoning Green and Gold at (09) 328-3300 or Black and White at (09) 328-8288.

Transperth operates the suburban **bus, train,** and **ferry services.** A Transperth ticket is valid for all public transport for two hours after the purchase time. There is a free City Clipper service around the CBD as well as regular services to the suburbs. Suburban train lines terminate at Fremantle, Midland, and Armadale, and they leave from the main station, Perth Central on Wellington St. A ferry service runs from the Barrack St. Jetty to South Perth, and this is a good way to travel to the Perth Zoo. Route and timetable information is available from Transperth's head office, 125 St. George's Terr., (09) 221-1211.

One novel way to see some of the city sights is on the Perth Tram (a bus actually), which plies between the city center and the Burswood Casino and takes in Kings Park en route. First tram leaves 124 Murray St. (near Barrack St.) at 9:30 A.M. and every 1½ hours until 6:30 P.M. Bell stops at major hotels. Tel. (09) 325-6893 for details. Fremantle has train tours daily from the Fremantle Town Hall. Tel. (09) 335-8487.

## ORGANIZED TOURS

A number of operators provide day and half-day tours of Perth and environs. Destinations include the Yanchep National Park and Atlantis Marine Park, 60 km (83 miles) north of Perth, tel. (095) 61-1600, where dolphins, sea lions, and seals perform; El Caballo Blanco Andalusian dancing horse stud farm, 60 km east of Perth, (095) 73-1288; historic city buildings, and Fremantle. You can also visit the Avon Valley and the Benedictine community of New Norcia by day tour, but both destinations are worthy of closer inspection and are covered in the Midwest section below. Recommended coach companies include Great Western Tours, (09) 328-4542, and Feature Tours, (09) 381-3780.

You can learn of Perth's history and have a glimpse of some of its more prestigious suburbs by **cruising on the Swan River.** The Captain Cook, (09) 325-3341, has lunch and coffee cruises daily from number 2 jetty, Barrack St. The paddle steamer *Decoy,* (09) 325-5269, also makes daily river trips and has jazz cruises on Friday evenings, departing from number 5 jetty, Barrack St.

Alternatively, cruise up river to the Swan Valley wine district and the home of two of the state's most prestigious labels, Houghton's and Sandalford. Lunch (weekdays) and dinner (Fri. and Sat.) cruises with tastings at the winery are included in the price, which is around $35. Book for the *Miss Sandalford* or *Lady Houghton* on (09) 325-6033. Both boats depart from the Barrack St. jetty.

The West is justly famous for its wildflowers and visitors can see them in full glory in **King's Park Botanic Gardens** from April to Oct. During this period, free guided tours leave at 10 A.M. Tues. and Wed. from the Karri log near the restaurant.

## ❦ ACCOMMODATIONS

Perth boasts more five-star hotels on a population basis than any other capital, and at slow times rates become very competitive. If you book through the Western Australian Tourist Centre even better deals and weekend packages are sometimes available. Unless otherwise indicated, hotels in this section accept all major credit cards.

**The Perth International,** 10 Irwin St., Perth 6000, (09) 325-0481, has standard rooms beginning at $120 and executive rooms from $160. The latter include a continental breakfast in the tariff and provide access to the executive business center, and complimentary afternoon tea, pre-dinner champagne, and canapés. The hotel has a pool and also contains one of Perth's finest restaurants, The Irwin Room, where the freshest local produce is prepared in cuisine moderne style, the modern French-style cuisine greatly favored by Australian chefs. Try the local marron with avocado mousseline, sugar-cured Tasmanian salmon, or the fresh goose liver en brioche with raspberry vinaigrette. Dinner will cost $65 a head without wine, and even if you're not staying in house, try to fit in a visit.

**The Merlin,** 99 Adelaide Terr., Perth 6000, (09) 323-0121, has its luxury accommodation around an atrium hung with massive kites. Room rates begin at $140, and its restaurant, Rama Thai, is highly recommended. There is a pool as well as a sauna.

The **Burswood Casino Resort** is located between the city (3 km, 2 miles) and airport (5 km, 3 miles) on the banks of the Swan River. If the gaming tables in the adjoining casino don't appeal, maybe the pool, surrounding parkland, golf course, and tennis courts will. The address is Great Eastern Hwy., Victoria Park, Perth 6000, (09) 362-7777, telex 92450, and double rooms range from $120 a night.

More moderately priced accommodation is available at **Miss Maud's European Hotel**—if you can cope with the decor which is Scandinavian cutesy. Single rooms are available from $60 and doubles from $75 and these rates include a hearty smorgasbord breakfast. It's located at 97 Murray St., Perth 6000, (09) 325-3900, telex 93176.

**The Adelphi,** 130a Mounts Bay Rd., Perth 6000, (09) 322-4666, telex 95080, is a few blocks from the CBD at the foot of Kings Park. It has apartments with separate bedrooms, living areas, and kitchens, for $50 double. Room service is also available and there's a deli on the premises.

Budget pub accommodation is available at the **Regatta Hotel,** right in the city center at 560 Hay St., Perth 6000, (09) 325-5155. A double room will cost $47, but you'll have to share bathroom facilities.

Scarborough is a 20-minute taxi ride along the West Coast Hwy. from the city center. Top of the range accommodation in the beach suburb 17 km (about 10 miles) north of Fremantle and 15 km from the city is available at the Bond development, **Observation City,** the Esplanade, Scarborough Beach, Scarborough 6019, (09) 245-1000, telex 95782. Every room has a balcony with an ocean view and standard double units begin at $120. Suites are available from $400 and the complex has a heated pool and health center, four restaurants, six bars, and two night clubs.

More modest self-catering accommodation in Scarborough is available at **West Beach Lagoon,** 251 West Coast Hwy., Scarborough 6019, (09) 341-6122, telex 93898. Each apartment has two bedrooms and a separate kitchen and living/dining area. Rates begin at $90 a night. The complex has a pool, spa, sauna, and gym.

Closer to Fremantle shopping precinct (about 10 minutes' walk) is the **Trade Winds Hotel,** 59 Canning Hwy., Fremantle 6160, (09) 339-8188, telex 93898. It overlooks the Swan River and is about five minutes' walk from Port Beach. The hotel also has a pool, spa, and gym. There is hotel (shared bathrooms) accommodation for $35 single and $45 double, or studio apartments (with kitchenettes) for $70 single and $80 double. Apartments with separate bedrooms are $80 single and $90 double. There are two bars, a restaurant, deli, barbecue area, and pizza shop on the premises.

The **Esplanade Plaza Hotel,** at the corner of Marine Terr. and Essex St., is right in the center of Fremantle 6160, (09) 430-4000, telex 96977, overlooking the fishing boat harbor which was the home of the America's Cup Defense Headquarters. It's a development from that era, based on a verandaed colonial building and so artfully managed that it's hard to determine which parts aren't original. Room rates are $80 double for a standard room, $120 for a superior suite, and $150 for an executive studio. There are several bars and restaurants in the central atrium, as well as a pool, spa, sauna, and gym.

Many buildings from Perth's pioneering days have been preserved and a stroll around the city center will show you a number of them. The **Barracks Archway** is a memorial to the early colonists, all that remains of what in the 1860s was headquarters for soldier settlers who opened up farming in the state. It's on St. George's Terrace (West), in front of Parliament House. **Perth Town Hall,** corner Hay and Barrack streets, was built by convict labor between 1867 and 1870, and it's said that the bricklayers left their mark on the clock tower since the windows are shaped like the broad arrows that marked the prisoners' clothing. Nearby on Barrack Street a tablet set into the footpath commemorates the founding of Perth in 1829.

The **Old Perth Boys' School** on St. George's Terrace, opposite King St., is a church-style stone building constructed in 1854 as the government school. In 1898 it became an annex to the Perth Technical College, and today it's the **gift shop** for the National Trust of W.A. It's open Monday through Friday from 10 A.M. to 3 P.M. and quality Australian is for sale; telephone (09) 321-2754.

**The Cloisters,** the first secondary school in the state, is also on St. George's Terrace, opposite Mill Street. It was built in 1858 and is noteworthy for the brickwork. **The Deanery** is farther down St. George's Terrace, at the corner of Pier Street. It was built for the first Dean of Perth in the 1850s and is one of few remaining residences from this period. The Cloisters is now a shopping arcade open from 8:30 A.M. to 5:30 P.M. Monday through Friday; Thursday till 9 P.M.; 8:30 A.M. to 1 P.M. on Saturdays. **Government House,** the official residence of the Governor of W.A., built between 1859 and 1864, is across the road. It's romantic in design with Gothic arches and turrets, reminiscent of the Tower of London. The **Old Courthouse** is in Stirling Gardens off St. George's Terrace. It's Perth's oldest surviving public building, constructed in Georgian style in 1836, and now serves as the offices for the Law Society of W.A.

The **Old Mill** is a little farther afield at Narrows Bridge, South Perth. Built as a flour mill in 1835, it now serves as a museum of the pioneer days with relics of agriculture and domestic items on display. Open Sunday, Monday, Wednesday, and Thursday from 1 P.M. to 5 P.M. and Saturday from 1 to 4 P.M. While you're in the area, visit the **Perth Zoo,** Labouchere Road, South Perth. Major exhibits are a walk-through aviary, an open wallaby park, and nocturnal native animal house. Open daily from 10 A.M. to 5 P.M., admission $4, telephone (09) 367-7988. To get there from the city take the ferry from Barrack Street jetty.

Be sure to take a stroll through **Kings Park,** Kings Park Road, 404 hectares of bushland just minutes from the city in West Perth. There are great views of Perth and the river and in September and October the wildflowers are at their best. Bikes can be hired near the kiosk.

If you'd like a taste of farm life but can't make it to the Outback, the **Agridome,** Southwest Highway, Munijong, (095) 25-5455, is open from 10 A.M. to 4 P.M. every day except Tuesday. You'll see sheep shearing, sheep dog trials, and a sheep parade at the farm. Admission $8. Special animal parade on weekends at 2 P.M. To get to the Agridome from Perth (an hour's drive) take the Albany Highway and turn off Armadale on Southwest Highway.

## Fremantle

As well as a dining and shopping mecca, Fremantle is a rewarding destination for those with an interest in history. It's there, at street level, in countless colonial buildings, and also in complexes such as the convict-built **Fremantle Museum and Arts Centre,** Finnerty Street, (09) 335-8211. Open Monday through Thursday from 10:30 A.M. to 5 P.M.; Friday through Sunday 1 to 5 P.M.; holidays 9:30 A.M. to 5 P.M. Admission free. The **Western Australian Maritime Museum,** Cliff Street, (09) 335-8211, contains displays chronicling the state's early visitors, from the Dutch in the 1600s to the British settlement in 1929. Open Monday through Thursday from 10:30 A.M. to 5 P.M., Friday through Sunday from 1 P.M. to 5 P.M., admission free. The **Round House** on High Street was built in 1831 as a jail and visitors can see the cells where convicts were chained at night. Open daily from 10 A.M. to 5 P.M. The **Warder's Quarters** on Henderson Street are a row of terraces built in 1850 to house the guards of Fremantle Prison. They serve the same purpose today and aren't open to the public.

# SHOPPING

Emu farming is a new Australian industry being developed in the West. The body leather is prized for its quality and the tanned feet skin has a reptilian appearance and is used for trims. You can buy **emu leather** garments, belts, wallets, and other accessories at Emu Tech, Shop 33, Peppermint Grove, (09) 384-0318. Fashion designer Dreske Somoss, 51 Queen Victoria Street, Fremantle, (09) 335-6851, specializes in the medium.

For **Aboriginal art and craft,** head for the government-sponsored Aboriginal Artists Gallery, Markalinga House, 251 St. George's Terrace, (09) 321-4440, or Ridji Dij, 101 South Terrace, Fremantle, (09) 335-5990. The latter also carries the Desert Designs range of clothing made from fabrics screen printed in brightly colored Aboriginal motifs.

Ceramic, porcelain, Western Australian hardwood, and metal **objects by local artists** are for sale at the Crafts Council of W.A., first floor, Perth City Railway Station; (09) 325-2799.

The Argyle mine in the Kimberleys yields white, smokey bronze, deep brown, and yellow **diamonds** as well as pink diamonds, unique to the area. You can buy them in Perth from Charles Edward Jewellers, corner of Piccadilly Arcade and Hay Street Mall, (09) 321-3319. High-quality **cultured pearls** from Broome are also available here.

The **Fremantle markets** are in a huge brick warehouse built in 1897. Stalls sell local produce, crafts, and ethnic food. The markets building is on the corner of South Terrace and Henderson Street, (09) 335-2515, open Friday from 9 A.M. to 9 P.M., Saturday from 9 A.M. to 5 P.M., and Sunday from 11 A.M. to 5 P.M.

# RECREATION

With such a pleasant climate Perth residents tend to make use of the great outdoors and go swimming, surfing, and picnicking in the city's many parks. Spectator sports are **Australian Rules Football** in winter and **cricket** in summer. Coordinating bodies for the former are the W.A.F.L. (Western Australian Football League, read "waffle") and the latter, the W.A.C.A. (Western Australian Cricket Association, read "wacker"). W.A.F.L. headquarters are in the suburb of Subiaco (five minutes in a taxi from the city center) and the W.A.C.A. homeground is in the inner city suburb of East Perth. The newspapers will advise current matches.

Popular ocean **beaches** north of Fremantle are City, Cottesloe, Floreat, Scarborough, and North beaches. These beaches have good surfing. The nearest to Perth center is

City Beach. Take Transperth bus 84 from Wellington Square opposite Raine Square. Port Beach and Swan River beaches are calm. Port Beach is at North Fremantle. Swan River beaches close to the city include areas at South Perth (by car take the Narrows Bridge). Parks in Midland have Swan River beach access. Take a taxi, or by car head southwest from the city on Mounts Bay Road. Transperth, (09) 221-1211, will advise routes and timetable for buses. You can also hire hobie cats and sail on the river from Mitchell Park, South Perth. (To get to Mitchell Park take the ferry from the Barrack Street jetty to South Perth. Walk west down South Perth Esplanade to the park. Or, better yet, take a taxi—it's much faster than using public transport. However, if you must, bus 36 or 38 from St. George's Terrace stops at Mitchell Park.)

The City of Perth **Golf Course,** The Boulevard, Floreat, welcomes visitors. Equipment can be rented at the golf course. Telephone (09) 387-1496 for details. (To get there, take Mitchell Freeway northwest of Perth city and get off at the Floreat Beach exit. There is no public transportation to the course, so, if you don't have your own car, take a taxi.)

At Cable Ski Park, Troode Street, Spearwood, **water skiers** are transported around the waterways by means of a cable tow rope. Instruction is available; skis, life jackets, wet suits, and lockers can be rented. Open from 10 A.M. to 8 P.M., (09) 481-6888. Spearwood is a 15-minute taxi ride from the city center, a short distance south of Fremantle. From Perth, take the Kiwana Freeway south across Narrows Bridge and turn west on Canning Highway to Fremantle. You can also **water ski** and **parasail** on the Swan River at Ski Craze, Narrows Bridge, South Perth, (09) 341-7304. **Boats** can be hired as well.

## ☙ RESTAURANTS

Seafood is high in quality and readily available in Western Australia. Scampi, a large deepwater prawn, is also caught off the coast, though most are frozen at sea and can have a mushy texture. Marron, large freshwater crayfish, are the most sought-after crustaceans, but hard to find and expensive.

Western Australia's major wine regions are the Swan Valley and Margaret River. Labels to look for from the former are Sandalford, Houghton's, and Evans & Tate, and from the latter, Leeuwin Estate, Cape Mentelle, Moss Wood, and Vasse Felix. Pub breweries are popular as well and at the Sail and Anchor Hotel on South Terr., Fremantle you can try made-on-the-premises ales and lagers.

Credit cards widely accepted are AE—American Express, V—Visa, MC—Master Card, DC—Diner's Club.

# Perth

Chinese restaurants account for nearly a third of the city's 1,500 eating places and **The Emperor's Court,** 66 Lake St., (09) 328-8860, is frequently accoladed for its Cantonese cuisine. It's licensed, open weekdays for lunch, and every night for dinner. Entrees range $10–$15 (for seafood). Major cards accepted.

**Farquies Restaurant,** 18 Glyde St., Mosman Park, (09) 384-2539, is licensed and BYOB and presents creative cuisine in an indoor/outdoor setting. Located in Mosman Park near north Fremantle; take the Stirling Hwy. from the city. Farquies is open for dinner Mon.–Sat. and on Sun. holds "paupers and princes" dinners with selections from pedigree hot dogs to caviar and truffles. Major cards accepted; dinner without wine will cost around $30 a head.

**Janica & Me,** 376 Fitzgerald St., North Perth, (09) 328-6220, located in an inner-city suburb just five minutes north of the city by taxi, has a garden setting for summer evenings, and is open for lunch Sun. and dinner Tues.–Sat. Food is innovative Australian; in particular there is an Indonesian influence on the menu here—try satays, and local seafood stir-fry. Three courses will cost around $30. Major cards.

**The Matilda Bay Restaurant,** 3 Hackett Dr., Crawley, (09) 386-5425, is an elegant establishment overlooking the river on one side and Kings Park on the other. Crawley is a river-side suburb 5 km (3 miles) west of the city. Take bus number 70 or 71 from St. George's Terr. or, save the effort and time, and take a taxi. The menu offerings include char-grilled buffalo steaks and baked avocado filled with seafood. The restaurant is licensed, open for lunch Mon.–Fri. and dinner Mon.–Sat. Major credit cards are accepted; dinner without liquor will cost about $35 a head.

**The Ord St. Café,** 27 Ord St., West Perth, (09) 321-6021, is a Perth institution for snacks and suppers. Located just five minutes from the city by car or taxi, the restaurant is open for cuisine moderne—a recent menu featured loin of pork with a red currant glaze and Asian-inspired chicken salad; lunch and dinner Mon.–Fri.; three courses cost about $30. Licensed, it accepts major cards.

**The Oyster Bar,** 88 James St., Northbridge, (09) 328-7888, has held its reputation as Perth's best seafood restaurant for more than twenty years. Located five minutes by taxi from city center, or walk over the Horshoe Bridge from the Perth Railway Station. No one could call the bar intimate but the atmosphere is always lively, and dinner will cost around $25 a head, more if you have crayfish. Open for lunch Mon.–Fri. and dinner Mon.–Sat.; BYOB; major cards welcome. No shortage of nightclubs in the area for after-dinner entertainment.

**Sabbadini's al Fogolar,** 231 Stirling Hwy., Claremont, (09) 383-1414, is between Perth and Fremantle, and specializes in Northern Italian fare with game, pasta, gnocchi, and polenta featuring. It's open for lunch Thurs. and Fri., dinner Mon.–Sat., is licensed, and has a cocktail bar. Three courses around $35; major cards.

For night owls, **Fast Eddy's Café,** corner Hay and Milligan sts., (09) 321-2552, has an upbeat atmosphere for snacks (burgers, nachos, sandwiches) 24 hours. Main courses around the $8 mark.

**Bernie's Café,** 140 Mount Bay Rd., is open 4 P.M.–4 A.M. for burgers in a garden setting. Among the claims this Perth institution can make are that it was Perth's first late-night eatery (opened 1939) and the first restaurant to serve hamburgers in Australia (to homesick U.S. servicemen during WW2).

## Fremantle

**The Bridges Seafood Restaurant,** 24 Tydeman Rd., North Fremantle, (09) 530-4433, is open for lunch Mon.–Fri. and dinner seven nights. To get there, take the Stirling Hwy. from the city. Specialties include local seafood—marron, scampi, and dhufish. Licensed, major cards, and three courses for about $30.

**Lombardo's Fishing Boat Harbour Complex,** Mews Rd., Fremantle, (09) 430-4343, includes a bistro, à la carte restaurant, fish-and-chip shop, and food stalls. Wander in and take your pick from elegant dining to take-away. The bistro and restaurant accept credit cards.

**The Oyster Beds Restaurant,** 26 Riverside Rd., East Fremantle, (09) 339-1611, is built over the water and surrounded by the fishing fleet. To get there, take the Canning Hwy. The restaurant features local seafood simply prepared and presented. Open every day for lunch and dinner, live music Fri. and Sat., licensed, and major cards welcome. Dinner will run around $35 a head.

## ENTERTAINMENT

Perth entertainment is as varied as its population, though with particular emphasis on catering to the young. Night-clubbing is popular with the young locals, as is the casino, but theaters and concert halls cater to more conservative tastes.

There are a number of **cinema complexes** throughout the city including the Hoyts Centre, St. Martins Arcade, 635 Hay Street, (09) 325-4922, and Cinema City, 580 Hay Street, (09) 325-2377. Check the entertainment pages of the morning paper, *The West Australian,* for current screenings.

His Majesty's Theatre, corner Hay and King streets, (09) 322-2929, has recently been restored and is the venue for **opera and ballet.** The Perth Concert Hall, 5 St. George's Terrace, (09) 325-9944, is the place for **orchestral recitals, folk music, and concerts** by visiting artists. The Perth Entertainment Centre, Wellington Street, (09) 322-4766, is a multipurpose auditorium for large audiences—**rock concerts, entertainment spectaculars.** Check the newspaper for current events.

The **Burswood Island Casino,** Great Eastern Highway, Victoria Park, (09) 362-7777, has more than 140 gaming tables as well as restaurants and bars and is open 24 hours except Christmas Day, Good Friday, and Anzac Day (April 25).

Northbridge, a suburb beside the city center is the spot for night owls. Catering to the under-thirty crowd, **nightclubs, discos, taverns, and pubs** with live music include Aurora, on William Street; Eagle One, popular with visiting American sailors, on James Street; Hannibals, which plays disco music for those age 18–25, on Lake Street; Red Parrot, on Milligan Street, with live rock; and the Perth Underground, on Newcastle Street. All of these clubs have loud music and small dance floors. More sedate entertainment can be found at Clouds in the Sheraton Perth Hotel, Adelaide Terrace, City.

# Rottnest Island

Rottnest, meaning rat's nest, was named by the Dutch explorers who mistook the island's unique quokkas, or small members of the kangaroo family, for large rodents. The island is 11 kilometers (about 7½ miles) long and 4½ kilometers (3 miles) at its widest point. Situated just twenty kilometers (about 13 miles) off the coast from Fremantle, it's a popular destination for Perth-ites for day and extended trips. Protected and surf beaches, salt lakes, great diving, and protected wildlife make Rotto, as it's affectionately dubbed, a great spot for R&R.

## TRAVEL

There are a number of day trips to Rottnest available for around $40. These include boat transfers from Perth, lunch, and a bus tour of the island. Contact Boat Torque Cruises, Pier 4, Barrack St. Jetty, Perth, (09) 325-6033, or (09) 430-6033 in Fremantle. Alternatively, you can fly on the Rottnest Airbus which leaves Perth airport daily for around $40 round-trip. Tel. (09) 478-1322 for details. But to soak up fully the island's gentle pace you'd be advised to extend your stay. You can travel to the island from Perth with one of the day-trip boats for about $25 round-trip.

Traffic is just one of the 20th-century hazards you'll abandon—favored transport modes on Rotto are foot or pushbike. The Rottnest Island Authority, which controls most business on the island, is based in the main settlement at Thomson Bay. They run a **bike rental** agency, (09) 292-5043, behind the Rottnest Hotel (better known as the Quokka Arms), and their information center, (09) 292-5044, is on Main Jetty.

## ✻ ACCOMMODATIONS

The Rottnest Island Authority rents more than 250 **villas and cottages** on the island on a ballot system. To book one you need to write, stating the number of rooms you require. Your name and a property will be matched in the draw. Address is Rottnest Island, W.A. 6161, telex 95033. You'll need to supply your own cutlery and linen, but these can be hired from the laundrette, (09) 292-5054, which also rents TVs, fans, beach umbrellas, golf clubs, and buggies. At peak holiday times demand for this accommodation can exceed availability, and you'd probably be better off booking rooms at the Rottnest Hotel or Rottnest Lodge Resort. Both take major credit cards.

In addition to its beer garden—the most popular watering hole on the island—the **Rottnest Hotel**, (09) 292-5011, has motel-style rooms for $50 single and $80 double. The **Rottnest Lodge Resort**, (09) 292-5018, has the island's most up-market accommodations centering around an entertainment hub, which was built by convicts in 1860 and served as a prison and reformatory until 1920. These days a stay in the renovated cells is a privilege rather than a sentence and dinner, bed, and breakfast in the superior units is $104 single or $154 double. The more spacious deluxe unit packages are $124 single and $174 double. There are cheaper standard units, but since these aren't air-conditioned, they're best avoided during the warmer months. The resort has a pool and both hotels are a short walk from the beach they overlook.

**Surfers** head for Transit Reef, just outside Thomson Bay, while those preferring **protected water** opt for the basin with its white sandy beach. The basin is a short walk from the Thomson Bay settlement; just follow the signs from the shopping area past the tennis courts. In the northeast section of the island are five **lakes** with water seven times saltier than the ocean. Certainly you'll notice its buoyancy, but the curative powers claimed for it are harder to prove.

Rottnest is a wildlife reserve and on the many **walking tracks** you'll see gulls, fairy terns, oyster catchers, a variety of ducks and, of course, quokkas. One of the walks leads to Cape Vlamingh on the west end. From here you can gaze out on the Indian Ocean and perhaps contemplate the swim to the next port of call heading west—Madagascar, nearly 6,500 kilometers (4,065 miles) away. For information and maps contact the Rottnest Island Authority information center, Main Jetty, Thomson Bay.

There are ten **tennis courts** and a nine-hole **golf course** on the island and bookings can be made at the Rottnest Island Authority at Thomson Bay. Most **water sports** are run from the Marine Services, (09) 292-5113. They hire scuba equipment, snorkeling gear, dinghies, canoes, and aquabikes. They are also the agents on the island for Diving Ventures, 384 South Terrace, South Fremantle, (09) 336-1664, who conduct four-day diving courses for beginners for about $250 and accompanied dives for certified divers for $45 including all equipment.

The island's environs are the graveyards for 12 wrecked ships, and the waters are also home to the world's southernmost brain and mushroom coral, so there's plenty to reward the diver. If you'd prefer to see it all without getting wet, a submarine, the *Underwater Explorer,* cruises from Main Jetty daily; (09) 335-8417.

# The Goldfields

The discovery of gold at Coolgardie, 500 kilometers (315 miles) east of Perth, in 1892 and the following year at Kalgoorlie, 40 kilometers (25 miles) farther east, was the salvation of the struggling Western Australian colony. The ensuing rush increased the population fourfold and dozens of towns sprang up on the goldfields. Many settlements lasted only ten years. Kanowna, with 12,000 people, lasted twenty and there are at least a dozen other ghost towns testifying to those heady days.

Today, even Coolgardie, once home to 15,000 in the town and 25,000 more in the area, has a population of only 700. Kalgoorlie, where every known mineral can be found and mining has never ceased, had a population in 1902 of 30,000 with 93 hotels and eight breweries. These days gold is still the major industry, and the town, the state's largest urban center outside Perth, boasts a population of 20,000, 29 hotels, and one brewery. Its Golden Mile, said to be the richest square mile on earth, has produced more than 40 million ounces of gold and is still yielding "paydirt" thanks to modern mining techniques.

## TRAVEL

Because of its size, Kalgoorlie is the ideal base for a visitor to the goldfields. Ansett Airlines and Skywest fly there from Perth daily, and Greyhound and Ansett Pioneer coaches have regular services. *The Prospector* train also provides a daily link with Perth. See W.A. Travel, at the beginning of this chapter, for more details. To drive from Perth takes about six hours. You can hire a car in Kalgoorie from Avis, 520 Hannan St., (090) 21-1722.

## ORGANIZED TOURS

Tom Neacy's Goldfields Highlight tour, (090) 26-6037, provides four days and three nights in the region from Perth, with all meals, choice of accommodation, and travel on *The Prospector* included. Cost is either $290 or $330 per person depending on accommodation. Book by phoning direct or through the Western Australian Tourist Centre offices.

Goldrush Country Tours in Kalgoorlie has a number of options including ghost towns, a chance to fossick with metal detectors, the two-up school, and a tour of Kalgoorlie with a mine visit.

Book at their office in Palace Chambers, Maritana St., Kalgoorlie (090) 21-2954, or at the Kalgoorlie-Boulder Tourist Bureau, 250 Hannan St., Kalgoorlie (090) 21-1413. All tours leave from Palace Chambers which is next door to the grand Palace Hotel. Costs are around $20 for each tour.

## ❦ ACCOMMODATIONS AND RESTAURANTS

For a taste of the 1890s heyday, you can stay in one of the gracious old pubs which give the streets of Kalgoorlie such distinction. The restaurants mentioned are the best in the area, but expect the Aussie bush standard fare—"meat and three veg." All of the Kalgoorlie pubs listed below accept major credit cards.

A young American, H. P. Hoover, managed a mine here and penned an erotic poem to one of Kalgoorlie's barmaids, an unconventional act by the Quaker who was to become president of the United States.

**The Palace Hotel,** on Maritana St., Kalgoorlie 6430, (090) 21-2788, has a sweeping carved jarrah staircase and is surrounded by ornate verandas. Air-conditioned rooms (with private bathrooms) range from $50 single and $60 double. Unfortunately the elegant dining room is now reserved for functions, but The Palace has a steakhouse where country breakfasts and lunches are served as well as dinner.

**The Old Australia** is another grand hotel with both pub and motel-style accommodations, all with air-conditioning. It's at the corner of Hannan and Maritana sts., Kalgoorlie 6430, (090) 21-1320, and pub rooms are $35 single and $45 double, while units are $50 single and $60 double.

**The Midas Motel,** 409 Hannan St., Kalgoorlie 6430, (090) 21-3088, has a pool, sauna, spa, and licensed restaurant, and room rates are $60 single, $75 double, and $85 for an executive suite. All rooms are air-conditioned.

Budget accommodation is available at **Surrey House,** 9 Boulder Rd., Kalgoorlie 6430, (090) 21-1340. Its rooms are $25 single and $36 double and a cooked breakfast is $6. There's a café on the premises and bathroom facilities are shared.

Start your tour of the Goldfields on Kalgoorlie's main street, Hannan, where there's a statue of Paddy who gave the street his name by being the first to find gold there in 1893. A tree and a plaque in the street mark the exact spot. You'll notice that the streets are twice as wide as in normal country towns. They were made that way to accommodate the camel trains which were the major form of transport in the early days. The **Golden Mile Museum** is also on Hannan Street, located in the former British Arms Hotel, reputedly the narrowest pub in the southern hemisphere. Inside, however, is a broad slice of goldfields history including old mining equipment, a working scale model of a stamp battery, and photographic records of the first gold rushes. The museum is open between 10:30 A.M. and 4:30 P.M. every day and admission is $2.

The **Hainault Tourist Mine** covers 6 hectares of the Golden Mile and tours conducted by ex-miners leave at 10:30 A.M. and 1, 2:30, and 3:30 P.M. daily. For information call (090) 93-1065. You'll see the power house, winding room, and boilers, and descend a shaft for demonstrations on how the mines used to be ventilated and gold ore extracted from the rock walls. When this mine ceased to be worked in 1968, it had produced 1,150,000 ounces of gold.

**Boulder,** Kalgoorlie's twin town on the Golden Mile, still has its town hall, post office, and courthouse. But the Boulder Block, which once held six hotels where liquor flowed around the clock for miners on shift work, has disappeared into goldfields legend. Not so the **Loop Line Railway,** once a vital link for taking miners to work and hauling equipment, now an interesting way for tourists to see the main mining area. The train is known as the *Rattler,* a reference to the quality of the ride. It's hour-long tours leave the Boulder Railway Station Monday through Saturday at 11 A.M. and Sunday at 1:30 and 3 P.M. Telephone the operators, the Golden Mile Railway Society, at (090) 93-1157 for details.

A Goldfields institution which existed illegally for a long time, but was recently sanctioned by the W.A. government, is the **two-up school,** on the Broad Arrow Road, just north of Kalgoorlie. The "game," as this distinctly Aussie form of gambling is called, is now played openly every day except race days and miners' pay days.

Many of **Coolgardie's** historic buildings have been faithfully restored, lending dignity to this town which has otherwise known much better times. Although a shadow of her 1890s self, spirits are once again high as the most significant strike in recent years in Australia was recently made near the town.

Although the days when nuggets littered the ground are long gone, fossickers still occasionally strike lucky. If you fancy trying your hand, you must first obtain a Miner's Right from the Department of Mines, Brookham Street, Kalgoorlie.

# W.A.'s Southwest

Ask ten people the reason for visiting W.A.'s southwest corner and you'll receive as many answers. This immensely varied region is a loose triangle formed by Albany, 412 kilometers (260 miles) south of Perth; Augusta, about 400 road kilometers (252 miles) west, where the Southern and

Indian Oceans meet, and the port of Bunbury, 175 kilometers (110 miles) south of Perth. Wine buffs regard its Mount Barker and Margaret River districts as some of the country's premium wine producers; those of a botanical bent go to see the wildflowers and the tall timbers of the karri and jarrah forests; surfers say the waves between Cape Naturaliste and Cape Leeuwin are Australia's best; while outdoor enthusiasts maintain that the same stretch of coastline has the most spectacular caves and, on the Blackwood River, the most challenging white water.

## TRAVEL

You can fly to Albany with Skywest or tour the region with Deluxe or Westrail coaches. The *Australind* train links Perth with Bunbury and coaches connect to the centers in the south. But this is an area best explored by car and it can be toured in a circuit by traveling from Perth south to Albany on the Albany Hwy., west along the South Coast and Brockman hwys. to Augusta, then north via the Bussell Hwy. to Bunbury. Return to Perth by the scenic Old Coast Rd., or the South Western Hwy.

## ORGANIZED TOURS

The Pinnacle Travel Centre, corner of Hay and Irwin sts., Perth, (09) 325-9455, conducts day tours to the jarrah forests and Margaret River vineyards and caves, but bear in mind that it's a long trip (about 12 hours) and much of your time is spent on the coach. Cost is around $50 including lunch.

Southern Haven Tours, (098) 41-1088, takes groups to the area's major attractions for $15 for half days and $30 full day. Tours leave from Albany Tourist Bureau. For bookings and information contact the Albany Tourist Bureau, Peels Place, Albany, W.A. 6330; (098) 41-1088.

## ❦ ACCOMMODATIONS AND RESTAURANTS

Albany is a popular holiday destination for Western Australians and there's a wide range of motels, guesthouses, cottages, and flats available. Details are available from the **Albany Tourist Bureau,** Peels Place, Albany, W.A. 6330; (098) 41-1088. Most accommodations in this area are air-conditioned and accept major credit cards. Recommended motels include the **Dog Rock Motel,** 303 Middleton Rd., Albany 6330, (098) 41-4422, which has single rooms from $60 and doubles from $75. There is no pool. If you prefer more personalized accommodation, the **Norman House** private hotel, 28 Stirling Terr., Albany 6330, (098) 41-5995, should appeal. This restored 1850 two-story residence has eight guest rooms with shared bathrooms for $28 single and $45 double including cooked breakfasts. A three-course home-style dinner is $15 and a picnic lunch $6.

Pemberton is between Albany and Augusta, home of majestic karri forests and rivers brimming with rainbow trout. You can stay near the town at the **Karri Valley Resort** and from your bedroom balcony watch trout jump in the lake below. They'll feature on the menu at the resort's restaurant, along with the freshwater crayfish, called marron, which are also found in the area. Accommodation is in motel-style units for around $75 double, or two-bedroom chalets with kitchens for $100 a night. The resort's address is Vasse Hwy., Pemberton 6260; (097) 76-2020.

While Augusta has an interesting history, spectacular coastal scenery, and limestone caves, it only has one motel, the **Augusta Hotel Motel,** Blackwood Ave., Augusta 6290, (097) 58-1994. The motel does have a pool. You might prefer to base yourself in the more central Margaret River area (about 45 km, 28 miles, north).

The **Captain Freycinet Motel,** Tunbridge St., in the township of Margaret River 6285, (097) 57-2033, has 62 units for $70 double. In addition to a pool, there are a cocktail bar and restaurant, but if you'd rather not eat in house, the **1885 Restaurant** is worth a visit. The name is a reference to the former residence's construction date, and it's located on Farrelly St., (097) 57-2302. The menu features local produce such as trout and marron and you'll also be able to sample the excellent Margaret River brie and many of the district's finest wines.

You'll learn even more about the quality of life in the southwest by staying at **Merribrook,** via Cowaramup, about 20 km (13 miles) north of Margaret River. Billed as an outdoor adventure farm, the 160-acre property is structured along ski resort lines with a central dining room and lodge surrounded by six rammed-earth chalets, a type of construction similar to mud brick—the walls are made of locally quarried compressed earth; the method was pioneered by a Margaret River local. At Merribrook, the lake was created by the excavation for this building material). Activities here range from bushwalking, canoeing, caving (they'll take you to some not open to tourists), abseiling, and cycling to less strenuous pursuits such as winery touring, bird watching, or simply reading a book by the lakeside. Expert instruction is available and guests are welcome to do everything or nothing. Meals are set menu, with the emphasis on fresh local produce and the waffles and museli at breakfast definitely justify working up an appetite. The retreat is BYOB, (097) 55-5490. Dinner, bed-and-breakfast rates range from $60 per person per day to $90 per person with all outdoor activities.

Another novel way of sampling the charms of the Margaret River district is to take your accommodation with you in the form of a vardo, or horse-drawn wagon. Each wagon is fully equipped with bedding and cooking equipment and the owners will supply hampers for $10 per person per day for all food requirements. They also provide maps of the area showing camp sites and call by at night to help with harnessing and care of the horses. **Vardo Horse-Drawn Holidays** is based on Bullant Dr., off the Bussell Hwy. between Augusta and Margaret River; (097) 57-7510. Three-day packages are around $350.

**Albany,** the site of W.A.'s first permanent European settlement in 1826, offers rugged coastal scenery, protected harbors and beaches for fishing and swimming, and relics of the pioneering days. Landmarks to visit in the area include the granite boulder in the shape of a canine head, **Dog Rock,** on the road to Middleton Beach; **The Gap,** a 24-meter sheer drop to pounding surf; and the **Natural Bridge,** a huge granite suspension which refuses to give in to the swelling seas and clings to the mainland.

**Albany Whaleworld** operated as the Cheynes Beach Whaling Station until 1978 and now functions as a museum to the state's oldest industry. The restored whale chaser, *Cheynes IV,* recalls the days when the boats could bring in up to 850 whales a season, a horrifying statistic when you realize that the station operated for more than 100 years. The museum is open daily from 9 A.M. to 5 P.M. and guided tours are available on the hour from 10 A.M. to 4 P.M. Call (098) 44-4347.

Safe swimming **beaches** include Middleton Beach (2 kilometers from the commercial center of Albany via Middleton Road), Emu Point (10 kilometers, about 6 miles, north of the center of town) and Ellen Cove (at the southern end of Middleton Beach), and there are also protected waters at Two People's Bay. Here a wildlife reserve protects a small colony of noisy scrub birds, which were thought to be extinct until they were found in the area in 1961.

If you want to **fish** in the area you'll need a license ($6) from the Department of Fisheries and Wildlife, 108 Adelaide Terrace, Perth, or the Pemberton Trout Hatchery on the outskirts of town. The trout season is from September 1 to April 30 and besides the Karri Valley Resort's lake, the Lefroy, Treen, Warren, and Donnelly rivers are likely grounds. The marron season extends from December 15 to April 30 and you might be lucky if you try the deep pools of the Donnelly, Warren, and Gardner rivers.

The **Mt. Barker wine district** is about 50 kilometers (31 miles) north of Albany and most wineries are open for tastings. Take the Albany Highway. Labels to look for include **Alkoomi,** (098) 55-2229, **Plantagenet,** (098) 51-1150, and **Chateau Barker,** (098) 51-1452.

The nearby **Stirling Range and Porongurup national parks,** (098) 53-1095, offer bushwalking trails where you'll have plenty of opportunities to see wildflowers during the season from September to November. You can buy **dried wildflowers** from Wilson's Wildflowers, 6 Marion Street, Mt. Barker, open Monday to Friday from 2 to 5 P.M. and Saturday from 10 A.M. to noon, other times by appointment, (097) 51-1690. Further information and maps are available at the ranger bases at the park entrance. Camping is permitted in Stirling Range National Park, but not in Porongurup. Book by phoning Stirling Range (098) 27-9230.

If you're staying in the Pemberton region, Forest Products Association takes private **tours through the tall timbers** for $25 an hour. You'll see virgin and control-logged karri forests, visit a sawmill, and climb 60 meters up a spiral staircase around Gloucester Tree, the highest fire lookout tree in the world. Book through the Manjimup Timber Park, (097) 71-2915, or the Pemberton Tourist Bureau, (097) 76-1133.

You can **tour the district by horse** with Shannon Horseback Adventures, R.M.B. 134, Manjimup, W.A. 6258; (097) 73-1234. They offer two- to seven-day rides with homestead or mustering hut accommodation and meals cooked over the campfire. Costs range from $150 for the shorter rides.

Augusta, on the southwesternmost tip of Australia, boasts spectacular windswept scenery which competes for visitors' attention with limestone formations in caves that riddle the coastline. The **Cape Leeuwin Lighthouse** was built from local stone in 1895 and its foundation stone is dedicated to the world's mariners. Today, it's also a major meteorological station, open to visitors every day except Monday from 9:30 A.M. to 3 P.M.

The main cavern of **Jewel Cave,** 8 kilometers (about 5 miles) north of Augusta on Caves Road, is 100 meters high and 91 meters long. Limestone formations include a 5.9-meter straw stalactite, and deposits resembling organ pipes and a jewel casket. There's an underground lake and the cave is lit and open for inspection daily. **Lake and Mammoth caves** are farther north along Caves Road, and are also open to the public.

The 64-kilometer (40-mile) stretch of coastline from Cape Leeuwin to Cape Naturaliste is a mecca for **surfers.** Most popular beaches are Point, Redgate, and Cowaramup bays, and the Margaret River Mouth, where national and international surfing titles are held. If you'd rather something between you and the water (this doesn't mean you won't get wet) Blackwood Expeditions offer **canoeing and camping trips** on the Blackwood River. The cost is around $90 per person per day, including all meals and equipment and accompanying guide. For more details contact Box 64, Nannup, W.A. 6275; (097) 56-1081 or 56-1209.

If you'd like to sample the fruits of the Margaret River vines, most **wineries** are open for tasting. Caves Road follows the coast from Yallin up to Cape Leeuwin and passes many wineries. Established names include **Leeuwin Estate,** (097) 57-6253, **Vasse Felix,** (097) 55-5242, **Moss Wood,** (097) 55-6266, and Cape Mentelle, (097) 57-2070. Further information is available from the **Augusta-Margaret River**

**Tourist Bureau,** Bussel Highway, Margaret River, W.A. 6285, (097) 57-2147.

# W.A.'s Midwest

While the midwest of the state abounds in natural wonders, they're often in remote locations and separated by vast distances. The region can be subdivided into the Avon Valley, the Batavia Coast, from Dongara to Kalbarri, and the Gascoyne, which takes in Shark Bay, Monkey Mia Beach, and the coastal centers of Carnarvon and Exmouth. Southern parts, such as the Avon Valley, the Benedictine community of New Norcia, and the eerie petrified forest of the Pinnacles, are within day-tripping distance of Perth, though, of course, more rewarding to explore at greater length.

If you plan to head north from Perth along the North West Coastal Highway to the rock lobster capital of Geraldton (425 kilometers, that's over 200 miles, north of Perth), the Kalbarri National Park (591 kilometers, about 366 miles, from Perth), the dolphin beach of Monkey Mia (833 kilometers, over 500 miles, from Perth), or Carnarvon (904 kilometers, 560 miles, from Perth) you'll need to allow several days just to do the driving. The world's largest monocline, Mt. Augustus, is a 900-kilometer (about a 500-mile) round-trip trek inland from Carnarvon and, even when you get back to the coast, you're 150 kilometers (less than 100 miles) short of being half-way to Broome, gateway to the Kimberleys, 2,296 kilometers (about 1,500 miles) north of Perth.

**Unless you're accustomed to long-distance motoring, or have heaps of time, leave the driving to a tour operator or plan your own itinerary with one of the coach companies.**

**Even if you do decide on your own transport, the remoteness of some of the attractions in the midwest means that it's advisable to visit them from the major towns with local tour companies.**

## TRAVEL

Greyhound, Ansett Pioneer, and Deluxe service all the ports on the North West Coastal Hwy., and Ansett Airlines has regular services from Perth to Geraldton, Carnarvon, Exmouth, and centers farther north. (See Western Australia: Travel section, at the beginning of this chapter, for telephone numbers.)

## ORGANIZED TOURS

Great Western Tours, Westrail Terminal, West Parade, East Perth, (09) 328-4542, telex 197284, offer coach and air packages to most of the destinations in the Midwest. One way to reduce the pain of the long haul north to the Kimberleys would be to tour the region with them, and upon return to Perth, fly to Broome.

Pinnacle Travel Centre, corner of Hay and Irwin sts., Perth, (09) 325-9455, telex 94435, conducts day tours to the Pinnacles (12 hours; cost $55) and three-day coach trips to Monkey Mia Beach (cost $221; meals and motel accommodation included).

Mid-West Tours, 274 Seventh St., Wonthella, (099) 21-5089, conduct seven-day (from Geraldton) and eight-day (from Perth) safaris to Mt. Augustus or Monkey Mia, Carnarvon, and Exmouth. Costs are around $700 per person for each tour (ex Perth).

## ❧ ACCOMMODATIONS

Because of its size there is no feasible single base for exploring W.A.'s Mid-West, so our recommendations on where to stay will be mentioned with the destinations as we travel, like most visitors, north from Perth. The exception is the sheep station **Thundelarra,** which, although in the region, is reached via the inland Great Northern Hwy. and requires a diversion from the route that takes in the attractions on the coast.

Visitors to this 156,000-hectare station, with its historic homestead, have a chance to sample Outback life by watching, or joining in, station work. It's 5½-hours' drive from Perth, or the owners will collect guests traveling by coach from the township of Paynes Find. There's a range of accommodations, from homestead rooms with dinner, bed, and breakfast for $60 per day, to a self-contained shearer's cottage for $40 a day, and twin-share rooms in the shearers' quarters for $10 a day. There's a tennis court and swimming pool and all rates include tours of the station. Address is Thundelarra, via Wubin, W.A. 6612; (096) 64-5056.

## AVON VALLEY

The Avon Valley is W.A.'s oldest area of inland settlement, an agricultural community with a faintly gentrified air, 100 kilometers (about 62 miles) north of Perth. Its scenic bushland, historic towns such as York, Northam, and Toodyay, and range of outdoor activities make it an appealing destination for a relaxing break in your itinerary.

## ❧ ACCOMMODATIONS AND RESTAURANTS

There are motels in the major towns, but the Valley specializes in more personalized accommodation in historic inns and guesthouses. In York, **Settlers' House,** 125 Avon Terr. (York 6302), (096) 41-1096, combines 19th-century charm with 20th-century comfort in its twenty air-conditioned rooms. The suites furnished in period style surround a central complex, which was built as a residence in the 1840s and served as a staging post in the 1860s. It now includes a saloon bar and the **Ensign Dale Restaurant,** while a row of shops at the front houses tea rooms, an art and craft gallery, and bookshop. Rates are $80 per room on weekend nights and $65 midweek. A country breakfast is $10, continental, $6. The house takes major credit cards.

**Buckland,** Irishtown via Northam 6401, (096) 22-1130, a stately 1870s residence which the owners operate as a bed-and-breakfast, is via Irishtown, 12 kilometers (about 8 miles) from Northam. It has only two guest rooms, and visitors are encouraged to treat the house, with its extensive art and antique collection, as their own. Rates are $50 single and $85 double including full breakfast. No credit cards. The house is also open for inspection 10 A.M.–5 P.M. every day except Fri., $3.50 admission. Dinner isn't served at Buckland, but the owners recommend **Byfield House,** 30 Gordon St., 6401, in Northam, (096) 22-3380, where Devonshire teas and light lunches are served as well as à la carte dinners Tues.–Sun.

---

**York**'s buildings are a tribute to the restorer's art. When completed in 1911 the Town Hall boasted the largest floor space of any municipal building in W.A.; the old hospital still has its steep, shingled roof and brickwork of richly colored local clay; and the **York Motor Museum,** (096) 41-1288, open every day, houses more than 150 classic and vintage cars, motorcycles, and horse-drawn vehicles. There's also the **Balladong Farm Living Museum,** 5 Parker Road, (096) 41-1279, the state's oldest continuously operating farm. You can see blacksmiths at work, sheep being hand-shorn with blades, and a Clydesdale team. York is also a craft center, and at **Squirrel Furniture,** in the Sandalwood yards, (096) 41-1656, you can see craftsmen working with oak, or at the **Glass Workers of York,** at the corner of View Street and Suburban Road, (096) 41-1440, watch leadlight and stained-glass windows being created.

York also hosts a calendar of special events including a theater festival and music festival in alternate winters, the Flying 50, an around-the-houses speed classic for sports cars and racing cars built before 1960, and the Perth-to-York veteran car rally. The progress of the Avon Descent, one of Australia's most grueling white-water boat races, held on the last weekend of July, can be watched from the river banks in the center of town. For further information, contact the **York Tourist Bureau,** 105 Avon Terrace, (096) 41-1301.

As well as home to a colony of white swans, **Northam** is the **hot-air ballooning** capital of the West. Flights can be organized by the **Northam Tourist Bureau,** Brabazon House, 3 Beavis Place, (096) 22-2100. Also in the valley are the **Blue Gum Camel Farm,** (09) 574-1480, where you can learn to oscillate to the gait, and the **Hoddywell Archery Park,** (09) 574-2480, on the Toodyay-Clackline Road. Instruction available for beginners, open every day except Monday.

# NEW NORCIA

The Benedictine community of New Norcia, is 132 kilometers (over 80 miles) north of Perth on the Great Northern Highway. (There are several minor roads from there joining the Brand Highway, which becomes the North West Coastal Highway.) Established by the Spanish monk Dom Rosendo Salvado in 1846, the township now serves as an education center run by the monastery. Of particular interest is the wealth of **Spanish architecture,** incongruously set in the Australian bush, and the **museum and art gallery,** (096) 54-8056, open 10 A.M. to 4:30 P.M. daily, which contains Aboriginal artifacts, religious art, exquisitely embroidered vestments, and an extraordinary collection of monastic effects recording the daily life of the monks for more than a century.

## ❧ ACCOMMODATIONS AND RESTAURANTS

You can stay at the **New Norcia Hotel,** New Norcia 6509, (095) 43-8034, originally built as a guesthouse for parents visiting their children in boarding school, now decorated with some of the furnishings from the monastery. Rates are $40 for un-air-conditioned doubles and bathrooms are shared. No credit cards.

Though not a gourmet experience, meals can be had at the pub or the **New Norcia Roadhouse,** (095) 43-8020, which serves 7:30 A.M.–8:30 P.M.

# PINNACLES

The curious limestone spires of the Pinnacles are found in the **Nambung National Park,** 250 kilometers (155 miles) north of Perth. The tallest measure up to three meters and some are estimated to extend below the desert surface for as much as eight meters. The area is gradually moving in a northeasterly direction. As scrub stabilizes one section, winds erode sands from another, exposing new pinnacles. You can get maps from the park headquarters at the entrance.

## ❧ ACCOMMODATIONS

Camping is not permitted in Nambung National Park and the nearest accommodation to the park is at Cervantes, 26 km (16 miles) away. The **Cervantes Pinnacles Motel,** Lot 227, Aragon St., Cervantes 6511, (096) 52-7145, charges $55 for an air-conditioned double room. The motel has a pool and takes major credit cards. You can also stay about 100 km (63 miles) from the park at the wildflower-and-emu-raising **Waddi Farms,** Koonah Rd., Badgingarra 6521, (096) 52-9071. They have self-contained chalets for $52 a night or cabins with share facilities for $25 double. No credit cards. Dried flowers and emu leather products are for sale.

# GERALDTON

Geraldton is the major port for the rock lobster fishermen who bring in their catch from the breeding grounds of the

**Houtman Abrolhos.** The islands are also the resting place for a number of wrecked ships that struck the surrounding reefs. Most notable are the Dutch vessels, *Batavia, Zeewyk,* and *Zuytdorp,* which sank during the 17th century. Relics from these disasters can be seen at the **Geraldton Museum,** open every day Monday to Saturday, 10 A.M. to 5 P.M., Sunday 1 to 5 P.M. Visitors can see the wrecks themselves by diving off Houtman Abrolhos. Arrangements must be made through a charter boat company. Because of the delicate ecology of the islands, visitors may not land on them, but boat and plane charters operate to the area. Since charter businesses open and close frequently, it's best to check with the local tourist bureau to find out who is operating at the time. Information is available from the **Geraldton Tourist Bureau,** Civic Centre, Cathedral Avenue, (099) 21-3999.

## TRAVEL

**Great Western Tours,** (099) 21-7144, run day and half-day tours of the district's points of interest.

## ❦ ACCOMMODATIONS AND RESTAURANTS

Geraldton has a range of hotel and motel accommodation, but for a taste of a gentler era, a stay at the **Hampton Arms Inn,** Company Rd., Greenough 6530 (30 kilometers, 18 miles, south of Geraldton), (099) 26-1057, is recommended. This century-old hostelry has three guest rooms and only one bathroom, with a huge old plunge bath. Rates are $55 double (no credit cards) and the inn has a licensed restaurant.

# KALBARRI NATIONAL PARK

The Kalbarri National Park, 160 kilometers, almost 100 miles, north of Geraldton, is traversed by the **Murchison River Gorge.** Towering red cliffs, crystal pools, abundant kangaroos and emus, and, from July to January, a blaze of wildflowers make this an essential stopover on the route north. Kalbarri coachlines, (099) 37-1104, takes visitors through the gorge country and also to the bizarre Hutt River Province. Prince Leonard and Princess Shirley of Hutt seceded from the rest of Australia in 1970 in protest against the introduction of wheat quotas. The province boasts a post office with its own stamps and church. Take your passport if you'd like to record your visit. Details are available from the **Kalbarri Travel Service,** Grey Street, Kalbarri, (099) 37-1104.

## ❦ ACCOMMODATIONS

Best accommodation in Kalbarri is at the **Kalbarri Beach Resort,** Grey St., Kalbarri 6536, (099) 37-1061, which has a licensed restaurant, swimming pool, tennis courts, spa, and sauna, and is located on the beach. Self-contained air-conditioned double units are $85. All credit cards.

# MONKEY MIA BEACH

The greatest attraction of the Shark Bay Shire is Monkey Mia beach, where **dolphins** appear daily to be hand fed. They will accept only whole fish (not gutted and gilled) and visitors are asked not to feed them anything else. The dolphins come up to be rubbed under the snout or along the belly, but will swim away if anyone attempts to swim or sit in the water with them. The **Shark Bay Visitor and Travel Centre,** (099) 48-1253, conducts four-wheel-drive tours for **fishing** enthusiasts and to **Steep Point,** the most westerly tip on the Australian mainland.

## ❦ ACCOMMODATIONS AND RESTAURANTS

The only accommodation at Monkey Mia is at the **Caravan Park,** (099) 48-1320, which has on-site vans for $20 to $35 a night. You can also stay about 75 km (46 miles) from the dolphin beach at **Nanga Sheep Station,** which has a homestead made from locally quarried shell-grit blocks, two-bedroom self-contained units for $60 a night, two-berth cabins for $30 a night, and four-berth cabins for $40. No credit cards. Nanga Station, (099) 48-3992, has a liquor store and BYOB restaurant.

Also in the area is **Shell Beach,** more than 100 kilometers (60 miles) long and 10 meters deep and composed of billions of tiny shells. At **Hamelin Pool** on Shark Bay is a rare stomatalite stronghold, coral formations said to contain the world's oldest "living" fossils. You can go snorkeling or wait until low tide to see the exposed formations from shore.

# MT. AUGUSTUS

If you plan to include Mt. Augustus on your itinerary, leave the North West Coastal Highway at Carnarvon and head for Gascoyne Junction. The turnoff to the world's largest rock is about 100 kilometers (62 miles) farther west at Dairy Creek.

Mt. Augustus, which is 8 kilometers (almost 5 miles) long, 4 kilometers (2½ miles) wide, and 700 meters (2,300 feet) high, straddles two Outback properties, **Mt. Augustus Station,** (099) 43-0527, and **Cobra Station,** (099) 43-0565. The giant sandstone-and-conglomerate formation closets wildlife, rock pools, and Aboriginal art sites. You can drive to the base of Mt. Augustus and explore on foot. The station management will either take visitors to see points of interest or provide directions. Both stations have visitor accommodation in self-contained units for around $40 per person. Food and petrol are also available.

# The Kimberleys

Australia's last real frontier, the rugged country of the Kimberley Plateau in the north of W.A., is surprisingly accessible. Ansett Airlines has regular services to the western gateway towns of Broome and Derby and the eastern entry point of Kununurra, on the Northern Territory border. Kununurra is also the access point for the Bungle Bungles, a 270-square-kilometer area of templelike domes of rock banded in multicolored layers of porous sandstone. The Great Northern Highway, more than 1,000 kilometers (over 600 miles) of road which links these centers, was finally fully paved in 1986, completing a bitumen route around Australia and opening the way for Ansett-Pioneer, Deluxe, and Greyhound coaches to service the area. Getting there is no problem, but the going gets tougher once you leave the highway to explore the region. For this reason many visitors opt to tour with one of the many specialized safari companies from the entry points. Operators to the area from Perth and Darwin are mentioned in Western Australia Travel, at the beginning of this chapter.

## ORGANIZED TOURS

Undoubtedly the most luxurious way to visit the Kimberleys is on the 33-meter *Kimberley Explorer,* which plies the coast between Broome and Wyndham (100 kilometers, 62 miles, from Kununurra). The vessel can accommodate a maximum of 34 passengers and its operators are justly proud of its amenities and cuisine. Guests are taken ashore to remote beaches, visit Aboriginal art sites, cruise up the Prince Regent River to see salt-water crocs from the safety of the deck. The price of these privileges is not for the faint-hearted—12-night cruises are $5,400 per person twin share, six-nights $3,000 per person. All meals, excursions, and accommodation in en suite cabins are included in the price but air fares to Broome or Kununurra are extra. Bookings for the vessel can be made at Kimberley Explorer Cruises, Suite 25, Merlin Centre, Perth, (09) 323-6200, or at the Roebuck Bay Hotel in Broome, (091) 92-1221, fax (091) 92-2390.

Aboriginal guide Sam Lovell and his wife, Rosita, of Kimberley Safari, conduct four-wheel-drive tours from Derby with tent accommodation and camp meals. Bookings can be made direct at 34 Knowsley St., Derby; (091) 91-1084. They have 14-day safaris to the Mitchell Plateau ($2,100), eight-day tours of the Bungle Bungles ($1,300), and six-day treks to the gorges of the King Leopold Range ($900).

Regional Safaris, 1664 Farrell St., Broome, (091) 92-1006, conduct three- and four-day four-wheel-drive treks to the western gorge country while Broome Bus Lines, (091) 92-1068, provide day and half-day tours of Broome's attractions.

Further information from the **Tourist Bureau in Broome,** corner of Bagot Rd. and Great Northern Hwy., (091) 92-1111, or the **Tourist Bureau in Derby,** Clarendon St., (091) 91-1426.

East Kimberley Tours, (091) 68-2213, have seven-day camping tours of the Bungle Bungles and eight-day tours to Wolf Creek meteorite crater from Kununurra.

If you'd prefer to see the East Kimberley on foot or horseback, Kimberley Pursuits conduct three-day bushwalks ($220) and three- and ten-day horse treks ($250 and $1,400 respectively) from Wyndham. You'll be accompanied by experienced local bushmen and the costs include all meals and camping equipment. More information from John Catchlove in Wyndham, (091) 61-1364, or Mountain Designs, 862 Hay St., Perth, (09) 322-4774.

SafariTrek Australia, (091) 68-1177, telex 99388, runs boat cruises on the Ord River, Lake Kununurra, and Lake Argyle from Kununurra. They also take groups on rafts down the Ord River. Further information on the East Kimberley is available at the **Visitors Centre**, Coolibah Dr., Kununurra, (091) 68-1177.

## ❦ ACCOMMODATIONS AND RESTAURANTS

In Broome, the new **Cable Beach Club,** Broome 6725, (091) 92-2505, has 75 one- and two-bedroom air-conditioned bungalows in palm-studded tropical gardens overlooking Cable Beach. The central complex contains a licensed **restaurant** and two bars and facilities include tennis courts, swimming pool, spa, sauna, sail- and paddle boards. Rates are $150 per day for one-bedroom bungalows and $195 for two-bedrooms. All major credit cards.

**The Roebuck Bay Resort,** Hopton St., Broome 6725, (091) 92-1898, also on Cable Beach, has air-conditioned motel units and two-bedroom villas. The resort accepts major credit cards. Dining options include the **Cherabin Restaurant,** (serves French-style food), or the less formal **Al Fresco** dining area, (serve-yourself BBQ with steaks, seafood, and salad), and the **Satay Hut** (Indonesian style satays with peanut sauce). Facilities include tennis courts, swimming pools, spa, sailboards, water skiing, surfcats, and moped and bicycle hire. Rates are $75 double for units, $85 double for studio units with separate living areas and $110 per day for villas.

Recommended in Kununurra is the **Overland Motel,** Duncan Way., Kununurra 6743, (09) 68-1455, which has rooms for $93 double, and a licensed **restaurant.** The **Kimberley Court,** corner of River Fig Ave. and Erythrina St., Kununurra 6743, (091) 68-1411, has cheaper accommodation for $64 double including a continental breakfast. Neither place takes credit cards.

At the beginning of this century **Broome** was the pearling capital of the world. Its fleet of 400 luggers employed Japanese, Chinese, Malay, and Filipino divers. The natural pearl industry has been replaced by cultured pearl farms, but the remnants of Broome's exotic past are everywhere—in the racial mix of the population, the houses built by master pearlers, the Japanese cemetery, and Chinatown with its "wild west" corrugated iron and timber buildings.

Pearling is still celebrated each year in August or September with the Shinju Matsuri Festival, which combines the Chinese feast of Hung Ting, the Japanese Bon Festival, and the Malaysian Merdeka. The festivals are designed to celebrate past successes and encourage the gods to provide continued good fortune in the future. Highlights include mardi gras, a float parade lead by a Chinese dragon, and lugger races.

Huge tidal fluctuations are a Broome phenomonen and at **Cable Beach,** the water recedes up to 500 meters at low tide. Occasionally during spring, when a full moon rises on the rippling mud flats, a curious lighting effect known by the locals as "the golden staircase to the moon" occurs. Cable Beach is also a popular spot with alternative lifestylers, more or less affectionately dubbed "mung beans" by Broome residents (for their partiality to sprouts and other health foods). Their daytime domain is "to the right" on the beach, a section unofficially reserved for nudists.

Residents from the other end of society's spectrum include British peer Lord Alistair McAlpine who spends about three months of the year in Broome. He's been responsible for much sympathetic development in the town, including the Cable Beach Club resort and the 20-hectare **Pearl Coast Zoological Gardens,** Lullfitz Drive, Cable Beach, (091) 92-1703, which has a large population of Australian animal and birdlife including the rare Palm Cockatoo. The gardens are open 9 A.M.–5 P.M. daily. Next door is the **Broome Crocodile Park,** (091) 92-1489, with a population of 35 mature crocs and their young. The park is open 10 A.M. to 12 P.M., 2:30 to 5 P.M. Monday through Saturday, Sunday feeding at 3 P.M.

Fossilized dinosaur footprints left more than 130 million years ago are visible at extremely low tides at **Gantheaume Point.** Cement casts of the tracks are displayed at the top of the cliff. On the north side of the point is a man-made rock pool which fills with the high tide, known as Anastasia's Pool.

Local lore has it that Cable House, which was built in 1888 to hold transmitting equipment for the submarine cable which in those days linked Broome with Java, is in fact a piece of misdirected mail. Pre-fabricated in Britain and destined for Kimberley in South Africa, it ended up in Australia. The mishap was Broome's gain and this charming colonial building now serves as the town's courthouse.

Of course, most visitors to Broome are en route to the natural wonders of the Kimberleys. Information on the Kimberleys is available from the Broome and Derby Tourist Bureaus, (see Organized Tours, above). The limestone walls of **Geikie Gorge** change from gold to crimson as they trace the path of the Fitzroy River. More than one hundred species of birds inhabit the gorge, also home to freshwater crocodiles and stingrays which adapted to fresh water when the ocean receded millions of years ago. **Windjana Gorge** is of deep significance to the Aborigines and contains splendid galleries of their art. Not far from Hall's Creek is **China Wall,** which runs several kilometers and looks like a man-made structure. In fact, it's a quirk of nature formed when a wall of quartz weathered more slowly than the surrounding stone. Also nearby, 106 kilometers, about 70 miles, south on the four-wheel-drive road to Alice Springs is the **Wolf Creek meteorite crater,** a circular depression one kilometer in diameter and deep enough to hold a 16-story building. Scientists estimate that the collision that created it occurred about a million years ago.

**Kununurra** in East Kimberley was established in 1960 to service the construction of the Ord River Diversion Dam. It's an Aboriginal name meaning "meeting of the waters," a reference to the lakes created by the scheme, **Lake Kununurra** on the town's doorstep, and massive **Lake Argyle,** a body of water eight times the size of Sydney Harbour. For **boating trips,** contact SafariTrek (see above); swim at your own risk—there are fresh water crocs in these waters. The Argyle mine at the southwest of the lake brought a new industry to this agricultural area—diamond mining. It has yielded the largest stone ever found in Australia at 7.03 carats, and also produces a unique pink diamond. **The Visitors Centre,** Coolibah Drive, Kununurra, (091) 68-1177, can provide information on East Kimberley.

# 12

# TRAVEL ARRANGEMENTS

The Australian Tourist Commission is a high-powered, very professional organization with lots of glossy information to help you plan your trip. Their specialty is the *Aussie Holiday Book* that can help with questions on transportation, tours, entry formalities, and the like. You can get one by contacting any ATC office. A list of their offices follows.

## AUSTRALIA

### Sydney
Level 3
80 William St.
Woolloomooloo. N.S.W. 2011
Tel.: (02) 360 1111
Telex: 22322 AUSTOUR
Fax: (02) 331 6469

## CANADA

### Toronto
2 Bloor St. West, suite 1730
Toronto, Ont.
Canada M4W 3E2
Tel.: (416) 925-9575
Telex: 06-21 8074
Fax: (416) 925-9312

## GREAT BRITAIN

### London
20 Savile Row
London W1X 1AE
Tel.: (1) 434-4372
Telex: 266039 ATCLON
Fax: (1) 734-1965

## NEW ZEALAND

### Auckland
Quay Towers, 15th Floor
29 Customs St. West
Auckland 1, New Zealand
(Box 166, Auckland 1)
Tel.: (09) 799 594
Telex: 21007 AUSTOUR NZ
Fax: (09) 373 117

## UNITED STATES

### Los Angeles
2121 Ave. of the Stars, suite 1200
Los Angeles Calif. 90067
Tel.: (213) 552-1988
Telex: 4720767 AUSTOUR
Fax: (213) 552-1215

### New York
489 Fifth Ave., 31st Floor
New York, N.Y. 10017
Tel.: (212) 687-6300
Telex: 421023 AUSTOUR
Fax: (212) 661-3340

## Chicago

150 N. Michigan Ave., suite 2130
Chicago, Ill. 60601

Tel.: (312) 781-5150
Telex: 170317
Fax: (312) 781-5159

The Australian states also have tourist offices which can be useful once you've narrowed down where you're going.

**New South Wales Tourism Commission**
2049 Century Park East, suite 2250
Los Angeles, Calif. 90067
Tel.: (213) 552-9566
Telex: 104905953

**Victorian Tourism Commission**
2121 Avenue of the Stars, suite 1270
Los Angeles, Calif. 90067
Tel.: (213) 553-6352

719 Yonge St, suite 205
Toronto, Ontario M4Y 2B5
Tel.: (416) 9603533
Canada M4N 3N1
Telex: 06218074

**Northern Territory Tourist Commission**
2121 Avenue of the Stars, suite 1230
Los Angeles, Calif. 90067
Tel.: (213) 277-7877
(800) 4 OUTBAC

**South Australian Tourism**
2121 Avenue of the Stars, suite 1210
Los Angeles, Calif. 90067
Tel.: (213) 552-2821

**Tourism Tasmania**
2121 Avenue of the Stars, suite 1200
Los Angeles, Calif. 90067
Tel.: (213) 552-3010

**Western Australian Tourism Commission**
2121 Avenue of the Stars, suite 1210
Los Angeles, Calif. 90067
Tel.: (213) 557-1987

**Queensland Tourist and Travel Corporation**
611 North Larchmont Blvd.
Los Angeles, Calif. 90004
Tel.: (213) 465-8418 U.S.A.
Telex: 188392
Canada call collect

# The Seasons In Australia

Yes, as you probably know by now, everything Down Under is turned around; and at no time is it more confusing for those of us from the Northern Hemisphere than when we try to figure out the seasons.

In general, it works this way:

summer:  Dec.–March
winter:  June–Aug.
spring:  Sept.–Nov.
autumn:  April–May

Australians like to boast that any time is the right time to visit—and in the southern areas of the country (New South Wales, South Australia, Victoria, Tasmania, and the southern areas of Western Australia) this is true. These areas are almost Mediterranean in climate: summers are hot, but not unbearable, and winters are generally mild—though days and evenings can get somewhat chilly—especially in the far southern areas, such as Melbourne and Tasmania. There is some snow to be found in the southern mountain areas. You can ski here—but we don't recommend foreigners travel to Australia just for skiing; you probably have better slopes closer to home; and good snow here isn't guaranteed.

Things are different in central Australia and the tropical northern areas. Summers can mean uncomfortably high temperatures. In the north they can also mean monsoonal rains and high humidity. In fact, in most of the north, they abandon seasons altogether—and divide the year into the Wet and the Dry. Go in the Dry—that's winter, where temperatures are still high, but the weather is infinitely more comfortable.

For people in the United States, the service WeatherTrak provides temperatures and the next day's forecast for 250 cities. Dial toll-free WeatherTrak (800-247-3282) for your local WeatherTrak number. Then, using a touch-tone phone, dial the WeatherTrak number and a computerized voice will ask you for the code for the city you'll be visiting. The United States and Canada use the city's area code; cities overseas use the first three letters of the city's name—for example, Sydney's code is SYD or 793, Melbourne is MEL or 635. To obtain a complete list of cities and codes send a self-addressed, stamped envelope to Cities, Box 7000, Dallas, Tex. 75209.

We included here a brief Climate Chart, with all average temperatures indicated in Fahrenheit. (Note that while averages are useful, they do not indicate temperature extremes—something to be wary of if traveling in the north in the summer.)

|  | Jan.–Mar. (Summer) min/max | April–May (Autumn) min/max | June–Aug. (Winter) min/max | Sept.–Nov. (Spring) min/max | Dec. (Summer) min/max |
|---|---|---|---|---|---|
| Adelaide | 59–85 | 51–73 | 45–61 | 52–77 | 59–82 |
| Alice Springs | 65–98 | 48–85 | 40–72 | 52–93 | 68–95 |
| Brisbane | 67–85 | 56–80 | 50–71 | 55–82 | 67–85 |
| Cairns | 74–89 | 68–85 | 62–80 | 66–87 | 74–88 |
| Darwin | 76–92 | 70–92 | 69–89 | 74–92 | 78–93 |
| Hobart | 50–71 | 43–63 | 40–55 | 43–65 | 51–68 |
| Melbourne | 57–80 | 47–68 | 44–59 | 46–70 | 55–75 |
| Perth | 64–86 | 53–76 | 48–65 | 50–76 | 60–81 |
| Sydney | 63–78 | 52–72 | 46–63 | 51–74 | 63–80 |

# SEASONAL EVENTS

Horse races, sailing competitions, even drinking competitions and boat races on dry river beds: Australia's annual events range from the historical to the ridiculous.

Check with local tourism offices for more events and make plans to join in the festivities whenever possible. The enthusiasm is contagious. Employers have come to recognize that it's often better to join in and admit defeat than to stand against the flow: it's possible that during a major "footy event" workplace no-shows can reach 60 percent. (During the country's celebration of their win of the America's Cup race, the prime minister said it was "downright unpatriotic" for any employer to sack staff who stayed home the morning after such a historic event. Remember: the race aired in the middle of the night in Australia; the country stayed up until dawn.)

As always, keep in mind that the seasons are the opposite of those in the Northern Hemisphere: springtime events take place in Oct. and Nov., winter events during July and Aug., and so on. We've tried to supply specific dates wherever possible, but at press time, many of the specifics had yet to be decided.

## January

**Cricket** is king: Throughout Australia's capital cities, cricket tournaments and matches take place to record crowds; international and interstate teams participate.

**The Australian Open Tennis Tournament** attracts internationally ranked professionals to play at the National Tennis Centre in Melbourne.

**Surf & Beach Carnivals:** Countrywide competitions of skill in surf-lifesaving by professionals and amateurs of all ages. Activities include surfing, surf rescue, and wind-surfing events, with on-shore entertainments to complement.

**The Perth Cup:** Jan. 2, Ascot, Perth, is W. A.'s major annual horse-racing event.

**The Royal Sydney Anniversary Regatta** is a sailing event in Sydney Harbour, in which anything that floats gets into the act. It's hard to tell the real players without a scorecard, yet onlookers don't seem to mind the confusion.

**The Festival of Sydney** lasts all month and features special events, parkside exhibits, and art displays throughout the Sydney area.

**Australia Day,** January 26, is a national holiday much like the 4th of July or Canada Day, with special events, fireworks, and national pride in full public display. Shops and banks are closed, pubs are open and doing a brisk business countrywide.

**Australians are the first to speak up about the problems of the country and government, but look unkindly on commentary from a visitor that reflects negatively on their Australia. Although it's not usually worn on the lapel, Australians are "fair dinkum" (that means "truly") patriotic.**

**The Melbourne Summer Music Festival,** Jan. 6–28, includes a full spectrum of music in open-air concerts: jazz, classical, folk, and contemporary all play a part, although jazz and contemporary are the strong favorites.

**The Hahndorf Schuetzenfest,** Jan. 14, takes place in Hahndorf, S.A., and includes a good bit of beer drinking, German music and food, dancing, and a variety of skilled competitions in marksmanship.

## February

**The Festival of Perth** runs all month long, and is a series of cultural events and open-air entertainments.

**Hobart Cup Day,** the first Wednesday in Feb., Elwick Course, and the **Hobart Regatta** are two events that mandate local merchants shut for "lack of interest" by patrons and employees. Tasmania, although low in population, turns out in full for the events.

**The Royal Canberra Show,** the last weekend in Feb., a national agricultural and industrial exposition, staged at the National Exhibition Centre, and attracts large numbers.

## March

**The Moomba Festival,** March 3–13, has the feel of Mardi Gras, and runs from late February to early March. The "let's party" theme spills over into the streets of normally conservative Melbourne. Elaborate floats and parades highlight the festivities.

**Adelaide Festival of Arts** takes place every even-numbered year, and includes three weeks of music and arts throughout Adelaide.

**The Canberra Festival** is a founding fathers' festival that celebrates the establishment of the capital city and includes a national food and wine "frolic," outdoor art show, a raft race, a "bird man" flying machines competition, open-air concerts, fairs, and outdoor markets.

**The Ballarat Begonia Festival,** March 10–19, in Ballarat, Vic., is nationally acclaimed for its flower shows, pleasant garden tours, and home tours.

## April

**The Sydney Royal Easter Show** is an Australian agricultural and industrial show that includes fireworks displays and parades. This is reputed to be Australia's largest annual showing.

**Sydney Cup Week,** April 1–8, Randwick Course: You guessed it, a week at the races which culminates in the Sydney Cup, a major purse event. The crowds dress to the nines.

**The Barossa Valley Wine and Vintage Festival** takes place every odd-numbered year, in the wine-growing area outside Adelaide, with tastings and cultural events that celebrate one-hundred-plus years of Australian wine-making.

## May

**The Bangtail Muster** is Alice Springs' equivalent of a round-up and rodeo. It's a major event which floods the town in the center of the center with well-dusted cattle and sheep hands from remote stations who test their skills and hoist their fair share of tinnies in the process. Open-air entertainment includes a rodeo and cattle muster. This is one of the Northern Territory's major annual events.

Also taking place in the Alice is the **Camel Cup,** May 13, the Outback's answer to the black-tie crowds of Sydney and Melbourne. Outbackers bring prize camels together to compete in a winner-take-all race, where anything can, and oftentimes does, happen.

**The May Day Holiday,** May 1, is officially recognized in the Northern Territory. Events take place side by side with the Muster and Camel Cup of the Alice. Pubs overflow, enthusiasts take to the streets, and organized chaos is the order of the event.

**The Adelaide Cup,** May 15, is South Australia's Day at the Races, where a statewide holiday is declared, spectators dress for the events of the day, and even the most conservative and straight of Australians is tempted to place a small wager on a favorite.

## June

**The Darwin Beer Can Regatta** is a classic event in which competitors take to the water in boats and floats, constructed almost entirely of empty beers cans. Craft come in all sizes and configurations, most everyone gets good and wet and adds to their vessel's size as they consume as they compete. Shoreline events such as open-air concerts and entertainment add flavor to a very wet event, of great spirit.

**The Townsville Pacific Festival,** in Qld., continues for two weeks and celebrates the history and culture of the Pacific region. Traditional dancing, artwork, and folk music highlight the event.

**The Rugby World Cup** seems to attract fans and fanatics from the woodwork. Rugby is one of Australia's lead spectator sports and the Rugby World Cup, held in the Concord Oval of Sydney, is a leading sports event series.

**The Queen's Birthday** is celebrated throughout Australia on June 8—with the notable exception of W.A. which prefers to celebrate the Queen's day on October 5. This is an official holiday, which finds shops closed, banks buttoned-down tight, and most Australians out and enjoying the day off. Statewide and local events often take place in honor of the royal birthday celebration.

## July

**The Darwin Show** is the Northern Territory's annual agricultural, industrial, and technical showing, held at the state fairgrounds.

Adelaide is host to the **Festival City Marathon,** which includes cultural happenings as well as sporting events in and around the city.

**Show Days** take place in July for Alice Springs, Tennant Creek, Katherine, and Darwin, which feature local events and are just another good excuse to celebrate in general.

July is also host to the **Rothmans' 100,000, The Grand National Steeplechase,** July 8, Flemington Race Course, Melbourne, and the **Forex Horse Races,** all of national interest.

## August

**The Brisbane Royal National Show,** Aug. 10–19, is Qld.'s annual agricultural and technical show, which takes place on the Exhibition Grounds, and features prize livestock and agricultural-methods programs. A good number of Qld.'s rural dwellers make the Brisbane show an event worthy of attendance every year. A good deal of peripheral activity is generated in Brisbane during this event.

**The Henley-on-Todd Regatta** is a good-natured event in which man-powered boats of all shapes and descriptions race without benefit of water, using as their course the very dry Todd River bed. Competition is fierce, yet friendly, among well-lubricated participants and well-wishers. Other non-aquatic events include waterless skiing and ski-jumping events. Not exactly punting on the Thames, but enjoyable nonetheless.

**Australian Ski Championships** take place throughout the month, and are staged in the Snowy Mountains.

Ballarat, Vic., famed for its gold strike and underground wealth, plays host to the **Royal South Street Competition,** a series of cultural and performing arts stand-offs, which show that Ballarat has come a long way from its early and rowdier pioneer days.

Both N.S.W. and the A.C.T. have declared **bank holidays** during the month of Aug., with banks closing up tight.

## September

Melbourne plays host to the **Spoleto Festival,** a month-long exchange of entertainment and cultural events, in conjunction with Melbourne's sister cities of Spoleto, Italy, and Charleston, South Carolina, in the U.S.

**The Royal Melbourne Show,** Sept. 21–Oct. 1, the **Royal Adelaide Show,** and the **Royal Perth Show** each represent their regions with agricultural displays and industrial exhibits and events during this month.

The **Warena Spring Carnival,** with its Mardi Gras atmosphere, parades, and processions, draws those of festive spirit to the annual event.

The **Carnival of Flowers,** at Toowoomba, Qld., is a springtime event favored by horticulturalists. It includes large floral displays, floral art, and garden tours.

The **New South Wales Horse Racing Carnival** takes place this month, and includes an auction, shows, and races.

## October

Tasmania's **Royal Hobart Show** is another of the annual agricultural and industrial events with livestock on display, method seminars, and industrial and technical exchanges.

The **Toohey's 1000** car race, Oct. 1, takes place in Bathurst, N.S.W., and the **Australian Grand Prix, with Formula One** races, take place, and draws large spectator crowds.

**McLaren Vale Wine Bushing Festival** is held the last week in August outside Adelaide, a week of wine-tasting, auctions, and displays which highlight the wine-growing areas.

The **Jacaranda Festival** of New South Wales, staged at Grafton, includes floral displays, garden tours, and open-air music and staged events.

Western Australia chooses October to celebrate the **Queen's Birthday,** on the 2nd. Local banks, shops, and services close.

## November

The **Australian Open Golf Tournament** takes place Nov. 23–26, one of the largest purse events in the country for golf—with a six-figure take. It's played in Sydney.

The **Victoria Spring Race Carnival** is a week-long racing form that culminates with the running of the **Melbourne Cup;** banks, shops, and other services close. The event gets top billing on national television, and spectators come dressed to kill. Everyone who is anyone gets seen at the Melbourne Cup.

Tasmania, not wanting to be left out, declares a **Recreation Day** the first Monday in November for the general well-being of its population. Services and shops shut tight, pubs and eateries do a brisk trade.

### December

The **Festival of Sydney** can begin in Dec. with special events, concerts, and exhibitions.

The **Sydney to Hobart Race** leaves Sydney Harbour the day after Christmas for a grueling and highly competitive sailing challenge. Boats mob the harbor to provide a real Aussie send-off to the competing flotilla.

**Carols by Candlelight,** Dec. 17, take place in the Domain, most notably in Sydney Domain.

**Boxing Day** is Dec. 26th, and an additional day is taken by the Northern Territory to add time to the holiday season.

# PACKING

When packing for your holiday in Australia, keep in mind that the social climate is casual. Also note that in most cases, what you bring along is what you'll be carrying. Unless your mode of travel is fully inclusive touring, you'll be toting your own gear. For this reason, we suggest you pack lightly. You can buy there anything you might have forgotten.

If you intend to sample the culinary delights of restaurants in the major cities, a smart dress or jacket and tie are recommended. In a few cases, you'll be asked to adhere to a dress code. For example, if you visit a casino, a collared-shirt and jacket is requested for gents and flip-flops are not allowed. Bring along a sweater for cool evenings and the air-conditioning at public places. We recommend you pack those items that are comfortable and easy to care for.

If you plan to travel to the Outback, plan to purchase in advance a small section of fly netting to wear over your hat. The flies are known to be plentiful and very persistent. Cork hats (hats with corks hanging from the brim) are available and make for good conversation pieces when you return home, but require constant head movement and take a bit of getting used to. Additional swim gear and sunglasses should also be included as a must. Suntan lotions are of excellent quality in Australia and can be purchased locally to assure protection from the strong rays of the Aussie sun.

Many of Australia's beaches are topless. So, if women want a top-end tan, they should pack a two-piece swimsuit. Australia also boasts a good number of totally bare beaches.

If you plan to take in the Great Barrier Reef, old sneakers are suggested to protect your feet from the coral. Most Great Barrier tour operators provide snorkels, flippers, and masks to their clients, but if you wear prescription eyeglasses, you might consider purchasing a mask with a special lens if you plan to spend any time exploring the reef.

Likewise, if you are going to spend time in the Outback and wear contact lenses, you might consider bringing along a pair of eyeglasses to prevent dust from irritating your eyes. Additional gear to bring along or purchase in Australia for Outback trips are binoculars, a flashlight, comfortable walking shoes, a hat, insect repellent, and a sense of humor.

The Australian government is very strict about drugs, narcotics, and controlled substances, and penalties for misuse are severe. If you intend to bring prescription medication into the country, it's also advisable to bring a doctor's prescription, which can be used to refill your own with an endorsement from an Australian physician. Up to four weeks' supply of prescribed medication is allowed for visitors.

Unless you're personally attached to your electric razor or hair dryer, you might consider leaving it at home. Manual shavers take up less room in your bag, are lighter to tote, and eliminate the problem of finding and bringing along adaptors. (See Electricity under Vital Information.) If you're staying in good hotels, you may well find hair dryers permanently mounted in bathrooms, or a call to the front desk will produce a local version of what you've left home. This also applies to irons, if you don't carry a portable, which will require an adaptor. (Most hotels, motels, guest cottages, and hostels will offer a loaner iron.)

We strongly recommend you wear a watch, to help make flights, buses, and show times and to keep track of the local scene. Another worthwhile investment is a travel alarm clock, which offers a safeguard to missing a wake-up call from the front desk.

If you plan to explore the Outback, or do a bit of bare-boat chartering (chartering a plain boat, which you will crew), a flashlight is suggested. Either bring one along or purchase locally.

When packing film for your camera, remember that there's lots of light in Australia and the bulk of your pictures will probably be outdoor shots; slower-speed film may suit you best.

# Formalities

Americans, British, and Canadians entering Australia will be asked to produce a valid passport and visa upon arrival for Customs and Immigration. (New Zealanders don't need one.) Assure that your passport will be valid for longer than the length of your stay, and have at least two open pages for stamps and validations. Although it's seldom requested, you might be asked to produce your onward travel tickets to verify your departure from Australia. En route to Australia, you will be given a short incoming visitor's card to complete. This document is not difficult provided your passport isn't stowed in a baggage compartment. With your passport and visa, these documents will be presented to the Australian authorities at your point of entry.

Entry personnel are in general business-like, yet recognize the fact that Australia is open and welcomes visitors. For purposes of tourism, a visitor's visa is relatively easy to obtain, but must be obtained prior to arrival in Australia; send for your application as early as possible. Visas are provided free of charge. Ask your travel agent about the nearest Australian Consulate. To obtain a visa, contact:

## Canada

The Australian High Commission
130 Slater St., The National Building
Ottawa, Ont.
K1P 6L2
Tel.: (613) 236-0841

Australian Consulate General
1066 West Hastings St./Oceanic Pl.
Vancouver, British Columbia
V6E 3X1
Tel.: (604) 684-1177

Australian Consulate General
Commerce Court West, suite 2324
Bay & King sts.
Toronto, Ont.
M5L 1B9
Tel.: (416) 367-0783

## Great Britain

The Australian High
Commission/Australia House
London
The Strand
London WC2 B4LA
Tel.: (01) 438-8000

Manchester
The Australian Consulate
Chatsworth House
Lever St.
Manchester M1 2DL
Tel.: (061) 228-1344

## United States

Australian Consulate General
636 5th Ave.
New York N.Y. 10111
Tel.: (212) 245-4000

Australian Consulate General
360 Post St.
San Francisco, Calif. 94108
Tel.: (415) 362-6160

Australian Consulate General
611 North Larchmont Blvd.
Los Angeles, Calif. 90046
Tel.: (213) 469-4300

The Australian Embassy
1601 Massachusetts Ave., N.W.
Washington, D.C. 20036-2273
Tel.: (202) 797-3159

Australian Consulate General
One Illinois Center
111 East Wacker Dr., suite 2212
Chicago, Ill. 60601-4675
Tel.: (312) 645-9440

Australian Consulate General
1990 Post Oak Blvd., suite 800
Houston, Tex. 77056
Tel.: (713) 629-9131

Australian Consulate General
1000 Bishop St., penthouse suite
Honolulu, Hawaii
Tel.: (808) 524-5050

When applying for your visa, you will be asked for confirmation of your travel plans, which will require either a travel agent's written itinerary or a valid ticket to and from the country. "Sightseeing and tourism" are generally accepted as explanation of your intent during a visit.

British and Canadian citizens between the ages of 18 and 30 may also be eligible for a "working holiday" visa, which allows employment in Australia for a period not to exceed three years. Applications for a working holiday visa must be made from the applicant's home country.

## Vaccinations

If you are traveling to Australia from Canada, the United States, New Zealand, or Great Britain, no vaccinations are required. A General Health Certificate is not required of visitors unless you've traveled through an epidemic zone (smallpox, cholera, typhoid, or yellow fever) within 14 days of your arrival in Australia. If your pre-arrival plans take you to areas where this health certificate will be required, consult your physician for advice.

## Have Your Tissues Ready

Because of Australia's unique location, it is pleasantly free from exotic diseases and non-native insect pests. Upon arrival in Australia, the interior of your aircraft will be sprayed to assure no incoming nasties enter the country. The aerosol mist is not very pleasant, so we suggest you have a tissue handy for the few moments it will take for the air to settle. It may not be the nicest welcome, but it is necessary.

Plan to leave the family pet at home when you travel to Australia. Quarantine requirements are lengthy, with the minimum being four months and, in many cases, upwards to nine.

## Customs

As a visitor, you are entitled to bring into the country 200 cigarettes or 250 grams of cigars or tobacco, and one liter of alcoholic liquor along with personal effects of clothing, toiletries, and camera equipment. Suitable goods valued at $200 or less and included in your personal baggage are exempt.

## The Departure Tax

Australia requires that every traveler departing the country pay a departure tax of $10 in local currency. If you are traveling with children under 12 years of age, the departure tax for them is exempted at the departure tax counter, but proof of age is required for the exemption sticker. If your itinerary calls for multiple entries and arrivals through Australia, you need only pay this departure tax once.

When planning your departure from Australia, arrive at the airport at least two hours prior to boarding your flight. The line at the departure tax counter at peak times can take a little time.

# Money Matters

Australia's currency is based on the dollar and, like Canada and the United States, a dollar consists of one hundred units. Coins come in one-cent and two-cent pieces (which are copper colored), five-, ten-, twenty-, and fifty-cent denominations (which are silver colored), as well as a relatively new issue of dollar coins. Australian notes are colored differently and range from one-, two-, five-, ten-, twenty-, and fifty-dollar bills. One-hundred-dollar notes are not widely circulated and can make change difficult for smaller retailers. Visitors are free to bring in whatever amount of currency they please, but a visitor may not take more than $5,000 from the country when departing.

You can change money at the airport and banks (9:30 A.M.–4 P.M., Mon.–Fri.).

At the time of publication, the current exchange rates for Australian dollars were as follows:

$A1=$US .8315
$A1=$Canadian .8087
$A1=British £ .5634
$A1=$NZ1.33

**Note: All prices quoted in this book are in Australian dollars.**

**Credit cards** are widely recognized and, in many cases, offer attractive conversion rates of exchange to the traveler. In this book we consider major credit cards to be American Express (AE), Visa (V), MasterCard (MC), and Diners Club (DC). In smaller rural areas, however, you may do well to have cash or traveler's checks on hand. Many taxi outfits accept payment of fares through most major credit cards.

Traveler's checks are the way to go. Your money is protected in the event of loss, and TCs are recognized, with identification, as legal tender throughout the country. Traveler's checks can be cashed easily (in Aussie dollars or other currency) in airports, at banks, hotels, motels, and many shops catering to off-shore visitors. We suggest you make your checks available in varied denominations, so if you want to cash a check for local currency and buy a small item, local merchants won't break their bank in order to make a sale. Plan to stay with the major forms of traveler's checks, like American Express. They are widely recognized and can be replaced more conveniently should you need to report losses. (Remember to record the numbers of your TCs separately, in case of loss.)

## Tipping
Tipping is never mandatory in Australia, but it is becoming more and more common, especially in the major cities. In better restaurants, generally tip about 10 percent of the bill. The same is recommended for taxi drivers.

# Transportation

## TRAVEL TO AUSTRALIA
Flights leave from North America for Australia from Los Angeles, San Francisco, Honolulu, and Vancouver. These are usually evening departures, so you can connect during the day. Or by taking advantage of stopover privileges available on some airlines, use an overnight stay in Hawaii or San Francisco (for example), to add a two-day mini holiday to your trip. In truth, it's a good idea to break up your flight with an overnight stop somewhere; the trip to Australia is a long one (about 17 hours from

L.A.), and can take a lot out of you. Hawaii is probably the best place to stop over—more midway between North America and Australia than other possible stops. Auckland, New Zealand, is another popular stopover—perhaps more exotic than the others—although the Auckland–North America flight can also be a grueling one.

Flights arrive in Australia in Sydney, Melbourne, Brisbane, and Cairns. Airlines connecting North America with Australia are Qantas, United, Continental, Air New Zealand, UTA French Airlines, and CP Air.

If you're planning to tour the north or west coasts of Australia, the most convenient route to Perth or Darwin might be via Europe. (Flights also connect Europe with Sydney and Melbourne.) Carriers currently running this route are Qantas, British Airways, Air India, Singapore Airlines, Lufthansa, and KLM.

**If there's any way your budget can stand it, consider flying business class rather than coach. Again, this is a long flight, no matter how you break it up, and you may be very grateful for the extra room and better service. No matter how you fly, get up and walk around the plane as much as possible (it's a good way to meet people, too—everybody on this flight gets antsy); carry your toothbrush on board to help you freshen up along the way—washing your face also helps. Some people even like to change into "lounge wear" (sweat pants and T-shirt, maybe?) for most of the flight. Dress in a couple of layers, as cabin temperatures will vary during the flight—leaving you cold sometimes, warm other times.**

You'll be crossing the international dateline if you're flying west to Australia; in which case you'll lose a day in the flight (and, of course, gain it back when you return). If flying to the most popular gateway, Sydney, you'll probably arrive in the morning. You'll be pretty exhausted, but perhaps excited enough so you won't give in and take a nap: just plan to look around a little; make it a light day and an early night. Otherwise, you'll confuse your body clock even further. Don't be surprised if you have to wait for your hotel room to be ready, too.

**If the weather is cold where your coming from, have some warm-weather clothes readily accessible: you can change in your hotel lobby bathroom, do some sightseeing, have lunch, and then come back to your room. You wouldn't want to be doing this in your December woolens.**

## DOMESTIC TRAVEL

Once you've arrived, you've got all the usual methods of transportation to choose from. Again, keep in mind that distances are great. But you can cut a swath across the entire country, chalking up miles in air-conditioned railway cars with lounges and modern amenities in just over sixty hours, or cover 10 km (6 miles) of Aussie Outback by camel in two days.

# Riding the Rails

Australia boasts over 9,500 km (6,000 miles) of major railway services between major city centers, many offering excellent services en route. These trainways provide air-conditioned cars and toilet facilities, as well as food-service cars and, in many cases, observation and skyway cars and berth accommodations. Train travel, like bus travel, is a good opportunity to meet traveling Australians. The locals have come to see rail travel as a viable alternative to relatively high-cost air travel and appreciate a ground-view perspective of the countryside.

Rail passes are a bargain, and, if you plan to travel by rail, consider a rail pass that can provide from 14 days to 3 months (economy and first class) of unlimited rail travel. These passes are available from outside Australia, so plan to book through the Railways of Australia office in your country but you can buy them from rail headquarters in Australian states if you produce your passport and outgoing air ticket. Two types of passes are available: Austral Pass, good for first class (seat and berth), and Budget Austral passes, good for economy seats. Keep in mind these passes must be used within six months of issue and refunds are available only if no rail travel whatsoever has been used. Sleeping berths and meals are not included in the rail pass system.

For general train information, call the office of Railways of Australia in Melbourne: 85 Queen St., Melbourne 3000, (03) 608-0811, or state rail headquarters offices in Brisbane, Perth, or Sydney; in the U.S., (818) 247-4564; in Canada, (416) 863-0799 (Toronto), or (604) 687-4004 (Vancouver).

# Flying

At one time, Australia was serviced only by one major air carrier, Trans Australian Airways (now Australian Airlines), which was government-owned and operated. As a result, service was non-competitive and prices for domestic travel by air were prohibitive. But now competition has provided the air traveler to Australia with tighter schedules and service, and prices have been made more pleasing, though still relatively expensive. If you intend to travel by air within Australia, airlines offer numerous passes at substantial savings to international visitors, available in Australia or before you leave home. Numerous smaller airlines operate with regions and states, such as Air New South Wales, Kendell, and Air Queensland.

Plan to arrive at the airport at least thirty minutes prior to local domestic flights, and assure you are in the correct terminal, often segregated by domestic and international flights. Contact your travel agent, or see below.

You can reach Australian Airlines in New York at (212) 986-3772; and in every major city and town in Australia.

Call Ansett and East-West toll-free in the United States at (800) 366-1300. Ansett also has offices all over Australia.

**Note:** ferries as well as planes connect Tasmania with the rest of the country. See the Tasmania chapter for details.

# DISTANCE CHART

| | | Adelaide | Alice Springs | Ayers Rock | Brisbane | Cairns | Canberra | Darwin | Hobart | Melbourne | Perth | Surfers Paradise (Gold Coast) |
|---|---|---|---|---|---|---|---|---|---|---|---|---|
| Alice Springs | km. | 1555 | | | | | | | | | | |
| | mi. | 964 | | | | | | | | | | |
| Ayers Rock | km. | 1597 | 446 | | | | | | | | | |
| | mi. | 990 | 277 | | | | | | | | | |
| Brisbane | km. | 1992 | 3026 | 3472 | | | | | | | | |
| | mi. | 1235 | 1876 | 2153 | | | | | | | | |
| Cairns | km. | 2858 | 2307 | 2753 | 1710 | | | | | | | |
| | mi. | 1772 | 1430 | 1707 | 1060 | | | | | | | |
| Canberra | km. | 1230 | 2785 | 2827 | 1315 | 2938 | | | | | | |
| | mi. | 763 | 1727 | 1753 | 815 | 1822 | | | | | | |
| Darwin | km. | 3261 | 1706 | 2152 | 3672 | 2953 | 4233 | | | | | |
| | mi. | 2022 | 1058 | 1334 | 2277 | 1831 | 2624 | | | | | |
| Hobart | km. | 999 | 2554 | 2596 | 1970 | 3291 | 903 | 4260 | | | | |
| | mi. | 619 | 1583 | 1610 | 1221 | 2040 | 560 | 2641 | | | | |
| Melbourne | km. | 747 | 2302 | 2344 | 1718 | 3039 | 651 | 4008 | 252 | | | |
| | mi. | 463 | 1427 | 1453 | 1065 | 1884 | 404 | 2485 | 156 | | | |
| Perth | km. | 2720 | 3639 | 3681 | 4314 | 5180 | 3950 | 4206 | 3719 | 3467 | | |
| | mi. | 1686 | 2256 | 2282 | 2675 | 3212 | 2449 | 2608 | 2306 | 2150 | | |
| Surfers Paradise (Gold Coast) | km. | 2028 | 3106 | 3552 | 80 | 1790 | 1235 | 3752 | 2074 | 1882 | 4393 | |
| | mi. | 1257 | 1926 | 2202 | 50 | 1110 | 766 | 2326 | 1286 | 1167 | 2724 | |
| Sydney | km. | 1475 | 2831 | 2873 | 1031 | 2636 | 302 | 4095 | 1141 | 889 | 3996 | 933 |
| | mi. | 915 | 1755 | 1781 | 639 | 1634 | 187 | 2539 | 707 | 551 | 2478 | 578 |

# Taking the Bus

The Australians refer to buses as coaches, and your driver is not a driver (don't call him that), he's a coach captain and proud of it. Buses are frequent; competition between big companies and small operators is keen. Because of this, coach travel is a bargain. These coaches run almost anywhere on the map and a good number of sites that aren't. If you're keen to meet Australians, this is a fine way to get on with it. Australians now fully accept this form of travel, to combat the cost of travel by the major internal airlines. Travel the big coaches, get the full stories layed on from your coach captain, and relax. (Do sit in front to hear it all.) They've been through it many a time before. Reclining seats, on-coach toilet facilities, and, in many cases, on-board videos for the slower times and longer hauls are yours to enjoy. You can also save on hotels by sleeping on the coach, and sightseeing is certainly part of the experience. Many coaches offer camping holidays with all the equipment provided including provision for food from point to point.

If you're planning to cover a good bit of ground, a number of national companies offer discounts for unlimited travel passes. The two biggest coach operations are Ansett Pioneer, Oxford Square, Darlinghurst, N.S.W. 2010 (02-268-1331, or toll-free in Australia, 1-800-366-1300), and Australian Greyhound (ask your travel agent).

**If you plan to travel by coach, bring along large and small plastic bags. Items stored below covered luggage compartments may be subject to dust, which on dirt roads finds its way into everything.**

# Driving Down Under

When driving in Australia, keep two important things in mind: Australians drive on the left side of the road, and it's a law that you must wear seat belts. Fines for not buckling up in the front seat can be steep. In and around major cities, the roadway systems are excellent but out of city centers roadways become less civilized. On many of the long-haul routes, don't be surprised to see a bit of dirt track. When you rent your vehicle, ask the advice of rental personnel explaining where you're most likely to travel. They can provide useful travel information and advisories for certain roadways and routes. If you are going to explore the more remote and Outback areas, it's wise to plan in advance. In some cases, water supplies are a necessity and food provisions may be required as facilities are sparse. Advisories given for long hauls are not to be taken lightly. We have given specific advice about driving in individual chapters.

All the major car-rental companies exist throughout Australia. Specific information is given in individual chapters. Be aware that drop-off charges may be applied if you want to pick-up the car in one city and leave it in another.

## Drinking and Driving

Australia has made great strides in improving its statistics on driving safety. As a part of this scheme, there is a war against drinking and driving which carries with it heavy fines, spot road checks, and mandatory jail terms. In response to this, Australians out for a night at the pub will "designate a driver" who refrains from imbibing. We heartily recommend you do the same. Around major urban areas, its not uncommon to find random road checks where you will be asked if you've had a drink and could be asked to "blow into the bag" to determine consumption and blood alcohol levels. Throughout Australia, if your blood alcohol level exceeds .05 percent alcohol, you'll be taking an unpleasant ride to the local hoosgow (police station) for a lock-up and risk the loss of your license. Our suggestion is simply, if you're driving, don't plan to be drinking.

# Cruising

It's a romantic notion, cruising the South Pacific; and it doesn't mean you necessarily have to take a year off to sail around the world. Instead, you usually fly to a South Pacific port and pick up a cruise ship from there. Usually a cruise combines Australian ports (with Sydney the major port) with ports of call on South Pacific islands such as Tahiti and Fiji, and stops in New Zealand.

You'll probably want to book through a travel agent, who can give you lots of information on cruising options. Or you can also call: Cunard, toll-free in the U.S. (800) 221-4770; or (212) 661-7777; in Canada (800) 268-3706, or (416) 924-1441. P&O Princess, (213) 553-7000; in Canada toll-free, except B.C., (800) 663-3591; or (604) 681-1311. Royal Viking, in the U.S. (800) 422-8000; in Canada (800) 233-8000.

# Taxis

Almost all taxis are fully air-conditioned and provide an eye-opening travel experience. Taxi drivers are a great source of local information. Ask questions on the ride from the airport to town.

Though it used to be common for passengers traveling alone to sit up with the driver, more and more Australian taxi drivers are getting used to travelers (women especially) who sit in the back seat—your choice. Tipping isn't mandatory—although, especially in major cities, it's becoming more and more common. Unless you have a gripe, give drivers in the major cities something like 10 percent.

# Touring

Australia has attractions and activities to satisfy every traveler's palate. Camel safaris, skin-diving, deep-sea fishing, bare-boat charters, and walking tours only scrape the surface of specialty travel opportunities available. We recommend, if you have a particular activity in mind, that you plan in advance. Be specific with your travel agent or the Australian Tourism Board about when you plan to travel, and ask for operators and schedules, costs and conditions *before* you actually depart.

*The Specialty Travel Index,* available through many Travel Agents or directly from the publisher (STI/9 Mono Dr., Fairfax, Calif. 94930, or tel. 415-459-4900) is in a magazine format, and features more than three hundred activities and two hundred tour operators in Australia, with short descriptions of each program, costs, and further contact details. *The Speciality Travel Index* is published twice yearly, and cost is $4 (U.S.).

In Great Britain, *Footloose* magazine offers similar listings to readers, and *LAM* (formerly *London's Australian Magazine,* now re-named *London's Alternative Magazine*) is free at pubs and travel agencies throughout areas of London, listing tours and details for specialty travel opportunities in Australia.

A comprehensive listing of adventure travel is available in Canada from Westcan Treks, 10918 88th Ave., Edmonton, Alberta T6G 0Z1. They will forward brochures and information on special touring opportunities in Australia. Other Australian Tour operators such as Australian Pacific, AAT Kings, Ansett Pioneer, 4 Wheel-Drive Discovery Tours, and Con TIKI are listed fully in the *Aussie Holiday Book* published by the Australian Tourism Commission, and available for the asking from the Australian Tourism Board: see above.

If you want to work at your special interest, consider an Earthwatch expedition in Australia—a not-for-profit group that places interested volunteers on field-research expeditions. For more information write: Earthwatch, 9 Juniper Dr., Belmont, Mass.

## WILDLIFE TOUR

For something unusual, consider a Wildlife Tour of Australia. Australian wildlife is among the most varied and unique in the world. Here are just a few examples around the country—big, small, famous and not. Starting in the southeast part of the country and heading north, you can explore the following:

- **Southwest National Park.** One forested corner of the Tasmanian island-state has been rated as among the most rugged wilderness areas in any temperate zone on the globe. White-water enthusiasts, backpackers, and adventure fishermen, take caution—and keep an eye peeled for such furry denizens as the Tasmanian devil. Tourist Bureau in Hobart, tel.: (002) 30-0211.
- **Phillip Island.** Victoria's best natural sanctuary for animals is about 90 miles southeast of Melbourne, accessible via a bridge, by air, or sea. Star attraction is the evening promenade along the beach by the fairy penguins. Fur seals and mutton birds also can be seen.
- **Rehwinkel's Animal Park.** A wide range of fauna can be seen here, from koalas and kangaroos to wombats and such introduced species as camel and water buffalo. Open every day, located 24 km (about 15 miles) north of national capital Canberra. Tel.: (062) 30-3328.
- **Waratah Park.** The former film set of Australian TV series *Skippy,* starring a kangaroo, now features descendants of

Skippy romping with emus in a large, open enclosure. You can go inside to feed the creatures but watch out for your fingers. At Duffy's Forest near Terrey Hills, a wooded suburb of Sydney. Tel.: (02) 450-2377.

- **Cape York Peninsula.** Heading north of Cairns in Queensland, you enter one of the world's only spots where pristine rainforest meets pristine coral reef. Along the way there are crocodile farms, a turtle rookery, a palm tree nursery, opals, sugar cane, and big game fishing. Much flora and fauna here are seen nowhere else on earth and many of the plants remain yet unnamed. To charter trips or go by public bus from Cairns, phone (070) 51-9533.

Moving west:

- **Aquascene.** Batfish, milkfish, bream, and many other finned fellows come from the open sea twice a day on the tide to be hand-fed by visitors at Doctor's Gully near downtown Darwin. The friendship with the fish was struck up years ago by a local resident and is now carried on by the wife of the Northern Territory's current Chief Minister. Tel.: (089) 81-7837.
- **Kakadu.** Perhaps Australia's most famous national park, this

---

## Kookaburra

The strangest sound made by any Australian animal comes from the laughing kookaburra. At first it's an ugly shock, as if the Wicked Witch of the West had escaped her watery fate after all, to haunt the antipodean twilight with a triumphant cackle.

Shock changes to pleasure after the bird that makes this deafening call is seen. The laughing kookaburra is one of the most plentiful and most popular of the more than 750 bird species found in Australia.

It has been nicknamed the "settler's clock" because it frequently is heard at dawn, but the laugh is a danger warning or a territorial defense rather than a wake-up call. Its brown and mottled blue body is about 18 inches long, making it the largest kingfisher. A close second is the blue-winged kookaburra, which frequents northern Australia and also has a bizarre voice, like the harsh yelping of a small dog.

Laughing kookaburras are found throughout the most populous parts of the country, including the east, south, and southwest. They frequent agricultural areas, forests, and heavily treed areas of cities. In wooded suburbs, they become·frequent guests of whomever leaves a bit of raw meat on the windowsill.

Normally, their diet consists of insects, fish, frogs, lizards, mice, and the like, but they'll also gobble small snakes and chicks. Because their massive beak isn't hooked like that of other birds of prey, they rather brutally beat their meals to death. Even so, with such big, staring eyes, a cocky style, and that insane cackle, everybody likes kookaburras.

—Steve Bunk

haven of birdlife, crocodiles, water buffalo, and ancient Aboriginal rock paintings is about two hours by road from Darwin. Tours of every description are available, to suit any budget. Phone the NT Tourist Bureau in Darwin, (089) 81-6611.

- **Kimberleys.** For those with either well-equipped vehicles or a good safari guide, the far northwestern corner of Western Australia is a mountainous region that many explorer-types pick as their favorite part of Australia. From the pearling port of Broome to the irrigated farms of Kununurra, the Kimberleys are rarely traveled and therefore full of surprises. The weird Bungle Bungle range in this area was only "rediscovered" in the early 1980s! Tel. the Western Australian Tourism Commission in Perth at (09) 220-6000.

# Outdoor Recreation

Throughout this book we give specific information on what to do where, where to rent equipment for it, and outfitters that will make an adventure holiday a bit less adventurous.

In general, if you want to camp in Australia, it's probably easiest to hook up with an outfitter who can take you into the country and set you up with all the equipment you may need. If, however, you want to camp on your own, consider buying your equipment when you arrive and then selling it or shipping it back home. Although it is possible to rent equipment, serious campers often don't like the idea of equipmental rentals—thinking about missing tent pegs, used sleeping bags, and the like. We've given specific camping information for national parks in appropriate chapters. In general, there are designated sites—and unless your trip is planned around a school holiday, you won't need to reserve a site in advance.

As for the rest of the activities possible in the Great Outdoors, it's become cliche now to say everything is possible in Australia. But it's true, some of the world's greatest diving is found along the Great Barrier Reef; surfing and sailing abound—especially along the east and southwest coasts; there's great fishing all through the country (except in the deserts, in the center); hikers can find bushwalking in national parks; and, for something a bit different, try your hand at fossicking for gems. Of course there are wonderful beaches (many are nude or topless).

You'll need a license for freshwater fishing; these are usually available through sporting goods stores and the national wildlife commission offices, located throughout the country.

You'll also need a fossicking license; contact the tourism office of the state you're going to for details.

The Sports Map here can generally orient you to what activities are available where.

# Accommodations

In addition to the full range of hotel/motel accommodations, Australia offers additional alternatives to the traveler. Major hotel chains throughout the country cater to the upper end of the market, as well as to the budget-conscious traveler, and your travel agent can best advise you on the packages available throughout the country. The range of accommodations is from Premiere Class, quality first-class hotels and motels with all the amenities on hand, through Moderate, well-maintained facilities with many of the amenities attributed to premier facilities. Other types of accommodations are rated Budget, with clean and well-kept facilities for the cost-conscious traveler, and Self-Catered Apartments with maid service, kitchens, and linen services provided. In many resort areas along Australia's coast, self-catered apartments can be booked in one- and two-bedroom varieties and offer a chance to use in-house kitchen facilities to cook and entertain. Most have additional facilities for sports, such as tennis courts and swimming pools. In a good number of cases, these self-catered apartments are part of a condominium complex used by the owners during holiday periods, and then rented on space-available basis when not in owner use. Most units include phone service, television, and air-conditioning/heating and laundry. Many pubs called "hotels"—because of old licensing laws that required drinking establishments to have rooms—do not have rooms for travelers. And then again, some do. As you may well guess, these are modest, budget accommodations (usually with shared bathrooms), and where we've felt one to be of good value, we have recommended it.

In all, comparative rates will please the foreign visitor to Australia. We strongly recommend that if you plan to travel during peak holiday periods, specifically around Easter holidays and Christmastime, you book in advance.

Australia also offers some creative and unusual forms of accommodation. **Home stays** allow you to live with a family in a bed-and-breakfast–type format in big cities and small township areas throughout the country. These stays allow you to see Australian home life up close, in a casual and informal manner, and sample the Australian mealtime fare as you go. Rates vary widely depending on the offering, from $18 per person per night to well over $100 per night in some of the more elaborate Australian home sites in major cities.

In a similar manner, **farm stays** offer a chance to mingle with the real Aussies in rural settings. These stays offer an opportunity to sample local foods, get involved in the day-to-day activities of rural Australia, or relax in an out-of-the-way setting. Accommodations vary from smaller farms to large stations, which can encompass large staffs and thousands of kilometers of land. Farm stays vary in cost, but currently run about $80 per day for all-inclusive room and board.

Most cities and towns have available smaller **bed-and-breakfast** accommodations with listings from the state or territory tourist boards. Costs vary from $14 to $35 per person per night. Specific farms and ranches are recommended in relevant chapters.

You can also contact one of the following organizations:

| | A | B | C |

Arafura Sea

Melville Island
Bathurst Island
Darwin
Kaka Natic Park
Katherine Gorge National Park
Katherine

Timor Sea

Kununurra
Kimberley

Indian Ocean

Derby

N O

T E

Port Hedland

Gibson Desert

WESTERN

Mount Ol
Uluru Yulara
National Park Ayers Roc

Carnarvon

AUSTRALIA

Great Victoria Desert

S

A U

Geraldton

Kalgoorlie

Rottnest Island
Perth
Fremantle

Esperance

Great Australian Bight

Leeuwin Naturaliste National Park
Bunbury

Albany

| diving | hiking | surfing |
| snorkeling | tennis | rafting |
| golf | racing | canoeing |
| sailing | football | hang gliding |
| fossicking | cricket | skiing |
| marlin fishing | fishing | game/trout fishing |

Southern Ocean

D · E · F

**1**

Gulf of
Carpentaria

Cape York Peninsula

Coral Sea

Cairns

Great Dividing Range

Great Barrier Reef

Townsville

**2**

Whitsunday
Islands

Mackay

**QUEENSLAND**

RN
ORY

Springs

Rockhampton

Great Dividing Range

Lake Eyre

Maryborough

Fraser
Island

ober Pedy

Sunshine
Coast

**3**

LIA

Flinders Ranges

Brisbane

Gold
Coast

Lightning Ridge

Flinders Ranges
National Park

Bourke

Glen Innes

Armidale

Port Augusta

Broken Hill

**NEW
SOUTH
WALES**

Dubbo

to
Lord
Howe
Island

Adelaide

Newcastle

angaroo
Island

Sydney

South
Pacific
Ocean

**4**

**A.C.T.**
Canberra

Kiama

Mount Gambier

**VICTORIA**

Ballarat

Melbourne

Geelong

Tasman
Sea

Wilson's Promontory
National Park

Bass
Strait

**5**

Launceston

N

**TASMANIA**

Hobart

**AUSTRALIAN
SPORTS**

0          miles          300
0       kilometers       400

**Australian Home Accommodations**
c/o ATS Sprint
1101 East Broadway
Glendale, Calif. 91205
Tel.: toll-free elsewhere
in the U.S.:
(800) 626-6665
Tel.: toll-free in Calif.:
(800) 336-9797

**Bed and Breakfast Australia**
c/o Islands in the Sun
760 West 16th St.
Costa Mesa, Calif. 92627
Tel.: (714) 645-8300

**Farm Holidays**
98 Fletcher St.
Woollahra, N.S.W. 2025
Australia
Tel.: (02) 387-6681

**Homehost Tasmania**
Box 550
Rosny Park, Tas. 7018
Australia
Tel.: (002) 44-5442; telex A57234

**Homestay of WA**
40 Union Rd.
Carmel, Wash. 6076
Tel.: (09) 293-5347

**Host Farms Association**
c/o SO/PAC
1448 15th St., suite 105
Santa Monica, Calif. 90404
Tel.: (213) 393-8262
Tel.: toll-free in Calif.:
(800) 445-0190
Tel.: toll-free elsewhere in the U.S.:
(800) 551-2012

**Toowoomba Tourism and Development Board**
541 Ruthven St.
Toowoomba, Qld. 4350
Australia
Tel.: (076) 32-1988

An alternative to consider is swapping houses. These **home exchanges** allow you to have a home-away-from-home, while someone from Australia stays at your place. We recommend these if you plan to concentrate your visit in one area or will be spending a long duration on holiday in Australia. Before swapping houses, make sure you're keen on the place or places being offered. The savings you gain by simply trading places might be consumed rapidly if you have to travel long distances for sightseeing, or incur additional accommodation costs to travel more extensively. For more information, contact the Vacation Exchange Club or Home Exchange in your country through directory assistance or your local travel agent. In the U.S. you can contact them at 12006 111th Ave., Young Town, Ariz., (602) 972-2186.

**Youth hostels** can provide an inexpensive form of accommodation with clean facilities throughout the country. More than 130 youth hostels dot the Australian map and are open to members (a nominal membership fee is required), and facilities are located in major urban areas, as well as off the beaten path. In general, these facilities appeal to youthful visitors, but many older travelers find them excellent value, allowing a substantial savings which can be applied to purchases and sightseeing opportunities. In many cases, common areas of hostels are open to members, with dormitories only open for use during nighttime hours. If you plan to use this form of accommodation, plan on spending your days away from the hostel facilities.

International youth and hostel organizations are listed in the yellow pages or through youth-oriented and university travel outlets. Plan to become a member in your home country and review the properties and locations of each. In the U.S. contact (202) 783-6161; in Canada, (613) 746-3844.

# Staying Healthy

The expression "you can't get there from here" ought to read, in the case of Australia—"you can't get there from wherever without getting a case of jet lag." Traveling to Australia holds strong odds that you'll be crossing the international dateline, and probably suffer from jet lag when you arrive. This turmoil in your body clock can create the unexpected and unwanted necessity of waiting for your body's time table to adjust to the local environment. We, therefore, make a few suggestions for dealing with jet lag.

No matter when you arrive Down Under, try to adapt to the local time format right off the bat. If you arrive in the early morning, try to stay up with the locals and avoid napping. A "just put my head down on the pillow" nap might last a few days and leave you groggy and disoriented. The same applies for all times of the day or night. Whatever the locals are doing, especially the first twenty-four hours after your arrival, you need to try and do. Its been proven that a degree of moderate exercise when you arrive is a good way to get the system set as well. Take a walk or jog, swim a lap in the hotel pool, and get the cardiovascular system pumping a bit. Within twenty-four hours you'll be on Aussie time and ready to roll.

## The Great Aussie Sunshine

We can't say enough about tanning carefully. The Aussie sunshine is year-round and strong. Plan to tan gradually and use sunscreens and blocks of a local nature—they are of good quality and value, and made for the conditions. Many of Australia's beaches are topless and females especially may need to be extra careful if their bodies aren't used to this. When you think you've had enough sun for one day but want to continue beaching it, be sure to cover up with a T-shirt or something, stay in the shade, and keep on a liberal application of block and lotion. You can continue to burn even through a T-shirt. Wide-brimmed hats aid in keeping the sun off the nose, a regular target of the Aussie sunburn syndrome.

When snorkeling, plan on wearing a T-shirt in the water. Reflection of light will also cause sunburn, and you'll not really feel it until you've dried off and the pain sets in.

Because the sand gets hot, plan to buy a pair of local flip-flops or thongs to avoid burning the bottoms of your feet. These rubber-type sandals are easy to find in stores, are easy to wear, and save you the effort of darting from one shady spot to the other when walking on the beach. Among the Australians, these flip-flops are common and can be worn almost anywhere—nicer restaurants, casinos, and the theater being obvious exceptions.

While at the beaches, the general rule of thumb is to check with the locals before taking a dip. In certain areas and during certain times of the year sharks are prevalent, and metal-mesh shark nets are put in place to keep the bathers and sharks segregated. In areas where netting is impractical, warning signs, much like traffic notices, indicate sharks present and swimming and wading prohibited. At certain seasons, bathers need take warning of "blue-bottles," a translucent blue jelly fish whose tentacles can produce a most uncomfortable sting. Fortunately, if one beach has blue-bottles, you normally don't have to travel very far to find another that is safe and clear. Again, we advise checking with the locals and lifeguards for any specific warnings and advisories when planning a dip. In some areas of the Top End (Darwin area) and Cairns (south along the coast), crocodiles can be found. They tend to be very localized in habitat, but again check with the locals if you plan to swim in nearby estuaries and river inlets.

When you travel into the interior and Outback areas of Australia, you're bound to run into hoards of friendly flies. You can either plan to keep one hand in perpetual motion (using the other for bodily functions such as eating, driving, and so on) or you can buy a wide-brimmed hat and some mosquito netting to go over your face—a type of screened-in porch for your face. This keeps the flies off you, and allows you to take a break from your arm swinging. Cork hats are typically Australian, but again, you've got to keep your head moving in order for them to really work. Plan to buy netting before you go to Australia, or pick some up in the big cities. It's a rare item in shops in the Outback and, if you buy a section big enough for a friend, he'll be very grateful when the flies come around to say, "G'day."

## Safety

Australia is no different from other countries and cultures around the world. By using good sense and keeping your wits about you, you'll find the people to be friendly, travel safe, and the experience a very positive one. A few suggestions however: Plan to carry a pouch-type purse or wallet, which frees your hands for toting other things. Money belts are often used, but are difficult to access. Modern developments in synthetic materials have provided a whole array of pouch-type belts that hold valuables and cash and allow you to walk or run unobstructed. If you do carry a purse with shoulder straps, turn your purse inwards so the flaps cannot be opened from the outside. If you plan to carry a conventional wallet, either turn the fabric inside the pants so you twist and lock the wallet into the rear pocket, or place your wallet in a front pocket rather than a rear. Plan whenever possible to leave valuables in a hotel safe, taking along only what you think you'll need. Traveler's checks are *strongly* recommended, as they can be replaced should they get lost or stolen.

When at the beach, set up your towel and so on and survey the area. You'll be able to determine a logical "watchdog" who will keep your items under surveillance when you take a dip or go for a stroll. You can then offer to reciprocate and make a friend. Remember, out of sight *is* out of mind. Cover up wallets and purses whenever possible, and keep cameras and equipment out of the sun and out of sight. When traveling in city centers at night, use the same awareness and caution you would in any other city.

With few exceptions, traveling in Australia is no problem for women. Having said this, we feel obligated to point out a few of the finer points regarding the Australian male. Australians in general enjoy the socialization process of the local pub, and have a reputation for being direct and to the point when it comes to forming liaisons with the opposite gender. Don't be put off if you get an abrupt offering in this setting—it's part of the male role and meant as a compliment. We advise that if you plan to travel independently, you do so by conventional means and avoid hitchhiking completely. In some parts of Australia, the male population dominates. For example, Alice Springs and Coober Pedy are communities where the male to female ratios are staggering in favor of males (though, the term "in favor of" probably depends on your perspective). As a result, when you encounter men in these remote areas, they'll work harder for your attention—in ways sometimes less than socially acceptable to the visitor. Use common sense as you would in other parts of the world and you'll be just fine. We suggest you don't play verbal fisticuffs if a slightly off-color comment is made, as in our experience this fuels the debate. Simply make it clear you're not interested (or are) and move on.

## TRAVEL INSURANCE

When planning your trip, you may want to consider travel insurance. Even if you have life or health insurance, you can benefit from travel insurance as it covers a number of items not dealt with in basic policies.

Travel insurance comes in a variety of packages, allowing you to choose the most appropriate policy: companies offer health insurance; health and trip insurance; and comprehensive programs. In addition, most packages come with emergency assistance services which can help you with legal matters in a foreign country, replace lost travel documents, pay on-site hospital expenses, and get emergency cash transfers. These services are also provided by many credit card companies; however these do not cover expenses: only an insurance policy holder receives financial aid. Contact your own credit card company for details.

While policies differ from company to company, many of the basics apply to all of them. Health insurance covers medical costs abroad, within certain limits, that basic health insurance only pays for in part. While some basic policies cover up to 80 percent of expenses incurred abroad as well as on-sight payments for hospital stays, many do not. You should check your policy before buying travel insurance, which is designed to supplement basic health insurance coverage. Check the restrictions here carefully as policies often cover only those illnesses/accidents that occur during the trip.

Trip cancellation/interruption insurance covers holders, within limits, for non-refundable trip payments and expenses if the trip is cancelled, delayed, or cut short due to circumstances beyond their control; it also provides for additional transportation expenses in order for holders to reach their final destination.

Comprehensive programs include the above as well as baggage and travel accident insurance. Baggage insurance covers loss, damage, or theft of baggage. Some policies include coverage for delayed baggage so holders can replace essential items until their luggage arrives.

Most companies offer a variety of program lengths, covering vacation lengths anywhere from a long weekend to a major expedition. Prices are determined by type of coverage, length of trip, and number of persons covered (e.g., family rates can mean a savings). Some programs cost as little as $40 while others are as much as $250. Once again, you should choose the package that best suits your needs.

In addition to restrictions and exclusions, find out exactly when the policy starts—some policies begin on the date the application is approved while others begin the day your trip starts—and ends, and how soon the tour operators and insurance company must be notified in order for you to collect benefits. You can obtain more information from the following companies:

**Access America**
600 Third Ave.
Box 807
New York, N.Y. 10163
(800) 851-2800

**Carefree Travel Insurance**
PO Box 310
120 Mineola Blvd.
Mineola, N.Y. 11501
(800) 645-2424

**HealthCare Abroad**
243 Church Street West
Vienna, Va. 22180
(800) 237-6615

**International S.O.S Assistance**
One Neshaminy Interplex
Trevose, Pa. 19047
(800) 523-8930

**Travel Guard International**
1100 CenterPoint Drive
Stevens Point, Wis. 54481
(715) 345-0505

# Business Brief

A typical Australian bumper sticker will read "I'd rather be sailing." In this vast, isolated country with spectacular beaches and beautiful harbors, inhabitants are particularly torn between how much time should be spent on recreation and how much time should be spent on work. Work is not an Australian's only priority: family and leisure activities play an important part in life here.

The following are tips on the business protocols of Australia that will assist you in the successful conduct of business with the Aussies.

- It is important that North Americans and Europeans traveling to Australia on business plan to arrive at least two days before meetings are scheduled. It's a long trip, and you should give yourself time to recover before getting down to serious business.
- Most Australian managers arrive at the office by 9:00 A.M. and work until about 5:30 or 6:00 P.M.
- Cultural sensitivities are few; however, it might be mentioned that older Australians are not used to dealing with women in business, despite progress made in fostering equality of the sexes in recent times.

- Engaging a local representative may be your key to success. An agent can assist with everything from marketing to breaking through many bureaucratic barriers. Good agents are both hard to find and also hard to keep.
- With the Aussies you must be straightforward. As negotiators they are very upfront; they do not respond to typical American tactics such as power plays. Their usual motivation is simply to make the deal.
- Avoid using the "I" approach when selling or presenting a business proposal. The Australians like to hear and know that they are a part of the opportunity being presented, and that you need their assistance and advice on how to accomplish your company's objectives in Australia's markets.
- Formal documentation is not as common in Australia as it is in the U.S.; here you may find your business negotiating partner utilizes informal and verbal agreements more readily.
- Where an American may inch toward his or her aims, stressing small points as negotiations proceed, the Australian prefers to view the entire scope of the transaction from the onset.
- Australians like to do business with people they consider friends. Their special word for a business relationship is "mateship."
- The Australians may be prepared to bargain, however make your initial price a realistic one. The price you open the bargaining process with will probably be close to the price finally agreed upon.
- Lawyers are far less important in business negotiations here than they are in the U.S. It is advised that if an attorney will be participating with you in negotiations, you inform your Australian counterparts so they do not misread your approach. In Australia attorneys are rarely brought in during the initial stages of negotiations.
- Gift-giving in the Australian business context is not usually practiced—although such thoughtfulness as bringing a bottle of wine to dinner in an Australian home is appreciated.

# CULTURAL TIME LINE

| 1770 | Captain Cook arrives at **Botany Bay** (present site of Kurnell oil refinery) |
|------|------|
| 1788 | First Fleet arrives at Botany Bay. **Sydney** colony founded |
| 1791 | **Experiment Farm** founded at **Parramatta** by first freed convict with government land grant as an experiment in self-sufficiency farming |
| 1793 | **Elizabeth Farm** built by John and Elizabeth Macarthur, **Parramatta** |
| 1803 | The city of **Hobart** (Tasmania) founded |
| 1804 | 200 convicts rebel against their treatment at Castle Hill; the largest convict uprising ever staged. Quelled in a few days |
| 1812 | Rum Hospital begun (now **Parliament House** and **Mint Museum**), Sydney |
| 1813 | Gregory Blaxland, W.C. Wentworth, and William Lawson cross the **Blue Mountains** for the first time |
| 1818 | First whaling station on Australia's mainland at **Twofold Bay**, N.S.W. |
| 1824 | Penal settlement founded at present site of **Brisbane** |
| 1825 | **Norfolk Island** set up as penal settlement |
| 1829 | **Perth** (Western Australia) founded |
| 1835 | **Melbourne** (Victoria) founded |
| 1836 | **Adelaide** (South Australia) founded |
| 1839 | Penal settlement at **Brisbane** closed; land opened for sale for civilian settlement |
| 1840 | Transportation of convicts ends in New South Wales, but continues to **Tasmania** |
| 1843 | First parliamentary elections in New South Wales |
| 1850 | Convicts first sent to Western Australia |
| 1851 | Gold rushes in New South Wales (near Bathurst) and Victoria (Ballarat) |
|      | **Victoria** becomes state, independent of New South Wales |
| 1852 | **University of Sydney** (Australia's oldest) is opened |
| 1853 | Last convicts sent to Australia |
| 1854 | Eureka Stockade (miners' rebellion against exorbitant taxes on their gold claims), Ballarat, Victoria |
| 1855 | **University of Melbourne** founded |
|      | First railway (Sydney to Parramatta) opened |
| 1857 | The wreck of the ship *Dunbar* at The Gap (near Watson's Bay) |
| 1859 | First paddle steamer up the Darling River as far as Brewarrina |

|      | **Queensland** separates from New South Wales to become independent entity |
|------|------|
| 1860 | Burke and Wills leave Melbourne for their epic journey across Australia from South to North and back |
| 1861 | Burke and Wills reach Gulf of Carpentaria—die near Cooper's Creek in the Centre |
|      | First **Melbourne Cup Race** run at Flemington racecourse |
| 1865 | Confederate warship *Shenandoah* calls in to Melbourne harbor for repairs and supplies |
| 1868 | Last convict shipment to Australia arrives in Western Australia |
| 1874 | American actor James Cassius Williamson arrives, founds theater company, J.C. Williamson Productions (still extant) |
| 1875 | **Sydney Town Hall** opened |
| 1876 | American whaling ship *Catalpa* rescues six Irish republican prisoners from Fremantle (Western Australia) jail—takes them to heroes' welcome in New York City |
|      | **University of Adelaide** founded |
| 1880 | Melbourne International Exhibition—**Exhibition Building** (similar to London's Crystal Palace) still standing in Exhibition Gardens |
|      | Bushranger Captain Moonlite hanged in Sydney, as is bushranger |
|      | Ned Kelly (the Wild Colonial Boy) |
| 1883 | Large deposits of lead and silver lead to founding of mining town of **Broken Hill** (New South Wales) |
| 1888 | First parachute jump in Australia (from balloon over Sydney) |
| 1891 | Convention of all governments to discuss unification of Australia; decide on "Commonwealth of Australia" |
| 1893 | Gold discovered at **Kalgoorlie** (Western Australia), Australia's richest goldfield |
| 1894 | Lawrence Hargrave's flight experiments using box kites over Stanwell Park, just south of Sydney |
| 1895 | "Waltzing Matilda" written and sung in public—Winton, Queensland |
| 1896 | Carl Hertz, an American magician, screened the first moving pictures in Australia—Melbourne |
| 1898 | **Queen Victoria Building** opened—Sydney |
|      | Sydney Powerhouse (now **Powerhouse Museum**) opened |
| 1901 | Commonwealth of Australia comes into being **Centennial Park** opened—Sydney |
| 1903 | Australian flag agreed upon |
| 1906 | First surf life-saving club in world formed at **Bondi** |
| 1907 | Norman Brookes is first Australian to win Wimbledon |
| 1908 | President Roosevelt sends "the great White Fleet" of U.S. Navy to Sydney; it draws huge crowds |
| 1910 | Harry Houdini gives aerial displays |
| 1912 | American architect Walter Burley Griffin wins competition to design city of Canberra |
| 1913 | **Canberra** founded as national capital |
| 1914 | Australia enters WWI |
| 1915 | Australian and New Zealand troops fight long, desperate, and ultimately losing battle at Gallipoli (now Istanbul, |

|  | Turkey)—since commemorated by public holiday on April 25 |
|------|------|
| 1920 | Queensland and Northern Territory Aerial Services (QANTAS) begun |
| 1928 | Australian Bert Hinkler makes the first solo flight from Britain to Australia |
|  | First flight of the Flying Doctor Service |
|  | Australian Charles Kingsford Smith makes first flight across the Pacific (California to Brisbane in Southern Cross—83 hours) |
| 1932 | **Sydney Harbour Bridge** opened |
|  | ABC (Australian Broadcasting Commission) publicly owned broadcasting is formed |
| 1939 | Australia is at war—WWII |
| 1941 | Australia and U.S. become allies at war |
| 1945 | Australian Howard Florey wins Nobel Prize for discovering penicillin |
| 1948 | Dr. H.V. Evatt, minister for external affairs, becomes first president of the United Nations General Assembly |
|  | The Holden, first mass-produced Australian car, leaves assembly line |
| 1956 | Television begins in Australia |
| 1957 | Danish architect Joern Utzen wins competition for design of Sydney Opera House |
| 1973 | **Sydney Opera House** opens |
| 1974 | Cyclone Tracy devastates the city of **Darwin** |
| 1983 | *Australia II* wins America's Cup at Newport |
| 1988 | Australia celebrates its Bicentennial |

# VITAL INFORMATION

## Clothing Sizes

**Women's Dresses**

| | | | | | | | |
|---|---|---|---|---|---|---|---|
| Australian | 10 | 12 | 14 | 16 | 18 | 20 | 22 |
| American | 8 | 10 | 12 | 14 | 16 | 18 | 20 |

**Men's suits, overcoats, and sweaters**

| | | | | | | | |
|---|---|---|---|---|---|---|---|
| Australian | 92 | 97 | 102 | 107 | 112 | 117 | 122 |
| American | 36 | 38 | 40 | 42 | 44 | 46 | 48 |

**Shirts and collars**

| | | | | | | | | |
|---|---|---|---|---|---|---|---|---|
| Australian | 36 | 37 | 38 | 39 | 40 | 41 | 42 | 43 |
| American | 14 | 14½ | 15 | 15½ | 16 | 16½ | 17 | 17½ |

## Communication

**Mail, Telegrams, Fax Machines.** Australia's Postal Service is not noted as one of the country's best public departments. Strong unions within the Australia Post have been known to slow the process to a crawl, and rates are not considered cheap by comparison with other countries. Stamps however, are attractive in design and well worth mixing and matching when writing to the home front. Post offices are numerous, and hours are set Mon.–Fri. 9 A.M.–5 P.M. A postcard home to Canada, the United States, or Europe and the U.K. will cost $.58–$.63, with airmail service for letters running $.90–$1. Figure that it will take two weeks to arrive. A letter sent within Australia is $.39 at this writing. Post offices also have facilities to send and receive telegrams and cables, with varying costs for general delivery or express rates. Forms for sending cables and telegrams are standardized, and available at post office countertops. If you expect to receive mail c/o general delivery, this can be done either through the Australia post offices or American Express offices. Mail can be collected after showing suitable identification. Fax machines are located in many major hotels and travel agencies, and they will send documents for a fee. Check with the front desk, or local phone book for details. Courier service (Federal Express for example) is easy to find in cities and reliable. Delivery to the United States takes about two days.

The country code for Australia is 61; when calling Australia from the outside, dial the country code and then the city code without the 0.

**Telephone System.** Public telephones can be found in towns and cities as well as hotels, restaurants, and other public places. A local call is a great value, costing $.30 for unlimited usage. Keep this in mind if you happen to be waiting to make a call and a local is ahead if you and chatting with another local . . . $.30 is good all day long. . . . Not all phones in Australia are alike; red phones known as STD (Subscriber Trunk Dialing) take larger coin denominations, and are used for local and long-distance calling within Australia. If you plan to call overseas, ISD phones (International Subscriber Phones) are located at airports, rail stations, and other traveler-related points, but are scarce by comparison to local dial phones. Many hotels now offer direct-dialing for international calls, or will place an operator-assisted call for you (they will book a call, and contact you when they've gotten through to your party) and charge an additional fee. Our suggestion is to keep the calls short, and pay the additional charges to have someone assist in placing your overseas call; it's worth the convenience. Recently, major credit-card-use phones have been installed in the major international airports on a trial basis; these are, unlike their counterparts elsewhere, easy to use. Long-distance calls made during business hours of 9 A.M. to 5 P.M. weekdays are made at a slightly higher rate to encourage usage during non-peak periods. If you know in advance where you're going to be, have calls made from the United States and Canada to you as the costs are considerably less; callers from the United Kingdom will pay more, so plan to call the United Kingdom from Oz.

## Electricity

The electrical current throughout Australia is 240/250 volts, AC 50 HZ. And, the Australian three-prong outlet is different from those found in the United States, Canada, and the United Kingdom, with two slanted slots at the top and a vertical one below, between the slanted ones. Many hotels provide a 240v/110 switch, but you'll still require an adaptor to the three-prong system. Converters for voltage differences are available in many hardware and department stores, and should be the "global converter" types to assure you get the right thing.

## Emergency Information

Nationwide emergency phone number: 000

### If you lose your credit cards:

American Express, tel. toll-free (008) 222-000
DC: tel. (02) 236-8923
MC: tel. toll-free: (008) 011-217
Visa: tel. toll-free (008) 224-402

## Metric Conversion

### Distance

1 meter = 39.37 inches
1 kilometer = .62 mile
1 millimeter = .039 inch

| Miles | Kilometers |
|-------|------------|
| 1 | 1.6 |
| 5 | 8.0 |
| 10 | 16.0 |
| 20 | 32.1 |
| 30 | 48.2 |
| 40 | 64.3 |
| 50 | 80.4 |
| 100 | 160.9 |
| 200 | 321.8 |
| 500 | 804.6 |
| 1,000 | 1,609.3 |

## Temperature

$°F = (°C \times 9/5) + 32°$
$°C = (°F \times 5/9) - 32°$

## Time Zones

Australia is large enough to require three very distinct time zones. These zones are cut zebra-striped along the North-South Latitudes, separating the country into Eastern Standard Time, Central Standard Time, and Western Standard Time. To confuse matters, not all the time zone changes are in hourly increments; Eastern and Central are separated by only a half hour, while Western Standard time varies two hours from the Eastern Standard Zones. This was not done intentionally to confuse visitors to Australia, but to confuse the locals, who when traveling long distances cross-country inevitably show up for a timely event either a bit too early, or a bit too late. Join the locals in this confusion and you'll have locked onto a good source of conversation.

Things get even more confusing in the summer (Oct.–March), when all states except Qld. and N.T. observe daylight-savings time. The information below is for non–daylight-savings time.

**Eastern Time** (N.S.W., Qld., Vic., Tas.) = Greenwich Mean Time + 10 hours = U.S. Eastern Standard Time + 15 hours

**Central Time** (S.A., N.T.) = Greenwich Mean Time + 9.5 hours = U.S. Eastern Standard Time + 14.5 hours

**Western Time** (W.A.) = Greenwich Mean Time + 8 hours = U.S. Eastern Standard Time + 13 hours

# USEFUL ADDRESSES AND PHONE NUMBERS

## AUSTRALIAN CAPITAL TERRITORY

### INFORMATION

**Canberra:** Visitor Information Centre, Northbourne Ave., Canberra 2600; (062) 45-6464. Open daily 9 A.M.–5 P.M.

### CONSULATES

**British** High Commission, Commonwealth Ave., Canberra 2600; (062) 70-6666.

**Canadian** High Commission, Commonwealth Ave., Canberra 2600; (062) 73-3844.

**New Zealand** High Commission, Commonwealth Ave., Canberra 2600; (062) 73-3611.

**U.S.** Embassy, Moonah Place, Yarralumla, Canberra 2600; (062) 70-5000.

## NEW SOUTH WALES

### INFORMATION

**Main Office:** Travel Centre of N.S.W., 16 Spring St., Sydney N.S.W. 2000; tel. (02) 231-4444.

### Offices throughout New South Wales

**Armidale:** Tourist Information Centre, 82 Marsh St., Box 75A, Armidale 2350; tel. (067) 73-8527.

**Bateman's Bay:** Bateman's Bay Tourist Centre, Princes Hwy., Bateman's Bay 2536; (044) 72-4225.

**Bega:** Bega Tourist Centre, Gipps St., Bega 2550; (064) 92-2045.

**Broken Hill:** Broken Hill Regional Tourist Association and Information Centre, corner of Blende and Bromide sts., Broken Hill 2880; (080) 6077 or 6078.

**Coffs Harbour:** Information Centre, Castle St., Coffs Harbour 2450; (066) 52-1522.

**Cooma:** Cooma Information Centre, Sharp St., Cooma 2630; (0648) 52-1177 or 52-1108.

**Coonabarabran:** Tourist Info Centre, John St., Coonabarabran; (068) 42-1441.

**Eden:** Eden Tourist Centre, Princes Hwy. South, Eden 2551; (064) 96-1953.

**The Entrance:** Tuggerah Lakes Tourist Assoc., Marine Pde., The Entrance 2261; (043) 32-9282.

**Glen Innes:** "The Railway Carriage," Church St., Glen Innes 2370; (067) 32-2397.

**Grafton:** Big River Tourist Assoc., corner of Duke and Victoria sts., Grafton 2460; (066) 42-4677.

**Jindabyne:** Snowy River Information Centre, Petamin Plaza, Jindabyne 2627; (064) 56-2444.

**Kiama:** Council Chambers, Princes Hwy., Kiama 2533; (042) 32-1122.

**Lightning Ridge:** Tourist Information Centre, Morilla St., Lightning Ridge 2834; (068) 29-0565.

**Merimbula:** Merimbula Tourist Information Centre, Town Centre, Merimbula 2548; (064) 95-2119.

**Mittagong:** Southern Highlands Visitors Centre, Hume Hwy., Mittagong 2575; (048) 71-2888.

**Murwillumbah:** Information Centre, Alma St., Murwillumbah 2484; (066) 72-1340.

**Nambucca Heads:** Tourist Information Centre, School of Arts Bldg., Ridge St., Nambucca Heads 2448; (065) 68-6954.

**Newcastle:** Hunter and Lower North Coast Tourist Authority, City Hall, Newcastle 2300; (049) 26-2323.

**Nowra:** Shoalhaven City Tourist Centre, Princes Hwy., Bomaderry 2541; (044) 21-0778.

**Port Macquarie:** Tourist Information Centre, Horton St, Port Macquarie 2444; (065) 83-1293.

**Tamworth:** Visitors Centre, CWA Park, Kable Ave., Tamworth 2340; (067) 66-3641.

**Tenterfield:** Tenterfield Visitors Centre, Tenterfield 2372. (067) 36-1082.

**Thredbo:** Thredbo Resort Centre, Thredbo 2627 (0648) 7-6360.

**Wollongong:** Leisure Coast Visitors Centre, Crown St., Wollongong 2500; (042) 28-0300.

## CONSULATES

**British** Consulate, 10th fl., Goldfields House, 1 Alfred St., Sydney Cove 2000; (02) 27-7521.

Consulate General of **Canada,** 8th fl., AMP Center, 50 Bridge St., Sydney 2000; (02) 231-6522.

**New Zealand** Consulate, 25th fl., State Bank Center, 55 Martin Pl., Sydney 2001; (02) 233-8388.

**U.S.** Consulate, 36th fl., Hyde Park Tower, Corner Park and Elizabeth sts., Sydney 2000; (02) 261-9200.

# QUEENSLAND

## INFORMATION

## Offices throughout Australia

**Adelaide:** Queensland Government Travel Centre, 10 Grenfell St., Adelaide, S.A. 5000; (08) 212-2399.

**Melbourne:** Queensland Government Travel Centre, 257 Collins St., Melbourne, Vic. 3000; (03) 654-3866.

**Perth:** Queensland Government Travel Centre, 55 St. George's Terr., Perth, W.A. 6000; (09) 325-1600.

**Sydney:** Queensland Tourist and Travel Corporation, 75 Castlereagh St., Sydney N.S.W. 2000; (02) 232-1788, telex 120404.

## Offices in Queensland

Queensland Government Travel Centre, 196 Adelaide St., Brisbane 4000; (07) 833-5300.

Tourism Brisbane, City Hall, King George St., Brisbane 4000; (07) 221-8411.

**Gold Coast:** Gold Coast Visitors & Convention Bureau, 115 Scarborough St., Southport 4215; (075) 91-1988.

**Sunshine Coast:** Sunshine Coast Tourism & Development Board, Alexandra Pde., Alexandra Headlands 4572; (071) 43-2411.

**Surfers Paradise:** Information Center, Cavill Mall; (075) 38-4419.

## CONSULATES

**British** Consulate, BP House, 193 North Quay, Brisbane 4000; (07) 221-4933.

**New Zealand** Consulate General, Watkins Place Bldg., 288 Edward St., Brisbane 4001; phone (07) 221-9933.

**U.S.** Consulate, 383 Wickham Terr., Brisbane 4000; phone (07) 839-8955.

# NORTHERN TERRITORY

## INFORMATION

### Offices throughout Australia

**Adelaide:** Northern Territory Tourist Bureau, 9 Hindley St., Adelaide 5000, S.A.; (08) 212-1133, telex 82506.

**Brisbane:** Northern Territory Tourist Bureau, 48 Queen St., Brisbane 4000, Qld.; (07) 229-5799, telex 42848.

**Hobart:** Northern Territory Tourist Bureau, 93 Liverpool St., Hobart 7000, Tas.; (002) 34-4199, telex 57012.

**Melbourne:** Northern Territory Tourist Bureau, 415 Bourke St., Melbourne 3000, Vic.; (03) 670-6948, telex 31450.

**Perth:** Northern Territory Tourist Bureau, 62 St. George's Terr., Perth 6000, W.A.; phone (09) 322-4255, telex 94467.

**Sydney:** Northern Territory Tourist Bureau, corner George & Barrack sts., King St., Sydney 2000, N.S.W.; (02) 262-3744, telex 26825.

### Offices in the Northern Territory

**Alice Springs:** Northern Territory Government Tourist Bureau, Ford Plaza Bldg., Todd Mall, Alice Springs 0870; (089) 52-1299.

**Darwin:** Northern Territory Government Tourist Bureau, 31 Smith St. Mall, Darwin 0800; (089) 81-6611.

# SOUTH AUSTRALIA

## INFORMATION

### Offices Elsewhere in Australia

**Melbourne:** South Australian Government Travel Centre, 25 Elizabeth St., Melbourne 3000; (03) 614-6967, telex 82487.

**Sydney:** South Australian Government Travel Centre, 143 King St., Box 1205 Sydney, N.S.W. 2001; (02) 232-8388, telex 82487.

### Offices in South Australia

South Australian Government Travel Centre, 18 King William St., Adelaide 5000; (08) 212-1644.

## CONSULATES

**New Zealand** Consulate, 8th fl., Standard Chartered Bank Bld., 26 Flinders St., Adelaide 5001; (08) 231-0700.

**U.S.** Consulate, 15 Nilpinna St., Burnside, Adelaide 5066; (08) 332-8886.

# TASMANIA

## INFORMATION

### Offices Elsewhere in Australia

Tasmanian Travel Centre, 129 King St., Sydney, N.S.W. 2000; (02) 233-2500.

### Offices in Tasmania

Tasmanian Travel Centre, 80 Elizabeth St., Hobart 7000; (002) 30-0211.

# VICTORIA

## INFORMATION

### Elsewhere in Australia

Victorian Tourism Commission, 150 Pitt St., Sydney N.S.W. 2000; (02) 233-5499.

### In Victoria

Victour, 230 Collins St., Melbourne, 3000; phone (03) 619-9444, telex AA 30868.

## CONSULATES

British Consulate General, Colonial Mutual Life Building, 330 Collins St., Melbourne 3000; phone (03) 670-5159.

Canadian Consulate-General, 6th fl., 1 Collins St., Melbourne, 3000; phone (03) 654-1433.

New Zealand Consulate, 330 Collins St., Melbourne 3001; phone (03) 670-8111.

U.S. Consulate General, 24 Albert Rd., South Melbourne 3205; phone (03) 697-7900.

# WESTERN AUSTRALIA

## INFORMATION

### Offices throughout Australia

**Adelaide:** Western Australian Travel Centre, 108 King William St., Adelaide 5000, S.A.; phone (08) 212-1344, telex 82812.

**Brisbane:** Western Australian Travel Centre, Level 2, City Mutual Building, 243 Edward St., Brisbane 4000, Qld.; (07) 229-5794, telex 41286.

**Melbourne:** Western Australian Travel Centre, 35 Elizabeth St., Melbourne, Vic. 3000; (03) 614-6833.

**Sydney:** Western Australian Tourism Commission, 92 Pitt St., Sydney 2000; (02) 233-4440, telex 24224.

### Offices throughout Western Australia

**Broome:** Broome Tourist Bureau, Bagot Rd. and Great Northern Hwy., Broome 6725; (091) 92-1176.

**Derby:** Derby Tourist Bureau, Clarendon St., Darby 6728; (091) 91-1426.

**Perth:** Western Australian Tourism Commission, 772 Hay St., Perth 6000; (09) 322-2999.

## CONSULATES

**British** Consulate, Prudential Building, 95 St. George's Terr., Perth, 6000; phone (09) 322-7674.

**New Zealand** Consulate, 10th fl. 16 St. George's Terr., Perth 6000; (09) 325-7877.

**U.S.** Consulate, 13th floor, St. George's Court, 16 St. George's Terr., Perth, 6000; (09) 221-1177.

# Index

# AUSTRALIA

© RV Reise- und Verkehrsverlag, München

INDIAN OCEAN · PACIFIC OCEAN

**Indonesia / New Guinea region:** Sumatra · Palembang · Banjarmasin · Greater Sunda Is. · Ujung Pandang · Celebes · Bandung · Jakarta · Surabaya · Java Sea · Surakarta · Flores · Sumbawa · Sumba · Timor · Timor Sea · Tanimbar · Aru · Buru · Seram · Banda Sea · Arafura Sea · Jayapura · New Guinea · P. Moresby

**Melanesia / Pacific:** Bismarck Arch. · New Ireland · New Britain · Rabaul · Bougainville · Honiara · Solomon Is. · Louisiade Arch. · Coral Sea · New Hebrides · Sta Cruz Is. · New Caledonia · Noumea · Fiji Is. · Suva · Tonga Is. · Nukualofa · Horne Is. · Niue · Samoa Is. · Rarotonga · Ellice Is. · Phoenix Is. · Tokelau Is. · Nassau · Suvorov · Norfolk · Lord Howe · Kermadec · Chatham · Antipodes Is. · Bounty

**Australia:** C. York Pen. · G. of Carpentaria · Arnhem Land · Darwin · Wyndham · Birdum · Cairns · Townsville · Mackay · Rockhampton · Ipswich · Brisbane · Newcastle · Sydney · Canberra · Mt. Kosciusko · Melbourne · Great Dividing Range · Gt. Artesian Basin · Alice Springs · Mount Isa · L. Eyre · Broken Hill · Bourke · Darling · Murray · Adelaide · P. Pirie · Gr. Austr. B. · Gr. Sandy Desert · P. Hedland · Meekatharra · Carnarvon · Geraldton · Perth · Albany · Kalgoorlie · Kosciusko

**Tasmania / New Zealand:** Bass Str. · Tasmania · Hobart · South East C. · Tasman Sea · New Zealand · North I. · South I. · North C. · Auckland · Wellington · Christchurch · Dunedin · Invercargill · Stewart I. · Southwest C.

**Oceans / basins:** West Austral. Basin · South Austral. Basin · Southeast Indian Basin · Indian Ridge · North Australian Basin · Northwest Australian Basin · Keeling Basin · Cocos · Christmas Trench · Sunda Trench · Macquarie Ridge · Tasman Rise · East Austr. Basin · Fiji Basin · Tonga Trench · Kermadec · Tropic of Capricorn · Nova Amsterdam · St Paul · Kerguelen

**Depths / heights:** 7315 · 5322 · 6035 · 5267 · 10882 · 9473 · 10047 · 7569 · 6650 · 7510 · 3758 · 1216 · 3764 · 2230 · 5998 · 5550 · 5850 · 8047 · 1125 · 5406 · 5706 · 6395 · 2152 · 3806 · 3455 · 3726 · 3616 · 7440 · 9140 · 5030 · 840 · 1227 · 3383 · 2300

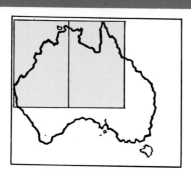